D0044181

The Queen

Also by Andrew Morton

17 Carnations: The Royals, the Nazis,
and the Biggest Cover-Up in History

Wallis in Love:
The Untold Story of the Duchess of Windsor,
the Woman Who Changed the Monarchy

Diana: Her True Story—In Her Own Words

Elizabeth & Margaret:
The Intimate World of the Windsor Sisters

The Queen

Her Life

ANDREW MORTON

**GRAND
CENTRAL**

New York · Boston

Grand Central Publishing
Hachette Book Group
1290 Avenue of the Americas, New York, NY 10104
grandcentralpublishing.com
twitter.com/grandcentralpub

First Edition: April 2022

Grand Central Publishing is a division of Hachette Book Group, Inc. The Grand Central Publishing name and logo is a trademark of Hachette Book Group, Inc.

The publisher is not responsible for websites (or their content) that are not owned by the publisher.

The Hachette Speakers Bureau provides a wide range of authors for speaking events. To find out more, go to www.hachettespeakersbureau.com or call (866) 376-6591.

Library of Congress Cataloging-in-Publication Data has been applied for.

ISBNs: 978-1-5387-0043-3 (hardcover), 978-1-5387-0044-0 (ebook)

Printed in the United States of America

LSC-H

Printing 1, 2022

To my mother, Kathleen, and all those
of the war generation.

Contents

Introduction

❧

Surfing with Her Majesty

We all remember the first time we ever saw the queen. I was on my first major royal tour as a royal correspondent for a British newspaper and recall watching with wonder as the royal yacht *Britannia*, pristine and glowing in the dappled sunshine, slowly sailed into San Diego Bay. It was February 1983, and those few days in the company of the queen and the Duke of Edinburgh transformed my life.

The royal yacht was surrounded by a raucous welcoming armada of speedboats, yachts, catamarans, skiffs, and canoes. It was a Saturday morning when the yacht docked and the royal party emerged. The queen's nine-day tour of California, land of surf, sun, and starry-eyed dreams, was supposed to be a carefully curated review of the best the Golden State had to offer, from the artifice of Hollywood to the natural splendor of Yosemite National Park. If the visit had been a Broadway play, however, it would have been named *The Tour That Goes Wrong*.

In those far-off days, when the royal family arrived in a new country they would, with some reluctance, hold a cocktail party for the press corps who dogged their every move. So, suited and booted, I found myself handing over my gold-embossed invitation card to a waiting navy officer and invited to take a proffered gin and tonic—measures naval and substantial—on the aft deck of the royal yacht.

It took me back to a foggy day in October 1965. I was aged eleven and, proudly wearing my freshly pressed Scout uniform, I took my place lining the route on the outskirts of Leeds to see the queen and Prince Philip pass by on their way to open the brand-new, brutalist Seacroft Civic Centre.

As they drove past, the dank claustrophobic fingers of fog combined with the bright interior light in their glass-domed Rolls-Royce only served to heighten the effect of two exotic beings dropped in from outer space, alien creatures come to view mundane municipal life. It was but a fleeting glimpse of the queen and her consort, but it stayed with me.

The queen had been part of my life forever. Growing up, the queen and her family were like the white cliffs of Dover, immutable, impregnable, there. A fact of life, like breathing.

Of course her picture appeared on postage stamps and coins, and looked down disapprovingly from behind the headmaster's desk just before punishment was administered. At the Regal cinema in Cross Gates we regularly mumbled through "God Save the Queen," the national anthem, after watching that week's children's offering—singer Cliff Richard's 1963 movie *Summer Holiday* about a group of friends singing and dancing their way across Europe on a London double-decker bus was a favorite. The queen, to my young eyes, was not a real human being. She was a distant faraway symbol, an occasionally smiling personage who spoke in barely understandable English when we gathered round the telly at three in the afternoon to watch her broadcast on Christmas Day.

For me the only human dimension was the fact that she was a few months younger than my mother and both had served in World War Two, my mother Kathleen in the land army, Princess Elizabeth in the Auxiliary Territorial Service or ATS.

On that Saturday in San Diego I have to confess that my first encounter with Her Majesty was less than memorable. The diminutive lady in a striking blue-and-white outfit listened with increased inattention as I went on about the impressive size of the American fleet lying at anchor in the harbor. She agreed and promptly moved on.

The next few days though did unpeel some of the mask of monarchy, revealing a somewhat different character from the stern visage on my postage stamps. The visit became the very antithesis of a royal program where every movement, every meet and greet was timed to the minute. What with gale-force winds, storms at sea, overflowing rivers, IRA demonstrators, washed-out roads, overserved celebrities, what didn't go wrong?

It seemed the queen positively relished it when the carefully crafted schedule was thrown up in the air. Years later her grandson Prince William made the same observation. "They love it when things go wrong," he said. "They absolutely adore it because obviously everything always has to be right, but when things go wrong around them, they're the first people to laugh."[1]

The first thing that went awry was the royal yacht. Storms were so bad the royal party left *Britannia* to make its roller-coaster way up the coast while they attempted to join the president and First Lady for a taco lunch and horseback ride at their ranch, Rancho del Cielo (ranch in the sky), above Santa Barbara.

It took a jouncing seven-mile switchback ride in a four-wheel-drive Chevrolet Suburban through a steep obstacle course of flooded streams, submerged roads, falling boulders, and downed tree limbs to reach their destination. It was all "terribly exciting," said the queen. Unfortunately a much-anticipated horseback ride in the scenic Santa Ynez Mountains was canceled and tacos were eaten indoors.

Then a tornado over Los Angeles prevented the royal yacht from leaving Long Beach and flooded roads in the dockyard where she was moored. The only way through the rising water was in a high-axle navy bus. The queen, not wanting to let people down, donned a pair of galoshes and climbed into the front seat. Secret Service agents were glad she didn't sit farther back as, during their cursory examination, they learned that the bus had more than its fair share of R-rated graffiti scrawled on the backs of the seats.

After that experience Reagan later wrote to the queen somewhat contritely: "I know your visit to our West Coast became a harrowing, tempest-tossed experience but through it all your unfailing good humor and graciousness won the hearts of our people."[2]

Given the organizational fiasco, it was an understandably visibly nervous Nancy Reagan who hosted a night of Hollywood stars at the M*A*S*H soundstage at Twentieth Century Fox in Beverly Hills. Though Frank Sinatra and Perry Como maybe sang one duet too many, it seems the queen enjoyed the entertainment, which included Dionne Warwick, comic George Burns, and meeting with stars like Fred Astaire and Jimmy Stewart.

It was another clue to the woman behind the mask. Her tastes in music and art were not elitist. She knew most of the lyrics to Rodgers and Hammerstein musicals. Unlike her sister Princess Margaret, she was no great fan of opera or ballet.

Though she has a good musical ear, she attended concerts infrequently.

On this night the British contingent was out in force, with Michael Caine, Roger Moore, Jane Seymour, and Elton John among the celebrities.

At a more intimate dinner for about thirty aboard the royal yacht in San Francisco Bay, the queen and Prince Philip hosted the president and First Lady as they celebrated their thirty-first wedding anniversary. The Royal Marines Band played the "Anniversary Waltz" on the pier and later the deputy White House chief of staff, Michael Deaver, serenaded the party on the piano, singing "True Love" for the couple. Reagan told the party that when he married Nancy, he promised her "a lot of things, but not this."[3] Among the guests at this intimate gathering were preacher Billy Graham and his wife, specially invited by the queen. It was another insight into her personality, the queen's Christian faith inspiring a long friendship with the charismatic American pastor.

The following day the royal couple went to Yosemite National Park, where they stayed at the exclusive Ahwahnee hotel with a spectacular view of a fourteen-hundred-foot-high rock wall formation called the Royal Arches.

When they went for a walk they were disconcerted to find the American Secret Service following closely. However quickly they walked, the agents were right behind. This was not the British way, where bodyguards knew to keep their distance.

At first the royal couple was irritated. Then they played a game, walking backward so that the Secret Service agents would have to mimic the couple. They walked back and forth, and finally everyone started laughing. Hardly the expected behavior of a head of state but another clue to the character of the queen, a woman with a fine appreciation of the absurd.

Here was a woman whose whole life was one of superlatives: the longest reigning, most traveled, and, for a shy person, the most gregarious, meeting more of her subjects face-to-face than any other sovereign in history. When the French president once asked if she ever got bored, she replied honestly: "Yes but I don't say so."[4] In an age of celebrity and artifice she has long been content with being down-to-earth and straightforward.

She regularly appeared on the *Sunday Times* Rich List but enjoyed donning rubber gloves to do the cleaning up after a barbecue on her Scottish estate at Balmoral. At her favorite log cabin it was once suggested that they install a plaque: QUEEN ELIZABETH SWEPT HERE.[5] Though she lived in palaces and castles, she seemed to relish a more normal life. She was a young woman cast into an extraordinary role. Even as a child she was one of the most talked-about people on the planet.

And early clues to who she was and what she became could be found on the top floor of a town house in the center of London almost a century ago.

1

❦

Shirley Temple 2.0

The young girl with the furrowed brow and intent expression bent furiously over her book. She carefully turned the pages and then, when she spotted her target, she grabbed her pen and scribbled and scratched out the offending words.

Doctor Simpson Scratch. *Doctor Simpson* Scribble. That he was but a character in one of the children's books in her nursery was irrelevant as far as the angry ten-year-old girl was concerned.

As Princess Elizabeth went about her solemn, destructive task, her younger sister Margaret played with the snaffles, bridles, and saddles of the wooden horses that crowded their nursery. She was focused on her make-believe world, unconcerned about her sister's silent rage over a certain Mrs. Simpson who, unbidden, was now changing all their lives. Disinterested, too, in the growing crowds that jostled and shoved in the winter gloom to watch the to-ing and fro-ing from 145 Piccadilly, the London home of their parents, the Duke and Duchess of York.

After all, they had spent a lifetime peering out from their

top-floor bedroom watching people looking at them, both sides wondering what the other was doing. It was a game that would last a lifetime.

This time, though, the crowds were bigger, the atmosphere inside the stone-fronted mansion tense and hurried. The front doorbells, labeled VISITORS and HOUSE, rang more frequently, and as the crowds of the curious and concerned grew, police were drafted in.

The name Simpson was first whispered and then became part of disapproving conversations that were abruptly ended when the girls hove into view. Much as her parents tried to protect Lilibet—the family name for the princess—and her sister, she was sensitive to moods and rhythms. She was adept at catching the conversational drift, especially because, since her tenth birthday, she'd enjoyed the privilege of taking breakfast with her parents and occasionally her grandmother Queen Mary. She was able to gather crumbs of information denied her younger sister. Not that Elizabeth was old enough to appreciate what was really going on.

She just knew that at the heart of the puzzle was that woman Simpson. The evidence was all around. Her father looked visibly ill; her grandmother Queen Mary, routinely ramrod-straight and imperious, seemed older and somehow shriveled; her mother's normally jaunty demeanor had for once deserted her. Nor did it help when, in early December 1936, the duchess came down with a nasty case of flu and was confined to bed.

When Elizabeth asked the three women in her life—her governess Marion Crawford, her maid Bobo MacDonald, and nanny Clara Knight, known as Alah—about what was going on their responses were evasive and dismissive. Indeed Crawfie often took the girls for swimming lessons to the Bath Club as a

necessary distraction. This down-to-earth triumvirate served as
the girls' window on the world, their genteel observations and
prim prejudices shaping Lilibet and Margaret's own responses.
As far as the princesses were concerned, the name Wallis
Simpson was taboo in the House of York. So Elizabeth went
through her books, scratching and scribbling in a futile attempt
to delete from her world the name of the woman who would
change her life, and that of her parents, forever.

Elizabeth had briefly met Wallis Simpson in the spring of
1936 after she had celebrated her tenth birthday. Not that she
made much of an impression. Simpson arrived with Elizabeth's
uncle David, the new King Edward VIII, to see her parents
at their weekend home, the Royal Lodge in the manicured
acres of Windsor Great Park. Her uncle came to show off the
two American interests in his life—a brand-new Buick sports
wagon and his other fascination, the twice-married lady from
Baltimore, Wallis Simpson. When they left Elizabeth asked
her governess Crawfie who that woman was. Was she responsible for the fact that Uncle David rarely came to see them
these days? Of all her father's brothers and sisters he had been
the most frequent visitor to 145 Piccadilly, after tea joining the
girls for card games of snap, happy families, and racing demon.
He was always fun, Elizabeth recalling the time he took the
duchess and the girls into the garden at Balmoral and taught
them how to perform the Nazi salute—to much hilarity.

While Crawfie's response to Elizabeth's questions about
the chic American may well have been noncommittal, the
Scottish governess found herself rather liking Mrs. Simpson,
later describing her as a "smart attractive woman, with that
immediate friendliness common to American women."[1] Not
so her employers. After spending a convivial hour discussing
gardening and taking tea with the new king and his paramour,

Wallis was left with the distinct impression that "while the Duke of York was sold on the American station wagon, the Duchess was not sold on the King's other American interest."[2]

At the time it was the presence of the York daughters that provided the chief talking point, not the American contingent. "They were both so blonde, so beautifully mannered, so brightly scrubbed that they might have stepped straight from the pages of a picture book," recalled Wallis in her memoir, *The Heart Has Its Reasons*.[3] Elizabeth and Margaret were, as children often are, used as the human equivalent of coffee-table books, their presence a neutral conversational diversion, a way of avoiding tricky grown-up issues. By the time they first met with Wallis Simpson, the girls had grown practiced at being used in this way, impeccably mannered children introduced to the visiting grown-ups to help break the conversational ice.

It was the same when they traveled to Scotland that fateful summer to stay at the modest Stuart house called Birkhall Lodge near Balmoral, the estate first purchased by Queen Victoria and even today rather like going back in time. The principal guest of the Yorks was the Archbishop of Canterbury, Cosmo Lang, who had accepted their invitation when the king, who traditionally invited England's senior Protestant prelate to Balmoral, left him swinging in the wind. Instead, up the road at Balmoral, he and Wallis hosted a jaunty party of aristocrats, Americans, and royal relatives, including his second cousin Louis Mountbatten and his younger brother Prince George, with his wife Princess Marina.

After tea on the second day of the prelate's visit, Elizabeth, Margaret, and their cousin Margaret Rhodes sang songs "most charmingly."

The archbishop noted: "It was strange to think of the destiny which may be awaiting the little Elizabeth, at present second from the throne. She and her lively little sister are certainly most entrancing children."[4]

The king was not so enamored. When he heard that the ecumenical head of the Church of England was staying with the Yorks he suspected his brother of attempting to set up a rival court. Their emerging conflict centered on the king's wish to marry Wallis once she had divorced her husband, shipping agent Ernest Simpson. In those days divorce wasn't just frowned on; it was deemed anathema in the eyes of the church. As the secular head of the Church of England, the king had no business marrying a divorcée, let alone a twice-divorced American of no standing or status. For his part the king threatened to renounce the throne unless he was allowed to marry the woman who had stolen his heart.

Though the British media had kept a lid on the blossoming romance—pictures of the king and Wallis during a summer cruise aboard the steam yacht *Nahlin* appeared everywhere except England—the potential constitutional crisis was finally made public early in December. It set in train a series of calamitous events that unintentionally placed Princess Elizabeth at the heart of the drama.

By then Wallis had secured a decree nisi from her husband but had to wait a further six months for the decree absolute, thus allowing her to marry the king and become his queen. Despite a dire warning from his principal private secretary Alec Hardinge—supported by Prime Minister Stanley Baldwin—that he would cause irrevocable damage to the monarchy, and probably provoke a general election, if he continued along this path, the king's mind was made up. At a tense meeting on November 16 he informed the prime minister that he intended to marry Mrs. Simpson as soon as he was legally free. If the government opposed he would simply abdicate. He later conveyed his decision to his mother and siblings, who were shocked to the core, Queen Mary seeking the advice of a therapist to verify her conclusion that her eldest son had been bewitched by a skillful sorceress. The prime minister was more sanguine, informing his cabinet colleagues that the elevation of the Yorks might prove to be the best solution as the Duke of York was rather like his much-loved father, King George V.

Not that Prince Albert, known as Bertie, would have agreed. He was slowly but surely being wound into a constitutional web that gave him no opportunity of escape. It was the stuff of nightmares. While there was some discussion that the Duke of Kent, the youngest of the brothers, could take over the throne as he already had a son, the fickle finger of fate pointed to the second-born, the hapless Bertie. For his part he had always assumed that his elder brother would marry one day and go on to have an heir who would become sovereign.

As the duke, shy, diffident, and cursed with a congenital stammer, reluctantly reviewed the hand he was now being dealt, his immediate thoughts went out to his eldest daughter whose position would change from second in line to the throne to heir presumptive, a future queen sentenced to a lifetime of duty and public solitude.

Though he had grave doubts about himself and his own capacity to take on such a great office of state, he quietly admired his eldest daughter. She had character, solid qualities that, as he told the poet Osbert Sitwell, reminded him of Queen Victoria. High praise even from a doting father who was, as Dermot Morrah, royal historian and friend of the new king, observed, "reluctant to sentence his daughters to the lifetime of unremitting service, without hope of retirement, even in old age, which is inseparable from the highest place of all."[5]

His daughter was rather more matter-of-fact and practical. When it became inevitable that the Duke of York was going to accede to the throne and that her beloved uncle Edward VIII, now the Duke of Windsor, was leaving for exile abroad, Princess Margaret asked: "Does this mean you're going to become Queen?" Her elder sister replied: "Yes I suppose it does."[6] She didn't mention it again except when her father casually mentioned that she would have to learn to ride sidesaddle for that time, hopefully in the far distant future, when she would have to appear on horseback at the annual Trooping the Colour ceremony at Horse Guards Parade.

While she was reluctantly resigned to becoming queen she did, according to her cousin Margaret Rhodes, think that moment would be "a long way off."[7] As an insurance policy, she added to her evening prayers the fervent hope that she would have a baby brother who, by dint of his sex, would leapfrog over her and become the heir apparent.

While Princess Elizabeth largely accepted her new station with the phlegmatic unconcern of youth, her father reacted differently. He "broke down and sobbed like a child" when he, Queen Mary, and the king's lawyer, Walter Monckton, were presented with the draft Instrument of Abdication.[8] On Friday, December 11, 1936—the year of three kings—the king's abdication was announced, the now ex-king driving to Windsor Castle where he gave his historic broadcast containing the memorable passage: "I have found it impossible to carry the heavy burden of responsibility and to discharge my duties as King as I would wish to do without the help and support of the woman I love." After praising his younger brother's many sterling qualities of civic leadership, he pointed out that "he has one matchless blessing, enjoyed by so many of you and not bestowed on me—a happy home with his wife and children."[9]

Not so happy for the family in question. The former Duke of York, now the new king described the momentous event as "that dreadful day"; his wife, the new queen, lay prostrate in bed with a nasty bout of flu; while the next day the hitherto ignored but now central characters in this unfolding drama greeted their new station in life with a mixture of excitement and irritated acceptance. When Princess Elizabeth saw an envelope addressed to the queen even her calm demeanor was punctured. "That's *Mummy* now, isn't it?" she commented, while her younger sister lamented the fact that they had to move into Buckingham Palace. "You mean forever?" she asked. "But I have only just learned to write 'York.'"[10]

On the day of the proclamation—December 12, 1936— both girls gave their father a hug before the new king, dressed in the uniform of admiral of the fleet, left for the ceremony. After he had gone, Crawfie explained that when he returned he would be King George VI and from then on, they would have to curtsy to their parents, the new king and queen. They had always curtsied to their grandparents, King George V and Queen Mary, so it was not a huge change.

When he returned at one o'clock both girls swept him beautiful curtsies, the behavior of his daughters bringing home to him his changed station.

Crawfie recalled: "He stood for a moment touched and taken aback. Then he stooped and kissed them both warmly. After this we had an hilarious lunch."[11]

Like her father, Elizabeth had now transitioned to become a living symbol of the monarchy, her name mentioned in prayers, her doings and her dogs now the daily fodder for the breakfast newspapers, her life owned by the nation. She became, along with the Hollywood child star Shirley Temple, the most famous face in the world, a subject of wonder and adoration.

Her life as a fairy-tale princess was, in reality, less Disney more Brothers Grimm. The sisters' new life in Buckingham Palace, a sprawling, echoing place of sinister shadows, scurrying mice, gloomy rooms, and portraits with eyes that followed as one tiptoed past, was a mixture of excitement, boredom, and isolation. It was a place where childhood nightmares came to life, where the daily round of the royal rat catcher and his deadly paraphernalia symbolized the gruesome reality behind the perceived regal glamour. Though Elizabeth was thrown into the circumscribed circle of her sister, governess, maid, and nanny with her parents a distant harassed presence, she became an object of fascination for millions.

ॐ

In some ways nothing really had changed for the heir presumptive. Elizabeth, with her glowing ringlets of blond hair, had been a national symbol all her life. Born on Wednesday, April 21, 1926, at two forty in the morning, just days before the general strike that crippled the British economy, she represented, in the midst of national crisis, values of family, continuity, and patriotism. Not only was her arrival a welcome diversion from the daily struggle for subsistence in a postwar Britain racked by dispute and want, it was also somehow medieval, mysterious, and rather comical.

Royal custom dating back to the seventeenth century decreed that the home secretary be present at the birth lest an imposter be smuggled into the bedchamber. In keeping with tradition the current occupant of that office, William Joynson-Hicks, whose agitated mind was occupied with thoughts about how to defeat the trade unions in the coming conflict, sat in a nearby room at 17 Bruton Street, the duchess's family's London home, during the royal birth.

Once the baby was delivered, royal gynecologist Sir Henry Simson gave Joynson-Hicks an official document outlining the bare details of the birth of a "strong healthy female." The certificate was then handed to a special messenger who hurried to the president of the Privy Council to make the official announcement. At the same time the home secretary informed the lord mayor of London, who posted the news on the gates of his official residence, Mansion House.

In the official bulletin, signed by Simson and the duchess's personal doctor Walter Jagger, they stated that before the confinement a "certain line of treatment was successfully adopted," decorously suggesting that the princess had been delivered by cesarean section.[12]

Though the sleeping infant was, by virtue of the 1701 Act of Settlement, third in line to the throne behind her father and the Prince of Wales, and not expected to reign, her lineage was a rich stew of the royal, the exotic, and the common.

While her great-great-grandmother was Queen Victoria, she was also linked, through her grandmother Queen Mary, to dentist Paul Julius von Hügel, who practiced in the Argentinian capital of Buenos Aires. On her father's side the blood of European royalty, notably the German Houses of Saxe-Coburg-Gotha and Hanover, predominated, though it was her mother's British heritage that intrigued.

Anthony Wagner, Garter king of arms, noted that among Elizabeth's many aristocratic ancestors were two dukes, the daughter of a duke, the daughter of a marquess, three earls, the daughter of an earl, one viscount, one baron, and some half a dozen country gentlemen. It was not only the aristocracy represented in her bloodline but also the world of commerce and religion.

According to Wagner, her hereditary pedigree included a

director of the East India Company, a provincial banker, two daughters of bishops, three clergymen—one related to America's first president, George Washington—an Irish officer and his French mistress, a London toyman, and a metropolitan plumber as well as a certain Bryan Hodgson, the landlord of The George, a coaching inn in Stamford, Lincolnshire.

Though her heritage demonstrated a wide social range, the names chosen by her doting parents—Elizabeth Alexandra Mary—suggested her future destiny as queen. Others agreed, the *Daily Graphic* newspaper observing presciently: "The possibility that in the little stranger to Bruton Street there may be a future Queen of Great Britain (perhaps even a second and resplendent Queen Elizabeth) is sufficiently intriguing."[13]

With Uncle David only thirty-two and expected to marry and produce an heir, that likelihood seemed remote. Yet there was no doubting the fact that the royal infant had been taken into the nation's bosom. Judging by the excited crowds gathered outside her Bruton Street home, there was something singularly special about Elizabeth Alexandra Mary, perhaps a reflection of the fondness felt toward her mother who, just three years after her marriage to Bertie, was held in high esteem and affection. In an authorized account of the duchess's life, biographer Lady Cynthia Asquith admitted that she struggled to find anything other than sweet perfection in the character of the new mother.

Early photographs revealed Princess Elizabeth as the quintessential bonny baby, with her clear blue eyes, perfect pink and white skin, and a mop of blond hair. Or as Queen Mary, one of the first visitors, put it, she was "a little darling with lovely complexion and pretty fair hair."[14]

Without uttering a word, she propelled her parents from the quiet backwaters of royal life to the front pages of newspapers and magazines. She was the Princess Diana of her day, every morsel of information turned into a banquet of gossip and speculation. Newspapers were merely supplying popular demand—weeks after her birth the pavement outside her London home was thronged with so many onlookers that often she had to be smuggled out of the back entrance in her pram for her daily airing.

On the day of her christening at Buckingham Palace on May 29, such was the crush to see the infant that well-wishers broke through the police cordon outside the palace. Until order was restored, a lucky few who surrounded the Yorks' car were able to catch a glimpse of the infant who had, it was later reported, cried throughout the ceremony, which was conducted by the archbishop of York.

After a few months the Yorks moved to 145 Piccadilly near Hyde Park, the five-story establishment coming complete with a ballroom, electric elevator, library, dining room for thirty, and around seventeen staff including a steward, two footmen, a valet, and three nurses to attend the new arrival. Yet in a collective case of myopia, media correspondents lovingly described how the Yorks had rejected the showy and ornate, opting for a life of simplicity, especially in the royal nursery. In this miniature kingdom, neatness, order, and a sensible routine reigned. There was much approving clucking when it was revealed that the princess was only allowed to play with one toy at a time. Ironically when her parents returned from a six-month tour of Australia in 1927, they brought with them three tonnes of toys for the little girl the media now dubbed Betty.

Thus the eternal paradox of royalty, or our perception of royalty, evolved, that they were and are different but the same as ourselves. Without even knowing it, the baby princess slept soundly beneath an imagined layette of magic and myth, a gossamer blanket where new threads were constantly interwoven into the patchwork of legend and reality. It was a blanket that would accompany her throughout her life.

By the time she could walk and talk the child dubbed the "world's best known baby" had appeared on the cover of *Time* magazine under the tagline PINCESS LILYBET—a reference to how she spoke her name. She featured, too, on postage stamps, boxes of chocolates, tea caddies, tea towels, commemorative mugs, and other goods. Songs were sung in her honor, Madame Tussauds installed a waxwork of her on a pony, while the Australians named a piece of Antarctica after her. Her only rival in this sea of adulation was her uncle David, the Prince of Wales, who was a bona-fide international pinup matched only, during his lifetime, by the Hollywood heartthrob Rudolph Valentino.

Her mother was concerned about the inordinate amount of attention she engendered. During a visit to Edinburgh in May 1929 she wrote to Queen Mary: "It almost frightens me that the people should love her so much. I suppose that it is a good thing, and I hope that she will be worthy of it, poor little darling."[15]

As the months and years passed, the contours of her personality, real and imagined, began to emerge. Frequently described as "cherubic" or "angelic," she was portrayed as a sunny, well-behaved girl with an innocent wit and engaging and endearing temperament.

When the royal family gathered at Sandringham for Christmas 1927 she was described by the *Westminster Gazette* as "chattering and laughing and bombarding the guests with crackers handed to her by her mother."[16] Even Winston Churchill was impressed. On a visit to Balmoral on September 1928, he wrote to his wife, Clemmie: "She has an air of authority and reflectiveness astonishing in an infant."[17]

Stories soon circulated about how the unafraid girl had tamed her irascible grandfather King George V, who was known to strike terror into the hearts of his children and senior staff. When Princess Elizabeth was in his presence, though, he was putty in her little hands. The Archbishop of Canterbury recounted an occasion when the monarch acted the role of a horse being led around the room by his "groom" and granddaughter, who clung to his gray beard as he shuffled along the floor on his knees.

"He was fond of his two grandsons, Princess Mary's sons," recalled the Countess of Airlie, "but Lilibet always came first in his affections. He used to play with her—a thing I never saw him do with his own children—and loved to have her with him."[18] The fact that she was a cherubic little girl with an unselfconscious and vivid imagination, particularly regarding the world of horses, probably sealed the deal—demonstrated by the fact that when she was just four, the doting monarch gave her a Shetland pony named Peggy.

Indeed, her ability to soothe the troubled brow of the sovereign—echoes here of the medieval notion of the healing royal touch—became a talking point of the nation in February 1929 when the king traveled to the seaside resort of Bognor, on the south coast of England, to recover from a near-fatal illness. The two-year-old princess kept the old man amused with her chatter and was widely appreciated for her role in helping to effect his recovery. He loved that she later called him Grandpa England and was always attentive in his company, listening gravely as he extolled the virtues of duty, decency, and hard work.

The constant company of indulgent adults encouraged a certain guileless precocity. When she was taking a walk with Archbishop of Canterbury Cosmo Lang in the gardens at Sandringham, she asked that the conversation not dwell on God. "I know all about him already," said the nine-year-old, solemnly.[19]

Elizabeth made her first friend outside the immediate royal family when she was in Hamilton Gardens and saw a girl of her age playing. It was Sonia Graham-Hodgson, the daughter of the king's radiographer. "Will you come and have a game with me?" asked the slender creature with the bell-like voice. They played French cricket for an hour under the watchful gaze of their respective nannies. Afterward they met virtually every day—until Elizabeth had to move to Buckingham Palace. Even so for a long time the princess considered Sonia to be her best friend. She even dedicated an unfinished novel, *The Happy Farm*, written when she was eight, to her friend. Her inscription read: "To Sonia My Dear Little Friend and Lover of Horses."[20]

Sonia had happy memories of their long friendship: "She was a sweet child and great fun. She always had a great sense of humor and a vivid imagination."[21] Most games involved horses but sometimes they imagined they were invited to a grand ball and the girls would earnestly discuss what they would like to wear. Before the Second World War they took dance lessons together; afterward Elizabeth was guest of honor at Sonia's twenty-first birthday. Despite Elizabeth's elevation they stayed in touch and saw each other from time to time at dinner parties or for afternoon tea.

On August 21, 1930, a playmate of a very different kind entered her life when her sister Margaret Rose was born at Glamis Castle, the haunted ancestral home of the Strathmore family, located north of Dundee in Scotland. Once the formalities were dealt with—the new home secretary, John Robert Clynes, had traveled to the northern redoubt to certify the birth—Elizabeth was introduced to the infant. She was suitably "enchanted," especially when she realized that it wasn't a perfectly formed dolly but a living, if sound asleep, sister.

Thousands of well-wishers, some driving from Glasgow and south of the border, joined the celebrations at Glamis Castle, where huge bonfires were lit.[22] As with the birth of her elder sister days before the general strike, Margaret's arrival served as a sunny counterpoint to the dark economic clouds that had blanketed the nation since the stock market crash the previous October.

The temporary feeling of disappointment that the duchess had given birth to a girl rather than a boy served once more to highlight Elizabeth's constitutional position. It led to earnest discussion about the proposition that the crown could technically be shared between the sisters or that the younger sister could take precedence. It became such a source of debate that the king ordered a formal investigation into the vexing issue. As common sense suggested, it was officially recognized that Elizabeth had seniority. The constitutional niceties of being a member of the royal family were further brought home to the duchess when it came to the naming of her second child. She had to accept that the final decision was that of the girls' grandparents King George and Queen Mary, not the parents. Initially the Yorks were set on naming their child Ann Margaret, the duchess thinking Ann of York a pretty name. Her in-laws demurred, preferring Margaret Rose, Margaret being a Scottish queen and family ancestor. The king and queen prevailed. It would not be the last time they interfered in the upbringing of the royal princesses. The mother bit her tongue and busied herself with the new arrival. She was eager to describe her personality to friends and family. In a letter to Cosmo Lang, the Archbishop of Canterbury, she wrote: "Daughter number 2 really is very nice, I am glad to say that she has got large blue eyes and a will of iron, which is all the equipment that a lady needs! And as long as she can disguise her will, and use her eyes, then all will be well."[23]

The arrival of Margaret Rose added a new actor to the royal melodrama. Now a neat quartet—"We four," as the duke repeated endlessly—they represented home, hearth, and family. In an age of uncertainty, mass unemployment, and poverty, they were the embodiment of an ideal of ordinary, decent, God-fearing folk who lived modestly and sensibly. Even though they resided in a grandly exclusive town house adjacent to Hyde Park, complete with ballroom and electric elevator, it was the fact that they preferred a cozy home life to café society that ensured their popularity.

This compact between the nation and the family was epitomized when the people of Wales, the most depressed kingdom of the realm, presented Princess Elizabeth with a miniature house called Y Bwthyn Bach—The Little House—for her sixth birthday. Designed by Edmund Willmott, the thatched cottage, two-thirds the scale of a normal house, was a magnificent creation that came complete with electricity, running water, and a flushing toilet. There were pots and pans, books by Beatrix Potter, food cans, and even a gas cooker—all reduced to scale. It was installed at the Royal Lodge, the Yorks' new if dilapidated home in the Windsor Great Park.

The princesses were enthralled with the present, spending hours cleaning, brushing, polishing, and "cooking." Elizabeth would wrap the silverware in newspaper so that it wouldn't tarnish while Margaret's great joy was running up and down the stairs and pulling the plug in the bathroom and listening to the water gurgle through the pipes. Official palace-sanctioned photographs of the girls standing outside the front door of their cottage or playing with their beloved corgi dogs in the house garden gave the watching public a window into their innocent lives, further cementing the generational bond between the royal family and their subjects. Assessing the public's covetous fascination with the two princesses,

Alan "Tommy" Lascelles, the king's private secretary, described them as "Pets of the World."[24]

The sense that the young princesses were somehow daughters of the wider national family was reinforced by the authorized publication in 1936—months before the abdication—of a picture book titled *Our Princesses and Their Dogs*, which lovingly chronicled the eight dogs, including two corgis, owned by the family and the central place they occupied in their daily lives. The book also stands as a heartwarming allegory of the intimate relationship between royalty and its people, the book symbolizing that immutable compact, one that was strained but not broken before the year was out.

While the girls' corgis, Dookie and Lady Jane, were constant companions, the animals that ruled Elizabeth's nursery kingdom were her horses, real, inanimate, and imagined. Though her corgis became synonymous with her life and reign, her first passion was for the equestrian world, and Anna Sewell's well-thumbed equine classic, *Black Beauty*, was her bedside testament to that love. "If I am ever queen I shall make a law that there must be no riding on Sunday. Horses should have a rest too," she once pronounced, gravely.[25] Equine creatures were all-consuming in her young life, from leading the king around the room by his beard, to turning a string of Woolworths pearls into a rein to perform the same maneuver on the duchess's biographer Lady Cynthia Asquith, to playing circus horses at Birkhall in Scotland with her cousin Margaret Rhodes where it was "obligatory to neigh."[26] Later injuries she sustained, notably when she was thrown against a tree and, on another occasion, kicked in the jaw, did nothing to dim her enthusiasm. When she was five she rode out with the Pytchley Hounds, her father hoping that she would be "blooded," if there was a kill. There wasn't.

When her new governess, Scottish-born Marion Crawford, walked into her bedroom at Royal Lodge in October 1933, their first conversation concerned the two abiding interests in Elizabeth's life, namely her horses and her baby sister Margaret Rose. She had been allowed to stay up late to meet the woman she would later call Crawfie and was sitting on her wooden bed driving imaginary horses around the park. For reins, she used cords from her dressing gown, which were tied to her bedhead. "Have you seen Margaret," said the princess. "I expect she is asleep. She is adorable but very naughty sometimes. Will you teach her too and will you play with us both? Will you let me drive you round the garden?"[27]

For several years Crawfie, as the girls' companion and teacher, played the role of a docile working horse, making deliveries of groceries and other goods to folk in the neighborhood. During these playtime diversions Crawfie gained an insight into Elizabeth's vivid imagination, especially when the princess delivered the goods herself. As Crawfie recalled: "Then the most wonderful conversation took place—about the weather, the householders' horses, their dogs, chickens, children, and menfolk."[28]

Crawfie quickly realized that Elizabeth's interest in all matters equine was more than a passion; it verged on an obsession, a first and lasting love. The princess often remarked that if she had not been who she was, she would like to be a lady living in the country with lots of horses and dogs.[29] A variation was to be a farmer with cows, horses, and children.[30]

When she moved to Buckingham Palace the highlight of her week was her riding lesson with instructor Horace Smith. She spoke knowledgeably about galling, girths, and currying, an indication that her interest in horses was not just on their care but also their management.

The princess was so protective of the thirty or so wooden horses that crowded the fifth-floor nursery that when the family was about to move to Buckingham Palace, she gave her favorite horse Ben to her friend Sonia for safekeeping. It was delivered two weeks later, after her other horses had been unpacked and lined up in the corridor outside her room.[31]

For Elizabeth horse riding was a chance to be herself, to enjoy control in a socially acceptable setting. So much of her daily routine was out of her hands: Bobo chose her clothes, Alah picked her menu, Crawfie organized her lessons, her parents, grandparents, and the men in suits at Buckingham Palace defined her future. She went through a phase where she would wake several times in the night and ensure that her shoes and clothes were folded and arranged just so. It was control but in another guise.

Her education was a classic example of the continual battle for the heart and mind of the heir presumptive. While her grandfather King George V barked at Crawfie, "For goodness sake, teach Margaret and Lilibet to write a decent hand, that's all I ask of you,"[32] Queen Mary was much more involved. She vetted Crawfie's academic timetable, the royal matriarch suggesting more Bible reading and dynastic history. Most Mondays she took the girls on educational excursions incognito to the Royal Mint, the Tower of London, the Bank of England, as well as art galleries. These visits didn't always go to plan. On one occasion the party was looking around the Harrods department store when a craning crowd gathered to catch a glimpse of the princesses. Elizabeth became so excited at the prospect of so many people wanting to see her that her grandmother, not wanting her moment of stardom to go to her head, gently ushered her out by a back door.

It was Queen Mary—leader of the palace faction, augmented by Owen Morshead, the royal librarian, and the formidable

Lady Cynthia Colville, the queen's senior lady-in-waiting—who felt that Elizabeth's education was too ladylike and easygoing. There was little cognizance in her syllabus, such as it was, of her possible future role and responsibilities. According to Lady Cynthia, "no Bowes-Lyon ever cared anything for things of the mind." It was a judgment trusted royal chronicler Dermot Morrah considered a tad harsh given the fact that the family had produced three female poets.[33]

The princesses' mother felt very differently. She and the duke were not overly concerned about their daughters' academic education. The last thing they wanted was a pair of bluestockings, girls too smart for their own good. As Crawfie observed: "They wanted most for them a really happy childhood, with lots of pleasant memories stored up against the days that might come and, later, happy marriages."[34] For her part the Duchess of York had been brought up on fresh air, a little French, and a smattering of German. Her own parents, the Earl of Strathmore and Kinghorne and his wife, Cecilia Cavendish-Bentinck, had educated their youngest daughter at home with a governess, only sending her to a private day school in London when she was eight. More emphasis was laid on arranging a vase of flowers, sewing, dancing a reel, and reciting poetry than learning Greek or Latin. Young Elizabeth Bowes-Lyon was taught to be polite, to look after visitors, where to cast for salmon, when to pick up dead birds during a shoot, and how to handle a shotgun. She was, however, no intellectual slouch. When she finally attended school, she passed the Oxford Local Examination with distinction when she was just thirteen.

Literature and Scripture were her scholastic strengths, and so it was no surprise that the duchess insisted on teaching the girls Bible stories in her bedroom every morning. Kindness, courtesy, and Christian values mattered, the duchess believing

that a decent character, a moral compass, and a sensitive awareness of the needs of others were as important as, if not more
important than, intellectual endeavors. In a letter to her husband she laid out her own strictures. She reminded Bertie that
his own father lost the affection of his children because he
shouted at him and his brothers.

Stuck in the middle was the hired hand Marion Crawford,
only twenty-two. Though a graduate of Moray House college
of education in Edinburgh—the future alma mater to *Harry
Potter* novelist J. K. Rowling and Olympic cycling gold medalist
Chris Hoy—she was out of her depth in the subtle back-and-
forth of palace politics. Indeed the Yorks had chosen Crawfie
precisely because she was young enough to enthusiastically
join in with the children's games.

Lessons, which included math, geography, poetry—anything
about horses captured Elizabeth's interest—and English gram-
mar, took place only in the morning between nine thirty and
twelve thirty, with a thirty-minute break for drinks and snacks.
There were also frequent interruptions for visits to the dentist,
hairdresser, and dressmaker, Crawfie sensing that education did
not come high on the list of the duchess's priorities.

Any attempt to extend the school day by Crawfie was
resisted as the duchess was keen for the girls to enjoy outside
play. Often the duke joined in games of hopscotch, hide-and-
seek, and sardines in Hamilton Gardens at the rear of their
home. As she grew in confidence Crawfie took the children
farther afield, organizing trips on the subway, boat rides on the
river Thames, and even, at Elizabeth's insistence, an excursion
on the top deck of a double-decker bus. It quickly became
clear to her that the girls were eager to experience what other
children enjoyed as a matter of course.

The girls as well as Elizabeth's friend Sonia Graham-Hodgson had weekly dancing lessons with Marguerite Vacani where Elizabeth proved a skillful Scottish dancer. It was, however, those Hollywood hoofers Fred Astaire and Ginger Rogers who were all the rage. For a time Elizabeth's favorite was the 1935 hit "Cheek to Cheek."

They were also enrolled for music lessons with Mabel Lander, a student of the Second Viennese School. Elizabeth, sometimes accompanied by her mother, would sing English ballads, African American spirituals, and Scottish airs—"The Skye Boat Song" was an enduring favorite. When Margaret was old enough to join in, her elder sister was immediately impressed by her ability to pick up a tune by ear. French lessons, which often took place when Crawfie was on holiday, were not so popular. On one occasion, presumably in protest at the dull teaching methods, a bored Elizabeth picked up a silver inkpot and turned it upside down on her blond locks. Their French mistress Mademoiselle Lander had an attack of the vapors and left others to sort out the inky mess.

Music, dance, and drawing classes interspersed with occasional French lessons were all very well, but Crawfie felt that the girls needed the stimulation and companionship of children their own age. "In those days we lived in an ivory tower removed from the real world," she recalled in her memoir, *The Little Princesses*.[35]

One of her most satisfying achievements was in 1937 when she set up a Girl Guide and Brownie troop that met at Buckingham Palace every week. For once the sisters were able to mingle with their contemporaries—the thirty-four-strong troop comprised children of palace employees, friends, and courtiers. Elizabeth was deputy to her older cousin Lady Pamela Mountbatten in the Kingfisher patrol while Margaret, who was too young for the Guides, was in the specially created Brownie patrol.

It was just as well they had children of their own age to play with as there was a steep change in their lives once they moved into their rooms at Buckingham Palace in the spring of that year. When Elizabeth went out and about she was now accompanied by a detective who had the ability, to the girls' amusement, of seemingly making himself invisible. Elizabeth now spoke of the king and queen rather than Mummy and Daddy and spent more time curtsying and being curtsied to than at 145 Piccadilly. Even the nursery menus were in French—just like those put before the king and queen. As for the nightly pillow fights and other high jinks that punctuated their lives at 145 Piccadilly, these were soon a distant memory. Their parents were just too busy.

Besides playing skittles in the long palace corridors, there was one perk to being a princess in a palace. The young princess discovered that the act of walking in front of the sentries guarding her new home meant that they had to present arms. Walking back and forth in front of a sentry was a new game Elizabeth never tired of.

Trumping this delight was the excitement surrounding the coronation scheduled for May 1937. Queen Mary took the event as a didactic opportunity, bringing a panorama of the 1821 coronation of King George IV into the nursery and proceeding to teach the princesses about the symbolism and meaning of the coronation. By the end Elizabeth was, according to Crawfie, an expert. Perhaps as enticing as these rites and rituals was the prospect of wearing their first long dresses and lightweight coronets designed by their father. "They came to me very shyly," recalled Crawfie, "a little overawed by their own splendour and their first long dresses."[36]

In her serious motherly way, what concerned eleven-year-old Elizabeth most about the coronation was whether her little sister, then six, would behave. She remembered that when she had been bridesmaid at the wedding of her uncle the Duke of Kent and Princess Marina of Greece and Denmark at Westminster Abbey in November 1934, Margaret was allowed to sit quietly with her mother. However, when her big sister first appeared, walking down the aisle and holding the bridal train, Margaret had waved at her, possibly in a mischievous attempt to distract her from her solemn duties. Elizabeth would not be swayed. She gave her sister a stern look and shook her head in order to discourage Margaret from further misbehavior. Elizabeth did not want a repeat at the coronation. In the end she was happy to report to Crawfie that her sister had behaved beautifully. It was all the more commendable as both girls had been awake most of the night due to the singing and chatter among the waiting crowds outside the palace.

Princess Elizabeth recorded her memories of that historic day in a lined exercise book neatly tied with a piece of pink ribbon with a touching inscription written in red crayon on the cover. It read: "The Coronation, 12th May 1937. To Mummy and Papa in memory of their Coronation from Lilibet by herself."[37]

She described how she was woken by the Royal Marines Band outside her bedroom window. Then, clutching an eiderdown, she and Bobo MacDonald "crouched in the window looking onto a cold, misty morning."[38] After breakfast they dressed and paraded themselves in their finery before visiting their parents who were themselves in the midst of dressing for the big day.

After wishing them good luck, the princesses and Queen Mary climbed into a glass coach for a "jolty" ride to Westminster Abbey.

The princess was mesmerized by the elaborate choreography of the coronation and was rather disappointed that her grandmother had not remembered much about her own big day. At one point in the proceedings when the prayers seemed interminable, Elizabeth looked through the program and pointed to the word *Finis*, the princess and her grandmother enjoying a conspiratorial moment together.

The coronation was living history, up close and personal, as well as a vivid and enthralling foretaste of the next stage in her royal education. This began with her attendance at her first Buckingham Palace garden party, followed by Trooping the Colour and finally the ancient royal ceremony of the Order of the Garter held at St. George's Chapel in Windsor Castle. With no baby brother on the horizon, Elizabeth's on-the-job training intensified. When Joseph Kennedy, the new American ambassador to the court of King James, arrived in London in March 1938, the king placed his eldest daughter next to him at a luncheon held at Windsor. So that she did not feel entirely left out, Margaret accompanied the Kennedys and her family on a walk through Frogmore Gardens. On another occasion, this time when President Lebrun of France made a state visit in March 1939, the princess joined her father and the French president on the drive from Buckingham Palace to Victoria Station, from which the French delegation departed.

Somewhat belatedly, the new queen now realized that her eldest daughter's academic education needed to broadened. After discussions with among others Sir Jasper Ridley, a banker and fellow of Eton College, it was decided that the princess should study constitutional history with Henry Marten, the vice provost of Eton. Although she was at first apprehensive about her twice-weekly visits to the all-boy college, she soon struck up a friendship with the dapper scholar, enjoying this grown-up introduction to politics, history, and current affairs. Indeed, political theater was playing out right in front of her when her parents appeared on the balcony of Buckingham Palace in September 1938 with Prime Minister Neville Chamberlain and his wife, Anne, to celebrate the famous Munich Agreement, which brought "peace in our time" with Nazi leader Adolf Hitler.

She was indeed growing up. Now thirteen, she was, according to Crawfie, "an enchanting child with the loveliest hair and skin and a long, slim figure."[39] Not that the Eton boys seemed to notice. If any boys needed to visit the vice provost's rooms or saw her in the corridors, they politely doffed their top hats and went about their business. For a girl who had been gawked at all her life this was a refreshing change, though it is possible that the growing adolescent, seeing boys en masse for the first time, felt their well-bred indifference was a tad too, well, indifferent.

Apart from her cousins George and Gerald Lascelles, the sons of her aunt Princess Mary, Elizabeth had had little to do with boys during her childhood. It is perhaps unsurprising, given her fascination with horses, that her first girlish crush was on Owen, the young stud groom. In her eyes he was the font of all wisdom and could do no wrong—much to the exasperated amusement of her parents, particularly her father.

The father-daughter relationship was by far the most significant. "The king had a great pride in her, and she in turn had an inborn desire to do what was expected of her," observed Crawfie.[40] Theirs was a loving, complex relationship, the king, a reserved, shy man, admiring her precocious maturity while gallantly trying to protect her from her lonely future. At times it seemed that he wanted to stop the clock, to keep his daughters as children rather than growing girls.

For her part her father brought out her mothering nature, especially when he suffered one of his "gnashes"—outbursts of temper caused by his frustrated inability to conquer his persistent stammer. Both girls learned how to bring their father out of these dark moods. They also learned to keep out of his way and let Mama deal with him.

In the summer of 1939, with prospect of war hovering over the horizon, the royal party sailed to naval college at Dartmouth in the southwest of England aboard the royal yacht, the *Victoria and Albert*.

It was here on July 22 that Elizabeth would meet the young man who would change her life. The omens were not propitious. Though the girls were due to attend a service in the chapel after an inspection of the cadets, it was decided that, because two cadets had mumps—which can cause infertility— the girls should spend time at the house of the captain of the college, Sir Frederick Dalrymple-Hamilton. His two eldest children, North, aged seventeen, and nineteen-year-old Christian, were deputed to keep them occupied. In the midst of playing with a clockwork train on the floor of the nursery, the quartet was joined by a good-looking boy with piercing blue eyes, sharp features, an offhand manner, and the look of a Viking. Enter Prince Philip of Greece, the Adonis-like nephew of the king's ADC, Lord Louis Mountbatten. The prince, then eighteen, was soon bored with trains and suggested jumping over the nearby tennis net instead. Though Crawfie thought him a "show off," her charges had a different perspective, admiring how high he could jump. Even though Elizabeth never took her eyes off him, he paid her little attention. He was simply doing his duty when his uncle Louis ordered him to keep the girls company. He would have much preferred to attend the main event where the king inspected the ranks of aspiring naval officers.

If he had been told by that incorrigible royal matchmaker, Uncle Louis, to befriend Elizabeth, then he made a halfhearted job of it. At lunch the following day, he exhibited a youthful enthusiasm for the extensive menu rather than make small talk with his royal companion. In short order the hungry cadet, who was more used to navy rations, devoured several plates of shrimp, a banana split, and anything else in his reach. "To the little girls, a boy of any kind was always a strange creature out of another world," noted Crawfie, who was somewhat censorious of his overconfidence in company. "Lilibet sat pink faced, enjoying it very much. To Margaret anyone who could eat so many shrimps was a hero."[41]

He was a strange, exotic creature indeed. After all, royal blood aside, the backgrounds and upbringings of Elizabeth and Philip could not have been more different. His was an extraordinary, scarcely believable early life. His grandfather was assassinated, his father imprisoned, his mother Princess Alice forcibly placed in an asylum. He was famously born on a dining table in a villa called Mon Repos on the Greek island of Corfu. Shortly after his birth, the infant, an orange box for his crib, and the rest of his family escaped the island aboard an English destroyer after his father Prince Andrea was sent into permanent exile; a death sentence imposed by a military tribunal was commuted following the intervention of George V.

From the age of eight he led a wandering lifestyle, seeing little of his father—who moved in with his mistress in a small apartment in Monte Carlo—and less of his mother. Within eighteen months his four sisters all married and had moved to Germany to be with their aristocratic husbands. Philip was enrolled at Cheam boarding school and studied at Salem in Germany before completing his formal education at Gordonstoun in north Scotland, the newly founded school run by Kurt Hahn, a German Jew who had escaped from his home country.

For all his travails, Philip was remembered as a cheerful,

lively fellow with an inquisitive mind and a natural sporting ability. He had no sense of self-pity about those days: "The family broke up," he told his biographer Gyles Brandreth. "My mother was ill, my sisters were married, my father was in the South of France. I had to get on with it. You do. One does."[42] At Gordonstoun he was made guardian or head boy; at Dartmouth he won the King's Dirk for the best all-around cadet of his entry.

He certainly caught the eye of the princess and the rest of the royal party as the *Victoria and Albert* slowly sailed along the estuary followed by a flotilla of rowboats while the excited cadets gave the ship a rousing farewell.

As the estuary broadened some boys still followed in the ship's wake. Finally the king, fearing that one of the cadets might get into trouble, told the commander of the royal yacht, Sir Dudley North, to signal them to go back. Eventually all the boys headed back to shore apart from one young blade who ignored all entreaties. It was Philip, who was watched intently through the binoculars by Lilibet. Eventually the young prince realized no one was impressed by his seaborne bravado and headed back to college.

Six weeks later Britain declared war on Germany. Shortly afterward Philip was appointed midshipman and assigned to the battleship HMS *Ramillies*. The girls first heard the news of the impending conflict when minister Dr. John Lamb preached an emotional sermon at Crathie Kirk near Balmoral where they were staying. He told the congregation that peace was over and Britain was once again at war.

As they left the service, nervous and excited, Margaret asked Crawfie: "Who is this Hitler, spoiling everything?"[43]

They would soon find out.

2

⚜

Bombs at Bedtime

Shortly after Winston Churchill became wartime prime minister in May 1940, a Nazi spy was parachuted into Britain. The Dutch-born agent who went by the name of Jan Willem Ter Braak carried with him a revolver, a radio transmitter, fake documents, and a bundle of cash. His orders were simple: find and kill Winston Churchill. For a time he lived with a couple in Cambridge and then, his money running out and fearing capture, he walked inside an air raid shelter and shot himself.[1] This was probably the earliest of at least three plots to kill the wartime leader, the conspirators sometimes killing the wrong target. As Churchill himself noted in his war memoirs: "The brutality of the Germans was only matched by the stupidity of their agents."[2] He was too dismissive. The German policy of killing or capturing political leaders and royal heads of state came within a whisker of success. George VI, the queen, whom Hitler later described as "the most dangerous woman in Europe," and their daughters were high on the list for imprisonment. One plan was for parachutists to drop into the garden of Buckingham Palace and other royal parks and hold the king and his family under "German protection."

The man behind this scheme, Dr. Otto Begus, had almost snared Queen Wilhelmina of the Netherlands during the Nazi invasion of the Low Countries. While troops parachuted over the royal residence at The Hague, Begus and his Kommando were involved in air-landing operations that led to a number of gliders crashing at the nearby Valkenburg airport.

Wilhelmina, with only the clothes she was wearing, just managed to avoid being caught, leaving behind all her personal belongings and making her way to the Hook of Holland. There, a British destroyer, HMS *Hereward*, was waiting to pick up the queen, her family, the Dutch government's gold and diamond reserves, as well as the Dutch government itself. The operation, code-named Harpoon Force, was a success though the destroyer was attacked by Stuka bombers during the passage to England. Eventually Wilhelmina safely arrived at Buckingham Palace, where the exhausted sovereign recounted her adventures to the king and queen.

The Belgian king, Leopold III, was not so fortunate. On May 28, days before the fall of France, he controversially surrendered his forces to the Nazis after the embattled troops were surrounded. He spent the rest of the war imprisoned in his château outside Brussels and was finally sent to Austria.

Throughout Europe, other crowned heads were on the run from the Nazi invaders. King Haakon of Norway spent weeks evading capture as he and his son, Crown Prince Olav, were chased by a one-hundred-strong squad of crack Nazi paratroopers. Like Queen Wilhelmina, he was eventually rescued, the exhausted sovereign and his son clambering aboard the British heavy cruiser HMS *Devonshire* and taken to England. Upon arriving at Buckingham Palace, they were so tired after their traumatic escape on June 7 that they fell dead asleep on the floor, the queen quietly tiptoeing around them lest she disturb their slumbers.

Farther south, the Duke and Duchess of Windsor, who were in neutral Portugal, narrowly avoided being kidnapped. Under a plan code-named Operation Willi, Hitler sent his top spymaster Walter Schellenberg to Lisbon to head a team who planned to capture the royal couple and spirit them across the border to Franco's Nazi-friendly Spain. In the nick of time Churchill got wind of the plot and ensured that the couple boarded a ship bound for the Bahamas, where the former king became the reluctant governor.

Hitler's grand scheme was based on the thinking that by installing the duke as a puppet king of the soon-to-be-conquered England or holding other European royals as hostages, they could be used as puppet-rulers or as surety for the continuing good behavior of their citizens. It was a strategy as old as warfare.

In the summer of 1940, with Britain on the ropes, its expeditionary force rescued at great cost from the bloodstained beaches of Dunkirk from late May to early June, Hitler was circling for the kill. Sometime in August 1940, as the invasion plan, code-named Operation Sea Lion, was being drawn up, Begus, according to his later testimony,[3] received written instructions to report for a special mission. His target this time was the British royal family. A specially trained Kommando of parachutists, including some from the Dutch mission, was readied to capture the king, the queen, and their daughters. The emphasis was on taking the royal hostages alive. Parachutists were briefed on the correct salute and form of address when seizing a member of the royal family.

In the grand German scheme it was Hitler's belief that if the airborne kidnapping attempt had succeeded, Britain would

have been forced to surrender. Only the failure of the Luftwaffe to win the Battle of Britain resulted in the plan being
scrapped. Even so, the prospect of German paratroopers landing in Buckingham Palace, the Tower of London, and other
royal residences was one taken very seriously by the royal
family and military planners.[4]

The queen, who was frightened of being captured, practiced her shooting skills with a pistol in the gardens of Buckingham Palace, using rats flushed from bombed royal outbuildings
as targets. Her niece Margaret Rhodes later recalled: "I suppose quite rightly, she thought if parachutists came down and
whisked them away somewhere, she could at least take a para-
chutist or two with her."[5]

King George VI, who now carried a rifle and a pistol when
he traveled, personally supervised the removal of the priceless
Crown Jewels from the Tower of London to Windsor Castle,
where they were wrapped in cotton wool, placed in leather
hatboxes, and hidden in the castle dungeons.

Behind the brave smiles and the confident public glad-
handing, both the king and queen felt a sense of impending doom during the most fateful summer since the Spanish
Armada threatened invasion in 1588.

Anticipating the grim uncertain days that lay ahead, the
queen wrote to her eldest sister Rose asking if she would look
after the princesses if anything happened to the king or herself.
Rose gladly agreed, saying: "I do promise you that I will try my
very best & will go straight to them should anything happen
to you both—which God forbid."[6]

Though both the king and queen spoke about going down
fighting should the Nazis invade, there was the distressing issue
of what to do about their precious daughters. Many of their
aristocratic friends had sent their offspring to Canada; others

had opted to evacuate their children to the country. After the declaration of war on September 3, 1939, following Germany's invasion of Poland, the princesses stayed at Birkhall Lodge in the Scottish Highlands—Balmoral was considered a target for Nazi bombers—while their parents, along with a skeleton staff, kept Buckingham Palace open. For the first few months of the so-called Phony War the girls rode their horses, played innocent games such as catching falling leaves and making a wish, and learned French under the watchful eye of Georgina Guerin. She later returned to her home country where she played a leading role in the Resistance. In addition, Elizabeth continued her history lessons with Henry Marten by post. The war seemed a long way away, though doubtless the girls, sensitive to parental moods, sensed the strain behind the lighthearted banter during the daily six o'clock telephone call. Even the fitting of gas masks seemed no more than a game, Princess Margaret, then nine, treating the rubber object as a strange toy.

Naturally the queen wanted to spare her daughters from worry as far as possible, telling Crawfie to monitor radio broadcasts and newspaper coverage. "Stick to the usual programme as far as you can Crawfie," ordered the king. Easier said than done, as the girls frequently tuned in to hear the loquacious pro-Nazi broadcaster Lord Haw-Haw, aka Irishman William Joyce, and his defeatist radio show. Often they were so appalled by his tirades that they pelted the radio with cushions and books.

The sinking in October of the *Royal Oak* battleship with the loss of 834 men and boys brought home to the girls the cruel reality of warfare. "Crawfie, it can't be," expostulated Princess Elizabeth. "All those nice sailors." It was a confusing and concerning time, especially as their parents were 520 miles away where, to their young minds, it seemed that Hitler could easily capture them.

Even though they were staying in the idyllic surroundings of royal Deeside, the tentacles of war touched everything. Every Thursday, Crawfie organized a sewing club in aid of the war effort, the girls serving refreshments for the roomful of local women. The king's decision to allow Craigowan Lodge on the Balmoral estate to be used to house evacuated children from the tenements of Glasgow certainly widened the girls' horizons. When they arrived, often with their mothers, Crawfie insisted that the princesses welcome them and offer the visitors a cheering cup of tea.

For the princesses, who had grown up in the country, it was like an encounter with creatures from an alien planet. Many of these youngsters, raised in poverty in the Gorbals district of Glasgow, had never seen a rabbit, a deer, or a pony or ever soaked up the silence of rolling hills—nor experienced the pleasures of a hot bath.

Another unusual presence at the time were Canadian lumberjacks who used their expertise to cut a swath through the Balmoral estate to provide timber for the war effort. Wartime made for odd friendships but ensured that both girls grew up much faster than they would have been allowed in peacetime. Though the queen liked to see her daughters in matching outfits, which inevitably made Princess Elizabeth seem younger than her years, the dislocation of their routine, the absence of her parents, and the uncertain grind of war made for a childhood cut short. At Christmas the girls enjoyed a welcome change of scene when the queen asked Crawfie to bring her daughters to Sandringham even though the flat Norfolk coastline was seen as a probable German invasion site. Indeed, while the girls were heading south, their near Norfolk neighbor the Earl of Leicester, who owned Holkham Hall, sent his daughters Anne and Carey to Scotland out of harm's way.

The royal children were different. Their whereabouts on mainland Britain were seen as a litmus test of the resolve of the nation's leaders. If they had been sent to Canada or a neutral country, it would have been a body blow to the country's morale and resistance. In late May 1940 when Prime Minister Churchill was shown preparatory plans for the evacuation of himself, the government, and the royal family, he flatly stated that "no such discussion"[7] should even be permitted. For once the queen outdid Churchill's rhetoric with her ringing phrase: "The children could not go without me, and I could not possibly leave the King, and the King would never go!"[8]

Yet the subject was discussed, despite Churchill's firm stance. In preparation for the potential arrival of the royal family following the expected German invasion, the Canadian government spent $75,000 purchasing Hatley Hall, a forty-bedroom mock-Tudor mansion on Vancouver Island, for the express use of the family. In his diary the Canadian prime minister William Mackenzie King wrote in May 1940 that the king and queen could be arriving shortly, implying that Britain would soon fall and Canada would be the refuge for the defeated government and what was left of the nation's armed forces.[9]

The debate about what to do with the heir presumptive and her sister, independently of the king and queen, occupied the minds of ministers and the military. It was accepted that the king and queen would want to stay with the resistance in Britain. However, if the fight were to continue from Canada, then the heir presumptive should be there as the legitimate head of the British state in exile. With a blackout on any discussion, some generals feared that a delayed departure would place Elizabeth and Margaret in unnecessary danger. The government would hear none of it, ministers alarmed that rumors were already circulating that suggested the princesses had departed for Canada.

At that time, in the summer of 1940, the princesses and the king and queen were being protected by different military units. In July, Major Jim Coats, MC of the Coldstream Guards, was assembling what King George would later call "my private army." Coats, a brilliant skier, skeleton racer, hotshot, skilled fisherman, and more important friend of the royal family, was in charge of the eponymous Coats Mission. Under the code name Operation Rocking Horse, he and his fellow Coldstream Guards were tasked with guarding the king and queen to "the last man and the last bullet." If they were in peril of being captured, it was their job to ensure a fighting retreat to one of four country houses in Worcestershire, Yorkshire, or Shropshire. Specially adapted armored cars were earmarked for the operation to ferry the royal couple to relative safety inland. Only when the country was in danger of complete collapse would they be flown to Canada via Iceland or alternatively sail to the Dominions from a destroyer anchored at the port of Liverpool. Members of the royal family were asked to keep a suitcase packed by their bedsides, ready for their possible evacuation. Queen Mary, safely ensconced in Badminton House in Gloucestershire, kept her most precious jewels—rather than clothing and toiletries—in her leather overnight baggage.

The strategy for the heir presumptive and her sister, who had been moved from Royal Lodge to Windsor Castle during the desperate days of May 1940, was somewhat different. Should there be a parachute attempt to kidnap the girls, on the lines of Begus's plan, it was up to Lieutenant Michael Tomkin of the 2nd Northamptonshire Yeomanry to ensure their safety. This company was effectively "Lizzie's private army." Such was the importance of their protective mission that shortly after receiving his orders, Tomkin and his troop found themselves in possession of four of the handful of armored cars left in the country—the retreating British army had left all their heavy equipment on the Belgian and French shoreline. They promptly adapted two for the princesses, removing the machine gun and installing two small armchairs for their comfort.

His troop then began practicing, usually at night, the routes they would take to a selected safe house—Madresfield Court in Worcestershire was initially earmarked as the base, known as Establishment A, for the royal family and government. As a special treat he took the two princesses as well as Crawfie and a corgi on a trial run around Home Park. It was, as far as the girls were concerned, an exciting and enjoyable experience.

Their father's rival private army did not fare so well. One evening he was discussing security with his temporary house-guest King Haakon, who asked what preparations were in place in case of a much-feared German parachute attack. With a flourish the king pressed an alarm signal and then invited the Norwegian monarch to join him and the queen in the garden to watch what he anticipated would be a rapid response from the designated defense force. In fact nothing happened. An equerry, who was eventually dispatched to discover what was going on, reported back that after the alarm had sounded the duty police sergeant told the officer of the guard that no attack was pending. Finally, after this bureaucratic delay, guardsmen began running into the garden. As far as the exiled king was concerned, their behavior did not inspire confidence. The king's biographer John Wheeler-Bennett took up the story: "To the horror of King Haakon but the vast amusement of the king and queen, they proceeded to thrash the undergrowth in the manner of beaters at a shoot rather than of men engaged in the pursuit of a dangerous enemy."[10]

The dire situation facing the country was no laughing matter. Several weeks later, on September 7, 1940, the code word

Cromwell was broadcast signifying that a German invasion was imminent. Church bells tolled through the night, several bridges were blown, and land mines were haphazardly laid on roads. The warning, which placed the men of the Coats Mission on high alert, marked the effective beginning of the Blitz, with the Luftwaffe sending wave after wave of bombers over southern England. London was the first target and the hardest hit, the royal family firmly in the front line. Buckingham Palace was bombed in the first attack though the explosion caused little damage. The second attack, on September 9, 1940, could have been far more serious. A bomb landed near the king's study but failed to explode. Thinking it was a dud, the king continued working. It was a foolhardy assumption as the bomb later exploded in the early hours of the night, causing considerable damage to the north front of the palace, breaking every window and dislodging much plasterwork. It was a lucky escape for the king—and the country.

An even more serious attack took place on September 13, when a single German bomber flew straight up the Mall and dropped six bombs, two landing near the king who was with his private secretary Alec Hardinge. "The whole thing happened in a matter of seconds," the king wrote later. "We all wondered why we weren't dead."[11] It was clear that Buckingham Palace was the target for this daring daylight attack, the king and others suspecting that the pilot was one of his many German relations. In total the palace was bombed sixteen times during the war, nine of which were direct hits. Thanks to the RAF and its decisive impact in the Battle of Britain, the fear of parachutists landing in the king's garden receded. In reality the bombing attacks on Buckingham Palace were a tremendous propaganda victory, cementing the emotional compact between the sovereign and his people and producing a worldwide wave of sympathy for the beleaguered royal family, especially in the United States. This patriotic sentiment was expressed in the queen's ringing phrase: "I'm glad we've been bombed, now I can look the East End in the face."[12] (The East End was a poor part of London that had taken the brunt of the damage.)

The sympathetic smiles and handshakes with victims and rescuers alike disguised the increased strain felt by both the king and queen. The queen found the air raid shelter at Buckingham Palace deeply claustrophobic, the nightly bombing terrifying, and the fate of herself and her family a constant source of concern. The war was all-consuming, physically and emotionally, and with every passing day there came another reminder of the transitory nature of life. The queen, whose beloved older brother Fergus Bowes-Lyon was killed during World War One, felt the suffering of others keenly. Every new dawn brought fresh horrors. In September 1940, for example, the queen visited a school in London's poor East Ham district that had been bombed. Scores of children waiting to be evacuated were among the dead and injured. "It does affect me seeing this terrible and senseless destruction. I think that really I mind it much more than being bombed myself," she wrote to Queen Mary.[13]

At least she and the king were able to see their children most evenings, the couple spending nights at Windsor Castle where a large reinforced air raid shelter under Brunswick and later Victoria Tower was prepared for the royal family. In the first few weeks Windsor was spared the worst of the bombing, the only excitement being the downing in September of a German Messerschmitt fighter in the grounds of Windsor Great Park. The princesses and their friend Alathea Fitzalan Howard, who lived in the park, found the downed plane in the woods and took souvenirs back to the castle. Most nights the ringing of the alarm bell inside the castle warned of an imminent air raid. Sleep was constantly disrupted by the bombing and retaliatory ground fire. "We seemed to be living in a sort of dimly lit underworld—again, with no central heating," commented Crawfie.[14]

In the early days the tardy arrival of the princesses in the air raid shelter caused anxiety among members of the royal household, fearful that they could be injured or worse if they didn't reach the relative safety of the shelter in time. On one occasion young Princess Margaret, then ten, was delayed looking for a pair of suitable knickers to wear. After the girls were provided with one-piece siren suits and their "treasures" put in small suitcases to bring with them, the journey time from their bedroom to the air raid shelter was much improved.

This was just as well, as for two consecutive nights in October the princesses suffered the unnerving sound of so-called whistle and scream bombs amid the thud, thud, thud of anti-aircraft guns, which were mounted around the castle. Though the castle was not hit that night, by war's end three hundred bombs had exploded in or around it. In her diary entry for early October, Alathea, who lived only a short distance from the castle, recorded her own terrifying experience as numerous bombs, some delayed-action, exploded nearby. "In my bed, I lay and shook with a wild terror I have never known before." A few hours later a time bomb went off. "I lay in speechless horror watching my walls rock violently from side to side."[15] Doubtless Alathea, who joined the princesses for drawing and dance classes every week, regaled them with her alarming experiences.

The noise of falling bombs and the strain and stress of constant anticipation of another air raid physically changed the princesses, the queen commenting later that her daughters

looked careworn and "different." "Though they are so good
& composed there is always listening & occasionally a leap
behind the door and it does become a strain," she wrote to
Queen Mary.[16]

That same month, October, Princess Elizabeth, then fourteen, made her first-ever radio broadcast, a word-perfect four-
minute chat about the trials and tribulations suffered by the
many children who had left their families behind for the relative safety of life in the far-flung Dominions. The princess,
who endlessly practiced her speech, reminded her worldwide
audience—special arrangements were made to broadcast her
talk in America—that children were full of cheerfulness and
courage in spite of having to "bear our share of the danger and
sadness of war."[17] The broadcast ended with Elizabeth urging
her sister to join with her in a wishing everyone good night.
Princess Margaret responded, "Good night, children."

As she listened to the broadcast from her temporary home
in Scotland, their playmate Anne Coke, who lived at Holkham
Hall, remembered thinking: "They were our heroines...there
were the two princesses still in England, in as much danger as us all."[18] And sharing the same privations. The king
was punctilious in abiding by the rationing and heating rules.
When they were older the girls were told that they should
never accept presents, especially such coveted items as nylons.
This life of necessary parsimony even affected the normally
compliant princesses. When the senior politician Sir Stafford
Cripps came to dine he asked for an omelet, which made a
considerable dent in the royal family's egg ration. As he tucked
in, the princesses scowled and pulled faces behind his back,
knowing that they would have to go without.

Like many in wartime Britain, the girls led a life of dramatic contrasts. On the days when Elizabeth met with her

history teacher Henry Marten, who arrived at Windsor Castle in his pony and trap, they would sit and discuss British history in one of the nation's most historic buildings while in the skies above them history was being made in the Battle of Britain.

Though a sure-footed teacher, Marten became rather hesitant when the topic moved firmly on to the British constitution. Given that the waning of the powers of the sovereign went hand in hand with the nation's unwritten constitution, he was worried as to how he should discuss the subject with the future monarch. When he asked Alan Lascelles for advice, he was told to "hide nothing."[19] For his efforts, in 1945 the king knighted Marten.

Less contentious was the academic assistance of Marie-Antoinette de Bellaigue, known as Toinon, who replaced Georgina Guerin, now a Resistance leader. She was hired to make the princesses proficient in spoken French. "In our general conversations," she later recalled, "I endeavored to give the princesses an awareness of other countries, their way of thought and their customs—sometimes a source of amusement. Queen Elizabeth II has always had from the beginning a positive good judgment. She was her simple self, très naturelle. And there was always a strong sense of duty mixed with *joie de vivre* in the pattern of her character."[20]

Princess Margaret translated her language tuition into French country and nursery songs, her clear young voice often heard ringing out from her room as she accompanied herself on the piano.

Their time in the classroom conferred a sense of routine and normalcy during the dark days of wartime Britain. Crawfie ensured that, far from being hidden upstairs with their governess, the young princesses were introduced to a wider cross section of the population than they ever would have met during peacetime.

She was particularly proud of inaugurating a Girl Guide troop at Windsor comprising daughters of household officials, local children, and youngsters from London's impoverished East End whose houses had been bombed or who had lost their parents and were living with families on the Windsor estate. There was no standing on ceremony. These young Cockneys, whose accents were as indecipherable as those of the children from the Gorbals in Glasgow, called Princess Elizabeth by her family-only pet name of Lilibet after hearing Margaret speak to her. "Margaret was the livelier one, full of fun and jokes," recalled fellow Sea Ranger Joan Scragg. Elizabeth was more reserved.[21]

Overfamiliar or not, everyone mucked in. When the girls went camping in Windsor Great Park, the king would sometimes join them, helping to erect tents and dig latrines. After cookouts and campfires the princesses, somewhat dolefully at first, did their fair share of washing up and foraging for wood. (Elizabeth enjoyed washing up so much that regular and enduring Christmas presents were pairs of rubber gloves.)

That winter the princesses left the Scout troop and spent Christmas with their parents at Appleton House, a retreat regularly used by the Norwegian royal family on the Sandringham estate. Here they mixed and mingled with the young officers from the Coats Mission, the eager young men soon seen as almost part of the wider royal family. They joined them at church, were invited for dinner and tea, and went pheasant shooting with the king on the estate's broad acres—though a four-star general objected when his soldiers were used as beaters to flush out pheasants for the guns.

Guards officer Major Malcolm Hancock recalled the occasion when the princesses came to have tea with his fellow officers: "We had a game of animal grab [a riotous card game] and Princess Margaret got so excited she jumped on the table."[22]

During their long winter sojourn the princesses played hide-and-seek and went on treasure hunts while Princess Elizabeth joined the men for a game of ice hockey on the frozen lake near York Cottage where George V had lived. Elizabeth scored a goal and then she and her sister joined in enthusiastically in the ensuing snowball fight.

Musical entertainment was also masterminded by the men of the Coats Mission, Temporary Captain Ian Oswald Liddell organizing the Christmas pantomime *Cinderella*, subtitled *So What and the Seven Twirps*. The royal family joined in heartily when "Old MacDonald Had a Farm" was sung, Margaret practicing the snorts and other farmyard noises for hours afterward. Some time later at a cocktail party for Coats Mission officers and their wives she sang the song again—farmyard noises included.

Such was the informality between the royal family and their military escorts that they had a collection and bought a box of chocolates for Princess Elizabeth's fifteenth birthday, which was on April 21, 1941.

Upon their return to Windsor Castle, Elizabeth and Margaret entertained officers from the Grenadier Guards, those recuperating from injury as well as airmen on leave. Though their father's preferred service was the Royal Navy, the daughters had a sneaking admiration for the magnificent men in their flying machines whose heroics had saved the nation from Nazi invaders. On the gramophone, the girls endlessly played the wartime dance favorite "Comin' in on a Wing and a Prayer," about a missing plane limping back to base. Like thousands of children, the princesses had memorized the characteristic sound and silhouette of every plane, German or British. In April 1941 they were thrilled to receive a model of a Spitfire, fashioned by a Czech pilot from the scrap of a downed

Dornier bomber. Given their sky-high passion for the RAF, it is not hard to imagine the excitement felt by both girls when they were introduced to a genuine, medal-wearing Battle of Britain fighter pilot who was to be a temporary equerry. He was the highly decorated squadron commander and ace Peter Townsend—as heroic and dashing a figure as the war ever produced in England. The queen described him as a "charming" man who "fits in beautifully."[23]

At teas and more formal luncheons in honor of the military men, some of whom were preparing for combat, Elizabeth arranged the seating plan, offered food, and opened the conversation. For the princess, who was appointed Colonel of the Grenadier Guards in February 1942 and whose first official public engagement on her sixteenth birthday two months later was an inspection of a regimental parade at Windsor, life at the castle was about keeping conversation bright and lighthearted, leaving dark thoughts of mortality for another day.

In her capacity as honorary colonel, she experienced firsthand the prosaic and arbitrary brutality of war, a profound sense of impermanence where she was now able to put faces to the names of those killed in action. Temporary Captain Liddell, for example—who in happier times organized the 1941 Sandringham pantomime—was killed in action a few days before VE Day, his heroism earning him the Victoria Cross, the highest award for gallantry.

The princess found herself writing to the families of those who never returned, describing the characters of their loved ones and how they were remembered during their time at Windsor Castle. Queen Elizabeth was sensitive to the effect the war was having on her daughters, aware, as she wrote to her brother David Bowes-Lyon in October 1943, that it was a "beastly time" for people growing up. "Lilibet meets young Grenadiers at Windsor and then they get killed and it is horrid for someone so young. So many good ones have gone recently."[24]

One positive side effect of her social leadership role was to force her to confront her chronic shyness head-on—with a little advice from her mother.

As Elizabeth's lifelong friend Prudence, Lady Penn, recalled: "Her mother said to her, 'When you walk into a room, walk through the middle of the door.' She meant, don't go in apologetically, walk like you're in charge. That was very good advice. And it's advice she's certainly followed to this day."[25] Crawfie also noted the transition. From being "a rather shy little girl," Elizabeth became "a very charming young person, able to cope with any situation without awkwardness,"[26] and she developed into "an excellent conversationalist."[27]

The princess was not one for gossip, though, as her best friend during the war, Alathea Fitzalan Howard, described. "She's the most ungossipy person I know. Placid and unemotional, she never desires what doesn't come her way; always happy in her own family, she never needs the companionship of outsiders; she never suffers, therefore she never strongly desires."[28]

The constraints and responsibilities of her position in wartime Britain emphasized and endorsed her stoical, reserved character and her somewhat solemn demeanor, qualities perceptively observed by First Lady Eleanor Roosevelt when she visited Britain in October 1942. She was staying in the queen's rooms at a bombed and freezing-cold Buckingham Palace and twice met the sixteen-year-old princess, who had officially entered the adult world after formally signing on at the labor exchange at Windsor, and during the First Lady's visit was strenuously lobbying her reluctant parents to let her face the same hazards as other girls her age. "If she were anyone's child that I met outside a palace, I would say she was very attractive, quite serious, a child with a good deal of character. Her questions put to me about life in this country were all serious questions. She has had to think seriously. I don't think they have kept her from seeing the seriousness of the war—after all, practically every window in Buckingham Palace is out!"[29]

The First Lady met the princess at a time when her father was gradually introducing her to the unique world of a reigning monarch through the interminable red despatch boxes, which contained top-secret cabinet and Foreign Office documents for the sovereign's perusal and signature. Unlike previous monarchs, notably Queen Victoria and George V, who very reluctantly allowed their heirs a peek into their destiny, George VI was eager and earnest in the training of his successor. As F. J. Corbitt who worked at the palace for twenty years as deputy comptroller of supply, noted: "I don't think any Sovereign of England has been taught so much in advance about his work by his predecessor as Queen Elizabeth was by her father. It was always a joy to see them together so happy in each other's company."[30]

The death of their uncle George, the Duke of Kent, in a plane crash in August 1942 further brought home to the princesses the sudden arbitrary reality of war. His death was the first time in more than 450 years that a member of the royal family had died in active service. It was all the more shocking as the king and queen, who were staying at Balmoral, had organized a Highland ball in his honor for later in that tragic week.

His death, the remorseless toll on the home and overseas fronts, and, in the latter stages of the war, the bombardment of London by deadly flying bombs or "doodlebugs"—which terrified the population more than the Blitz itself—made both the king and the queen aware that if their turn was next, they had better make preparations. In June 1944, days after a flying bomb scored a direct hit on Guards' Chapel near Buckingham Palace, killing 121 civilians and soldiers and leaving hundreds trapped beneath the rubble, the queen wrote to her eldest daughter about what to do should she get "done in" by the Nazis' doodlebug bombs. The tone was typically jaunty and light but betrayed her serious concerns.

"Let's hope this won't be needed but I *know* that you will always do the right thing & remember to keep your temper & your word & and be loving—sweet—Mummy."[31] No one was immune from thoughts of mortality. In July that year, shortly before leaving on a secret flight to visit the troops in Italy, the king outlined to his wife where she should live if he did not return.

Though Princess Elizabeth's stoical and phlegmatic character matched the make-do-and-mend mood of the times, on the flip side was the growing desire to spread her wings. The princess chafed at the cordon of caution that surrounded her. As family friend Veronica Maclean noted: "The quiet determination which is part of her character, and which is perhaps a variation of her father's patience and steadfastness, was beginning to emerge."[32] The teenage princess would be driven— under escort and in a group—into London for dinner or to watch plays and concerts. Her first opera was Puccini's *La Bohème* at Sadler's Wells. On another outing she listened to a Bach and Handel program at the Royal Albert Hall.

She and her sister were enthusiastic members of the weekly meeting of the madrigal choir under the leadership of Dr. William H. Harris, the organist at St. George's Chapel in Windsor Castle. The choir's genesis began during a musical session when the girls discovered *My Ladye Nevells Booke,* a collection of sixteenth-century virginal music. This expanded into a madrigal choir every week with, at the invitation of Dr. Harris, Guards officers and boys from Eton joining in. Because of her natural love of music, it was entirely fitting that in May

After more than a decade of war and grinding austerity, the prospect of a young and glamorous new Queen lifted the spirits of a weary nation. For the Queen and Prince Philip, their new duties and responsibilities exacted a high price. The Queen placed duty before family, while her husband resigned from his promising career in the Royal Navy. Here she is in 1953, at a concert in central London organized by the governments of Australia and New Zealand, who were expecting a six-month visit Down Under by the royal couple. Prince Charles and Princess Anne were left behind for the duration of the visit.

Left: Princess Elizabeth, an enchanting curly haired blonde, with her parents, then the Duke and Duchess of York. Only Hollywood child star Shirley Temple could match the royal infant for international appeal. Her winsome features appeared on stamps, plates, mugs and tea towels.

Right: A rare picture of eight-year-old Princess Elizabeth and her sister Margaret, then four, with other children. Here they are at a fancy dress party, Elizabeth dressed as a Tudor lady, Margaret as a fairy. For most of their day-to-day lives the sisters were in the company of adults who controlled every aspect of their welfare.

Left: After the shock of the abdication in 1936, when King Edward VIII gave up the throne to marry the twice-divorced American Wallis Simpson, the Windsors were keen to re-establish themselves as models of home, hearth, and humble family life. Here are what the new King, George VI, called "we four" posing for happy family snaps with their dogs in the setting of "Y Bwthyn Bach," or "The Little House," a miniature cottage given to Elizabeth by the people of Wales.

Above: For the coronation of King George VI, their father designed lightweight coronets and gowns for his daughters. Margaret, however, complained that her train was shorter than that of her elder sister. On the morning of the coronation, Elizabeth looked out from her bedroom at Buckingham Palace at the crowds who had waited all night to watch the ancient ceremony.

Below: The King and his daughters out riding in Windsor Great Park. Ever since she was a little girl, Elizabeth was fascinated by horses. She not only enjoyed riding horses but became involved in their management and care. Those in the racing community believe that if she hadn't become Queen she would have made an excellent trainer.

Left: The Second World War changed the lives of most, none more so than that of the future Queen. It was vital for morale that the country knew that Princess Elizabeth and her sister remained in England rather than seek safety in Canada or elsewhere. In 1940, with Britain on the ropes, the Princess, Margaret by her side, made her first broadcast to the nation's children, speaking with words of good cheer to those forced to leave their homes and families in the cities and move to the countryside or abroad.

Right: After months of badgering her parents to let her do her bit for the war effort, in early 1945 the King and Queen finally allowed Princess Elizabeth to join the ATS (Auxiliary Territorial Service). She learned to drive trucks, change tires, and perform mechanical repairs. The Princess showed off her skills when she drove a truck through central London to Buckingham Palace.

Left: This was the moment when sharp-eyed journalists realized that Princess Elizabeth was dating the handsome naval lieutenant Prince Philip of Greece, when he helped her off with her fur coat prior to the wedding of Lord Brabourne and Patricia Mountbatten at Romsey Abbey, Hampshire, in October 1946.

Left: On her 21st birthday, April 21, 1947, Princess Elizabeth gave the most important address of her life when she dedicated her future, "whether it be long or short," to the service of the nation and the Commonwealth. Many listening to the radio broadcast, relayed from Cape Town in South Africa, were moved to tears by her simple humility.

Right: Princess Elizabeth and the newly minted Duke of Edinburgh celebrate their wedding day on November 20, 1947. The duke soon realized that he had not just married a Princess, he had taken on a dynasty. In the early years he found the going difficult.

Left: Princess Elizabeth cradled baby Prince Charles, who was born on November 14, 1948, during his christening at Buckingham Palace shortly before Christmas. The happy event was overshadowed by general concern regarding the King's health.

Above: The royal couple dancing reels at the Phoenicia Hotel in Valetta, Malta, where Philip was stationed in 1949. Princess Elizabeth was able to lead a relatively normal life away from the shadow of the palace. She handled money for the first time, went to the hairdresser on her own, and drove or sailed around the island unnoticed. It was one of the happiest periods of her life.

Below left: Bareheaded, the King sees off his daughter from London Airport, before she and Prince Philip headed to Australia via Kenya on a much-delayed royal visit. He died in his sleep at Sandringham days later, on February 6, 1952. Below right: Elizabeth, now Queen, walks down the aircraft steps to be greeted by Prime Minister Winston Churchill and other senior politicians.

Left: During the three-hour coronation, the Queen, now wearing St. Edward's Crown, accepted the formal declaration of loyalty from her husband. Initially the Queen had opposed the televising of this historic event but in the end she gave in to popular demand.

Right: The newly crowned Queen Elizabeth II waves to the crowds from the balcony of Buckingham Palace, alongside Prince Philip and three of her six maids of honor. It was hoped that the new reign would herald a dynamic Elizabethan age of change, innovation, and reform.

Left: Princess Margaret inspects the troops followed by (far left) her secret lover Group Captain Peter Townsend, a war ace who held the post of comptroller inside the Royal Household. Her sister's affair with a divorced man would present the Queen with an early problem that tested her character in full measure.

Above: The Queen, shortly before giving her first televised Christmas broadcast, in 1957. Her broadcast came at a time of mounting criticism of the "tweedy sort" who made up the Queen's court. Her critics, though, were very much in the minority as the broadcast attracted a substantial audience of sixteen and a half million viewers in a nation where television ownership was still in the minority. With the success of the first broadcast, the queen's Christmas message became a festive must-watch.

1943, shortly after her seventeenth birthday, she became the president of the Royal College of Music.

Other cultural entertainments were less successful. A poetry recital organized by the queen's friend Osbert Sitwell at Windsor Castle was an unmitigated disaster. One drunk female poet had to be removed from the makeshift stage, the diminutive Walter de la Mare was obscured by the lectern, and another bard declaimed his rhyming couplets for so long that he was asked to cut short his reading. It was all too much for the princesses, who were barely able to keep a straight face. Many years later the by-then queen mother described the somewhat surreal, unintentionally comic affair to biographer A. N. Wilson: "We had this rather lugubrious man in a suit, and he read a poem...I think it was called 'The Desert.' And first the girls got the giggles, and then I did and then even the King."

A somewhat perplexed Wilson interjected, "'The Desert,' ma'am? Are you sure it wasn't called: 'The Waste Land'?"— referring to the now classic work by T. S. Eliot.

The queen continued: "That's it. I'm afraid we all giggled. Such a gloomy man, looked as though he worked in a bank, and we didn't understand a word."

"I believe he DID once work in a bank," responded Wilson.[33]

More notable than this poetic interlude were the pantomimes staged at Christmas and starring the young princesses. While the endlessly dramatic Margaret Rose was a natural on stage, the real revelation was the heir presumptive who showed a confidence, vigor, and command before audiences of five hundred or so. Her tap-dancing skills—she skittered her way through the American hit "In My Arms"—were widely admired because her stagecraft came as such a surprise.

Even the cynical Tommy Lascelles was impressed, deeming the 1942 Christmas pantomime *Sleeping Beauty* worthy of the

West End. "The whole thing went with a slickness and confidence that amazed me," he wrote.[34] He was equally impressed the following year when Princess Elizabeth starred as a "charming" Aladdin, although the king thought her breeches way too short and somewhat indecorous.

Equally memorable was a ball that George VI organized to celebrate Elizabeth's seventeenth birthday. It was such a success that it did not end until dawn. Toward the end of the war the king would also give smaller dances in the Bow Room on the first floor of Buckingham Palace. On one occasion the monarch led a conga line through the palace rooms and corridors, leaving the band playing to an empty room.

One of the guests at these events was Lieutenant Mark Bonham Carter, who had made a daring escape from an Italian POW camp. He recalls twice dancing with the teenage Princess Margaret and later reported that she was "full of character and very tart in her criticisms."[35] Bonham Carter, whose mother was daughter of Prime Minister Herbert Asquith, boasted unusual royal connections; decades later his actress niece, Helena, would play Princess Margaret in the TV show *The Crown* and the queen in *The King's Speech*. At the time he was an instant hit with the sisters and kept them amused with a string of jokes and an ability to slide down banisters without using his hands.

He was one of a number of eligible young Guards officers, usually with a stately home lurking somewhere in the family background, who were invited by the king and queen to Windsor Castle and later in the war to Buckingham Palace to amuse their daughters. The queen referred to them as "the bodyguard."

Besides Bonham Carter, other eligible young men put in the path of the princesses included Andrew Charles

Elphinstone—the son of the queen's sister Lady Mary Bowes-Lyon—who became a vicar after the war. Princess Elizabeth thought he would make an ideal husband for some lucky woman. In November 1943 Elizabeth wrote to her cousin Diana Bowes-Lyon: "I saw Andrew for a moment last week. And the more I see of him, the more I wish he wasn't my first cousin. As he's just the sort of husband any girl would love to have. I don't think one could find anyone nicer."[36] Andrew felt that he was being left behind in the marriage stakes by his friends and asked Lilibet outright if she knew anyone he could marry.

But there were plenty of other potential suitors, including Lord Rupert Nevill, ADC to Sir Brian Horrocks during the invasion of Germany, Lord Wyfold, and handsome Irish Guards officer Patrick Plunket, who later became the king's equerry. The presence of so many eligible bachelors gave rise to newspaper speculation in America suggesting that Elizabeth was about to announce her engagement either to Charles Manners, the Tenth Earl of Rutland, or to Hugh FitzRoy, also known as the Earl of Euston.

Apparently Manners ruined his chances at a union by making a pass at the princess, which she found greatly offensive. Eminently safe in taxis was Henry Porchester, known as Porchie, later the Seventh Earl of Carnarvon, whose home Highclere Castle became rather more famous than the family itself when, years later, it became the setting for the long-running saga of aristocratic life *Downton Abbey*. Porchie, who shared Elizabeth's love of horses, was not a serious threat to win her heart and eventually became her racing manager.

It was, however, South African–born Hugh FitzRoy, the Earl of Euston—a descendant of King Charles II and later the Duke of Grafton—who, unknown to himself, caused something of a romantic rivalry between Princess Elizabeth and her wartime friend Alathea Fitzalan Howard. Alathea, two years older than the princess, was utterly infatuated with Euston, who was a regular guest at social events organized by the king and queen at Windsor Castle. To her chagrin, he was often seated next to Elizabeth at meals or to watch movies, and they would regularly lead off the dancing at parties. Alathea suspected that the king and queen were trying to make a match between Euston and their daughter. She confided in her diary: "They're so pointedly nice to him that one wonders if there's anything behind it; he gets on so well with all of them—I'm sure he likes Lilibet better than me."[37] Not that Elizabeth was immune to jealousy herself. At one party in July 1941, the princess quizzed Alathea about how often she danced with Euston as, she complained, he had only danced the first dance of the evening with her out of obligation. This genteel rivalry came to a natural conclusion in 1943 when Euston was posted to India as the ADC to Lord Wavell, the viceroy of India.

Long before that day, however, the princess and her sister had let Alathea into the secret of the man who genuinely made her heart beat a little faster. In April 1941 she confided that Prince Philip of Greece and Denmark was the genuine beau— or as Princess Margaret put it, "boy"—in her life. Her flirtation with Euston was a distraction. Quietly and very privately the princess was writing letters to the prince and even cut out relevant newspaper articles about the activities of his ship.

Her cousin Margaret Rhodes recalled, "I've got letters from her saying: 'It's so exciting. Mummy says that Philip can come and stay when he gets leave.' She never looked at anyone else. She was truly in love from the very beginning."[38]

Her beau had a good war. His first wartime posting was aboard HMS *Ramillies* escorting convoys of Australian and New Zealand troopships bound for Egypt. At the beginning of his posting he told his captain, Vice Admiral Harold Baillie-Grohman, that he was in correspondence with the princess and confided that his uncle Dickie had ideas for him. "He thinks I could marry Princess Elizabeth." Somewhat surprised the captain asked: "Are you really fond of her?" "Oh, yes," replied Philip, "I write to her every week."[39] As the sweethearts were only eighteen and thirteen respectively, Baillie-Grohman advised him not to mention his friendship to any of his shipmates. When *Ramillies* arrived in Sydney, Baillie-Grohman, mindful of the possible marital plans for the prince, sent Philip to a remote sheep farm rather than let him spend his leave amid the temptations of the big city.

Though the correspondence was platonic, Lady Myra Butter, Philip's cousin, was convinced that it was the intention of the ambitious Lord Mountbatten, Philip's uncle, to engineer a royal marriage and burnish the House of Mountbatten in the process. Myra recalled: "Philip would never have married her if he hadn't been in love with her, I can tell you that, because I knew his other girlfriends."[40]

Philip, five years older than his royal pen pal, was a popular bachelor, squiring any number of eligible ladies around town. Beautiful Osla Benning, a dark-haired Canadian, was a regular girlfriend. Years later Osla's daughter Janie Spring described Philip as her mother's first love.[41]

As Alexandra, daughter of Aspasia, Princess of Greece and Denmark, noted wryly: "Blondes, brunettes and redhead charmers, Philip gallantly and I think quite impartially squired them all."[42] However, it was to Princess Elizabeth that he dashed off notes about his military life—subject to the censor's pen. He had much to relay. After deciding to commit to the British rather than the Greek navy, on New Year's Day 1941 he joined the battleship HMS *Valiant* at Alexandria and sailed to Athens where he spent some time with his mother Alice as well as George II of Greece. One of the guests at a cocktail party attended by Philip was the American-born diarist Henry "Chips" Channon. He described the prince as "extraordinarily handsome" and then noted: "He is to be our Prince Consort, and that is why he is serving in our Navy."[43] Channon implied that Philip's decision would make him more acceptable to the British public should he and Princess Elizabeth marry.

At the time Philip was more concerned with matters naval than marital. In March 1941 the *Valiant* was part of the three-day Battle of Cape Matapan, which saw the prince mentioned in dispatches for his handling of a searchlight to outline targeted Italian warships. King George II of Greece subsequently awarded Philip the Greek War Cross for his actions.

In June 1941 he returned to Britain to take his sub-lieutenant examination. During this time ashore he stayed at Coppins, the home of his cousin the Duchess of Kent, where he enjoyed his first dance with Princess Elizabeth who was, according to her friend Alathea Fitzalan Howard, "very excited" at the prospect of seeing her beau again.

He was also a guest at Windsor Castle, where he regaled the king and company about his adventures in the Mediterranean. His Majesty was impressed by Philip's crisp summary of the Battle of Cape Matapan, which effectively crushed the Italian navy. Later he wrote to the prince's grandmother Victoria, Marchioness of Milford Haven. "What a charming boy he is, & I am glad he is remaining in my Navy."[44] After passing his sub-lieutenant exams, in June 1942, he was posted to HMS *Wallace* on the Firth of Forth in Scotland, tasked with escorting merchant navy ships along Britain's eastern coast. In June 1943 the *Wallace* sailed for Sicily, where it was attacked in the open waters by the Luftwaffe. After the first wave of enemy planes had departed, it was obvious that further bombardments would follow. They only had twenty minutes or so to fashion an escape. Philip had the presence of mind to have a raft thrown overboard with smoke floats attached to create the impression that the German bombs had hit their target, hence the billowing smoke and debris ablaze on the water. Attacking German pilots would be duped into thinking that the first bombers had sunk the ship. His ship steamed away from the burning debris and then the captain ordered the engines stopped so that marauding bombers would not see the telltale wake. Philip's ruse worked. The next wave of bombers flew past the *Wallace* and attacked the smoking raft instead. Years later crew member Harry Hargreaves recalled: "Prince Philip saved our lives that night. I suppose there might have been a few survivors, but certainly the ship would have been sunk. He was always very courageous and resourceful and thought very quickly."[45]

It surprised none aboard when Philip was promoted to lieutenant, one of the youngest in the Royal Navy. He was, however, able to accept an invitation to stay at Windsor Castle for Christmas 1943. This news delighted the princess.

"Who *do* you think is coming to see us act, Crawfie?... Philip!" said an excited Elizabeth.[46] Though he was unable to attend the dance the king had organized for his daughters as he had the flu, he did appear for the pantomime, laughing along with the rest of the five-hundred-strong audience at the dreadful puns and the ham acting.

Elizabeth, in the title role, made her entrance by jumping out of a laundry basket. Her tap-dance routine—she skittered her way through the American hit "In My Arms"—earned general applause though this was clearly a performance for one particular member of the audience. Crawfie was surprised at her animation and unmistakable sparkle—here was a young woman in love.

Her suitor was no longer the brash and boastful cadet who jumped the tennis net at Dartmouth college but, to Crawfie's critical eye, a young man who was sober, serious, and charming, his wartime exploits clearly tempering and maturing him. He joined the royal family for Christmas and played games of charades, watched film shows, and danced to the gramophone until the early hours. It was time together both would cherish. Her friend Alathea Fitzalan Howard watched the evolving romance with quiet satisfaction. She remembered the summer of 1942 when Elizabeth, who normally kept her feelings to herself, wondered aloud if she would ever marry and resolved to run away with the man of her dreams if necessary. Now eighteen months later she had seemed to have found a fitting partner. "He seems so suited to PE [Princess Elizabeth] and I kept wondering today whether he is her future husband," she noted in her diary entry of December 18, 1943. "I think it is the most desirable event that could possibly happen. She would like it and, though he would not be in love with her, I believe he is not averse to the idea."[47] The following year when he sent her a photograph of himself for Christmas, the princess "danced round the room with it for joy."[48]

The war had changed everyone, whether they were on the front line or not. Elizabeth was no longer a little girl in white ankle socks but a shapely young woman who knew her own mind. She was branching out.

For her eighteenth birthday in 1944, she received a diamond tiara from her mother and a sapphire and diamond bracelet from her father. That year she shot her first stag; caught her first salmon, a sturdy eight-pounder; launched her first ship, HMS *Vanguard*, on Clydebank; gave her first public speech as president of the National Society for the Prevention of Cruelty to Children; attended her first official Buckingham Palace dinner; and took on the role of counselor of state when her father made a top-secret flight to see the troops in Italy.

Elizabeth's elevation drove her sister wild with jealousy and validated her feeling that she was always left out of anything of substance or interest. She had previously railed against the decision to leave her out of the history lessons with Sir Henry Marten. Now Elizabeth had been made a counselor of state at eighteen when the normal age was twenty-one.

There was further sisterly jealousy when, in March 1945, Princess Elizabeth was allowed to join the Auxiliary Territorial Service (ATS) as a second subaltern. Every day, after first learning to drive, she drove her commandant to their base at Camberley fifteen miles from Windsor Castle. Along with the other girls, she learned how to strip an engine; change a tire, spark plugs, and oil; and read a map and navigate at night. The high point was when the princess, who looked, according to Alan Lascelles, a "duck" in her ATS uniform, drove her commandant from Aldershot to the courtyard of Buckingham Palace.

At long last she had been allowed to contribute to the war effort, which made her feel that she had earned the right to join in with the wild celebrations following the German surrender on May 8, 1945. The princesses accompanied their parents and war leader Winston Churchill on the balcony of Buckingham Palace to wave to the huge cheering, delirious crowds.

The girls, who had spent a lifetime looking out at the passing parade, pleaded with their parents to allow them to join the celebrating multitude. After some hesitation, the king agreed. The fact that, on this of all nights, she and her sister had to beg to be allowed out vividly demonstrates what sheltered lives they led, their every movement, every desire fretted over by the king, the queen, and their courtiers.

The girls, though, were not allowed out alone; instead they

were escorted by sixteen chaperones, including Group Captain Peter Townsend, Lord Porchester, and the king's starchy equerry Captain Harold Campbell, who was dressed in a pin-striped suit and bowler hat and carried a rolled umbrella. He strongly disapproved of the impromptu jaunt, which Elizabeth described as "one of the most memorable nights of my life."[49]

Perhaps he had a point. Though Pathé News showed the crowds taking part in cheerful conga lines, the real picture was rather more salacious. Aristocratic army wife Diana Carnegie was part of the throng and later wrote to her husband James, who was still in Germany, that she and her party "stumbled across fucking couples in the dark" as they made their way from the West End to Buckingham Palace.[50]

Years later the queen told veteran BBC war correspondent Godfrey Talbot that her overriding emotions that night were "thrill and relief." The queen, who gave a rare interview to commemorate the fortieth anniversary of VE Day, recalled: "My parents went out on the balcony in response to the huge crowds outside. I think we went on the balcony every hour—six times. And then, when the excitement of the floodlights being switched on got through to us, my sister and I realized we couldn't see what the crowds were enjoying . . . so we asked my parents if we could go out and see for ourselves."[51]

The princess recalled being "terrified of being recognized" and pulled her cap over her eyes. But the Grenadier Guards officer with her refused to be seen in the company of another officer improperly dressed.

"So I had to put my cap on normally. We cheered the king and queen on the balcony, then walked miles through the streets. I remember lines of unknown people linking arms and walking down Whitehall [the main street of British government], all of us just swept along on a tide of happiness and relief."[52]

3

❧

A Walk in the Heather

S he was an unlikely Cupid. Princess Marina of Greece and Denmark was the chilly beauty who captured the heart of King George V's youngest son, the wild and willful Prince George. Though she was titled the Duchess of Kent, that most English of Home Counties, she remained resolutely European, so proud of her Greek and Russian heritage that she never truly allowed herself to be absorbed into the British royal family. She had contempt for the middle-class American Wallis Simpson, whom she met at Balmoral in 1936, and referred to the queen and her sister-in-law, the Duchess of Gloucester, as "those common little Scottish girls."[1]

She was less judgmental of her European relations. The duchess and her husband Prince George regularly invited her first cousin Prince Philip of Greece and Denmark, the son of her uncle Prince Andrew, to stay with them at Coppins, their converted Berkshire farmhouse in the charming village of Iver situated a few miles from Windsor Castle.

Philip stayed with the family during breaks from his boarding

schools of Cheam in southern England and Gordonstoun in
the far north of Scotland as well as Dartmouth naval college
in Devon. With his lively mind, positive attitude, and energy,
the prince proved himself to be an entertaining houseguest.
When the Duke of Kent was killed in an air crash in August
1942, Philip's sensitive if no-nonsense approach to life was crucial in raising Marina's spirits. After a brief initial collapse, the
Duchess of Kent not only took on her husband's royal duties
but also trained as a nurse. She acted as chaperone when she
hosted the prince and a "certain young lady" over Easter 1944.
The presence of the king and queen at the gathering indicated
a degree of parental approval. Clearly romance was in the air.
When Elizabeth drew compliments from the prince for wearing a particular blue dress, the next time they met at Coppins
she made sure she wore a similar style and color. As the historian Sir Steven Runciman, a friend and confidant of both
Princess Marina and the queen mother, would later reveal: "It
was Princess Marina, not (Louis)Mountbatten, who was the
marriage broker between the Queen and Prince Philip."[2]

Indeed, in the early months of the royal romance, Mountbatten had his hands full in the Japanese theater of war where he
was Supreme Allied Commander South East Asia Command.
During his occasional visits to London, however, Mountbatten
continued to press the case for his nephew. He wrote to influential figures, including independent member of Parliament Tom
Driberg, stressing his nephew's Englishness. At times his chirpy
and irrepressible ambition on behalf of his nephew exasperated
the king. "I know you like to get things settled at once, once
you have an idea in mind...but I have come to the conclusion
that we are going too fast," the king told him. He was concerned
that his eldest daughter was too young and inexperienced to be
content with the first eligible bachelor to cross her path.[3]

Even Prince Philip felt that his uncle's relentless lobbying on his behalf was a double-edged sword. He wrote to him in earnest: "Please I beg of you not too much advice in an affair of the heart or I shall be forced to do the wooing by proxy."[4]

Though he had the support of his influential uncle as well as the steadfast devotion of the princess, Philip's acceptance as the favored suitor for the hand of the future queen was by no means assured. The royal family and their courtiers were suspicious and wary when this penniless, rather rough interloper who, some thought, would not be faithful arrived on the scene. Inevitably there were all kinds of salty rumors about the flotilla of girls who had crossed the prince's path. Most gossip emanated from Sydney and Melbourne in Australia, where he was ashore for three months in May 1945 while his ship HMS *Whelp* underwent a refit. He attended parties and other social gatherings where there was no shortage of attractive young ladies. Two girls in particular who caught his eye were society belle Sue Other-Gee and singer and model Sandra Jacques. He remained friendly with Other-Gee for many years. She even kept a scrapbook recording their occasional meetings. As for Sandra Jacques, film producer Robin Dalton, who met the prince during the war, recalled that his relationship with Jacques was "a terrific love affair. A very full love affair."[5] Just to complicate matters, romance novelist Barbara Cartland, a former girlfriend of Mountbatten, claimed that, following one intimate liaison with an unnamed woman, he fathered a child who was born in Melbourne. She always refused to give further details.[6]

Though his title, striking good looks, and easy charm ensured that he was a target for a stream of society gals, those who knew the man, rather than the rakish image, regarded him as a cautious, cagey fellow who kept his feelings to himself.

In this regard he was similar in manner to Princess Elizabeth. Even her family described her as "the cat who walks alone." His friend and fellow officer, the Australian Mike Parker, described Philip as a "reserved" young man who never really played the field. "We were young, we had fun, we had a few drinks, we might have gone dancing but that was it."[7]

Perhaps the king was looking for a reason, however spurious, to reject his daughter's long-distance suitor. Whether he wanted to admit it or not, the king was possessive and had found a happiness and completion in family life that had been missing from his own chilly childhood. He also felt his daughter, not yet twenty-one, was too young to make such a life-changing choice. His redoubtable mother, Queen Mary, disagreed. She told her close confidant Lady Airlie, "Elizabeth would always know her own mind. There's something very steadfast and determined about her."[8]

The queen wanted her daughter to be happy but fretted that Philip, self-confident, independent-minded, and ambitious, would find it difficult to accept the junior role in a marital partnership with the future queen. She favored a well-born Guards officer for her eldest daughter, preferably a duke but an earl would do, with a family stately home lurking in the background. Her brother David Bowes-Lyon supported her view. In his eyes a British aristocrat rather than a foreigner with family married to Nazi officers was an infinitely preferable choice.

On this weighty matter the queen had the endorsement of the king's influential private secretary, Alan "Tommy" Lascelles, who was firmly opposed to Princess Elizabeth marrying Prince Philip.[9] According to Edward Ford, the newly appointed assistant private secretary, Lascelles's choice was Hugh Euston, who became the Duke of Grafton. It seems that Alathea Fitzalan Howard's suspicions that the king, queen, and their courtiers were quietly and deliberately pushing together Elizabeth and Hugh, upon whom Alathea had developed a huge crush, were well founded.

Hugh Euston remained friendly with both the princess and Alathea. He may never have realized the romantic consternation he caused every time he arrived at Windsor Castle during the war. Alathea, too, accepted that it was not meant to be and eventually came to terms with the fact that he was the one who got away. In October 1946 the romantic door was closed for good when he married Fortune Smith, the daughter of Captain Eric Smith, a member of the Smith banking dynasty. She was later appointed mistress of the robes at the court of Queen Elizabeth II.

By the time Hugh married, the princess's own romance was in full swing.

Philip had arrived back in Britain in January 1946 after witnessing Japanese leaders formally sign the instrument of surrender on September 2, 1945, in Tokyo Bay, aboard the aircraft carrier USS *Missouri*.

On his final voyage, he brought British prisoners of war safely home to England. Then he was tasked with decommissioning HMS *Whelp*. A few months later he was posted to an officers' training college at Corsham in Wiltshire, around a hundred miles west of London. Here he lectured petty officers on seamanship.

On free weekends or on leave, he scrounged gas coupons—petrol was still rationed—from his fellow officers and drove his little black MG sports car at reckless speeds to London where he stayed at Chester Street in Belgravia, the central London home of the Mountbattens. Philip also became a regular and welcome visitor to Elizabeth's suite of rooms at Buckingham Palace.

As she later wrote to journalist Betty Shew: "We first started seeing more of each other when Philip went for a two-year job to the RN Petty Officers' school at Corsham—before that we hardly knew each other. He'd spent weekends with us, and when the school was closed, he'd spend six weeks at Balmoral—it was great luck his getting a shore job first then! We both love dancing—we have danced at Ciro's and Quaglino's as well as at parties."[10]

During his visits to Buckingham Palace, Crawfie, who acted as chaperone, looked on indulgently as she watched the nascent romance grow and blossom. She liked Philip's breezy and informal manner but felt that the young couple had too little time alone together especially as Princess Margaret was always the third wheel. She was ever present unless Crawfie cooked up some reason to leave the couple on their own.

Philip's presence in Elizabeth's life had an immediate effect. Her circle could not help but notice the changes. She was more confident and humorous with an ear for a funny anecdote. At a party given by the Grenfell family at their Belgravia home in February 1946 to celebrate the peace, the princess impressed Laura Grenfell with her natural conversational style and her close observation. She amused fellow guests with her rendition of a sentry losing his hat while presenting arms. Her eye for oft-overlooked details and keen sense of the ridiculous would serve her well in her future role.

Others were equally impressed by the princess's choice. At a dinner held at the home of the Elphinstone family at Beaconsfield, fellow guest Sir Michael Duff described Prince Philip as "charming" and argued that he had all the right qualities—handsome, intelligent, and a brave sailor—to be a popular consort to the future queen. The fact that he only spoke English was, Duff believed, "admirable and necessary" especially "when one considers the point of view of the man in the street, who has an innate prejudice against any language but his own."[11]

It was a shrewd observation, as Philip was seen in some quarters as too Continental. Even though his mother was born at Windsor Castle, and he had been educated in England and served courageously in the Royal Navy, he was often dismissed as "the hun" or "Charlie Kraut" by some in court circles. This knee-jerk hostility was understandable; one brother-in-law, Prince Philipp of Hesse, was then under Allied detention and another, Prince Christoph of Hesse, was widely, though falsely, suspected of being the mastermind behind a daring daylight bombing raid on Buckingham Palace.

During his first summer back in Britain, Philip was, as Elizabeth recalled, invited to spend a few weeks at Balmoral. While the examination wasn't as rigorous as those he taught at Corsham, the Balmoral test was and continues to be an important assessment by the family of a potential bride or groom. Essentially the intention was to assess, quite informally, the sailor prince to see if he would fit in to a country lifestyle where deer hunting, grouse shooting, and salmon fishing are an essential part of the royal round—as, too, are frequent wardrobe changes.

Philip did not get off to the best of starts. His wardrobe was as threadbare as his bank balance, his father Prince Andrew only leaving him several suits, an ivory-handled shaving brush, and a signet ring after his death in 1944. He had borrowed a kilt for his sojourn on the fifty-thousand-acre royal estate. As it was just a wee bit too short the prince, in attempting to turn a fashion faux pas into a moment of levity, dropped a cute curtsy rather than a neck bow when he greeted George VI. The king who, like his brothers, was a stickler for the correct attire and formalities, was not amused. Philip's behavior added to the sense among his detractors at court that this rather unpolished, overly confident young man, without a home, a fortune, or a kingdom to bolster his credentials, was little more than a Continental carpetbagger.

During his stay his shooting was as wayward as his dress

sense, with the ghillies and beaters declaring his marksmanship "erratic and poor."[12] He did, though, hit the target in matters of the heart. This was where it really mattered. Forthright and to the point, he took Elizabeth out for a drive on the estate and then, as they walked alone on the heather, the sound of a distant curlew adding to the sense of solitude, he asked if she would be his bride. The princess, who had inserted pictures of the prince in her photograph album and had kept a framed picture of her bearded navy beau on her desk for months, accepted on the spot. It was only later that the prince separately sought the formal permission of the king, his consent required under the 1772 Royal Marriages Act, which was passed by Parliament to prevent unsuitable or improper marriages that would diminish the standing of the royal house.

During his six-week stay the king formed a warm attachment with the young prince. Like any father he was happy to see his daughter blossom thanks to the love and support of her future husband. In the dynastic juggling act this was, caveats aside, deemed to be a good match, and he willingly gave his permission. There was one condition.

A royal tour of South Africa, which had been months in the planning, was scheduled for early 1947, and the king asked the couple to wait until the royal family returned in May before making a formal announcement. The palace even issued a statement in early September denying the rumor that there was an engagement between the two. This prevarication left the princess bewildered and crestfallen. She knew her own mind; it was her parents who were being indecisive, using the excuse of the South African tour to test the couple's resolve. In fairness the prince still needed to become a naturalized British citizen before any announcement, and that was not going to be a straightforward application.

Reluctantly the couple agreed to hold off on the announcement and to continue disguising their feelings for each other in public for just a little longer. In his letter of thanks to Queen Elizabeth, dated September 14, 1946, the emotionally circumspect prince offered a window into his feelings. He wrote: "I am sure I do not deserve all the good things which have happened to me. To have been spared in the war and seen victory. To have fallen in love completely and unreservedly makes all one's personal and even the world's troubles seem small and petty."[13]

Though the couple had agreed to keep their betrothal a secret, the public sensed that a romance was blossoming between the heir and the naval officer when they appeared at the wedding at Romsey in Hampshire of Philip's first cousin Patricia Mountbatten to Captain Lord Brabourne in October 1946. Sharp-eyed onlookers noticed that Philip and Elizabeth were probably more than just friends. Not only did he walk with the royal family to the church but, at the entrance, he also solicitously helped Princess Elizabeth, who was a bridesmaid, with her fur coat. Over the next few months well-wishers, who read media speculation about the couple, took to asking "Where's Philip?" when Elizabeth appeared in public, much to her embarrassment and irritation.

In late January 1947, just a few days before the royal family sailed for South Africa aboard HMS *Vanguard*, some of those genuinely in the know attended a small dinner party at Chester Street hosted by Lord Mountbatten. Noël Coward serenaded the party and guests toasted Philip and Elizabeth with champagne, except for the king who always drank whiskey. The royal family would be away for four months and at least two of those present were counting the days until their return.

༄

A key member of the traveling party was the *Times* journalist Dermot Morrah, a passionate monarchist. When he was four years old his nanny found him in floods of tears after learning of Queen Victoria's death. A mathematician, classicist, historian, and fellow of All Souls College who went by the title Arundel Herald of Arms Extraordinary, he became a lead writer for the *Times*, always ready with a high-flown phrase or lofty sentiment. If a Latin simile was required, Morrah was your man. During the war he came to the notice of the king who, his stammer under control, felt much more comfortable about speaking in public. Frequently the gentleman journalist was drafted in to prepare, construct, and polish His Majesty's utterances.

As one of the journalists on the White Train which was the royal family's home for the next few weeks as they visited hundreds of towns and hamlets throughout South Africa, Morrah was frequently called upon during the 11,000 mile tour to craft speeches for the king. Though the visit was ostensibly to thank the South Africans for their sacrifice and support during the war, it was also hoped that the sunshine and temperate climate would give the king, visibly gaunt after the tribulations of the conflict, a much-needed tonic. The optics of the visit were important, too. Not only was it hoped that the presence of the royal family would bolster the moderate government of General Jan Smuts against racist nationalists, but the palace considered Princess Elizabeth's planned coming-of-age speech, which was due to be broadcast on her twenty-first birthday, to be the high point of the trip.

The speech would touch on the time-honored values of monarchy—service, loyalty, and tradition—while articulating the continued significance of the institution in a rapidly changing world. It was an important address of commitment and connection that needed careful thought and memorable prose, as the speech would serve as a manifesto for the postwar monarchy. The king's private secretary assigned the delicate task to Morrah, who worked assiduously on a draft throughout the tour. At one point, the precious manuscript went missing somewhere aboard the train, but it was finally located among the bottles of booze in the bar of the "Protea" dining car.

The normally gruff Alan Lascelles was mightily impressed by the speech. "I have been reading drafts now for many years," he wrote to Morrah, "but I cannot recall one that has so completely satisfied me and left me feeling that no single word should be altered. Moreover, dusty cynic though I am it moved me greatly. It has the trumpeting ring of the other Elizabeth's Tilbury speech, combined with the immortal simplicity of Queen Victoria's 'I will be good.'"[14]

Others were not so impressed. For once the king disagreed with his private secretary. According to BBC radio correspondent Frank Gillard the monarch found Morrah's original "too pompous and full of platitudes."[15] As it was likely to be one of the most important royal speeches ever made, it deserved everyone's full attention. One Sunday, following a church service held at the Victoria Falls Hotel, the king, queen, and Princess Elizabeth as well as Frank Gillard took deck chairs into the garden and for the next two hours worked on the speech, page by page, line by line, the princess reading out passages and changing words here and there to improve clarity and meaning. As Elizabeth would be the one reading this declaration of intent, she was an important voice literally and figuratively in the shaping of the historic speech.

Once everyone was satisfied, the princess rehearsed the finished product under the watchful gaze of Gillard. Unlike her stuttering father, the radio veteran deemed the princess "composed, confident and extremely cooperative."[16] The speech was then secretly recorded and filmed under the trees in the hotel garden, the proceedings watched by a curious troop of baboons. On the princess's birthday, April 21, the speech was broadcast as if it were live from Government House in Cape Town, with an audience of more than two hundred million, including America, tuning in to listen to her words.

She made clear from the opening sentence that her life, which she voluntarily yoked to the growth of the Commonwealth of Nations, would not be an all-white affair. "On my twenty-first birthday, I welcome the opportunity to speak to all the peoples of the British Commonwealth and Empire, wherever they may live, whatever race they come from and whatever language they speak."

The climax to the seven-minute speech came as she dedicated her life to the service of the crown and the people. It was an almost nun-like vow and brought Elizabeth to tears when she first read the draft.

"I should like to make that dedication to you now. It is very simple. I declare before you all that my whole life whether it be long or short shall be devoted to your service and to the service of our great imperial family to which we all belong.

"But I shall not have the strength to carry out this resolution alone unless you join in it with me, as I now invite you to do. I know that your support will be unfailingly given. God help me to make good my vow and God bless you all you who are willing to share in it."[17]

Many around the world paused in their daily round to listen to the princess's speech, which clearly came from the heart. It brought tears to the eyes of the king and queen as well as Queen Mary, who confided to her diary: "Of course I wept."[18]

She was not alone. Churchill, a romantic to the tip of his Romeo y Julieta cigar, admitted that he, too, was moved to tears.

Tory grandee Viscount Templewood, formerly Sir Samuel Hoare, wrote in the *Times*, "It may well be that the Crown will make possible a Commonwealth of free peoples and many races far more varied than any that may exist today."[19]

During her radio address she stated that while she was six thousand miles away from her birthplace she was not six thousand miles away from home. That was a cute compliment to her South African hosts but something of a stretch. While the ever-loyal Bobo MacDonald brought her morning calling tray and her sister and parents gave private gifts over breakfast, her twenty-first birthday was spent in the company of strangers who, though they wished her well, were not her friends or family. Her coming of age reminded her that in a lifetime of duty, personal happiness and pleasure came a poor second.

For most of the day she nursed a headache. She found herself surrounded by overeager outsiders while the man she loved was thousands of miles away.

As the final insult, at the first of two balls in her honor, her dance partner, a clumsy if good-looking rugby player called Nellis Bolus, not only trod on her toes with his size-thirteen shoes but succeeded in dancing her into the fender in front of the ballroom mantelpiece. At the end of the dance, departing revelers recall seeing the two princesses, their shoes off, sitting on the staircase giggling and rubbing their sore feet.[20]

There were, though, glittering compensations. At the second ball, which was held at Government House, General Jan Smuts had presented her with a beautiful necklace of twenty-one flawless diamonds with fifty-two facets. She forever referred to them as her "best diamonds."[21]

Though her birthday speech was a personal triumph, the opening sentiments of inclusion and racial integration fell on stony ground, at least in South Africa. Within a year the National Party was in power and the cruel apartheid system voted into law. An informal policy of racial segregation was already in effect when the tour began. It infuriated the king that he was prevented from personally pinning medals on black ex-servicemen or shaking the hands of chiefs and elders at gatherings. During walkabouts and open car tours, the indigenous black population was on one side of the road, the whites on the other. It was an eye-opening experience for the princess. Already learning to see beyond official bromides, during the tour Elizabeth began to appreciate the reality of life in South Africa and understand why her father, who was frustrated by the way he was controlled by the tour organizers, referred to their white police guard as "our Gestapo."

She wrote to Queen Mary: "The Zulus nowadays are a broken people not at all what one expects to see after hearing about the 'huge Zulus' [of military folklore]. The Union government has been very ruthless with them, which is sad and have removed a lot of their customs."[22]

As the tour progressed, the king, far from relaxing and reviving, became increasingly tetchy. Even Smuts was alarmed by his deteriorating health and his frequent uncontrolled outbursts of temper. During what his family called his gnashes, the king was notorious among his entourage for kicking wastepaper baskets and twisting bath sponges to destruction. On one occasion the White Train stopped on a remote bay by the Indian Ocean so that the king could go for a swim on his own. "The loneliest man in the world," journalist James Cameron described him.[23] The experience was far from a rest cure: When the king returned to Britain he was seventeen pounds lighter and looked much frailer.

If the rigors of the seemingly endless tour and the constant pain in his legs distracted him, it was his family who provided consolation. As their equerry Peter Townsend observed: "A perpetual current of it [affection] flows between them, between father and mother, between sister and sister, between parents and their daughters and back again." He mused, somewhat optimistically given the hostility of the Nationalist Party to the tour, that the affection felt among the royal family had an impact around the globe. "Then it [affection] radiated outward to the ends of the world, touching thousands of millions of hearts who sent, rolling back, a massive wave of love to the royal family."[24]

This romantic image perhaps expressed his own feelings toward the royal family—and one member in particular. It was during this visit to the land he described as a "paradise" that Townsend, who was then still married with two boys, fell in love with Princess Margaret, nearly sixteen years his junior.

Theirs was a love affair that began in plain sight of the rest of the family, their courtiers, and the accompanying media. Every morning and evening, the princesses, accompanied by Townsend and assistant private secretary Michael Adeane, went riding through the rolling countryside or along the seashore. "We sped in the cool air, across the sands or across the veldt, those were the most glorious moments of the day," wrote Townsend. It was during these exhilarating and much-anticipated daily rituals that the sixteen-year-old princess, as she admitted years later, fell "madly in love"[25] with her riding companion.

In her sensible way, her elder sister would have initially

dismissed her sister's mooning over the married group captain as a juvenile crush. Only later would she be obliged to take their burgeoning relationship more seriously.

Elizabeth was the great success of tour, the princess seen as sensible, solicitous toward others, a skillful conversationalist, with a well-developed sense of fun and a briskly business-like attitude to bread-and-butter royal engagements. Her let's-get-on-with-it approach was often at variance with her mother's dilatory if more theatrical style.

She developed a habit of jabbing the queen on her Achilles' heel with her parasol if she was overrunning the schedule. Nor was Elizabeth—known by some as the colonel—averse to putting her father on a "charge" if he was being too difficult. In short she was a courtier's dream. Yet, and this was mentioned time and again, she was always solicitous with regard to the well-being of others. Elizabeth's chief cheerleader, Dermot Morrah, described watching her scrambling up a granite hillside in her stocking feet because she had handed over her own pair of shoes to her mother after her heels broke.[26]

Tommy Lascelles wrote to his wife about the "remarkable" development of Princess Elizabeth. "She has come on in the most surprising way and all in the right direction."[27] It was her father who struck a poignant and knowing observation about his beloved daughter during a visit to Cecil Rhodes's grave. He was asked by a government minister if he should accompany the princess. With a brief shake of his head, the king watched her walk away from the monument and said, "There she goes, Elizabeth, poor lonely girl, she will be lonely all her life."[28]

As they sailed back to Portsmouth in May, little did Princess Elizabeth think that she would not return to South Africa for nearly half a century. However, the vibrant colors, the endless skies, and the banquet of exotic food left an indelible impression. It was a nation, as the princess concluded, where some lived like kings.

She had her own treasure waiting patiently for her return. As the *Vanguard* approached the south coast port, Elizabeth was seen doing a jig of glee on deck, knowing that her own engagement could not be long delayed. Her father, recognizing his daughter's stalwart patience on this important matter of the heart, later wrote to her: "I was rather afraid that you had thought I was being rather hard-hearted about it. I was so anxious for you to come to South Africa as you know."[29]

On their return the royal family realized that the trials and tribulations of their long tour were as nothing compared with the catastrophic weather experienced by their subjects. In the worst winter in memory the country had suffered dreadful flooding, towering snowdrifts, transport chaos, dwindling coal supplies, and food rationing worse than during the war.

At Corsham naval base Prince Philip took to wearing a heavy greatcoat in the freezing classroom, where he delivered his lectures by candlelight.

Before the royal party left for South Africa he had accepted that the king was right to ask them to delay their announcement. Now he was eager to end the secrecy. He had not been idle while Elizabeth was away. The prince was all too aware that his exotic surname and family background might be a cause for criticism. In February, in order to deflect these concerns, he had become a naturalized British subject. No longer Prince Philip of Greece and Denmark, he was known as plain Lieutenant Mountbatten RN. It had been a close-run thing and the matter needed all of Mountbatten's legendary string pulling to encourage an indifferent court and civil service to thread the administrative needle and formally make him a British citizen.

It would, however, be another two frustrating months before the official engagement was announced. The king and queen still had their doubts, with the queen expressing her ambivalence to Tommy Lascelles. She wrote: "One can only pray that she has made the right decision, I *think* she has—but he is untried as yet."[30]

Finally, on July 9, their engagement was announced. It was a brief pick-me-up for a nation on its knees, a country where rationing was so severe that concerned folk from the Dominions sent food parcels to help out. Britain may have won the war but was rapidly losing the peace. This was the age of austerity, a pervasive attitude that cast a long shadow over the planning for the wedding, which was officially set for November 20, 1947.

If the royal family and their courtiers had their reservations about the untested prince, as the wedding day approached Philip, too, had doubts about the prospects of marrying the future queen. A week after the engagement was announced, he and the princess traveled to Edinburgh, where she was given the freedom of the city. As the princess made her acceptance speech, he dutifully stood two steps behind her. It was to be his default public position in the years ahead.

Over breakfast at Kensington Palace after the second of two stag nights, the prince asked his cousin Patricia Mountbatten, "I don't know if I'm being very brave or very stupid going ahead with this wedding." His cousin, sensing that his question was nervously rhetorical, told him, "I am quite sure you are being very brave."[31]

As she later recalled, "We were well aware that he wasn't just taking on the immediate family; he was taking on all the outer aspects of the Court life. He was very well aware, I think, that there were going to be difficulties."[32] For her part Queen

Wilhelmina of the Netherlands likened Philip's situation to "entering the royal cage."[33] And she told him so.

During his first Balmoral summer as the princess's fiancé, he had a taste of what he was up against. Many fellow guests, including the queen's brother David Bowes-Lyon, the Eldons, and the Salisburys, had been doubtful of the match. The prince, knowing he was in hostile territory, was perhaps more combative and "chipper" than usual. Courtiers who ran the rule over the couple concluded that she was in love with him but they were not too sure about her erstwhile fiancé. They found him too offhand toward the princess for their tastes. For his part, Philip found the courtiers, particularly that gnarled and grizzly palace infighter, Tommy Lascelles, patronizing and dismissive.

As the wedding day approached, he concluded that he was simply seen as a cypher, albeit a dashing one. All the big decisions about the wedding were taken out of his hands. Even though he had fought loyally during the war, the king deemed it too soon to invite his sisters, who had married Nazi royalty. "So soon after the war you couldn't have the Hun," said Lady Pamela Hicks bluntly.[34] It was a disappointment to both the prince and his sisters, but he completely understood the king's reasoning.

On the big day itself Philip's Nazi family was forgotten in the euphoria of the wedding. When Princess Elizabeth looked out from her second-floor bedroom window, she was amazed by the scene that greeted her. In the dawn November light she saw hundreds of people lining the Mall, some lying on mattresses and blankets now sodden with the rain that had fallen during the night. At Kensington Palace, where Philip Mountbatten RN spent his last night as a bachelor, he seemed remarkably relaxed for a man who had just given up smoking—at the urging of his fiancée. He decided to wear his somewhat careworn navy uniform, a move admired by the queen and her friends. Though he wore a pair of darned socks on his big day, he now had enough to buy himself a new pair as his £11-a-week navy pay ($600 at today's prices) had been augmented by an award of £10,000 a year from the Civil List. His bride was awarded £50,000 by the government with a further grant of £50,000 to restore Clarence House, which was bombed during the war and was now earmarked as their London residence.

That wasn't the only bounty the navy officer received. On the day before the royal nuptuals the king had bestowed upon him the Order of the Garter. In addition, on the day of the wedding, the king awarded him the titles of Duke of Edinburgh, Earl of Merioneth, and Baron Greenwich.

Once again Dermot Morrah had come to the rescue. When the king was agonizing about what his future son-in-law should be called, Morrah compiled a list of appropriate names and ranked them in order of historical relevance and suitability. Several found favor with the sovereign.

By contrast with the groom's modest preparations, his bride and her eight bridesmaids were being fussed over by couturier Norman Hartnell and his team. It took them two hours to fit the princess into her ivory silk satin wedding dress, a creation that had taken a team of 350 dressmakers seven weeks to make. The dress, with its theme of rebirth and renewal, had even been discussed in the cabinet, where the Labour prime minister Clement Attlee had expressed concern that the silk may have come from a country recently at war with Britain. Hartnell tartly pointed out that the silkworms were from Nationalist China, an ally of Great Britain.[35]

Inside the palace, as the princess was carefully eased into her wedding dress, there was subdued panic. First the bride's bouquet went missing, only to be discovered in a cool cupboard after a footman recalled he had left it there for safekeeping. Then, as the princess's veil was fitted, the frame of the sun-ray tiara, lent to the bride by the queen, snapped off.

Fortunately the crown jeweler was on hand. He was escorted by police to his workshop to effect running repairs. Finally Elizabeth's double string of pearls, given to her by the king and queen, went missing. Fortunately a courtier recalled that the absent pearls were on display with the other 2,583 gifts at St. James's Palace. So the princess's private secretary Jock Colville commandeered the official car used by King Haakon of Norway and raced to St. James's where, after a tricky conversation with police guarding the wedding gifts, he was able to retrieve the precious piece of jewelry.[36]

As the drama took place backstage, Westminster Abbey itself saw the largest gathering of royalty since before the outbreak of war in 1939. Crown Princess Juliana of the Netherlands scanned the other royals, many looking distinctly down-at-heel, and commented: "Everyone's jewelry is so dirty."[37] Besides Philip's sisters there were three other telling omissions from the guest list—the Duke and Duchess of Windsor and the princess royal, the king's sister. She boycotted the ceremony because she felt that the Windsors' exclusion was unfair and un-Christian. It was the first public example of a pattern that would continue for the rest of their lives, the duke and his American wife exiled from the land he once ruled.

By contrast his friend Winston Churchill, who had played a telling role in the abdication crisis, was treated as the all-conquering hero. He deliberately arrived late and almost stole the show as everyone in the congregation, including royalty, rose to their feet in acknowledgment of his contribution to securing victory, liberation, and peace in Europe. As the war leader had predicted, the royal wedding was a "a flash of color on the hard road we have to travel," as more than two hundred million tuned in to the radio broadcast and thousands lined the streets leading to the abbey.[38] For many it was a chance to escape grinding austerity and soul-destroying drabness just for a day. For others it was a renewal of the ancient compact between the public and the royal family, a chance for the nation to pat itself on the back, to celebrate an eternal ceremony that speaks of commitment, love, and hope.

The star of the show arrived to a fanfare and the hymn "Praise, My Soul, the King of Heaven," Elizabeth and her father walking slowly down the red carpet—secondhand to save money—to the high altar where Philip and his best man, David Milford Haven, were waiting.

"I was so proud and thrilled at having you so close to me on our long walk in Westminster Abbey," the king later wrote to his daughter. "But when I handed you to the Archbishop, I felt that I had lost something precious."[39] At the wedding breakfast Philip made a short speech saying: "I am proud—proud of my country and of my wife," while the new bride wished for nothing more than that "Philip and I should be as happy as my father and mother have been, and Queen Mary and King George before them."[40] Acknowledging that "we four" were now "we five," the latest arrival to the House of Windsor wrote tenderly to reassure the queen that her daughter was in good hands.

"Lilibet is the only 'thing' in the world which is absolutely real to me and my ambition is to weld the two of us into a new combined existence that will not only be able to withstand the shocks directed at us, but will also have a positive existence for the good."[41] Perhaps the suspicious courtiers had misread the royal romantic.

Though "blissfully happy," Elizabeth considered the first

few days of her honeymoon on the Broadlands estate a most "vulgar and disgraceful affair," particularly their attendance at Sunday service.[42]

Curious crowds arrived on foot or by car to watch them at Romsey Abbey. Those who couldn't get inside climbed on gravestones or propped ladders against the walls so they could peer through the church windows. One family even brought a sideboard they used as a makeshift stand to watch the royal newlyweds at prayer.

Royalty as celebrity, monarchy as circus. It was a sign of things to come.

4

The Barefoot Princess

Marriage changed Elizabeth. She seemed more womanly, more assured, and more confident. The family dynamic had changed. Her world now centered on her husband and rather less so her parents and sister. Nonetheless in the early going Elizabeth's instinctive reaction to a troubling decision was often to consult her mother first and her husband second. It was a difficult habit to give up and one that the queen continued to encourage as she felt Philip challenged her authority as the family matriarch. Philip bided his time. History professor Jane Ridley has argued that the queen viewed him as "rather an enemy." She added, "One would see those early years as being a tug-of-war and a tussle" for the ear of Princess Elizabeth.[1]

As forthright and tactless as he could be, the prince was in no hurry to clash with his formidable mother-in-law. It was perhaps inevitable that in any close family, royal or non-royal, the arrival of a newcomer upsets the existing power balance. It was particularly the case when "we four" turned into five.

In their day-to-day life Philip ruled the roost domestically, choosing menus, giving orders to staff, placing furniture, and organizing private engagements. For her part Elizabeth consulted with her private secretary Jock Colville on matters of state, royal engagements, official signatures, and the like. Philip kept his nose out just as he avoided conflict with the third wheel in the marriage, his wife's companion and dresser Bobo MacDonald, who was in attendance during their honeymoon at Broadlands and afterward at Birkhall on the Balmoral estate.

The dour Scot, who dressed just like her mistress, was the guiding hand behind the princess's daily wardrobe. She kept an inventory of her handbags, hats, dresses, and shoes and ensured that everything coordinated and fitted.

She was the one who brought the princess her calling tray with a cup of tea every morning and, more important, passed on the palace gossip. Her presence occasionally grated, but for the most part Philip held his peace.

In the meantime the princess was excitedly plotting her departure from Buckingham Palace and starting married life at Sunninghill Park, a rambling country house set in 665 acres on the boundary of Windsor Great Park. For a young woman who wanted to be surrounded by dogs, horses, and eventually children, the early-nineteenth-century country house estate was ideal. Shortly before they were due to move in, however, the rambling pile, which had been invaded by squatters, caught fire and burned down. Arson was initially suspected though after an investigation the police concluded that the fire began during repairs. With their London home of Clarence House under construction, the homeless royals lodged for a time at Kensington Palace before returning to Elizabeth's suite of rooms at Buckingham Palace. The couple had separate bedrooms and exchanged jolly banter while they were being dressed by, in Philip's case, his valet John Dean while the ever-present Bobo dressed the princess. And of course the newlyweds were under constant scrutiny, watched by silent footmen, judged by knowing courtiers, and minded by their police bodyguards.

Even so, compared with today, it was a relatively relaxed ambience. Prince Philip was able to walk to work along the Mall to the Admiralty where he had a desk job working for the naval director of operations. Often he would take a break during the day to oversee the works at Clarence House. It was Philip who was responsible for the installation of the latest gadgets including washing machines, televisions, an intercom system, and an electric trouser press. As the place neared completion the princess would join in, busying herself by mixing the paints for the green walls of the Adam-style dining room.

Her private secretary Jock Colville was active, too, trying to mix and match the newlyweds, who were still royal apprentices after all, with a swatch of different events that would help paint for them a more authentic picture of modern Britain. The couple attended a debate in the House of Commons, visited a juvenile court, and had dinner, hosted by Prime Minister Clement Attlee, with young politicians and their spouses.

But it was not all serious matters of state. On February 28, 1948, the family went en masse to the London Palladium to watch the American entertainer Danny Kaye. For the first time, the royal family sat in the front row of the stalls rather than the royal box. The king joined in with a sing-along and was the one to shout a warning to the comic in a skit about missing his tea break. The royal family loved Kaye's zany, often improvised routines. Over the decades the comedian became a regular and welcome visitor to royal homes. Elizabeth was such a fan that the American poet Delmore Schwartz wrote the poem "Vaudeville for a Princess," which was subtitled "Suggested by Princess Elizabeth's Admiration of Danny Kaye."

On their first overseas tour together, in May 1948, the couple visited Paris, which gave the princess the chance to put all those French conversation lessons to good use. While they enjoyed watching the horse races at Longchamp and danced at a fashionable nightspot, the princess was nursing a secret. She was in the early stages of pregnancy and prone to morning sickness. On several occasions during the visit she only just managed to maintain her composure. Most spectators thought that her indisposition was due to her depth of feeling.

In the meantime the couple appointed a comptroller and treasurer, General Sir Frederick "Boy" Browning of Battle of Arnhem fame and husband of novelist Daphne du Maurier. One of his first jobs was to secure a lease on Windlesham Moor, a country manor set in fifty acres of leafy Surrey. Philip immediately turned the tennis courts into a cricket pitch and organized matches with friends and locals during the summer. They had eight staff when they were in residence, including a footman whose job was to bring the corgis their food on a silver tray at four thirty precisely.

Regular weekend visitors were Philip's great naval friend Michael Parker and his wife Eileen who, like the princess, was pregnant but with her second child. Though the two wives did not know each other at all well, they had a common topic of conversation—babies.

Eileen Parker recalled that the princess often spoke about her dreams and ambitions for her children, wanting her sons and daughters to have less restricted lives than she had had. The word *normal* was frequently used—as it would be by future generations of royal mothers. As Eileen recalled: "She longed for them to be brought up under what she called 'normal' circumstances."[2] "I would like them to be able to lead ordinary lives," the princess said, confiding to Eileen that her idea of happiness was to live quietly with her children, dogs, and horses. Her ambition was something of a pipe dream.

No sooner did the palace announce her pregnancy on Derby Day, June 4, than she and her husband were showered with layettes, booties, blankets, and toys sent by well-wishers. The princess gave up royal duties at the end of June and spent her days in the then-traditional way of mothers-to-be, namely organizing the nursery at Clarence House and developing a craving for her favorite chocolate cake.

The princess insisted on having the baby in her own rooms at Buckingham Palace and was relieved when the James Chuter-Ede made it clear that a presence of a senior government minister at the birth was no longer required. Neither, it seemed, was her husband, who played squash with Michael Parker in the palace courts as the princess, attended by four doctors, was in labor. The prince was interrupted by Tommy Lascelles who told the duke that, as of 9:14 p.m. on November 14, 1948, he was now the father of a baby boy. They named him Charles Philip Arthur George.

As the new parents celebrated with flowers and champagne, a cloud hung over the palace. The king, increasingly irascible and fragile, had been harboring a serious medical complaint. Throughout his daughter's pregnancy, he had been suffering from wrenching cramps in his feet that made standing—part and parcel of his job—agonizing. Not wishing to cause a fuss, the stoical sovereign had soldiered on until the pain became too much to bear. He had relied on the remedies prescribed by his homeopathic doctor, Sir John Weir, and this dubious course of treatment was suspected of delaying more conventional investigation. On October 30—two weeks before the birth of his first grandchild—doctors established that he was indeed seriously ill. Once he had given himself up to the ministrations of the orthodox medical fraternity, the king, exhausted and distressed, slept for two days straight.

After further tests he was diagnosed as suffering from Buerger's disease, a chronic inflammation of the major blood vessels. There was such a severe danger of gangrene in his right leg that surgeons discussed amputation.

During these anxious few days, secrecy and evasion were the order of the day to ensure that nothing would upset the heavily pregnant princess.

No word of the king's condition became public before the princess gave birth. Two days later, on November 16, he accepted that a long-anticipated tour of Australia and New Zealand would have to be postponed. He also gave permission to release a medical bulletin and announced that he was canceling all engagements for the foreseeable future. He was, however, sufficiently well to attend the christening of Prince Charles at Buckingham Palace on December 15. Besides other members of the royal family, the ceremony was also attended by Elizabeth's former governess Marion Crawford and her husband George Buthlay, the couple having married in September 1947.

As the Buthlays watched Archbishop of Canterbury Geoffrey Fisher pour water from the river Jordan over the infant's head in the Music Room at Buckingham Palace, they were planning a stratagem that would rupture the lifelong relationship between Crawfie and Elizabeth.

The recently wed Mrs. Buthlay planned to write her memoirs about her time with the princesses and their parents. It was an incendiary idea especially as it soon became crystal clear that the royal family was wholly opposed to former or existing members of the royal household writing or talking about their experiences.

Even though her memoir, titled *The Little Princesses*, depicted Elizabeth and Margaret and their parents as a virtuous family who extolled wholesome fireside values of duty, love, and fidelity, their former governess was deemed to have betrayed their trust. In a letter sent to Mrs. Buthlay in April 1949, the queen made the family position clear: "I do feel most definitely, that you should not write and sign articles about the children, as people in positions of confidence with us must be utterly oyster."[3] That is to say, stay silent. When she defied her former employer and went ahead with a series of articles in the American magazine *Ladies' Home Journal* and then published her memoir, the royal family was furious and shocked. Even though, to modern eyes, the book is anodyne and highly complimentary, Princess Margaret felt sick and her sister deeply upset at the perceived betrayal by their governess.

Elizabeth accused her of having "snaked"—betrayed the family—and advised any ladies-in-waiting who received letters from Mrs. Buthlay to hold them with a long pair of tongs. It was not what she wrote that concerned the royal family—the governess conjured up a world that was human yet dignified and where love, duty, and obedience were the currency of everyday life—but her deliberate act of disloyalty. In a six-page letter to Lady Nancy Astor the queen lamented that "our late and completely trusted governess" had "gone off her head."[4] The phrase *to do a Crawfie* was now used to describe any member of royal staff who subsequently sold stories about their royal service.

This unhappy episode vividly illustrated a royal family trait: At any sign of danger, the royal family immediately circled the wagons. Cross one and, as Crawfie found to her cost, cross them all. There was no going back, the onetime royal employee was cast into the outer darkness forever. Shortly after publication of *The Little Princesses* she vacated her "grace and favor" cottage inside the grounds of Kensington Palace and moved to Aberdeen just a few yards from the road to Balmoral.

She longed for a reconciliation but it never came. In her later years she twice tried to take her own life. On one occasion she left a note that read: "The world has passed me by and I can't bear those I love to pass me by on the road."[5]

That said, the former governess should have anticipated the stern unforgiving reaction of the young woman whom she loved and adored like her own child. When Jock Colville, who was Elizabeth's private secretary for two years before working for Winston Churchill, asked the princess if it were possible for him to write about his experiences in her office, he was given short shrift. His request cast a pall over the remaining months of his secondment to the royal family in 1949.

Just as Elizabeth was completely loyal to her family and the institution, so she expected complete loyalty from those she worked with. The long-term effect of the Crawfie affair was to place a distance between the princess and those in her employ, no matter how loyal. At times of crisis the royal family instinctively withdrew into themselves.

If the Crawford affair marked the end of childhood innocence, so the ailing king's incapacity—he underwent a major spinal operation in March 1949 to restore the circulation to his legs—firmly propelled the twenty-two-year-old princess into the front line of the monarchy.

As he slowly recovered it was Princess Elizabeth who grew in stature, taking over many of his formal duties. In June 1949 the king was driven in an open carriage to watch the Trooping the Colour ceremony while his eldest daughter rode at the head of the horse parade.

Though endlessly concerned about her father, she was beginning to lead the life of an independent married woman, a process that accelerated when the couple moved from Buckingham Palace to Clarence House that summer.

Earlier in the year, when the princess celebrated her twenty-third birthday, she went to the fashionable Café de Paris on Coventry Street after watching Laurence Olivier and Vivien Leigh in *School for Scandal*. Then the glamorous thespians joined the royal party for an evening of tango, quick-step, and samba at a nightclub. At a ball held at Windsor Castle that summer the royal newlyweds stole the show. Chips Channon commented that they looked "like characters out of a fairy tale."[6] In July they arrived in fancy dress—Elizabeth as a Edwardian parlor maid and her husband as a waiter—for a summer party hosted by the American ambassador Lewis W. Douglas, whose daughter Sharman was a close friend of Princess Margaret. Determined to make an impact, Margaret came as a Parisian can-can girl complete with lace knickers and black stockings. In her thank-you note she told Douglas: "I was feeling so over-excited by the time our Can-Can was due that I could hardly breathe." That didn't stop the "ecstatic" royal from putting on her costume and repeating her routine for her mother when she got home to Buckingham Palace.[7]

Improvements in the king's condition coincided with the end of Philip's sojourn ashore. He was appointed first lieutenant and second-in-command of HMS *Chequers*, which was based in Malta, and he left for the island in October 1949. Elizabeth joined him a month later with the king's blessing. Malta was a place that had become dear to George VI's heart in the war. In April 1942 during the brutal siege of Malta he awarded the gallant defenders the George Cross and visited the island himself in June. The queen, who had a photograph of the king arriving at Malta on her bedroom dressing table, later recalled, "The King was so determined to get to Malta somehow, to try and convey his gratitude and admiration to the brave citizens for their courage and tenacity under endless attacks."[8]

The feeling was entirely mutual as thousands thronged the streets to catch a glimpse of the king's eldest daughter and their future queen. Such was the fascination with and adoration of Princess Elizabeth that Mabel Strickland, the owner of the *Times of Malta*, wrote an article asking the public to leave them alone on private occasions.

The princess, who arrived on her second wedding anniversary, November 20, hardly had a chance to join her husband to celebrate before she was plunged into a round of engagements. During her six-week stay she visited the island's cathedrals, the national library, the dockyard, the Mediterranean fleet, an industrial exhibition, and numerous hospitals; she presided over the annual children's toy tea at the palace and inaugurated a monument to the victims of two world wars.

For all the formality and protocol—Prime Minister Paul Boffa and the Archbishop Michael Gonzi were a seemingly constant presence—this was one of the happiest periods of Elizabeth's life. Malta was where her second child, Princess Anne, was conceived and where she and her naval husband were able to spend time alone, exploring the fascinating coastline on a loaned Navy cruiser appropriately named the *Eden*. To keep seasickness at bay, she would take a bag of Maltese galletti, a wafer biscuit, which she nibbled on. She and the duke found time to go dancing aboard his ship at an officers' mess shindig and at the Phoenicia hotel where the band leader dutifully played her favorite tune, "People Will Say We're in Love" from the Rodgers and Hammerstein musical *Oklahoma*.

She was also able to properly thank Philip's fellow officer, Lieutenant Bill O'Brien, who had graciously given the prince his petrol ration coupons when they were stationed at Corsham together so that he could drive to London to court the princess. He and his wife Rita were regular guests at the dinner parties hosted by the royal couple at Villa Guardamangia, a limestone villa with commanding views of Grand Harbor. The current occupants, Lord Louis and Edwina Mountbatten, moved rooms in the rambling establishment in order to give the royal couple the best suites in the house.

Another fixture in Elizabeth's life was Mabel Strickland, the colorful, controversial character who ran the *Times of Malta*. She brought the princess into her circle and helped her with guest lists for social events. When the royal couple finally moved into Villa Guardamangia, Mabel attended their first dinner party. Fellow guest Vice Admiral Guy Grantham, who eventually became the governor of Malta, recalled: "We had a local dish as a second course, and we were using gold plated fish knives and forks—and the first thing that happened was that one of the knives used by the ADC snapped off. The Princess told him not to worry, [saying] 'It was a wedding present' but before we had finished the course another couple of handles had gone too! This amused the princess frightfully."[9]

The atmosphere at the villa was warm and friendly, and Edwina Mountbatten enjoyed coddling the young mother. "It's lovely seeing her so radiant and leading a more or less human and normal existence for once."[10]

As a reminder of the responsibilities to come, Philip got an earful from his uncle when he kept his wife out late once, which caused them to miss the start of a dinner party hosted by the Mountbattens. He summoned the prince to his office where he told him, "Don't you dare do it again. Remember, she is the Queen of tomorrow and please never forget that."[11]

This turned out to be one in a series of clashes between two hard-driving men who liked to have their own way. After several weeks of brusque, offhand behavior toward the older man, Philip sat down with his uncle for a heart-to-heart to resolve their issues. The prince admitted that he was trying to resist his dominating uncle's influence in the only way he knew how—by fighting back. In response Mountbatten agreed to back off. Once the issues were aired, the two men resumed their previously friendly and affectionate relationship.

Mountbatten was desperate to be liked and admired by the future queen, and he was thrilled when he discovered that she found him rather good company. He told his sister Patricia, "Lilibet is quite enchanting and I've lost whatever of my heart is left to spare entirely to her. She dances quite divinely and always wants a samba when we dance together."[12]

The dancing came to an end in December when the princess waved farewell to her husband as his ship HMS *Chequers* was sent with six other warships to patrol the Red Sea, following tribal clashes in Eritrea. It was a salutary rite of passage experienced by all navy wives, including Edwina Mountbatten, who felt a surge of sympathy for the young woman standing on the docks watching her man sail away. Shortly afterward the princess and her small entourage flew back to London on a Viking prop plane.

"Lilibeth has left with a tear in her eyes and a lump in her throat," Edwina told Pandit Nehru, India's first prime minister, with whom she enjoyed a long and intimate romance. "Putting her into the Viking when she left was I thought rather like putting a bird back into a very small cage and I felt sad and nearly tearful myself."[13]

The consolation was that she was reunited with her son, who had spent Christmas with his grandparents at Sandringham. Elizabeth, who was later joined by Philip, spent the next few weeks at the Norfolk retreat, helping entertain the numerous guests who came for what was called a dine and sleep, effectively staying the night after dinner. It was a way of efficiently hosting important guests, such as politicians and diplomats, as Sandringham was well off the beaten track. During a visit in February, Cynthia Gladwyn, the wife of the former English ambassador to Paris, observed the contrast between Elizabeth's youth and her exalted position. She noted that she had "a most charming mixture in her expression of eagerness to please and yet a serious awareness of her rank and responsibility. Her charming diffidence was very appealing, for a touch of genuine gravity was always the traditional barrier which separated royalty from the common herd, warning them that no liberty should be taken. But all this with a sweet smile, a very pretty soft voice, and a certain gaucherie in her walk, showing her still to be a young girl."[14]

Shortly afterward she left for Malta again to be reunited with her husband. The princess spent her twenty-fourth birthday at a polo field on the island, where she watched her husband and her uncle joust for bragging rights in their highly competitive games. She turned a deaf ear to her husband's language, which, if the game were going badly, was of the industrial variety. These were happy days for the pregnant princess who, according to Mike Parker, spent only 10 percent of her time being a royal. For the rest she "mucked in" with other naval wives, organizing tea parties and other social events.[15] For the most part she was left alone, the islanders heeding the urgings of Mabel Strickland and others to respect her privacy. All too soon that carefree spring and early summer came to end as the princess left for Clarence House, where thousands of curious onlookers gathered to catch a glimpse of the princess before she gave birth to her second child. On August 15, 1950, the waiting multitude were rewarded for their noisy patience when Princess Anne was born. Normally in robust health, the princess spent longer than expected recovering from the birth, her doctors advising her to cancel public engagements until November. That month she returned to Malta to spend Christmas with her husband and left Charles and baby Anne behind at Sandringham with her sister and her parents—as well as a small platoon of nurses and nannies.

When she arrived, Philip was eager to show her around his new "baby." In September, shortly after the arrival of Princess Anne, he had been given command of the frigate HMS *Magpie* and was gazetted to lieutenant-commander. Only twenty-nine and now in command of a frigate, it was clear Philip was on a fast track to much greater things.

Shortly after she joined him in Malta, Elizabeth and the duke sailed to Athens on a goodwill visit to the Greek royal family, King Paul and Queen Frederika. Elizabeth made the journey aboard HMS *Surprise*, the commander in chief's dispatch vessel, the prince on *Magpie*. During the voyage the royal couple exchanged humorous signals that are still preserved in the navy log. One famous example was: *Surprise* to *Magpie*: "Princess full of beans." *Magpie* to *Surprise*: "Can't you give her something better for breakfast!" Others related to biblical texts, the princess on one occasion signaling "Isaiah 33:23," which says "Thy tacklings are loosed." Her husband rapidly responded with "I Samuel 15:14"—"What meaneth then this bleating of the sheep?"[16]

Their highly successful visit, which was sanctioned by the Foreign Office, was the perfect union of Philip's naval and Elizabeth's royal duties.

This longer stay—without Uncle Dickie interfering—was probably the happiest, especially when her sister Margaret arrived to join in the fun. In a memo to her staff the princess made it clear that she wanted a life that was sunny-side up. "I sincerely hope that full cooperation will exist between all members of the staff as to create a happy atmosphere at the Villa Guardamangia."[17] She was relaxed enough to walk round the tiled mansion barefoot. Nor did she stand on ceremony. Tony Grech, the son of her maid Jessie, took to calling her Auntie Liz.

He was not the only one. Long after she had left Malta she sent Christmas cards to her Maltese staff and later invited all of them to celebrate her twenty-fifth wedding anniversary at Westminster Abbey and Buckingham Palace.

While Philip raced his yacht *Cowslip* across the bay or honed his polo skills on a wooden practice horse, the princess went riding herself, drove around the island in her Daimler with her lady-in-waiting or detective for company, or visited other navy wives for tea and sandwiches.

She is also remembered for trying local dishes like rabbit pâté; pastizzi, a pasta dish; lampuki, a fish pie; or hobz malti, a local bread.

On one occasion in April 1951, she visited Sannat on the tiny island of Gozo, where she watched lace making.[18] Though a plaque now commemorates the occasion, at the time her visit attracted only local interest. Hers was a life barely imaginable in England and an experience that she always looked back on with affection and gratitude.

Even in January 1975, a year after Malta became a republic, she waxed lyrical about the place. "I have been thinking so much about Malta and the happy times we had there as a Naval family—something I shall never forget," she wrote to Mabel Strickland, who sent her an annual gift of avocados, oranges, lemons, and other exotic fruits from her garden.[19]

It was hard to give up such a happy and contented berth. But give it up they did. By the summer of 1951 it was clear that the visit to Greece on HMS *Magpie* had been nothing more than a happy coincidence. Both the Royal Navy and the royal family were full-time commitments. Something had to give. Philip was forced to accept the inevitable. Looking wistfully at his navy whites, he told his valet John Dean, "It will be a long time before I want those again."[20]

Shortly afterward he was put on indefinite leave.

A bout of influenza that caused the ailing king to cancel a visit to Northern Ireland in May 1951 rather sealed his fate. As he recuperated, the queen, Princess Elizabeth, and Princess Margaret took on his duties, his eldest daughter representing the king at Trooping the Colour in June. During the summer the king's condition deteriorated, news that cast a pall over Princess Margaret's twenty-first birthday celebrations at Balmoral in August. Several weeks later, in September, seven doctors issued a short but dramatic bulletin saying that the condition of the king's lung gave cause for concern and he had been advised that he needed an operation soon. Elizabeth and Philip, who were due to sail to Canada for a five-week tour of North America, postponed their sailing and decided to fly instead so that they could be in London during the king's operation on September 23.

The news was not good. After the operation the king's surgeons informed the queen and Elizabeth that cancer had been found in the removed lung. This news was withheld from the king. As the monarch made a slow, painful recovery, he insisted that their tour of Canada and America go ahead.

After a farewell lunch at Buckingham Palace on October 7, they boarded a BOAC Stratocruiser for the seventeen-hour flight to Montreal. It was the first time an heir to the throne had made a long-distance flight, and such was the concern that Royal Navy ships took up strategic positions across the Atlantic route in case of an emergency. Among their baggage were the black clothes of mourning as well as a sealed envelope containing the draft Accession Declaration should the worst happen and the king die.

Their arrival in Montreal was a far cry from those halcyon days of untroubled anonymity in Malta. A friendly but boisterous crowd of around fifteen thousand welcomed the royal couple, and such was the crush of photographers that glass from exploding flashbulbs splattered over Princess Elizabeth's fur coat. The pace on the thirty-three-day visit was relentless and exhausting, and the princess was so unnerved by the good-natured mayhem that accompanied their every move that a muscle in her right cheek twitched constantly. She also reverted to her default pose of polite but contained interest. As a result critics complained that she was too distant and formal. These sentiments troubled the princess, who told her entourage that her jaw was aching from all the smiling. It would not be the only time that people mistook her impassive demeanor for aloofness, even though it was her way of keeping her natural emotions in check. This understandable misreading would dog her throughout her reign. As her former private secretary Lord Martin Charteris, who knew her for fifty years, observed, the key to her character was that she was actually afraid of her emotions because they were very strong and she always tried to keep them under iron control.[21]

When they returned home in November, the princess was relieved to see that her father had gained weight and was even talking about shooting with a light gun. She agreed with the plan for him to travel to South Africa in March 1952 to enjoy the winter sunshine and hopefully regain his strength. He was still so weak that when he recorded his Christmas message he could only manage one exhausting sentence at a time.

As a result of the King's continuing poor health, it was decided that the Duke and Duchess of Edinburgh would finally embark upon the oft-postponed trip to Australia and New Zealand in his place, departing on Thursday, January 31, with a stopover in Kenya. The last evening the royal family spent together before the tour was at the Theatre Royal Drury Lane where they saw a performance of *South Pacific* by Rodgers and Hammerstein.

The next day, Thursday, January 31, he ignored the advice of his doctors, and stood for half an hour hatless on the wind-blown airport tarmac at London airport to say goodbye to his beloved daughter. "He is like that," the princess later remarked, "he never thinks of himself."[22] Though the king and queen chatted to Churchill and other members of the official group, pictures showed a haggard and strained King George VI, which shocked and disturbed the nation. "I felt with foreboding that this would be the last time he was to see his daughter, and that he thought so himself,"[23] remarked the colonial secretary Lord Chandos. He was not alone.

After Lord Casey, Australian minister for external affairs, met Princess Elizabeth around Christmas 1951, he told his wife Marie: "I am not sure that Elizabeth doesn't know that practically at any moment she may become Queen of us all. She has such a serious demeanor that I think she was warned or has some instinctive knowledge that at any time she might have this burden thrust upon her." When he mentioned this impression to Churchill, he said, "Yes there is too much care on that young brow."[24]

Back at Sandringham on Tuesday, February 5, the king was in exuberant spirits and went shooting on a bitterly cold but blue-skied day. Over dinner that night he listened attentively to his racing manager Charles Moore as he described his adventures in Kenya at the Treetops Hotel in the Aberdare Forest where at that very moment Elizabeth and Philip were sitting in a little cabin perched in a giant fig tree watching elephants and rhinos and other big game in the moonlight.

The king retired early. The next morning, February 6, at seven fifteen his undervalet James MacDonald took the king his tea but he couldn't rouse him. After pulling back the curtain, he realized that the fifty-six-year-old sovereign was dead. It was discovered later that he had suffered a coronary thrombosis, a blood clot that had reached his heart. The queen was told and immediately went to the king's bedroom. He looked so peaceful that she thought he was just in a deep sleep. Then she realized what had happened. She stood for a moment by his bedside and gently kissed the king on the forehead. Then she went to tell Princess Margaret the dread news while putting into motion the mechanics of "Hyde Park Corner"—the code phrase used to inform senior courtiers at Buckingham Palace as well as top government officials that the king was dead.

In Kenya that morning, the sky was shimmering with a pale-blue light and the whole atmosphere around the princess was vibrant and tinged with magic. As she looked over the iridescent landscape in wonder, a majestic eagle circled overhead for some time and then dipped as though in salute before disappearing from view. Mike Parker thought it an uncanny experience, and it haunted him for a long time afterward.

Without communication of any kind, Elizabeth was blithely unaware of the drama unfolding at Sandringham. The previous evening, the small group, their faces illuminated by kerosene lamps, had listened intently as the princess had spoken proudly of her father and his battle to regain his health. The princess remembered the day he put a walking stick to his shoulder and said: "I believe I could shoot now."[25] His daughter hoped his forthcoming visit to South Africa would do him good and that he would have made a full recovery by the time she returned home.

After breakfast the party returned to Sagana Lodge, the cabin given to the royal couple as a wedding present by the Kenyan people. Here the princess sat at her desk writing a letter to her parents about the excitements of the previous night. Philip was having a rest before a planned trout-fishing trip.

Along the corridor Mike Parker took a phone call that left him thunderstruck. It was from the princess's private secretary, Martin Charteris, who was staying at a local hotel. He had been informed by a journalist about wire reports from London announcing the king's death. Parker's first instinct was to wake Prince Philip. Instead he waited in his room quietly listening to a shortwave radio for more information. Once he was doubly certain, he broke the news to Philip. The prince looked as if the world had dropped on his shoulders as he absorbed the full import of the king's death. After he composed himself, he went into his wife's room and took her out into the garden. There in the dappled sunlight against the soft background of a rippling stream she learned of her father's death and that she was now queen.

Her response revealed the caliber of the young woman, only twenty-five, who had inherited the throne. She seemed almost prepared for this dread event, because her reaction was almost matter-of-fact and business-like. There were no tears or any emotional outburst as she began to grasp the full import of losing her beloved father while accepting the inevitability of her destiny. Certainly she was pale, almost translucent, very tense and strained, but those who traveled with her remember the new queen as being remarkably contained, clear-sighted, and in control. There was much to reflect on. Some days later hunter Jim Corbett, who accompanied the princess, captured the mood when he wrote in the visitors book: "For the first time in the history of the world a young girl climbed into a tree one day a princess and the next day she climbed down from the tree a Queen."[26] When she reappeared at the lodge, her cousin and lady-in-waiting Lady Pamela Mountbatten went up to her and impulsively gave her a hug. "What can one say?" she said to the new queen. Elizabeth simply shrugged and said: "It's one of those things."[27] Moments later she dropped in a deep curtsy, realizing that Elizabeth was no longer her friend but her new sovereign.

For the next few hours the new queen's lifetime of training went into action as she busied herself with her new and onerous responsibilities. Her own emotions were placed in deep freeze, subordinated entirely to her duty. She remained dry-eyed and focused on the job ahead. As Edward Windley, the provincial commissioner for Nyeri district, later recalled: "She was very pale. She was like ice; just like ice." Asked how she received the news he replied: "She took it like a queen."[28]

When her private secretary Martin Charteris arrived at the Sagana Lodge still wearing his sports jacket, she looked up from her desk and said: "Australia must be told."[29] Then she wrote a note to Governor General Sir William McKell expressing her regret for the postponement of the forthcoming tour. As part of the procedural formality Charteris had to ask by which name she wished to be known: "My own name, Elizabeth, of course."[30] To underline her decision she signed some photographs of herself and her family with her new signature: "Elizabeth R."[31] Though time was of the essence—thunderstorms were gathering near their airport at Nanyuki—she insisted in thanking the assembled lodge staff.

Their chauffeur James Cosma A. Gabatha knelt to kiss the new queen's feet when she said goodbye. As her mourning clothes were aboard the SS *Gothic*, which was moored at Mombasa Harbor, she left Sagana Lodge in her day clothes, namely a white-and-beige dress and white gloves as well as a black armband, which was always carried in the official royal bag.

As they drove to Nanyuki, they marveled at how many villagers lined the side of the road with their heads bowed in respect. Clearly the bush telegraph had been working overtime. When they arrived at the grass airfield, the queen was pleased to note that the covey of photographers had agreed to her request not to take pictures and had instead placed their cameras on the ground in a mark of respect.

When she climbed the aircraft steps she paused at the top for a long time, as if drinking in the electric, primal atmosphere of this rugged land. Writer John Hartley described the moment: "She stood in the gathering darkness, unmoving and totally removed. Everyone and everything was silently poised, waiting breathlessly and listening."[32]

Then it was down to business. During the endless flight to London they were in sporadic radio communication with the government and palace. Prime Minister Winston Churchill sent a message of condolence on behalf of the cabinet.

Her mother, too, sent a message, which read: "All my thoughts and prayers are with you, Mummy."[33] During the long flight the queen had plenty of time to review the draft of a speech she was due to make to the Privy Council the following day.

By the time they reached London airport, the queen was tightly controlled, composed, and rested, ready to face the official welcoming party.

With her mourning clothes still aboard SS *Gothic*, she waited before disembarking so that she could change into a black dress and veil, which were brought for her from Clarence House. When she was ready to meet Prime Minister Churchill and other politicians, she took a last look out of the aircraft window before descending the steps.

During their tenure at Clarence House the royal couple had eschewed the outsize and cumbersome royal Rolls-Royces and Daimlers for a more modern and modest fleet of Austin Princess cars. As they taxied along the runway the queen looked out at the row of black official Daimlers and Rolls waiting for her. "Ah," she said, "they've sent those hearses."[34] Her sense of entombment was complete.

5

⚜

Crowning Glory

As the new queen and her entourage drove through the streets of the capital back to Clarence House, a new blackout was in progress. On the silent streets, men were in black suits; women wore black dresses or at the very least black armbands. On fashionable Bond Street a haberdasher dressed his window display with black lingerie. Avuncular historian John Wheeler-Bennett, who became George VI's official biographer, recalled how "the people of England made no secret of the depth and sincerity of their sorrow. I saw many in tears."[1]

Queen Elizabeth II, now "the Most High, the Most Mighty and Most Excellent Monarch," had no time for sentiment. When she arrived at Clarence House, her grandmother, Queen Mary, was waiting for her. She stood erect and dignified as the new sovereign entered the reception hall. Then the old queen, who had seen five reigns and had now lost another son, dropped a deep curtsy and kissed the young queen's hand. It was such a powerful moment of family intimacy and royal symbolism that her lady-in-waiting Lady Cynthia Colville struggled to keep her composure. Not so the unflappable royal, who reminded her granddaughter that her dress was too short for official court mourning.[2]

Later Elizabeth and Prince Philip, in his capacity as privy councilor, attended a twenty-minute meeting of the Privy Council, comprising some 175 dignitaries, at St. James's Palace where the queen signed her oath of accession. After proclaiming herself Queen Elizabeth II, she told the council: "My heart is too full for me to say more to you today than I shall always work, as my father did throughout his reign, to advance the happiness and prosperity of my peoples, spread as they are all the world over."[3]

While Prime Minister Churchill confided to his joint private secretary Jock Colville that the new queen was "only a child,"[4] he gave her a rousing oration in a packed House of Commons. "With the new reign we must all feel our contact with the future. A fair and youthful figure—princess, wife and mother—is the heir to all our traditions and glories never greater than in her father's days, and to all our perplexities and dangers never greater in peacetime than now. She is also heir to all our united strength and loyalty."[5]

With the initial formalities dealt with, the new queen drove to Sandringham to help console her grieving mother and sister and to bid a private farewell to her father. When she arrived at the twenty-thousand-acre Norfolk estate her first act was to go to her father's ground-floor bedroom, where his body lay in a simply carved oak coffin crafted from a single tree felled some months before. She quietly promised that she would follow in his footsteps and make him proud. It would not be easy. Beyond the teachings of Sir Henry Marten in constitutional history, and the limited insights her father had given her, she felt that she had had incomplete training for her role though on reflection she was the same age—twenty-five—as the first Elizabeth when she ascended the throne. In those turbulent days she had no father to guide her, relying instead on her experienced and forthright private secretary Tommy Lascelles, her husband, and of course Mr. Churchill. She placed her private doubts to one side, knowing that she had to be the strong member of the remaining trio for the sake of her mother and sister who, as she later acknowledged, "had the biggest grief to bear, for their future must seem very blank while I have a job and family to think of."[6]

The king and queen had been an emblem of hope and unity during the war. They were a partnership, Queen Elizabeth, now the Queen Mother, as dependent on her husband's "wisdom, his integrity, his courage" as he had relied on her confidence and support.[7] Now she was alone. She felt worthless and empty, her sense of loss "beyond description."[8]

Elizabeth's sister was equally despairing. The king, second-born himself, always had a soft spot for his youngest daughter, calling Margaret his "joy" and Elizabeth his "pride." An indulgent father, a convivial friend, and a wise counselor, he had been the center of her universe. In return she had been the one able to calm him when, in his later ailing years, he had given in to angry gnashes. Margaret explained "the awful sense of being in a black hole" as she tried to come to terms with his loss, the first time she had lost someone really close.[9] She wrote to her friend Veronica Maclean thanking for her "support at this time of anguish." The princess continued: "One is happy to think that he is safe in Heaven away from everything that can hurt or harm him and soon we will feel him nearer to us than he has ever been."[10] Even her faith—Margaret, like her sister, knew and reflected upon her Bible—could not help her through the dark nights of the soul. Instead feeling "tunnel visioned," she turned to sedatives, hard liquor, and cigarettes and lost a worrying amount of weight.

Elizabeth felt guilty and helpless but had to soldier on, aware, too, that the sailor in her life was grieving as well. While he certainly mourned the loss of his father-in-law, he was also bidding farewell to a career just as it was really taking off. Though he had taken sabbaticals to accompany the princess on overseas visits, he assumed that he had another twenty years or so in the navy before retiring from the service. According to his cousin Pamela Mountbatten, the couple had planned their life with the view that Elizabeth would not be on the throne until they were in their fifties.[11] Four years was simply too soon for Philip to give up everything with regard to his naval ambitions. Now he was his wife's subject, obliged forever to walk two paces behind her in public.

She may have been the one to wear the crown but she was not head of the household. That was Philip's dominion. While it had been that way from the beginning of their marriage, it became even more pronounced now that she was queen. Not only was he in command of their domestic world, but as the children grew older he would be the first parent with whom they would discuss personal matters. "He was the boss man," a former close aide told me. "She left all the decisions about family and home to him. Anything royal, symbolized by the red boxes, was her department and he kept out."[12]

Before the funeral on February 15, it was the new queen, not her consort, who had an awkward meeting with the black sheep of the family, the Duke of Windsor. Little effort had been made by the palace to inform the duke, who was in New York, of his brother's death; he only learned of his passing as a result of media inquiries. He sailed to England alone as he realized that his wife would find a chilly reception from those who now ruled his former kingdom. His main purpose was to ensure that the £10,000-a-year income (around $380,000 in 2021) he received from his brother would continue. He was grievously disappointed. In one of her first acts as sovereign, his niece cut his allowance completely. It was a bitter blow to the duke, who expected a little leniency from the new monarch. After receiving the news he wrote to Wallis: "It's hell to be even this much dependent on these ice-veined bitches."[13] Not that he was about to live in penury, having made nearly $2 million for his memoir, A King's Story, which was published in 1951. To no one's surprise, the king's death did not end the duke's exile or the family feud, which would continue almost until the day he died.

On a bitterly cold winter's day the once and former king did, however, accompany the funeral cortege to Westminster Abbey. In a radio address Archbishop of Canterbury Geoffrey Fisher described how the king had made two perfect marriages: one to his queen, the other "to his people."[14] One mourner remarked that the funeral was "a great tribute to him and it's a great tribute to us. Because George VI is *us*. He is *us* and we are him. He is the British people, all that is best in us, and we all know it."[15]

With silent dockyard crane jibs dipped, flags at half-mast, transport at a standstill, and sporting fixtures suspended, there was no doubt as to the extent of national mourning. At the head of his coffin, Elizabeth left a white wreath of flowers. It was inscribed, simply, intimately and lovingly, TO PAPA, FROM LILIBET. Her sister's was equally modest: DARLING PAPA FROM HIS EVER LOVING MARGARET.[16]

From then on, whenever she was in doubt the new queen would refer to how her father did things. If it was good enough for him then it was good enough for her. He was her test, silently looking over her shoulder as she pondered the many difficult decisions she now faced. In any case change was not part of her emotional lexicon. Her motto then and for some time to come was "Safety first." One of her first acts was to appoint her dour, traditional, but loyal maid, Bobo MacDonald, as her official dresser. As the iconography of royal fashion and styling essentially defines a reign, it was arguably a more important appointment than that of a private secretary. It certainly described her in the public imagination: a tight helmet hairdo, intimidating handbag, twinset, pearls, and white gloves. It was only after the retirement of Bobo and the arrival of Angela Kelly during the 1990s that the queen's clothes became more sophisticated and imaginative.

Even though everyone still carried identity cards and, more than six years after the war's end, sweets and eggs remained rationed, change was in the air with excited chatter about a "new Elizabethan age." The nation was in vigorous dialogue with itself about its past and the future. It was more than just a nostalgic harking back to the glory days of Elizabeth I and the Tudor dynasty, but an embrace of the new, the playful, and the vibrant as symbolized by the Festival of Britain—which, though opened in 1951, caught the appetite for change and challenge. Provocative operas such as Berg's *Wozzeck*, controversial literature like Graham Greene's novel *The Power and the Glory*, which criticized the Catholic church, and Graham Sutherland's avant-garde portrait of media magnate Lord Beaverbrook showed that Britain was not afraid to address difficult and perplexing issues.

The left-leaning *New Statesman* magazine hoped that the new monarch, described as "capable, energetic, and sensibly progressive," would "seize the opportunity to sweep away the old order at court and substitute a way of life that matches the times they live in."[17] As the palace was still a place where footmen and other servants powdered their wigs with flour and water and it took fifteen minutes for a pot of tea to arrive from the kitchens to the royal apartments, it was asking a lot.

While Britain was a nation on the cusp of profound social change, it was also a country at war yet again, this time in the Korean conflict. At the same time the world seemed to be teetering on the brink of nuclear annihilation with the arms race between Communist Russia and the capitalist United States. In one of her first acts as queen, Elizabeth invested fusilier Private Bill Speakman with the Victoria Cross, the highest military award for gallantry. It was a reminder that Britain had over eighty thousand men fighting on the Korean Peninsula. After his investiture at Buckingham Palace, Speakman remarked: "I think she was nervous and I was very nervous!"[18]

She was learning on the job, and learning quickly. Her courtiers were impressed by her dedication, attention to detail, and brisk no-nonsense approach. Practical rather than poetic, she read documents more quickly and thoroughly than her father had, and she retained information more accurately. She was balanced, detached, and cool under pressure, her attitude reminiscent of the far-flung British colonial administrators who had held together the greatest empire the world had or has ever seen. Self-controlled, cautious, and conscientious, she was keen to ensure that she got everything right.

In the early months the problem she faced was that there weren't enough hours in the day, and her schedule was so jam-packed that her role of mother was neglected. "Why isn't Mummy going to play with us tonight?" Charles and Anne would protest.[19] One solution was to delay her Tuesday audiences with the prime minister by an hour so that she could play and bathe the toddlers before leaving them in the care of their strict Scottish nanny, Helen Lightbody, known as No Nonsense Lightbody because of her stern ways.

The queen soon learned that hers was a very lonely position, continuously in demand but always alone. Her corgis were her constant companions and a useful diversionary tactic if conversations became too difficult. She needed Dookie and company for her first meeting with Churchill, three times her age, an esteemed war leader and Nobel Prize winner. Would he take her seriously? Little did either realize during that first tentative official meeting that they would become good friends and confidants.

With hindsight Churchill was the perfect first prime minister for Elizabeth. Given her lack of training for the position, Churchill's shrewdness, experience, and understanding of the role of the sovereign in relation to government proved invaluable. As a dedicated monarchist, he became her willing and enthusiastic mentor. His wife, Clementine, once described her husband as "the last believer in the divine rights of kings."[20]

When a former courtier, Richard Molyneux, asked Elizabeth whether her relationship with the prime minister could be compared to that of the "over-indulgent" Lord Melbourne and Queen Victoria, she replied: "On the contrary, I sometimes find him very obstinate."[21] Churchill was the authoritative yet devoted father figure that the young queen needed. The watery gleam in his eye suggested that he might even have been somewhat infatuated with her. His joint private secretary Jock Colville described him as being "madly in love" with the queen, the prime minister stretching out his weekly audiences from the regulation thirty minutes to an hour and a half.[22] He found her cautious, astute, and in the best sense of the word, conservative. While courtiers could not hear what was said, Tommy Lascelles noted in his diary that the conversation was "punctuated by peals of laughter, and Winston generally came out wiping his eyes. 'She's *en grande beauty ce soir*,' he said one evening in his schoolboy French."[23] The much younger woman, unschooled in government, accepted his advice while he came to respect her judgment.

Elizabeth's first crisis was not long in coming. As was to be the case throughout her reign, it concerned her family, on this occasion the family name. Two days after the funeral, the editor of *Debrett's*, the bible of the aristocracy, had written that, as Philip had taken the name Mountbatten as his surname, the royal house was now the House of Mountbatten rather than the House of Windsor. Churchill and his ministers made it clear that this "appalling fact" be amended.[24] It was not so simple. The issue went to the heart of the relationship between Elizabeth and Philip. As the wife of Philip Mountbatten, it was tradition that she indeed took his name. What was more, he expected it.

However, as with so many aspects of daily life, the royal family is literally a law unto itself. Members of the royal family can be known both by the name of the royal house and by a surname that is not always the same. Until 1917 members of the British royal family had no surname, only the name of the house or dynasty to which they belonged. Hence Henry VIII or Henry Tudor, he of the six wives fame.

This all changed during World War One. With anti-German feeling at its height, King George V changed the name of the dynasty from Saxe-Coburg-Gotha, which was Germanic in origin, to Windsor so as to appear more British. At a meeting of the Privy Council on July 17, 1917, George V declared that all male descendants of Queen Victoria would bear the name of Windsor.

As the queen came from the female line of the family, it was argued by Lord Mountbatten and Prince Philip that the family name should reflect his surname as well.

The matter came to a head at a dinner party held at Broadlands where Mountbatten boasted that since the funeral of King George VI a Mountbatten was sitting on the throne and the "House of Mountbatten now reigned."

When this piece of gossip was passed on to Queen Mary she was horrified. The steely-eyed matriarch contacted Churchill and convinced him, not that he needed much convincing, of the necessity of continuing the House of Windsor. She insisted that Churchill formally ask the queen to confirm the continuation of the House of Windsor now and in the future. This also applied to the royal offspring.

Despite her husband's furious protests, the queen, as she was obliged to do, took the government's formal advice and, on April 9, 1952, signed an Order in Council confirming the ascendancy of the House of Windsor.

At a time when she needed Prince Philip's support, she found herself living with a morose, resentful husband who exclaimed that he was "nothing more than an amoeba— a bloody amoeba" as he was the only husband in the land not able to confer his surname upon his children.[25] For such an alpha male, it was a bitter pill to swallow. Even after the announcement he continued a rearguard action. He sent a memo to Churchill arguing that the royal house be called Edinburgh-Mountbatten. Queen Mary's view was typically robust. "What the devil does that damn fool Edinburgh think that the family name has got to do with him?"[26] That "damn fool Edinburgh," though, would not let the matter drop.

Precedent was on his side as Queen Victoria had taken Prince Albert's surname when they married. His opponent, the prime minister, also relied on British history. He and Queen Mary argued that the name Windsor had been created by King George V in 1917 not only, at a time of conflict, to disassociate the monarchy from its German origins but also to convey native grit and stoicism in the face of a redoubtable enemy.

The queen as sovereign and wife was left in a difficult position, with her implacable grandmother, mother, and Churchill on one side ranged against her husband and her uncle on the other. This rancorous family debate was, as politician Rab Butler recalled, the only time he had seen the queen close to tears. In the end, much as Philip and Mountbatten might seethe, Churchill and the queens would prevail.

Churchill had bested Philip on one contentious issue. It was not long before he was to usurp his domestic authority again. This time the argument concerned where the royal family should live. Clarence House was currently their home, a place where they had invested time and energy making it their family nest. They had chosen the soft furnishings, mixed the paint colors, and the picked the curtains. Philip's interest in technology ensured that their home boasted the latest labor-saving devices including a wardrobe that could eject the required shirt or jacket at the touch of a button. For a young man who had led a rootless existence, the chance to build a home for his wife and family was naturally appealing.

During lunch one day it was suggested that the queen and her family stay at Clarence House and use Buckingham Palace as an office. Philip was enthusiastic, the idea making practical sense especially as Queen Elizabeth, the Queen Mother, and Princess Margaret were still in residence at Buckingham Palace and the queen mother, at least, showed no desire or inclination to move out. She had been mistress of the grand residence since 1936 and clearly wished to stay on for as long as possible. Discussions about a move from Buckingham Palace were awkward and emotional. On at least one occasion the queen mother uncharacteristically burst into tears. Elizabeth was sensitive to her mother's profound personal loss as well as her sudden demotion in the court hierarchy. For the first few months she had selflessly taken the junior role, even though their regal positions were now reversed. At Sunday church services, for instance, the queen encouraged her mother to sit in the monarch's seat. There was an "awkwardness about precedence," one courtier remembered. "The Queen not wanting to go in front of her mother and the Queen Mother used to going first."[27] Elizabeth knew that her mother wished to stay on at Buckingham Palace for as long as possible and, for the sake of family happiness and unity, the young woman went along with the proposal, especially as her husband was keen to remain at Clarence House.

Churchill and the queen's crusty but knowledgeable private secretary Alan Lascelles would have none of it: "The flagpole [at Buckingham Palace] flies the Queen's Standard and that's where she must be," Churchill decreed.[28] Philip reacted badly. He stayed in his room, depressed and gloomy, the prince dreading the move from Clarence House to Buckingham Palace.[29] It was easier for Elizabeth to accept Churchill's edict as she was simply moving back to her former home albeit in the grander surroundings of the Belgian Suite. Philip, on the other hand, would be moving from the only home he had ever known and giving up the last remaining realm in his life where he still had control. "It was bloody difficult for him. In the navy, he was in command of his own ship—literally," Mike Parker explained. "At Clarence House, it was very much his show. When we got to Buckingham Palace, all that changed."[30]

The move, in May 1952, while the surname battle was at its height, was as bad as Philip predicted. Now under the constant scrutiny of courtiers there were, as he recalled, "Plenty of people telling me what *not* to do. 'You mustn't interfere with this.' 'Keep out.' "[31] In a reference to his previous role as a ship's captain, he confessed: "People used to come to me and ask me what to do."[32] Now he was ignored. Churchill, who had fallen out with Mountbatten over his unnecessarily hasty handling of Indian independence. He seemed to take out his antagonism out on his royal nephew by blocking his every suggestion.

The elderly statesman told an aide that while he wished Philip no ill he neither liked nor trusted him and hoped he would not do harm to the country. As Philip's cousin Pamela Mountbatten recalled: "Prince Philip was completely excluded and unwelcome at Buckingham Palace. Everybody closed ranks. Churchill made him feel totally apart from the whole thing. Although the Duke of Ediburgh had never expected to be king, nor had he expected to be so brutally and cruelly sidelined."[33] In a matter of months, Philip had lost his career, his name, his paternal rights, his home, and his authority as a husband. As a pitiful consolation he bought himself an electric frying pan so that he could fry his eggs and bacon in the morning without waiting for his breakfast to be brought from the kitchens.

The queen who, as Lascelles noted, was unusually sensitive to others, could see that her husband was struggling. She had married a dynamic, ambitious naval officer, not a man who felt sorry for himself. It was clear that he needed to stop brooding and be put to work on a project.

Initially the queen asked him to oversee the construction and design of the new royal yacht currently being built at the John Brown shipyard at Clydebank in Scotland. It was the perfect job for the former commander with an interest in design and an eye for detail. He liaised with Sir Hugh Casson who was commissioned to lay out the interiors of the 412-foot yacht, which the queen named *Britannia* at the launch in April 1953.

While his work on the royal yacht channeled his love of architecture and technology, the queen's request that he chair the committee organizing the coronation, which was due to take place on June 2, 1953, a few days before the famed Derby horse race at Epsom, plunged him once more into conflict with the Establishment. This time it included his wife. The queen was dead-set against the televising of the coronation. Her husband thought otherwise. The queen's attitude was supported by the queen mother, Churchill, Lascelles, and the Archbishop of Canterbury, who worried that the queen's habit of licking her lips would look indecorous on such an august occasion. Philip, as a man of science and innovation—he was the first royal to fly in a helicopter—supported the opening up of this solemn ceremony to the common man via the new technology of television.

The queen's objections were both practical and personal. She recognized that the coronation was a profound and sacred moment, an ordinary mortal transformed into a potent symbol, half man, half priest, in a solemn ritual going back over a thousand years. At the same time she was concerned that television coverage would mean that millions would see her blushing embarrassment if anything went wrong.

She vividly remembered her father's memories of his own coronation which had been beset by numerous mishaps: a priest fainted and in so doing held up the procession; the oversized Bible proved too heavy to carry and had to be replaced; a bishop accidentally covered the words of the oath when the nervous King was about to read it; another bishop stood on George VI's robe as he tried to stand; and lastly the crown seemed to have been handed to the Archbishop of Canterbury the wrong way round, which created more tension. His experience made for an amusing story—after the event. It was

funny until she had to accept her own dread destiny. She had
no intention of turning the sacred into slapstick.

Philip, a man of progressive temperament, was convinced
that opening the coronation to the people via television was
the simplest and surest way of maintaining the monarchy.
He turned the argument of Victorian constitutionalist Walter
Bagehot on its head as he argued that "daylight should be let in
on magic." Despite his reasoning, the old guard won out. On
October 20, 1952, the palace announced that the coronation
would be broadcast live on the radio alone. The mass media
and politicians immediately attacked the decision, blaming
the men in gray rather than the queen. "Truly astonishing,"
the *Daily Express* complained. "The people will be denied the
climax of a wonderful and magnificent occasion in British history."[34] In the face of overwhelming criticism, the government
gave the nation an early Christmas present, on December 8
performing a U-turn and declaring that the ceremony would
now be televised. The new queen was praised for her, falsely
perceived, role as the "people's queen," as the public believed
that she had stood firm against the ancien régime who sought
to exclude her subjects from her big day. It was an early example of collective projection. The queen was cautious rather
than progressive, cleaving to the past and precedent, just like
her father. It was her husband who was the agent for change
in their partnership. It was not a complete victory for people
power as the queen insisted that there were no close-ups of
her face and that the sacred act of communion and anointing
would not be filmed by the TV cameras.

Around the time of the great television debate in December, Margaret made an appointment to see her sister alone
in the Belgian Suite. Another crisis was in the making. After
dropping an abbreviated curtsy, she joined her sister over

tea and explained her deep feelings for Peter Townsend, the king's former equerry who had since been made comptroller of the Queen Mother's household, a father of two young boys, who was nearly sixteen years her senior and very shortly to be divorced. Though his age and existing family may have been frowned upon, it was the D-word—divorce—that presented the greatest obstacle. After all it was only sixteen years (almost to the day) that their uncle David, King Edward VIII, had abdicated the throne so that he could marry the twice-divorced American Wallis Simpson. That crisis had rocked the monarchy and had changed the trajectory of both their lives. Under the Royal Marriages Act of 1772 Margaret, third in line to the throne, had to obtain the sovereign's permission before she could marry. Once she reached twenty-five she could marry whomsoever she wished—dependent on the verdict of the Privy Council. Marriage to a divorcée, as Margaret knew full well, was a big no-no in the eyes of both the church and the state.

The queen, a great noticer of social nuance, was seemingly unsurprised by Margaret's admission. Perhaps Margaret and her war hero lover had not been as careful as they thought.

Her response was muted and sympathetic but ultimately noncommittal. She was acting both as Margaret's sister, who naturally wanted her to be happy, but also her queen who had obligations to the institution of monarchy. She was placed in an extremely difficult position by her younger sister, one where she would be obliged to accept the formal advice of her government.

Some days later she invited Margaret and her lover to dine with her and Prince Philip to discuss the matter in a less formal setting. Philip's behavior was disconcerting. He seemed to find what Townsend described as a "poignant situation" most amusing, cracking jokes and making merry throughout supper. While the irony of the late king's daughter falling in love with a divorcée so soon after the abdication was lost on no one, the loving couple felt that, given the queen's benign reaction, there was hope that they could one day fulfill their dream and marry. After all, they had secretly played out their romance for the best part of five years, ever since the tour of South Africa in 1947 when Margaret, then sixteen, admitted she fell in love with the former fighter pilot. Over the months and years, what had begun as indulgent friendship gradually blossomed into a full-blown love affair. People noticed. During a weeklong visit to Balmoral in 1950 young socialite Lady Jane Vane-Tempest-Stewart observed their social interplay and concluded they were in love. When she returned to London she told her mother of her suspicions. Her mother would have none of it. "Don't be so romantic and ridiculous. He's the king's servant. She can't be in love with the king's servant, that would be utterly wrong."[35]

At the time he was not just a servant but also still married— though in name only. The death of George VI in February 1952 brought the couple closer, Townsend's sympathetic presence helping to fill the void left in Margaret's life.

Whatever hopes they harbored that they could be eventually accepted as a married couple were brutally dashed by Tommy Lascelles during a bruising encounter in his office. He bluntly told Townsend that he was either "mad or bad" for even contemplating such a match.[36]

Yet rather than dismiss Townsend or ask for his resignation, he was promoted. The queen mother asked him to become the comptroller of her household, which included Princess Margaret. In this capacity he was in even closer daily proximity to the princess than when he was the king's equerry. It was his responsibility to organize the transition for the queen mother and Princess Margaret from Buckingham Palace to Clarence House.

As confusing as this was for the romantic protagonists, the back-and-forth continued during the Christmas break at Sandringham in Norfolk, where Lascelles had further discussions with the queen, her sister, and Prince Philip about the Townsend affair. They came to no definitive conclusions although the queen did ask Margaret to wait until after the coronation in June before taking any further steps. Her policy of delay, delay, delay was to become a mantra during her reign, a policy that was epitomized by her habit of taking her dogs for a long walk rather than face awkward encounters.

Everyone agreed, however, that the coronation must come first. It was an all-consuming event. In the months leading up to the big day, arguably the most important day in the reign of the sovereign, the queen was concerned to ensure that the televised ceremony went with "balletic" precision. No fainting clergymen wanted here.

At Buckingham Palace, she spent hours in the White Drawing Room rehearsing her lines and practicing walking down a makeshift aisle, several sheets tied to her shoulder. She listened to recordings of her father's coronation and even wore the St. Edward's Crown while going through her daily tasks, getting used to the five pounds on her head.[37] On other occasions she walked, unembarrassed, with a bag of flour of her head as a substitute crown. The young queen even pulled aside the bishop of Durham and beseeched him not to wiggle his eyebrows as, if he did, she could well fall into a fit of giggles.

With the pitfalls of her father's coronation in mind, no detail was too small to escape her notice. She had a shortened length of pile made for the carpet in Westminster Abbey so that her heels and train would not get stuck, had two silver stars secured on the crown so that the Archbishop of Canterbury would know the front from the back, and had armrests installed in the Gold State Coach so that she could appear to be freely holding the weighty orb and scepter for the five-mile procession around London. She carefully scrutinized the guest list, chose the flowers, floral hangings, and color scheme for the abbey, examined seventy-three coronation stamp designs, and, though not a vain woman, scrutinized dozens of photographs of herself to see which makeup and lipstick suited her best for her television appearance.

Even her husband was brought to heel. At a rehearsal at the abbey Prince Philip made a hash of swearing the oath of allegiance to the new queen. He knelt, mumbled his words, gave an air kiss, and backed off rapidly. "Come back Philip and do it properly," she said patiently.[38] Though the preparations had every contingency covered, just in case, dressmaker Norman Hartnell sewed a little sequined four-leaf clover in her gown for good luck.

On March 24, 1953, preparations paused for a time following the death of the queen's grandmother, Queen Mary. She was eighty-five and as dutiful in death as she was in life. At the end she insisted that the forthcoming celebrations should not be halted or delayed due to court mourning. Queen Mary may not have been the most outwardly affectionate grandmother, but she showed her love and devotion in other, more practical, ways. She taught Elizabeth the secret of good posture and how high heels and big hats help royal women assert themselves. She also advised her that the best way of dealing with overly intimate questions or inappropriate remarks was to keep smiling at the presumptuous individual as if hearing nothing and then gracefully moving on.

By contrast Princess Margaret, like the Duke of Windsor, shed few tears for the chilly matriarch. She never forgave her for her constant criticism of Margaret's short, rather plump figure, especially when she was an adolescent, as well as her disapproval of the princess's love of singing, dancing, and lively company.

Queen Mary would, however, have very much approved of the patriotic singsongs that erupted spontaneously among the milling crowds around Buckingham Palace as they waited expectantly in the chill and rain for a glimpse of their new queen. The universal feeling was that the new reign would usher in a new Elizabethan era of dynamism, abundance, and hope. ALL THIS—AND EVEREST TOO, announced the *Daily Express* front page after news that a British and Nepalese climber had scaled the world's highest mountain in time for the big day.[39] The new queen caught the mood. At a luncheon with Commonwealth leaders on coronation eve, the queen appeared exultant and triumphant. She later confided: "The extraordinary thing, I no longer feel anxious or worried. I don't know what it is—but I have lost all timidity."[40]

As the big day loomed, she continued to be in high spirits. When a lady-in-waiting asked if she was feeling nervous, she responded with a straight face, "Of course I am, but I really do think Aureole will win"—a tongue-in-cheek reference to her horse, which was due to run in the Epsom Derby the following Saturday.[41]

The queen was serenely composed as she and Prince Philip rolled along in the opulent but uncomfortable Gold State Coach for the brief journey—which she later recalled as "horrible"—to Westminster Abbey. Before she made her grand entrance, the queen, with a big smile on her face, turned to her maids of honor and asked, "Ready, girls?"[42] With that, she made her way forward, never looking back, ready for a ceremony of consecration and coronation that would last for nearly three hours.

It was the thirty-eighth coronation held at Westminster Abbey, and while the arcane ritual still conveyed an aura of magic and authority, the queen's youth and femininity suggested the promise of new beginnings, as well as a requiem for the old aristocratic order. "It is the most solemn thing that has ever happened in her life,"[43] Canon John Andrew later observed. "She cannot abdicate. She is there until death."[44] His thinking was based on the solemn oath she had taken before not just the nation but also God. It was a nun-like vow of service.

The royal family's favorite journalist, Dermot Morrah, observed that "the sense of spiritual exultation that radiated from her was tangible."[45] As the St. Edward's crown came down upon her head—the right way around this time—the queen felt the weight of monarchy being placed on her. But she held herself high, and ever since then, the crown has remained firmly in place.

The long coach procession back to Buckingham Palace surrounded by exultant crowds was every bit as moving and profound as the intimate ceremony. "The sound reached fever pitch, so loud it felt as if the whole nation was entering into one massive long cheer," recalled maid of honor Anne Glenconner.[46] She returned to the palace, her eyes shining with relief and jubilation. The wife of a palace courtier recalled the "extraordinary impact which the crowded streets and cheering people had had on her." She (the Queen) said that she had never guessed it would be like that, the feeling of elation and joy, of being carried forward on a great wave.[47]

An even greater wave had watched the ceremony in black and white as they crouched around television screens. More than twenty-seven million people, twice the BBC estimate, tuned in, fully endorsing Prince Philip's democratic instincts.

Once back at the Green Room at Buckingham Palace, the queen and her maids of honor fell onto the sofa with a sigh of glee and relief before trooping off for Coronation Chicken, a dish invented specially for the event. As they reviewed the day they acknowledged a few minor hiccups. Elizabeth forgot to curtsy at one point, preventing the rest of her maids from doing the same. When she went to sign the text of the oath, she found there was no ink. "Pretend you're signing," the lord chamberlain whispered in her ear. Even though the queen had ordered a gold rug with a shallow pile, it was laid the wrong way and the nap caused the queen's mantle to get stuck. Fortunately the Archbishop of Canterbury was alert to the situation when the queen hissed: "Get me started."[48]

Her husband, after his halting performance during rehearsal, was faultless, kneeling before her and pledging to be her "liege man of life and limb."[49] He kissed her cheek so firmly that she had to steady the crown. Back at the palace he was at his most officious, bossing everyone around for the photographs. Eventually an exasperated Cecil Beaton put down his camera and said: "Sir, if you would like to take the photographs please do."[50] The queen and queen mother looked on horrified and the duke, realizing he had gone too far, retreated.

As the camera clicked and everyone chatted excitedly about the events of the day, Prince Charles, then four, saw his mother's crown and made a beeline for it. The little boy got as far as picking it up, but an alert lady-in-waiting managed to grab it before any harm came to either the Prince or the royal headgear.

His time would come.

6

Hearts and Coronets

Every new generation of the House of Windsor walks with a shadow. The good royal versus the naughty royal. The royal rebel and the sensible prince. Or princess. Harry the wild child, William the straight-shooter, Diana the demure, Fergie the roustabout. Nonconformist Meghan, levelheaded Catherine. Once that narrative is shaped, it becomes accepted wisdom. Yet this endless exercise in perceived character contrasts disguises as much as it reveals.

In her day Princess Elizabeth was a competent singer and actress who enjoyed concerts and dancing. In social situations she was able to winkle out the amusing and unusual or weave a funny story around a royal encounter. On one occasion she kept a member of the Privy Council in fits of laughter as she performed the contortions of a wrestler she had watched during a televised bout. Yet these qualities were often overlooked because her younger sister was more overtly theatrical. Princess Margaret would eagerly join Hollywood stars to sing around the piano late into the night, the blue-gray plume from her cigarette holder giving her sitting room the feeling and smell of a downtown nightclub.

Margaret was "a girl of unusual intense beauty who was capable of an astonishing power of expression," observed her lover Peter Townsend, who described the royal comedienne as both "coquettish and sophisticated."[1] It was a description that, by and large, stuck—even though in pictures of the sisters, Elizabeth was taller and slimmer with more open, welcoming features. Her younger sister often seemed as if she were only present at public occasions by force. She was the royal bachelor girl who was catnip for the gossip columnists, linked to thirty-one different suitors by the time she was twenty-one. Her public image was that of the excitable young girl out for a good time in the nightclubs of Mayfair in central London surrounded by a coterie of the frivolous sons and daughters of the aristocracy.

Margaret was different from her sister but similar in so many ways. Romantically they both fell for the first man they met and ignored the wishes of their parents, particularly their mother, to find happiness with a duke or an earl. Elizabeth was just thirteen when she first met Prince Philip, and Margaret was only sixteen when she realized that she had fallen for a married man many years her senior and father to two children.

Her parents had no inkling of the secrets hidden deep in Margaret's heart. They made sure she mixed with the "right sort," men who would not be overawed by her class or position. Even Tommy Lascelles joined in the romantic guessing game. After watching Johnny Dalkeith, later the Ninth Duke of Buccleuch, making "cow eyes" at the princess as she celebrated her twenty-first birthday at Balmoral, he gave him the thumbs-up, telling Townsend that the young aristocrat was the chosen one. Townsend smiled inwardly, knowing where Margaret's true feelings lay.

These emotions were expressed perhaps unconsciously as Group Captain Townsend stood outside the abbey at the end of the coronation ceremony. Margaret, looking sparkling, ravishing, and pink-cheeked with the excitement of the day, came up to him and casually smoothed his lapel, brushing a little fluff from his immaculately pressed sky-blue RAF uniform. It was a moment of tenderness and routine familiarity caught by the cameras. The following day this affectionate gesture received the same front-page coverage in several New York and Continental newspapers as the coronation itself.

Although the British media focused on this unique and profound ceremony, in the offices of national newspapers wheels were in motion. Just as the palace feared, the story was about to become public. The queen agreed for Lascelles to travel to Chartwell, Churchill's country home, to alert the prime minister. Once briefed Churchill's initial reaction was, according to his private secretary Jock Colville, typically romantic. "What a delightful match! A lovely young lady married to a gallant young airman, safe from the perils and horrors of war." His redoubtable wife Clementine immediately put her foot down. "Winston if you are going to begin the Abdication all over again, I'm going to leave. I shall take a flat and go and live in Brighton."[2] An ironic remark, given that their own son Randolph was divorced and remarried and that three members of Churchill's cabinet were also divorced.

Clemmie was perhaps overstating the situation—Margaret was third in line to the throne with no realistic chance of ever becoming queen and Townsend, though divorced, was a bonafide war hero liked and admired by his adopted family. Once the romance became public he rapidly assumed the status of a folk hero. The crown was not in existential peril as it had been during the abdication of King Edward VIII, but the conflict between the couple and the Church of England—which would not countenance divorce or divorced couples marrying in church—remained. In those days the stigma of divorce was such that a divorced man was not allowed to read the news on the radio or television for the British Broadcasting Corporation.

Two weeks after the coronation, the *People* newspaper backed into the story with the headline THEY MUST DENY IT NOW. They pointed to the "scandalous" and "utterly untrue" rumors of the love affair between the princess and a divorcé named Group Captain Peter Townsend. The newspaper editorialized that it was "quite unthinkable for a royal princess to even contemplate a marriage with a man who has been through the divorce courts."[3] When she heard the news, the Duchess of Windsor, who blamed the queen mother for their exile from Britain, could barely contain her delight. She telephoned one of her friends in Paris and gloated: "So now it's happened to her own daughter."[4]

For the most part the man in the street wished them well. They were an attractive couple; she a beautiful princess, he a gallant fighter pilot who helped save Britain in its darkest hour. A poll in the *Daily Mirror* attracted seventy thousand responses to the question: Should they be allowed to marry? Ninety-seven percent answered yes.[5] Though Churchill's first instincts reflected popular opinion, that opinion was no match for precedent, the law, the church, and Tommy Lascelles. He had already advised the queen that Townsend should leave and take an appointment abroad, preferably a good distance abroad. In this way the scandal would be diluted and contained. It was not advice the queen was at all keen to hear.

She was having to cast judgment on her shadow self, a sister who, for all her faults and foibles, she loved and supported in the same way that Margaret had supported her when doubting Thomases at the palace wrinkled their noses at the arrival of Prince Philip. The sisterly bond remained strong. During Ascot week they were seen cheerfully racing each other along the Royal Mile, riding neck and neck, and both laughing as Margaret rode out the winner.

They were aware that whatever their personal feelings, the monarchy was bigger than both of them, and that the queen must be guided by her ministers. It was her get-out-of-jail card that spared her from a jolting and potentially acrimonious confrontation with her sister. Though the princess would later complain, somewhat disingenuously, that she was unaware of the consequences should she marry Townsend, it seems that Lascelles had, with the queen's agreement, been punctilious in fully briefing her about her options. Indeed she even sent him a note of thanks after he explained that, under the Royal Marriages Act of 1772, if she wished to marry without the queen's permission she would have to wait until she was twenty-five and even then obtain dispensation from the two Houses of Parliament. He further pointed out that she would lose her position in the line of succession and of course be obliged to marry in a civil ceremony. In the worst-case scenario she would also have to relinquish her title, give up her Civil List payment, and possibly live abroad as plain Mrs. Townsend. As her friend and biographer Christopher Warwick observed: "We now know that far from keeping her in the dark, Lascelles clearly outlined the obstacles to her."[6]

On June 16, at his weekly audience with the queen, Churchill advised her that, for the well-being of the nation and the crown, Group Captain Townsend should be posted abroad without delay. The royal lovers should not be permitted to see each other for at least a year. It was one of the most difficult decisions she had had to make, weighing the happiness of her sister against the prerogatives of the crown.

As the wheels were set in motion, the queen asked for one concession, that Townsend not leave the country until after the queen mother and Princess Margaret had returned from a visit in July to Southern Rhodesia, now Zimbabwe.

With that agreement, Lascelles summoned Townsend and abruptly informed him that he was being sent abroad for two years and that he had the choice of postings in Brussels, Johannesburg, or Singapore. Townsend was utterly stunned by the turn of events. One moment he was enjoying dinner with the queen and the Duke of Edinburgh; the next he was facing exile. Once he had regained his composure, he opted for the post of air attaché in Brussels. At least he was near to his two boys, who were at a boarding school in Kent. After Princess Margaret and her mother left for Africa, the queen asked Townsend to accompany the royal party on a visit to Belfast in Northern Ireland. Townsend saw it as the queen's way of ensuring that he was still seen as part of the wider royal family. Unfortunately the queen's press secretary Commander Richard Colville (no relation to Jock Colville) announced Townsend's departure to Brussels during the visit, a move that ensured Townsend unwittingly received more media attention than the queen. Upon the return of the royal party to London, the queen deliberately sought out Townsend after she had alighted from the plane. She wished him good luck and shook his hand—a move that was seen by many as a gesture of friendship and goodwill. Still, Colville's announcement accelerated Townsend's departure from Britain, the newly appointed attaché sent to Brussels before the return of the princess from Africa. It would be a year before he saw her again. When she heard the news Margaret broke down and wept, and Townsend needed all his soothing influence on a scratchy telephone line to calm her down. She completed the rest of the tour in low spirits.

In the meantime the queen had to endure a sorrowful parting of her own. She and Prince Philip spent the summer at Balmoral on holiday with their children before undertaking the much-delayed visit to Australia, New Zealand, and all points west. It was not the happiest of holidays. The weather was miserable, Charles was confined to bed with an ear infection, and his sister had a fever. Princess Margaret, glum and missing her lover, was moody and overcast. Understandably the queen, out of sorts at the prospect of not seeing her children for half a year, was not as sympathetic as she might have been. In her absence her sister and mother supervised the education of the queen's children. Charles traced his parents' route on their tour of ten Commonwealth countries with the aid of a globe in the palace classroom. It was scant consolation for missing the real thing. The prince celebrated his fifth birthday and Christmas with his parents on the other side of the world. For the most part communication was by letter as the time difference and technical difficulties made phone conversations something of an ordeal.

The six-month tour, which began in November 1953, was truly a marathon, arguably the popular high point of the monarchy. In Australia such was the wild delirium that more than three-quarters of the population turned out on the streets for a glimpse of the royal couple as they passed by. During the prolonged tour the royal couple traveled forty-three thousand miles; the queen gave 102 speeches and was personally introduced to more than thirteen thousand people. Constantly on parade, the royal couple developed into a smooth double

act, with Philip making the jokes, the queen accepting the
flowers—and the plaudits. This facade was punctured only
once on the lengthy visit when an Australian camera crew
captured a royally undignified scene on film. This unexpected
insight into the royal marriage occurred on the shores of the
O'Shannassy Reservoir in Victoria where they were staying in
luxury chalet during a rare weekend off duty. They had agreed
to a brief filming session for an official movie about the visit
titled *The Queen in Australia*. Outside their chalet cameraman
Loch Townsend and his deputy waited patiently for the royal
couple to emerge so that they could be filmed admiring kan-
garoos and other indigenous wildlife. Suddenly the chalet door
flew open and out came a distinctively ruffled Prince Philip
followed by an irate queen, who threw a pair of tennis shoes
and a tennis racquet at the rapidly disappearing royal figure.[7]
She shouted at her husband to come back, dragged him into
the chalet, and slammed the door. All this was captured on
film. As Townsend and his crew debated their next move, they
were confronted by the queen's press secretary Commander
Colville, who abruptly ordered them to hand over the footage. They duly obeyed his command. Shortly afterward the
queen, smiling, calm, and grateful, emerged from the chalet
and apologized for the domestic altercation. "I'm sorry for that
little interlude but, as you know, it happens in every marriage.
Now what would you like me to do?"[8] Then she posed for the
camera. While we shall never know the background to the row,
the incident indicated that beneath the composed, controlled
image the couple enjoyed a rumbustious, sparky relationship—
and that Philip did not entirely rule the roost.

Ironically, though the visit was a tremendous success, once
again critics complained that the queen didn't smile enough.
The narrative of a distant sovereign was beginning to take

shape. She was ruled by her head, her willful younger sister was ruled by her heart. Or was she? As her twenty-fifth birthday approached in August 1955, the world wanted to know if she would give up her royal status for the love of a divorced war hero. It was a seductive story. When Margaret celebrated her birthday at Balmoral Castle the estate was surrounded by around three hundred journalists and photographers waiting for some kind of signal from the beleaguered inhabitants. "Please make up your mind," urged the *Daily Mirror*.[9]

The princess, though, was not quite the romantic of popular imagination. Six days before her birthday she wrote to the new prime minister Anthony Eden, himself a divorcé, and coolly explained her thinking. She told the prime minister that she had no intention to seeing Townsend until October when he had annual leave and only then would she be in a position to make up her mind as to whether or not she wanted to marry him. The princess wrote: "But it is only by seeing him in this way that I feel I can properly decide whether I can marry him or not. At the end of October or early November I very much hope to be in a position to tell you and the other Commonwealth Prime Ministers what I intend to do.

"The Queen of course knows I am writing to you about this, but of course no one else does, and as everything is so uncertain I know you will regard it certainly as a confidence."[10]

This letter, which lay undiscovered until 2009, recasts the orthodox view that Margaret sacrificed her romance on the altar of duty and monarchy. As her biographer Christopher Warwick argued: "This was a determined and confident young woman in control of the situation, telling the Prime Minister that she has not decided and is wavering, which is at odds with what the public was led to believe and certainly with what she told me."[11]

While the limitations of her royal position hemmed her

in, it was the church that had perhaps the dominant role in her eventual decision. As a committed Christian she found the idea of being prevented from marrying inside the Church of England deeply distressing. At the same time that she was ruminating upon her future, a rangy, blond farmer's son from North Carolina with a passion for hamburgers and the word of God came into her life. He made a deep and lasting impression, not just on the conflicted princess but on the whole royal family. The charismatic Christian crusader Billy Graham first visited London in March 1954. By the time he left in May he had preached to two million Britons, his services the largest outdoor gatherings since the coronation. When he returned the following May, just three months before Margaret was twenty-five, he was invited to join the queen mother and Princess Margaret for coffee at Clarence House. That successful first meeting resulted in an invitation to preach before the queen at Windsor Castle.

He accepted and busily prepared a punchy sermon from Acts 27:25: "Sirs be of good cheer for I believe God that it should be even as it was told me."

After his sermon he and his wife Ruth were invited for luncheon at Windsor. On entering the castle Graham heartily shook the hand of the butler who was reaching to take his hat. It was a rather clumsy beginning to what would become a long-lasting friendship among the queen, Princess Margaret, the queen mother, and the American preacher.

Over the years he sent the queen regular reports of his ministries, especially if he was preaching in a Commonwealth country. As his son Franklin Graham observed: "There's no question, she's very devout in her faith and very strong in her faith. Her faith has been consistent not just with conversations with my father but throughout her life."[12]

Their relationship, which continued until Graham's death in 2018, was anchored not just in faith but also by their distinct yet similar stations in life. Both were yoked for life to organizations that were demanding of their every breath, Graham with his allegiance to the word of God, the queen to the monarchy. It was both a calling and a confinement, Graham describing the life led by himself and his wife Ruth as akin to being prisoners.

Marshall Frady's biography recalled the occasion when he and the queen were looking out of the window, perhaps at Buckingham Palace, observing the huge crowd peering at the royal edifice. "I asked Queen Elizabeth if she ever felt sometimes she would like to be able to just go down and join them. She said: 'With all my heart.' I said to her: 'That's just the way I feel.'"[13] The little girl who looked out at the passing parade from her bedroom window at 145 Piccadilly had not changed overmuch. Just as the world was curious about her life, she remained intent on knowing about theirs.

At the same time the arrival of Billy Graham that fateful summer reminded both sisters of the role of faith in resolving their conflicts.

It was the new prime minister Anthony Eden, though, who teased a pathway through the secular and spiritual jungle on behalf of the princess. When he arrived at Balmoral in early October 1955 for the customary weekend visit by the prime minister, he was able to inform the queen and the princess that, after reviewing the situation, Margaret would have to give up her right of succession but not her title or Civil List moneys, or go into exile. In fact, should she decide to marry Townsend he might be conferred with his own title and receive a Civil List allowance. Of course conflict with the Church of England would remain, but the state now stood aside from her decision.

This was all very different from the dire prognostications of Tommy Lascelles and Winston Churchill. There were potential pitfalls—but for the queen and the monarchy. An unsigned Downing Street memorandum suggested that the crown could sustain some damage, but not fatal damage, should the match go ahead. There would be objectors among the wider population, which could have an effect on the institution. Eden encouraged Margaret to make up her mind sooner rather than later in order to end the uncertainty for herself, her sister, and the monarchy. He made it clear in a letter to other Commonwealth leaders that the queen did not wish to get in the way of her sister's happiness.[14] With Townsend now on leave and preparing to see Margaret, the queen gave her sister license to meet discreetly at Clarence House and at the homes of known friends.

For the next two weeks the couple wined and dined and wooed and tested the water. Townsend, though, seems to have been kept in the dark about Eden's revision of the penalties faced by the princess and her paramour. There is no indication in either his memoir, *Time and Chance*, or subsequent interviews that he had the faintest idea that Margaret would only have to give up her position in the line of succession and marry in a civil ceremony. He labored under the impression that she would have to give up everything—and Margaret did little, if anything, to correct that view during their time together. He was on the outside looking in.

As Eden anticipated, with public hysteria building to a crescendo, the Princess Meg question had to be resolved one way or another. As Peter Townsend admitted in his memoir: "Everyone was by now impatient, and critical of a situation which was fast becoming ridiculous." The two people at the center of this maelstrom were "exhausted, mentally, emotionally and physically."[15] Decisions had to be taken.

Margaret spent the weekend of October 22, 1955, in an emotional reckoning with the queen mother, her sister, and her brother-in-law at Windsor Castle. Tensions were running high. Margaret had barely spoken to her mother who was in great distress about this entire affair. At one point she asked where Margaret and Peter would live should they marry. This earned the crushing reply from Prince Philip that it was still possible to buy houses.[16] The queen mother walked out, slamming the door behind her. The tension within the royal family was matched by the uproar without. After just a few days in the company of Townsend, Margaret came to the conclusion that she no longer felt as strongly about him as she had before their long parting. Ultimately the choice was hers. The queen had put no pressure on her. If anything, she had been prepared to accept criticism of the crown for the sake of Margaret's happiness. She chose faith and family. Townsend himself, though not in possession of the full facts, independently came to the same conclusion.

During a restless night's sleep he jotted down what would become the spine of her public statement. When she read his draft at Clarence House she was in complete agreement.

He recalled: "For a few moments we looked at each other; there was a wonderful tenderness in her eyes which reflected, I suppose, the look in mine. We had reached the end of the road. Our feelings for one another were unchanged, but they had incurred for us a burden so great that we decided together, to lay it down. As we did so, we both had a feeling of unimaginable relief. We were liberated at last from this monstrous problem."[17]

After speaking with the Archbishop of Canterbury, Margaret released her statement on October 31, 1955: "I would like it to be known that I have decided not to marry Group Captain Peter Townsend. I have been aware that, subject to my renouncing my rights of succession, it might have been possible for me to contract a civil marriage. But mindful of the church's teaching that Christian marriage is indissoluble and conscious of my duty to the Commonwealth, I have resolved to put these considerations before any others. I have reached this decision entirely alone and in doing so I have been strengthened by the unfailing support and devotion of Group Captain Peter Townsend. I am deeply grateful for the concern of all those who have constantly prayed for my happiness."

She received more than six thousand letters of support, with sympathies ranging from laments over her decision to give up her relationship to congratulations for accepting the strictures of the church.

As family friend Veronica Maclean observed: "It was the first time that Queen Elizabeth, a very private person, had to face up to a personal dilemma in the full glare of the public's gaze and it had been an unpleasant, painful experience for her and for the whole family."[18]

Though still in her early years as queen, Elizabeth had handled the family crisis with care. She had adhered to the formal advice of her ministers while giving her sister as much latitude as she was able. While the queen did not want to be the one to stand in the way of Margaret's happiness, this was the abiding narrative in the popular imagination. It was only the release of letters and government papers some fifty years after the event that showed how much Margaret enjoyed the support of her big sister.

Just a few months later the queen herself needed her sister

to stand by her when her own marriage came under scrutiny. It all arose out of the best of intentions. She had seen how her energetic husband had been frustrated by the solemn pace of change at court and had encouraged him to sail to Melbourne, Australia, to open the 1956 Olympics aboard the royal yacht *Britannia*. As she perceptively remarked: "There's nothing worse than to fence a man in and stop him from doing what he wants."[19]

With a visit to Antarctica and other remote corners of the Commonwealth, the four-month voyage was a unique chance to put the yacht, which he had been involved with at the design stages, through its paces.

Certainly, with a crew of 240 and a twenty-six-piece Royal Marines Band, nothing could evade scrutiny aboard the royal yacht *Britannia*. Yet it was his famous 1956 voyage to visit obscure corners of the Commonwealth that placed the royal marriage firmly under the international microscope.

Though the queen affectionately mentioned his absence in her Christmas broadcast and the duke made an informative forty-minute documentary about his travels, the fact that he was voluntarily away from his family for so long sparked a spate of rumors that resulted in a rare official comment about their marriage. The American weekly *Time* reported in February 1957 that "the [rumor] mongering winds were howling louder around Buckingham Palace than they had since the day of Wallis Warfield Simpson and Edward VIII."[20]

The gales of speculation began with unsubstantiated stories about wild parties aboard the royal yacht. Given the large complement it was unlikely that shipboard shenanigans would have passed notice. It was the departure at Gibraltar of Philip's equerry, Mike Parker, before the yacht had completed the journey that really created a hurricane of innuendo. During the voyage his wife Eileen had filed for divorce, and her lawyer had helpfully tipped off a Sunday tabloid as the yacht completed the last leg of the journey. It was rumored that Parker was being punished by the palace for leading the prince astray. In fact Parker decided, in the light of the Townsend affair, to leave the ship's company early in order to save Philip or the royal family from any embarrassment. Philip was furious that one of his oldest and most loyal friends had his private life plastered all over the tabloids.

Parker's decision was juxtaposed with stories in the American media about the queen and Prince Philip in a "rift" over an unnamed party girl he had met regularly at the home of a society photographer, presumably his friend Henry "Baron" Nahum.

This was an old story that gained new legs thanks to the prince's long absence. During the 1940s he joined the all-male Thursday Club, a regular social gathering held at Wheeler's fish restaurant in Soho, central London, and presided over by Baron.

It was an eclectic group that included newspapermen, actors, artists, and the odd politicians who liked ripe conversation, white wine, practical jokes, and oysters. With brilliant raconteurs like actors Peter Ustinov, James Robertson Justice, and David Niven present, no one stood on ceremony.

Besides organizing the club, Baron was notorious for late-night parties held at his Mayfair flat, which was also the venue for Philip's alternative bachelor night party before his wedding at Westminster Abbey. It was Baron who first got the prince into hot water after a night out that didn't end until dawn. The photographer was infatuated with the celebrity singer and actress Pat Kirkwood and took the prince and his equerry to her dressing room after she had finished her performance in the musical *Starlight Roof.* The quartet went for dinner and then out dancing at the Milroy nightclub. When Philip took to the dance floor with the glamorous actress, there was a palpable hush among the other partygoers. Tongues wagged and word reached George VI, who was outraged that his son-in-law had been so indiscreet.

Even though Kirkwood always vigorously denied the rumor that they had an affair—there was talk that she had been given a Rolls-Royce car by the prince—her brief association with the queen's consort followed her to the grave.

Her name was prominent in the list of Philip's potential paramours as the marriage of the queen and the prince came under the media microscope.

So too was that of the vivacious nightclub owner Hélène Cordet. Philip had known the former Hélène Foufounis since he was three and spent holidays with her at her parents' villa in Le Touquet in northern France. When she had two children while separated and refused to name the father, Philip's name was in the frame, especially when he agreed to be their godfather. In fact the father was a French fighter pilot. In Philip's defense Cordet riskily argued: "Of course he likes women. What the hell can he do to have a decent reputation? If he doesn't look at women, they say he likes men. He likes women. So what. It's a good thing."[21]

Over the years he was linked variously to the novelist Daphne du Maurier, whose husband Sir Frederick 'Boy' Browning was his comptroller; the actresses Merle Oberon and Anna Massey; TV celebrity Katie Boyle; and Susan Barrantes, the mother of Fergie, the Duchess of York.

A sign of the queen's dismay at the marital headlines was her decision to authorize her press officer, Commander Colville, to issue an official statement denying the scurrilous stories. "It is quite untrue that there is any rift between the Queen and the Duke," was the official palace line.[22]

The rumors of infidelity continued to haunt the prince for the rest of his days. When I first started royal reporting in 1982, within a year I was told that Prince Philip had secret families in Wales, Norfolk, Germany, and Melbourne. When a female journalist summoned up the courage to ask him about these rumors, his response was typically robust. "Have you ever stopped to think that for the past forty years I have never moved anywhere without a policeman accompanying me? So how the hell could I get away with anything like that?"[23] Of course that didn't stop his eldest son Charles from conducting a longtime affair with Camilla Parker Bowles, now his second wife.

It was a sign of just how seriously the story of a royal estrangement was taken that, when the queen flew to Lisbon in Portugal to be reunited with her husband before a state visit to England's oldest ally, there were 150 media members waiting on the airport tarmac eagerly watching their every move.

During the voyage the prince had grown a splendid full beard, which he had shaved off shortly before the end of the trip. When Philip went aboard the royal plane, to his surprise the royal entourage, including his wife, were sporting false ginger whiskers. They apparently hadn't got the memo that he was now clean-shaven. But it broke the ice, a continuation of the practical jokes the couple played on each other. During their tour of Canada in 1951, for instance, he left a booby-trapped tin of nuts for his wife to open, while on another occasion he chased her down the corridor wearing a set of joke false teeth.

Princess Margaret summed up the feelings of the royal

family in a letter to her American friend Sharman Douglas. "I see the fine old press in your country tried to make out the Queen wasn't getting on with my b-in-l [brother-in-law]. So of course the stinking Press here repeated it all sheep-like, like the nasty cowards they are. However, all is well and he's terribly well and full of fascinating stories of his journeys and it's very nice indeed to have him home again. The children are thrilled."[24]

Others noted that far from being estranged, the royal couple had become a team who worked instinctively together. At least that was the conclusion of Cynthia Gladwyn, the wife of the British ambassador to France, who entertained the couple during a four-day visit to Paris and Lille in April 1957.

She wrote in her diary: "Prince Philip is handsome and informal, creating an easy democratic atmosphere in the wake of the Queen. This informality makes him very popular. He shines out as a breezy sailor who has known what it is like not to be royalty. He handles a difficult position in a remarkably successful way, and I cannot think that any other person, whom the Queen might have married, would have done as well."[25]

Not everyone felt the same way. Since the coronation, Princess Margaret and Prince Philip had been in the media firing line. Now it was the queen's turn. Criticism of her style and personality came from an unlikely quarter—one of her own, a member of the House of Lords.

In a trenchant article published in August 1957, Lord Altrincham took the queen and her "tweedy set" of courtiers to task. Writing in his own periodical, *National and English Review*, he described her speaking style as "a pain in the neck," her personality that of a "priggish schoolgirl," and her speeches as "prim little sermons." Altrincham wrote: "Like her mother she [the queen] appears to be unable to string even a few sentences together without a written text."[26]

His attack echoed that of other artists and intellectuals who gave the "new Elizabethan age" short shrift. Playwright John Osborne, one of the so-called Angry Young Men of the 1950s, described the monarchy as "a gold filling in a mouth full of decay."[27] Loquacious TV personality Malcolm Muggeridge dismissed the passion for the royal family as a kind of substitute or "ersatz religion."[28] As a result the BBC banned him from appearing on their TV station.

It was, however, Altrincham who created the biggest stir. Such was the national uproar that after he was leaving a television studio in central London he was punched in the face by an incensed sixty-four-year-old member of the British Empire Loyalist pressure group.

Some of Altrincham's own jabs hit home, notably his criticism of the presentation of debutantes at court. This outdated ritual was indeed scrapped—but the queen delayed her decision by a year so as not to seem to have been pushed around by the errant peer.

Of course what all three men were saying was that the institution of the monarchy was behind the rapidly changing times and that the queen, artificially buoyed by the worship she had received during and after the coronation, was encircled by a coterie of men who did not remotely represent modern Britain. This prevented her authentic personality from shining through, stifled as it was by sonorous platitudes and outdated ritual. In a note to *Ladies' Home Journal* publishers Bruce and Beatrice Gould, Altrincham, who years later gave up his peerage, wrote: "For the sake of the institution and for that matter of the Queen herself, changes are long overdue, and I hope the recent controversy may have helped to force the pace. Certainly I had given up all hope of achieving results by argument behind the scenes."[29]

This debate, which was given so much prominence and weight, was a way of obliquely approaching Britain's precipitous military and political decline and fall in the modern world. The monarchy served as the lightning rod for the calamity that was Suez. When Altrincham wrote his infamous article, the nation was still licking its self-inflicted wounds.

The debacle took place in October 1956 when Israel, Britain, and France tried to take control of the Suez Canal waterway, which had been nationalized by Egyptian president Nasser. Although the invasion was condemned by the United Nations, fellow Commonwealth countries, and, most important, the United States, the triumvirate went ahead with military action against the nationalist leader.

Prime Minister Eden, in power for less than two years, ignored the warnings from President Eisenhower and paid the price. He resigned in ignominy after being forced to withdraw his troops. Internationally Suez signaled the end of Britain's position as a major world power while domestically it gave license to question and criticize hitherto inviolable institutions such as the monarchy.

The tectonic plates in society were shifting but not quite as fast as some hoped. While the religion of royalty had its critics, they were few in number. After the Altrincham episode, the queen addressed the criticism in her own way. Although she was shy in front of the television cameras, she agreed to give her first-ever live Christmas broadcast during which she acknowledged that it was inevitable that she would be seen as a remote figure. "I very much hope that this new medium will make my Christmas message more personal and direct," she said from the Long Library in Sandringham. Although she recognized that she never really touched the personal lives of her subjects, she continued, "But now at least for a few minutes I welcome you to the peace of my own home."[30]

At that time television sets were still not universally owned, yet she attracted an eye-watering audience of sixteen and a half million. The royal family's embrace of the mass media had begun.

7

✤

Secrets, Scandals, and Spies

While the dawning of a new Elizabethan age proved to be something of a chimera, the queen and her husband initiated a quiet revolution inside the House of Windsor. For the first time in history they decided to send their children to school rather than having them taught by tutors inside palace gates. Their decision did not meet with wholesale approval. The queen mother, who had effectively been mother and father to Charles and Anne while their parents were on their many travels, lobbied for the children to be educated at the palace. The queen and Prince Philip were resolute. As he later explained on American television: "The Queen and I want Charles to go to school with other boys of his generation and learn to live with other children, and to absorb from childhood the discipline absorbed by education with others."[1]

It was a genuine break from the past, a step change that the queen had long dreamed about. She had often talked about her children being able to lead relatively "normal" unrestricted lives. This unique trial to integrate young royals with other children began in November 1956 when Prince Charles was enrolled at Hill House, a small private school in Knightsbridge, just a five-minute drive from the palace. In the first few days it was an experiment that seemed doomed to failure as the eight-year-old prince ran a noisy gauntlet of photographers and curious onlookers when he arrived for school. This was not what the queen had hoped for.

After three days of this mayhem the queen kept Prince Charles at home and ordered her press secretary Commander Colville to contact every newspaper editor and ask them to call off the dogs. The ploy worked. This editorial compact was the first of many future informal agreements between Fleet Street and Buckingham Palace that allowed royal children to go to school without undue harassment.

Not that Prince Charles saw it that way. He agreed with his grandmother and craved the protection and certainty of life behind the palace gates, the young prince safe in the hands of his devoted nannies. When he was in the presence of other children, Prince Charles was so afraid of their company that he would cling to nanny Lightbody for support. She was his surrogate mother, the first to wake and feed him in the morning and the one to kiss him good night. As a toddler he played in the nursery until he was taken downstairs to spend thirty minutes with his mother or his father. While it was a distant parenting style, it was one that other members of the aristocracy and the upper classes found familiar. When Princess Elizabeth was in Malta with her husband it scarcely raised an eyebrow that Charles and his sister were left behind at Buckingham Palace and Sandringham for months at a time, cared for by the triumvirate of nanny Lightbody, the queen mother, and Princess Margaret—as well as a small army of nursery staff.

In the informal agreement the queen and Philip made at the beginning of their marriage, the prince took control of important family matters while she embraced matters of state, taking on the responsibilities of her ailing father, George VI. Neither parent expected the king to die so young, and it meant that the new queen was plunged into her royal duties with very little time for her children. She constantly had to choose between red boxes and bath time. Duty always triumphed. Godfrey Talbot, a royal correspondent of the period, recalled: "She immediately had to take on the responsibilities of state. She had been trained since the cradle by her father that duty came before everything, including family. She reluctantly had to abandon her children and they virtually didn't see their parents for months on end."[2]

Charles, a shy, sensitive, solitary, and rather overweight boy, worshipped his mother but from afar. As his father ruled the roost domestically, he and his sister Anne spent much more time with Philip—when he was available.

As a youngster Anne, innately aggressive and competitive, more readily responded to her father's blandishments while Charles wilted under Philip's tirades. His method of teaching his children to swim, for example, was to throw them in at the deep end of the Buckingham Palace pool. Anne surfaced all giggles; Charles spluttered and choked, terrified.

While Charles would later describe his father as a bully— a criticism his siblings rejected and told him so—there was method in Philip's tough aggressive behavior. In his own way he was trying to find one sport or activity that his children, especially Charles, would master and that would give them confidence as they grew and developed. Lady Kennard, a family friend, thought Philip a "wonderful parent." "He played with his children, he read them stories, he took them fishing, he was very involved," she recalled.[3] Eventually Charles joined his siblings in praising his father's parenting skills. "My father was marvelous at arranging silly games," he said in a 2001 tribute program to celebrate Prince Philip's life. "There was lots of chasing around and mad things."[4]

While Charles initially struggled with this robust parenting style, Anne thrived. Put her on a horse and she purred, the princess becoming the first-ever member of the royal family to compete in the Olympics when she rode for the British equestrian team at the 1976 Montreal games.

While Anne was something of a tomboy growing up, her elder brother struggled. He was neither sporty nor especially horsey. Everything seemed designed to humiliate and belittle him. When he first started lessons in the palace nursery he was diligent and persevering but baffled by the basics of mathematics, found English a chore, and floundered with dates in elementary history, much as he loved the subject. Charles was a "trier" who seemed happiest with a brush and a box of paints to experiment with.

His modest academic ability, retiring nature, and unathletic appearance and ability did not help him fit into Hill House. The prince struggled during his time there. If he thought Hill House was difficult, his next school was his worst nightmare. He was enrolled at Cheam boarding school, his father's alma mater. Philip had survived and excelled, becoming school cricket captain and first-team soccer goalkeeper.

Not so his eldest son who was utterly miserable and homesick. Timid and sensitive, he found it difficult to make friends or to join in and invariably found himself on the edge of any activity. These were among the most wretched years of his life. Even though the queen supported her husband wholeheartedly in this project, she did have to steel herself when, at the end of the Balmoral holidays, Charles would plead with her not to return to the house of "misery."

Nor did it help when, in the summer of 1958, the queen decided, for no apparent reason, to announce that her son was now "Prince of Wales, Earl of Chester and Knight Companion of the Most Noble Order of the Garter." The plump pupil blushed bright red and wished the earth could swallow him up as he watched the announcement on television with his classmates.

As the queen's biographer Sarah Bradford observed: "Nobody had even thought of warning him about it beforehand, which seems an extraordinary lack of sensitivity on Elizabeth's part."[5]

Much as she sympathized with her son's plight, she not only supported her husband but also felt that Charles's boarding school experiences were good training for the ups and downs of his future position. While the queen took a benign, though imperturbable, view of her son's education, she showed little interest in her daughter's academic progress. Anne was schooled in the nursery by a governess, Catherine Peebles. Even though her schoolroom was just above her mother's rooms at Buckingham Palace, the queen never came to see how she was faring. Instead it was Princess Margaret who reviewed her niece's work, discussed her curriculum with her tutor, and even tested Anne herself. What she considered to be her own inadequate education rankled, so she was pleased when eventually Princess Anne became the first daughter of a reigning sovereign to attend a boarding school, this time Benenden, an all-girl school in Kent.

While Anne recalled her "pleasant" schooldays, her brother

memorably referred to his senior school, Gordonstoun on the northern Scottish coast, as "Colditz with kilts."[6] (Colditz was a notorious prisoner-of-war camp.) He had wanted to go to Eton, the private boys' school near Windsor Castle. In this ambition he was supported by the queen mother, who lobbied her daughter and son-in-law. Her arguments fell on deaf ears, Philip arguing that Eton was too close to London meaning that Charles would inevitably be hounded by the media. So Gordonstoun it was. Despite his early misgivings, eventually he made the best of his time there. He joined the theater group and was made the school's guardian—or head boy—just like his father.

Charles never really got over the detached parenting of his childhood. His official biographer Jonathan Dimbleby described the queen as "cold"—a sentiment with which his siblings strongly disagreed. More tactfully, a friend explained the queen's parenting skills this way: "Motherhood is not the Queen's long suit. She likes getting on with her job and she is extremely busy."[7]

This long-running narrative of parental distance first started following the release of news footage of the famous reunion aboard the royal yacht *Britannia* in the port of Tobruk in Libya at the conclusion of the queen and Prince Philip's six-month 1954 Down Under tour. When the royal parents first saw their children on deck, Charles and Anne solemnly and politely shook their hands. At least they recognized their parents—there was a fear that after such a long absence they wouldn't know who they were. Though the welcome belowdecks was much more affectionate, this muted maternal display would come to define the queen's cool approach to motherhood. Much later, her emotional reticence would be seen as a stark contrast with Princess Diana who, during a similar reunion halfway through a tour of Canada, ran down the deck and scooped her two boys into her arms—right in front of the cameras.

Others who have known the queen for years take a different tack. They view her as a woman of powerful emotions who has been forced to keep herself under iron control because of the relentless demands of her position. Or as writer James Pope-Hennessy put it: "One feels that the spring is wound up very tight."[8]

There have been numerous occasions when she had had to subsume her strong maternal instincts in favor of the crown. At times of family crisis, notably her sister's marital breakdown and the death of Diana, Princess of Wales, her first thoughts were always for the well-being of the children.

During her teenage and adult years she spoke often of her somewhat conventional ambition to be a lady living in the country surrounded by dogs, horses, and children. It was no idle pipe dream. Her father George VI was a knowledgeable horseman, but his eldest daughter took it to quite another level. She has earned the respect of the racing community because she is an acknowledged authority on the breeding and rearing of race horses. In 1954 and 1957 she was the flat racing Champion Owner, the first reigning monarch to reach this milestone twice. "If she had been a normal person, she probably would have become a trainer, she loves it so much," observed trainer Ian Balding.[9] At Balmoral she breeds Shetland ponies; at Hampton Court her interest is in Fell ponies. As a breeder of gundogs, she won numerous prizes over the years for her professional handling in competitive trials. When she gave her brother-in-law Anthony Armstrong-Jones (later Lord Snowdon) one of her gundogs as a present, he immediately recognized what a special gift it was.

Over the years dogs and horses helped keep her sane. They responded to her for who she is as a human being, not her title.

In a world where she was regularly surrounded by people she barely knew, animals gave her a sense of normality and help explain why even into her nineties the queen rode out every day, accompanied only by a groom and a detective. It was a chance to be alone, at least for a time. Just as she was sincere in her enthusiasm for dogs and horses, so, too, she was serious about starting a second family now that she and Philip had evolved into a professional working couple able to cope with the demands of "the job." Though the watching world was surprised when she fell pregnant in the spring of 1959, she and Philip had considered the issue several years before, after Philip returned from his controversial circumnavigation of the globe.

The arrival of Prince Andrew Albert Christian Edward in Belgian Suite at Buckingham Palace on February 19, 1960, made him the first child born to a reigning monarch for more than a hundred years. His predecessor was Princess Beatrice, the fifth daughter and youngest child of Queen Victoria and Prince Albert. Both were thrilled by the new arrival, particularly Prince Philip, as they named their third child after his father.

There were considerable advantages to having a child later in her reign. No longer the monarchical ingenue, the queen felt able to spend more time with her baby son—to the point that his big sister Princess Anne thought he was being spoiled, at least compared with her upbringing. The queen taught him the letters of the alphabet, showed him how to tell the time on one of the palace clocks, and gave him riding lessons on Mr. Dinkum, his first pony. Sometimes she would work at her desk in her study while Andrew played on the floor. If the queen told nanny Mabel Anderson to leave her to look after the toddler, there was always a page and a footman present to help out. Where diary engagements permitted, the queen would take charge at bath time while Prince Philip read or made up a bedtime story. Andrew grew to be a boisterous, noisy boy, racing along the corridors with a football or stick. Despite—or perhaps because of—his energetic antics, he has always been referred to as the queen's favorite child, the son who could do no wrong. Prince Philip called him "the boss" after he arrived at a charity engagement sporting a black eye.[10] He later explained it was the result of a bedtime boxing match with his second son that got out of hand.

The arrival of Andrew also helped to heal a long-standing marital wound. For years Philip had resented the fact that his children did not bear his surname, Mountbatten. Since the coronation there had been back-and-forth among the various parties to resolve this vexatious matter. In January 1960, shortly before Prime Minister Harold Macmillan left for South Africa where he gave his famous "Winds of Change" speech, he came to Sandringham to discuss the issue with the queen. He recognized that she wanted to placate her husband and heal the rift in their marriage.

"The Queen only wishes, (properly enough), to do something to please her husband, with whom she is desperately in love," he sighed. "What upsets me is the prince's almost brutal attitude to her in all this."[11] The prince finally got his wish: Eleven days before the birth Buckingham Palace issued a proclamation that in future certain members of the royal dynasty would bear the surname Mountbatten-Windsor. The royal house, however, would still be called Windsor.

It was a happy time domestically for the queen. She was nursing her third child, her husband was content, and finally her sister, so unlucky in love, had found the man of her dreams and had accepted his proposal of marriage. Though photographer Antony Armstrong-Jones did not come from the serried ranks

of the aristocracy—as Margaret's parents would have wished—
he was eminently acceptable. Not only was he courteous and
charming, but he seemed to make Margaret happy. He even got
on with Prince Philip, who tended to be dismissive of photographers as a breed. "If he hasn't got what he wants by now, he's an
even worse photographer than I thought," was his regular—and
disconcerting—complaint at formal photo sessions.[12]

When the Old Etonian traveled to Sandringham in January
1960 to ask the queen for her formal permission, she gave it
with the caveat that the engagement announcement wait until
after the birth of her third child.

Just two weeks after Andrew's birth, the queen mother formally posted the engagement notice in the august Court Circular, the venerable record of daily royal business. The news
sent shock waves through the shires and European royalty who
felt that the freelance photographer was not *ebenbürtig*—not
equal in either rank or birth—to the princess. His newspaper colleagues were equally nonplussed as they never had an
inkling that one of their own was about to join the royal family.

Yet the general response by the queen and the rest of the
Windsors to this new suitor was welcoming. There was collective guilt among the family—the feeling that because Margaret
had had to relinquish the love of her life in Peter Townsend,
they would tolerate any sensible marital pick. Throughout her
reign, the queen rarely interfered with or commented on the
marital partners chosen by her family. Unlike some mothers
she was quite passive, content to watch the romantic drama
play out. There was no sense of the sovereign encouraging her
offspring to marry the rich and the titled. Modestly well-to-do
commoners were the typical choices—apart from Lady Diana
Spencer, the daughter of an earl.

However, with regard to her sister's match, the queen would

not have been so accommodating had she been aware that, several months before the wedding, the society photographer was conducting a three-way affair with his first choice of best man, the inventor Jeremy Fry, and his wife Camilla. She became pregnant with Armstrong-Jones's child and gave birth to a daughter she named Polly while the photographer was on honeymoon aboard the royal yacht *Britannia*.

Though in smart circles he divided opinion, for the most part the British public were thrilled that Princess Margaret, so often a loser in love, had found happiness at last—and with a man who represented, along with celebrity hairdressers and models, the most "with it" profession of the Swinging Sixties. For the first time a royal wedding was televised live and more than three hundred million viewers tuned in to watch a lavish spectacle that featured twenty wedding cakes, a sixty-foot floral arch, and a dress made from over thirty yards of fabric by the royal family's favorite designer, Norman Hartnell.

During the service at Westminster Abbey on May 6, 1960, it was noted that the queen looked less than enthusiastic about the happy occasion. "Everyone has commented on the black depression on the Queen's face," observed the publisher Sir Rupert Hart-Davis, "and the mind likes to invent the causes of it—jealousy, snobbery?"[13] Other royal watchers made similar comments; "a sulking Queen Victoria face throughout the entire service," noted Kenneth Rose.[14]

As the queen recognized early on in her life, she has the kind of face that looks angry when she is trying not to smile. On this day she could wave farewell to one long-standing family difficulty—her sister. She may have looked severe, but inside she was quietly rejoicing.

Once she had waved goodbye to her sister as she boarded the royal yacht *Britannia* anchored in the Port of London, it was back to her role as CEO of Great Britain Inc. For all the talk of the Swinging Sixties and sexual equality, there were few working mothers who held high-ranking positions. The queen was one of that rare breed. In an era made famous by the TV series *Mad Men*, about the chauvinism and sexual prejudice in a Manhattan advertising agency, even the queen was given few concessions in her role as mother and executive. When she was at the palace she was able to spend time with her third child; nonetheless she still missed many of the waypoints of her baby son's life—notably his first birthday. That year, 1961, she embarked on a grueling schedule of visits that took in Nepal, India, Pakistan, Cyprus, Iran, the Vatican City, Italy, Liberia, and lastly Ghana. Her frequent absences were something her older children simply had to get used to.

"I miss them when I'm away for long," the queen told scientist Niels Bohr, "but they understand why I have to go."[15] Anne later echoed her mother's remark, saying that her children accepted the demands on her time, adding: "I don't think that any of us, for a second, thought she didn't care for us in exactly the same way as any mother did."[16]

Her overseas visits weren't just so much smiling and glad-handing; they were a visible arm of foreign policy, her presence helping to cement allegiances particularly among those nations that were once part of the British Empire but now played a role inside the Commonwealth of Nations.

In November 1961 the queen and Prince Philip were scheduled to make a much-delayed visit to Ghana, the first British colony to gain independence. Under the socialist rule of President Nkrumah, the country was edging toward the Soviet sphere of influence. With the country riven by factional violence—two bombs exploded in the capital Accra days before the queen's arrival—the visit hung in the balance. Prime

Minister Macmillan and even Winston Churchill were worried about the queen's safety.

After much soul searching Macmillan sanctioned the visit on the grounds that to cancel would give Nkrumah an excuse to leave the Commonwealth and align with the Soviet Union.

The queen agreed, firm in her resolve. "How silly I should look if I was scared to visit Ghana and then Khrushchev [the Soviet leader] went and had a good reception. I am not a film star. I am the head of the Commonwealth—and I am paid to face any risks that may be involved. Nor do I say this lightly. Do not forget that I have three children."[17] Her attitude reflected her settled view that she did want to be treated any differently because she was a woman and a mother. She was firmly backed by the queen mother, for whom the spirit of the Blitz was second nature. "I am sure that if one listened to all the faint hearts, one would never go anywhere," she wrote.[18]

It proved to be the right decision—and, given the febrile atmosphere, a brave one. The queen demonstrated her serious commitment to the Commonwealth, an organization nurtured during her reign, as well as her robust response to the prospect of personal danger. The short tour was such a triumph that the Accra *Evening News* trumpeted, somewhat optimistically, that the queen was "the world's greatest Socialist Monarch in history!"[19]

Her deft diplomacy culminated at a state banquet where the bejeweled queen and the president, all smiles, danced together. The picture of the dancing queen went around the world, for once the queen knocking her glamorous younger sister, now the face of the Swinging Sixties, off the front pages.

Not only was the photograph a symbolic demonstration of the altered relationship between Britain and the former colony, but it underlined that though the monarch's authority was much reduced, she still had global reach and influence.

This Cold War warrior in ermine had a close encounter of a rather different kind shortly before her trip to Ghana when, in July 1961, she met the first man in space, Soviet cosmonaut Yuri Gagarin. Once again realpolitik was at play—and the queen was drafted in at short notice to play a part. Gagarin's Russian masters had sent him on a worldwide goodwill mission in order to extol the virtues of communism. The tour's success alarmed ministers so much that when he arrived in London to a tumultuous reception it was thought prudent to invite the cosmonaut to Number 10 Downing Street to meet Prime Minister Macmillan and to Buckingham Palace for breakfast with the queen.

After the initial introductions, a clearly nervous cosmonaut took his seat next to the queen and then, to her utter astonishment, put his hand forward and stroked her leg just above the knee. The queen followed Queen Mary's advice and kept smiling while sipping her coffee. He later explained, through interpreters, that he touched her leg to make sure that she was real and not some animated doll.

The former foundryman also struggled with the rules of dining etiquette, baffled by which cutlery he should use. The queen responded kindly: "My dear Mr. Gagarin, I was born and brought up in this palace, but believe me, I still don't know in which order I should use all these forks and knives."[20]

One Cold War couple who knew their way around the table settings for a formal dinner were President Kennedy and his sophisticated First Lady, Jacqueline Kennedy. They came to dinner at Buckingham Palace at the end of a whirlwind European tour and received a similarly rapturous welcome as the Russian cosmonaut.

The rapport between the First Lady and the queen was not quite as intimate as her close encounter with the Russian cosmonaut. Mrs. Kennedy later complained that she found the queen "heavy going." When writer Gore Vidal passed on the remark to Princess Margaret, she exclaimed loyally, "But that's what she's there for."[21]

At a later visit, in March 1962, when the First Lady was returning from Pakistan after a successful official visit, the two women bonded over lunch at Buckingham Palace. If the queen had heard some of the First Lady's remarks—she criticized her clothes and "flat" hair style—she never showed it.

The chilly emotional temperature warmed up once they discovered their mutual love of horses. During her stay in Pakistan, President Ayub Khan presented the First Lady with a ten-year-old bay gelding called Sardar, whom she called her "favorite treasure."[22] Like many others before and after her, the First Lady saw the queen's face light up and become more animated when others shared her passion for the equine community.

While they were never going to be best friends, the queen and First Lady shared many characteristics besides a love of horses. Both had married extrovert, aggressive, alpha husbands while they were quite private, quite shy women who found themselves in positions where they had to mask their personalities with a calm reserve. When Kennedy was assassinated on November 22, 1963, the queen was unable to console or pay her sympathies to the grieving widow in person as she was pregnant with her fourth child. Doctors advised her not to travel to the funeral, which took place in Washington. Prince Philip went in her stead.

༄

A few days before Kennedy's assassination, Liverpool-based pop sensation the Beatles appeared at the Royal Variety

Performance before Princess Margaret, Lord Snowdon, and the queen mother, who was standing in for the pregnant sovereign.

Before their final song, John Lennon asked those in the cheap seats to clap along. "And for the rest of you," he added, looking pointedly at the royal box, "if you'd just rattle your jewelry."[23] Irreverent, iconoclastic, and homegrown, they represented the 1960s zeitgeist, the quartet becoming rock-and-roll royalty.

The arrival of the Beatles and other bands, the explosion of satire, with shows like *That Was the Week That Was*, and the glamorization of creative professions contributed to the sense that the times really were a-changin'. Even the queen and her consort were daringly modern with the birth of Prince Edward Anthony Richard Lewis. He was born in the Belgian Suite of Buckingham Palace on March 10, 1964, and for the first time Prince Philip was present at the birth—a move encouraged by their birthing expert Betty Parsons. Barely a week later Elizabeth was writing to her old friend Mabel Strickland in Malta: "The baby is flourishing and is a great joy to us all, especially to Andrew, who is fascinated by him."[24]

The tectonic plates were genuinely shifting in society. Britain's ruling class was under consistent attack, its decline epitomized by the Profumo scandal, which centered on war minister John Profumo who had an affair with a sex worker, Christine Keeler. At the same time she was sleeping with a KGB spy, Eugene Ivanov. Eventually the affair became public knowledge. In a statement to the House of Commons, Profumo lied and formally denied the affair. Once the truth emerged, Profumo resigned in disgrace. The tentacles of the affair spread throughout high society as Keeler's amateur pimp, Stephen Ward, was a well-known osteopath and portrait artist who rented a cottage on the Cliveden estate where riotous naked pool parties regularly took place. Moreover Ward, who was a member of the Thursday Club, had made drawings of Prince Philip and other members of the royal family. Though the media worked valiantly to link Philip with the sexual shenanigans at Cliveden, there was lots of smoke but no fire. Prime Minister Macmillan wrote a painful apology to the queen for the behavior of his minister and others. "I had, of course, no idea of the strange underworld in which other people, alas, besides Mr. Profumo have allowed themselves to be entrapped."[25] While the queen sympathized with his plight, it wasn't long before the inexorable tide of scandal came lapping along the red-carpeted corridors of Buckingham Palace once again. It flowed from the most unlikely of sources, concerning as it did her long-serving surveyor of the royal pictures, the noted art historian Sir Anthony Blunt.

The queen had never been close to Blunt, who was appointed to his position by her father. He was a chilly ascetic who was perfectly proper, but one could sense the contempt in his eyes. Blunt found court life dreary and told friends that the royal family's idea of a cultural evening was playing indoor golf with a piece of coal on a precious Aubusson carpet. He only accepted a knighthood in 1956 to please his mother. As his biographer Miranda Carter noted: "Blunt's social mode, polite but distant, was not unlike the Queen's polite unreadability."[26]

Sometime during 1964, after the birth of Prince Edward, Elizabeth's private secretary Sir Michael Adeane delivered the jaw-dropping news that MI5, Britain's security agency, acting on information from the FBI, had unmasked him as a Soviet spy. Before and during the Second World War he had been sending information to Moscow.

When Adeane briefed the queen, he emphasized that Downing Street advised that she do nothing and leave him in place. He had been granted immunity from prosecution on the proviso that he agreed to cooperate and tell the authorities everything he knew.

There were also concerns that any publicity would severely damage British intelligence's relations with the Americans, which were already at a low ebb thanks to the Profumo scandal and the unmasking of the so-called Cambridge spy ring of which Blunt was a member. His fellow spies Guy Burgess, Donald Maclean, and Kim Philby had all been discovered and had fled to Russia.

Though preserving Anglo-American relations was top priority, there was also suspicion that keeping the status quo would save the embattled government further embarrassment. Little if any thought had been given to protecting the good name of the House of Windsor when, inevitably, the presence of a traitor at Buckingham Palace was later revealed. Over the years the queen showed herself a doughty defender of the institution, always ready to prod her ministers should she feel the monarchy's authority was under threat. Though Blunt was not unmasked until November 1979 in the House of Commons by Prime Minister Margaret Thatcher, courtiers have subsequently questioned why he was kept in post until his retirement, his knighthood intact. It was said that the queen mother, who never liked Blunt as he was an atheist, would have presented a stouter defense of the monarchy. "The queen mother, whose judgment was usually less good, wouldn't have worn it for a moment, but the queen did," recalled one senior royal official.[27] Another former adviser remarked: "I am amazed that the decision to keep Blunt didn't do the monarchy more damage when the facts eventually became public in 1979. I do know that we spun it with great difficulty." Though she was forced to take the formal advice from Downing Street there was a feeling that the queen was too passive in accepting the official line and that, as the custodian of the institution, she should have insisted that, at the very least, Blunt be removed from his post. One happy outcome from the affair was a brilliant play by Alan Bennett called *A Question of Attribution*, which focused on the delicate philosophical duel between the sovereign and her surveyor about truth, image, and reality.

࿂

No longer the ingenue of the early 1950s, the queen was comfortable and experienced, more relaxed in her position as monarch and mother. She gave a telling insight into her world when she allowed Pathé cameras to film her and her family as they walked through the grounds of Windsor Castle at Easter 1965, the queen pushing the pram containing baby Prince Edward. Though the commentary pointed up the frequent absences the queen faced because of her demanding job, it was clear that she was very much enjoying the days and hours with her second family. She brought forward her Tuesday-evening prime ministerial audiences so that she could bathe Edward and insisted on blocking out time in her diary so she could be with Andrew. She told a friend that it was "such fun" to have a baby in the house. Indeed the main theme of her Christmas broadcast in 1965 was "the family," which she described as "the focal point of our existence."

The image of a modern mother only went so far—there was still a platoon of nannies, nurses, and other staff to care for the infant. If not backward-looking the queen was seen as upholding tradition, the perception being that she was a dragging anchor as the Swinging Sixties, democratic and daring, sailed on. When Prime Minister Harold Macmillan resigned in October 1963, he suggested the queen call for a member of the House of Lords, Scottish landowner the Fourteenth Earl of Home, rather than his deputy Rab Butler.

The move was a public relations disaster. Home was a card-carrying member of the "tweedy" set criticized years earlier by Lord Altrincham. With his weak chin, speech that sounded like he was gargling with a mouthful of marbles, and an Old Etonian background, Sir Alec Douglas-Home, as he became after relinquishing his peerage to become prime minister, was a satirist's dream.

Conversely the queen felt very comfortable with the new prime minister, with a family tree that stretched back to the fifteenth century and grouse moors near her own estate. As a courtier confided: "She loved Alec. He was an old friend. They talked about dogs and shooting together. They were both Scottish landowners—the same kind of people, like old school friends."[28]

A decade after Altrincham, the queen still surrounded herself with landowning aristocrats, all men naturally, whose conservative outlook bolstered her own natural caution. Her long-serving press officer Commander Richard Colville, for example, thought the media were "little better than a communicable disease."[29] His basic rule, one that he had adhered to during his twenty years of service, was that anything that did not appear in the Court Circular was not to be filmed, photographed, or even discussed. This approach was comforting for a monarch who was shy in front of the cameras and had an ingrained wariness of personal disclosure. It was, though, out of step with the rapidly changing times.

The growing gulf between the monarch and her subjects was highlighted when Labour leader Harold Wilson won, by a slender majority, the October 1964 general election, which was called amid growing industrial unrest.

Their first encounter inspired neither trust nor confidence. Her new prime minister was a pipe-smoking former Oxford University don and the son of a works chemist and a schoolteacher. He was a far cry from the urbane Tory landowners and aristocrats who had come before him. For their first meeting at Buckingham Palace, the new prime minister brought along his political secretary Marcia Williams as well as his wife, Mary, his father, Herbert, and two sons, Robin and Giles. They waited outside the audience room while Wilson discussed matters of State within.

It was an unpromising beginning. As Marcia Williams, later Lady Falkender, recalled: "A number of anonymous palace officials were there and to me they all looked exactly alike. As I recall it, the conversation centered on horses. Perhaps it was assumed everyone was interested in horses, though my knowledge of them was minimal, and the Wilson family's less."[30]

Nor did things go well in the traditional thirty-minute briefing conversation between the sovereign and her first minister. He arrived unprepared and fluffed a question. She responded sharply, and both withdrew from this initial encounter ruffled and annoyed. It was going to be a steep learning curve.

∽

The death of Winston Churchill in Wilson's first months in office, on January 24, 1965, showed how far the nation had changed. Churchill was born in Blenheim Palace with a lineage of dukes and knights in his family. His rattle had been saved for posterity. Wilson was delivered at Number 4, Warneford Road, a small terraced house in the mill town of Huddersfield in West Yorkshire. When wartime prime minister Churchill offered only "blood, toil, tears and sweat" to his beleaguered people, Wilson was able to promise "the white heat of technology."[31] At St. Paul's Cathedral where the state funeral took place, the queen responded to the enormity of the event by waiving the precedent that she always arrived last.

Instead she awaited the arrival of her greatest subject. Her simple act of humility, a sovereign standing aside for her subject, served to make the farewell even more poignant. Churchill's grandson Nicholas Soames observed: "It is absolutely exceptional if not unique for the Queen to grant precedence to anyone. For her to arrive before the coffin and before my grandfather was a beautiful and very touching gesture."[32]

His death marked the end of an era and the passing of perhaps Britain's greatest statesman and leader, a man whose loyalty and counsel had been invaluable during Elizabeth's early years on the throne. As actor John Lithgow, who studied Churchill's life before playing him in the TV series *The Crown*, observed: "Churchill's relationship with the queen follows a beautiful trajectory. She's this completely untutored queen who, arguably because of his instructions, gradually realizes her role and sense of her own power, eventually coming to overrule and discipline him. His last audience with her in 1955 is extremely moving, when age and infirmity force him to step down."[33] While numerous men of stature advised kings and queens during their reigns—Henry VIII and Cardinal Wolsey, Queen Elizabeth and William Cecil, Queen Victoria and Lord Melbourne—Churchill was unique in helping to shape an entire royal dynasty.

8

A Family Affair

At nine fifteen on a clear blue-skied morning on October 21, 1966, the mining village of Aberfan in south Wales was devastated when a man-made mountain of coal waste collapsed and slammed into a primary school and nearby houses, killing 116 children and twenty-eight adults.

It was one of the worst peacetime disasters in British history, a national tragedy of epic proportions. The village looked like a scene from hell as frantic parents, some just using their bare hands, dug in the mud in a futile attempt to rescue their infants. Elsewhere stunned survivors stood or sat, their eyes and faces blank with shock. Prime Minister Wilson was one of the first dignitaries to reach the village, assessing, correctly, that this was a calamity where both consolation and prompt action were required.

While the queen hesitated about traveling to Wales, her brother-in-law showed no such reticence. Without waiting to consult officials, Tony Snowdon packed a bag and grabbed a spade before catching a train to Wales. In a scribbled note to his wife, he wrote: "Kiss the children for me."[1] For a time he became consoler in chief, visiting the bereaved and sitting in silence with them as they grieved mightily for their lost sons and daughters.

He visited local hospitals, talked to doctors, nurses, and survivors, and tried to keep up flagging spirits. Prince Philip arrived the next day, bringing with him the sympathies of the nation. At a moment of national grief, the queen held back, preferring to wait on events rather than acting on instinct. This was part of her temperamental makeup and it normally served her well. Though she did not want to hamper recovery work or to intrude into intense private grief, at the time it was seen by some of her advisers as an opportunity missed.

As a courtier told historian Ben Pimlott: "She regrets that now—she would say it was a mistake, that she should have gone at once."[2]

Eight days after the disaster, when recovery work was complete, the queen did visit the devastated village, where she was greeted by a young girl with a posy of flowers for her. The card's stark message read, "From the remaining children of Aberfan."[3] She came as a monarch but also as a mother, and the attendant media and watching villagers appreciated her presence in that light.

As she walked slowly through the largely silent crowd and witnessed the full extent of the carnage, reporters noted that she looked pale and that tears pricked her eyes. During her tour she visited the home of Councilor Jim Williams who had lost seven relatives in the disaster. As she spoke to those who had lost loved ones, a visit scheduled for an hour stretched to two and a half.

While they derived considerable comfort for the queen's presence, neither the villagers nor media were privy to the internal debate among her advisers about whether she should have gone earlier. Her hesitation, some insiders believed, originated from her recognition that, unlike her more theatrical mother, she was not a touchy-feely person. That did not mean that she cared any the less, but she didn't show her feelings in obvious ways. She was, as veteran royal correspondent Grania Forbes observed, "very tightly wrapped."[4] The queen did not have, as one courtier noted, "outward humanity," that instinctive rapport with strangers exhibited years later by Princess Diana and then her younger son, Prince Harry. Over the years the queen has visited Aberfan on four separate occasions, these visits cast by some as atonement for what she acknowledged as an excess of caution.

This overwhelming tragedy came at a time when inquiring minds inside the palace were considering how best to recast the monarchy for modern times. The sheen of glamour and glitter of the coronation was well worn and the queen, now forty, and the institution over which she presided were seen as middle-aged, dull, and remote. To use the parlance of the day, it was "square." That of course was no bad thing. In a rapidly changing Britain where the abolition of the death penalty and the legalization of homosexuality and abortion were all under intense discussion, the monarchy was a security blanket of certainty and stability.

With the prospect of Prince Charles's investiture as Prince of Wales looming, thoughts turned to how best to showcase the monarchy to take advantage of the arcane spectacle.

Fortuitously there was a changing of the old guard at Buckingham Palace with the affable Australian William Heseltine taking over from the dead hand of Commander Colville. The new press secretary argued that there was nothing between the dull prose of the Court Circular and the gleeful exaggerations of the tabloid press to explain and illustrate the work of the monarchy and its relevance to the modern world.

Even with Princess Margaret and her photographer husband adding glamour and contemporary luster to the crown, the queen recognized that the crowds were dwindling, interest was waning. Just as television had turbocharged the monarchy during the coronation, Heseltine suggested it was time to approach that magic box in the corner of the sitting room again to give the monarchy a much-needed jolt. He was supported by Mountbatten's son-in-law, noted filmmaker Lord Brabourne, and Mountbatten himself. Prince Philip had long been an exponent of the virtues of television. Not only did he make the argument—against his wife's wishes—to employ television at the coronation, but in the intervening years he had made or featured in several documentaries himself.

Philip, the eternal modernizer, argued that a carefully controlled fly-on-the-wall television documentary would open the world's eyes to the normal way the royals lived their lives. It would document their official life and the remorseless call of duty while pulling back the curtain to give viewers an edited glimpse into their private world. Princess Anne thought it was a "rotten idea."[5] Initially the queen, too, was not keen. Not only did she feel self-conscious in front of the cameras—which is why she delayed televising her Christmas broadcast until 1957—but, mindful of her Bagehot, she was reluctant to let too much daylight in on the magic of monarchy. Eventually she agreed with the proviso that an editorial committee chaired by Philip would give her ultimate editorial control. Whatever her reservations she felt, something must be done to arrest the slow drip, drip, drip of popularity. This then was the genesis of the show that arguably changed the monarchy forever, filmed over twelve months during 1968. Brabourne's central problem was to encourage the queen to be more natural when the cameras were whirring. Eventually he succeeded, the queen relaxing and becoming more herself. As the film was titled *Royal Family*, part of the idea was to show the queen as wife and mother as well as monarch and head of state. She was filmed at Balmoral taking Edward for an ice cream, joining in with a barbecue picnic, and chatting over the breakfast table. More formally she was shown entertaining the British Olympics team at drinks, receiving Prime Minister Harold Wilson at his weekly audience, and welcoming President Nixon to lunch.

She came across as even-tempered, quite serious, but always ready to see the funny, wry side of a situation such as American ambassador Walter Annenberg's agonizing circumlocution when describing building work at the embassy in London. Moments such as the queen and Prince Charles exchanging affectionate smiles while preparing a barbecue salad truly gave a sense that the 110-minute film was unrehearsed and authentic.

Scriptwriter Antony Jay, who was later made a commander of the Royal Victorian Order for his efforts, gave the film an intellectual underpinning with his crisp summary of the value of the monarchy and its relevance to modern times. The queen's very existence, he argued, was a bulwark against overambitious generals and politicians. "The strength of the monarchy does not lie in the power it gives the Sovereign—but in the power it denies to anyone else," he wrote.[6]

Worldwide response to the TV show was extraordinary and unprecedented. It was watched by over 350 million people including 23 million in Britain, more than half the adult population.

While it brought the royal family closer to their public and showed them as three-dimensional human beings, critics felt the exercise had been a huge mistake by making them seem too ordinary and accessible.

The broadcaster and anthropologist David Attenborough, since knighted, told director Richard Cawston: "You're killing the monarchy, you know, with this film you're making. The whole institution depends on mystique and the tribal chief in his hut. If any member of the tribe ever sees inside the hut, then the whole system of tribal chiefdom is damaged and the tribe eventually disintegrates."[7]

On the other hand the audience was delighted to be invited into the headman's hut to take a guided tour. They eagerly anticipated a sequel though the queen, who was happy with the documentary, was in no mood to turn her family—or herself—into a cast member of a television soap opera. She felt the documentary, which was broadcast two weeks before the investiture, had fulfilled its principal function, namely to whet the public's appetite for the colorful ceremony, scheduled for July 1, 1969. If the TV documentary showed a family at work and play, the investiture described a dynasty with roots dating back centuries.

Everyone at the palace strained to ensure that the much-anticipated event went off without a hitch. With bomb threats from radical Welsh nationalists, nerves were on edge. Though the investiture was designed as a kind of coronation, it had no place in the constitution and little precedent in history. Only two of the previous twenty-one Princes of Wales had had a similar celebration, and that included Edward VIII when he, too, was Prince of Wales. It was a ritual with modern antecedents masquerading as an ancient ceremony. Given that it had been sixteen years since the coronation, courtiers were anxious to bring a little razzle-dazzle back to the venerable institution.

The queen asked Tony Snowdon to take on the task of re-creating the spirit of the investiture held in 1911 when the Prince of Wales, now the Duke of Windsor, was crowned. Though he had a tiny budget of £50,000—the equivalent of

She may be the Queen and Head of State of Britain and the Commonwealth but that means nothing to her dorgis and corgis who appeared reluctant to follow her lead as she prepared to board an aircraft of the Queen's Flight at Aberdeen Airport, near her private estate of Balmoral in the Scottish Highlands. Her corgis, a breed which she had since childhood, were instantly recognizable symbols of her reign.

Above: The Queen in her favorite habitat – the countryside. Here she is chatting away with an unconcerned Highland shepherd at a gun dog trial in the early 1960s. If she hadn't been the Queen, she wanted to live in the country surrounded by children, horses, and dogs.

Above: Photographer Cecil Beaton captured the domesticity of motherhood in the grand setting of Buckingham Palace. The birth of Prince Edward in 1964 completed her family. Prince Andrew, who was intrigued by his baby brother, looks on.

Above: The Queen tours the site of the mining disaster in the south Wales village of Aberfan, when a slag heap collapsed and slammed into a school and local houses, killing 144, mainly children. The Queen always regretted not going earlier.

Above left: Prince Charles pledges his loyalty to the Queen at his investiture as Prince of Wales at Caernarfon Castle, July 1, 1969. The ceremony helped reignite interest in the monarchy. Above right: In the unlikely setting of a fair in the New Zealand town of Greymouth in March 1970, the Queen made history when she mingled with her subjects, the first monarch since Charles II to do so.

Below: The Queen at her desk in her study at Windsor Castle in May 1977 as she prepared for her Silver Jubilee celebrations. Note the picture of her father, King George VI, with his grandson Prince Charles, placed prominently on her desk.

Above: Prince Charles kisses his bride, the newly minted Princess of Wales, after first asking his mother for permission. Their wedding, watched by 750 million people globally, was described by the Archbishop of Canterbury as a "fairy tale."

Left: The Queen had a tricky relationship with Princess Diana, especially as the latter's marriage began to collapse. While Diana respected the Queen, she felt that she should blame her son for their marital breakdown. Here they are at Victoria Station in 1986, preparing for the arrival of a foreign dignitary.

Right: The Queen, accompanied by a young Prince William on the forecourt of Buckingham Palace, bids farewell to the Duke and Duchess of York as they embarked on their honeymoon on July 23, 1986.

Above left: The Queen, desolate and clearly upset, inspects the damage to her beloved Windsor Castle following a devastating fire in November 1992, the year she described as her "annus horribilis," which saw the separation and divorce of three of her children. Above right: The Queen and Prince Philip inspect the mountain of flowers outside Buckingham Palace following the death of Princess Diana in a car crash in a Paris underpass in August 1997.

Left: The Queen wipes away a tear during the decommissioning of the royal yacht *Britannia* in December 1997. The yacht was the Queen's much-loved home away from home on arduous official tours.

Below: The Queen, together with the rest of the royal family, bids a final farewell to the Queen Mother at her funeral on April 9, 2002, at Westminster Abbey.

Left: In 2002 the Queen and Prince Philip in the Gold State Coach on their way to St Paul's Cathedral for a service of Thanksgiving to celebrate the fiftieth anniversary of Her Majesty's succession.

Right: One is quite amused. Prince Harry essays a joke with his grandmother as they watch a flypast over Buckingham Palace during the 2008 Trooping ceremony. Harry seemed to have the ability to convince the Queen to go along with some of his jaunty schemes.

Below: The Queen took an early interest in Prince William's romance with Catherine Middleton and liked that she loved him for himself, not his position. Here they are on their wedding day, April 29, 2011, on the Buckingham Palace balcony.

Left: The Queen and other senior members of the Royal Family watch an armada of waterborne craft as part of the Thames River pageant to celebrate her Diamond Jubilee in June 2012. One casualty from the constant chilling rain was Prince Philip, who was taken to the hospital with an infection and missed the rest of the festivities.

Right: The future is assured. The Queen and Prince William point out aircraft to Prince George, then aged two, whose arrival pushed Prince Harry down the line of succession. The Duchess of Cambridge and baby Princess Charlotte look on during the traditional Trooping tableaux in 2016.

Below: Happy families? Prince William cracks wise as the latest recruit to the Royal Family, Meghan Markle, joins in the merriment as the Royal Air Force stage a flypast in July 2018 to celebrate their centenary. Unity did not last long. Harry and Meghan moved to California after leaving the Royal Family, the couple trailing accusations of racism behind them.

Left: At the funeral service for Prince Philip, who died peacefully on April 9, 2021, the Queen was forced to sit on her own due to strict Covid regulations. The sight of the Queen, hunched and diminutive, saying her final farewells to her husband of more than 73 years without any member of her family nearby to comfort her, was for many the most poignant moment of a brief but moving ceremony at St. George's Chapel, Windsor.

Above: The Queen is in the handshaking, people-meeting business. So, when the pandemic took hold, she was forced to adapt, using modern technology to speak remotely to those she would otherwise meet in person. Here she is in her study at Windsor Castle, where she remained for much of the crisis.

Left: Thrilled to be back. In one of her first public engagements since the death of Prince Philip, the Queen attended Royal Ascot week. She genuinely loves the turf, a passion that began when she was a little girl. It was no surprise when, in 2021, she was one of the first to be inducted into Flat racing's Hall of Fame.

$1.5 million today—Snowdon, whose family was Welsh, was thrilled at the challenge he had been given of interpreting the ancient and the modern and molding it into dramatic harmony with Caernarfon Castle, a massive medieval fortress used as a backdrop to dramatize Prince Charles's coming of age.

He was careful to show the queen and Prince Philip his designs, including sketches for the thrones and the Perspex canopy to shield the modern dais of Welsh slate for the crowning ceremony. The race to provide a spectacle fit for the queen was played out against escalating violence by Welsh nationalists, who made death threats to officials and attacked public buildings with petrol bombs. Uncharacteristically the queen, normally phlegmatic in the face of danger, told Prime Minister Harold Wilson that she feared for her son's safety and asked whether the ceremony should be canceled. Wilson assured her that he would do everything in his power to ensure the occasion took place without incident. All police were issued with firearms although, fearing the worst, the BBC pre-recorded a full-length TV obituary of Prince Charles. On the Royal Train the queen mother told her grandson that the event was going ahead but he was going to be replaced by a stunt double. Her jovial remark did little to dissipate the tension.

"Charles," Lord Snowdon told writer Gyles Brandreth, "was shit-scared."[8] With justification. On the eve of the big day, two activists were killed by the bomb they were planting on the railway track that would carry Charles to Caernarfon Castle. They were immediately dubbed the Abergele Martyrs. Half an hour before the ceremony was due to start there was a loud bang near the castle. The bejeweled and uniformed audience, already settled in their seats, tried to pretend they hadn't heard it.

As the clock ticked toward the ceremony the guests fell silent. Among the crowd of four thousand were foreign royalty, ambassadors, politicians, local Welsh gentry—and a handful of modern-day druids, who were playing ancient Celtic priests, clad in nylon capes.

Then it was showtime. Heart in mouth, the royal party made its way into the castle and all was well. The ceremony went off precisely as planned. There was no repetition of the clownish antics of the dress rehearsal where Prince Charles's oversize crown slipped down over his forehead, obscuring half his face. It was the cue for the queen and her son to try and stifle their giggles.

The actual ceremony, though, was both moving and believable, the most affecting moment when the Prince of Wales knelt before the Queen and after placing his hands between hers, swore: "I, Charles, Prince of Wales, do become your liege man of life and limb and of earthly worship, and faith and truth I will bear unto thee to live and die against all manner of folks." It was an echo of Prince Philip's own oath of allegiance during the coronation.

More than five hundred million worldwide watched the ceremony, a magnetic combination of the feudal and the modern, the symbolic and the familial. The queen was thrilled with Snowdon's creative vision and awarded him the GCVO, Grand Cross of the Royal Victorian Order, in the investiture honors. In a long handwritten letter she admitted that she was initially skeptical that his dramatic vision would work but was admiring of his "spectacular and breathtaking achievement."[9]

The success of the investiture and the *Royal Family* documentary had a real impact. The queen personally noted the increased size and enthusiasm of the crowds, anecdotal evidence matched by favorable opinion poll findings.

With a positive wind at the queen's back, the dawn of the 1970s marked another waypoint in the measured modernizing of the monarchy. During a visit to Wellington in New Zealand in 1970 the royal car came to a halt and the queen, Prince Philip, Princess Anne, and Prince Charles got out and started shaking hands and making small talk—"Have you been waiting long?"—with the somewhat startled crowds. Thus began the walkabout, the name derived from the term used by indigenous people meaning "to go wandering." A little piece of history was made as the queen became the first sovereign since Charles II, more than three hundred years before, to mingle with her people. Back in Britain she successfully repeated the trick during visits to Manchester and Coventry. "There was a clear policy of making her much more accessible," observed the BBC's court correspondent Ronald Allison. "Suddenly, the lady on the schoolroom wall, on the postage stamp, was a real person."[10]

A real person who cost the taxpayers money, a lot of money. It was not some radical politician who first raised the sensitive issue regarding the cost of the monarchy but Prince Philip, four months after the investiture in November 1969 during a conversation with American TV journalists on *Meet the Press*.

He told the surprised TV inquisitors that the royal family was about to go into the red and went on to explain that they had already sold their private yacht *Bloodhound*, they may have to move into smaller premises, and he might have to give up polo. It was a classic example of what the duke himself called "dontopedalogy"—putting one's foot in one's mouth—as he was wildly mistaken if he thought he would find any sympathy from the British public.

The country, on the brink of a tumultuous decade of industrial action and political radicalism that culminated in the miners' strike and the imposition of the three-day working week, was angry and hostile. Though the queen's response is not recorded, she cannot have been happy that her husband had exploded this sensitive issue in such a blunt headline-grabbing manner. Though she lived in palaces, castles, and stately homes, had the world's finest collection of jewelry, and took her holidays aboard a royal yacht that came complete with a twenty-six-piece Royal Marines Band, she carefully projected an image of frugality and modesty. She was the monarch who turned off lights to conserve electricity, sent her eldest son to look for a lost dog leash with the ringing rebuke that "dog leads cost money," and stored her morning breakfast cereal in a plastic Tupperware container. Less welcome was the story that she was the world's richest woman—an unwanted accolade that her senior advisers insisted was way wide of the mark.

In May 1971, against this background, lawmakers set up a committee to review the Civil List, the payment agreed at the beginning of every reign to finance the upkeep of the monarchy, including payment to staff and maintaining the upkeep of the royal households. Inflation had eaten into the original Civil List, which made it difficult to balance the royal books. Hence the genesis of Prince Philip's provocative comments.

However, lawmakers were in a fighting mood. Firebrand member of Parliament Willie Hamilton described the request for greater royal funding as "the most brazenly insensitive pay claim made in the last two hundred years."[11]

Ultimately the royal family got the raise they required, but it was a surprisingly confrontational process. During its review the inquiry inadvertently illuminated the relationship between the queen and her mother after lawmakers pointedly asked why the queen mother's personal allowance had increased even though, at seventy-one, she was well past retirement age and undertook far fewer engagements than previous years. It was a question that perplexed even long-serving royal courtiers.

The issue of the queen, the queen mother, and their financial relationship began in earnest following the death of George VI. As queen consort, Elizabeth had grown used to being the star of the show. When the king passed she struggled to accept second billing. Her eldest daughter, who was the reluctant agent of her demotion, felt guilty about her mother's unhappiness and as a result found it difficult to deny her anything, especially when it concerned the royal coffers.

In the beginning of the reign there was much internal correspondence about the queen mother's desire to live in the palatial splendor of Marlborough House, the home of Queen Mary who died shortly before the coronation. A review of royal finances concluded, much to the queen mother's disappointment, that it was too expensive to renovate this imposing Grade One listed building for her sole use. Over the years, however, the new queen indulged her in other ways.

She restored several properties for the queen mother's use, namely Clarence House in central London and the Castle of Mey, a desolate pile in the far north of Scotland that she bought on a whim; she also expanded her home of Birkhall on the Balmoral estate and confirmed her mother's continued occupancy of Royal Lodge, the country house in the middle of Windsor Great Park that she and her husband, then the Duke of York, were given in 1931 by King George V.

Even years after the king's death, the queen just couldn't say no to her mother's extravagances. She always felt that it was a tragedy that she had been widowed at the young age of fifty-one. As a result the queen mother was given the equivalent of an open checkbook, which she used to the full. "She had none of the usual Scottish carefulness," recalled former assistant private secretary Edward Ford. "She didn't seem to know anything about money."[12]

With half a dozen or so limousines and a staff comprising, among others, three chauffeurs, five chefs, and numerous pages, footmen, and butlers, the queen mother was cocooned in an Edwardian time warp of excess and indulgence. Admonishment came there none. The most the queen could muster was a plaintive note, saying "Oh dear Mummy" after she had spent a small fortune on new bloodstock for her stables.[13]

When it was finally reported in public that she had a staff of fifty and an overdraft of $5.6 million, most observers, including the Prince of Wales, thought the figure way too low.

Just as during Princess Margaret's romantic vacillation regarding Group Captain Peter Townsend, the queen was prepared to accept a degree of short-term criticism of the crown in exchange for her sister's ultimate happiness, she was also willing to accept some public censure of her mother's finances if it kept her content and avoided personal confrontation.

The queen mother was the unseen power behind the throne, a matriarchal figure who wielded enormous influence. Beneath the twinkly, somewhat exaggerated personality was a strong-willed, deeply conservative woman who enjoyed the ear of her daughter in daily phone calls that in themselves were a kind of vaudeville act as the operator intoned, "Your Majesty, Her Majesty, Your Majesty." What is more, the queen listened and took note of what she said. As exasperating as she might be at times, the queen usually found it easier to go along with her mother's wishes than oppose her will. Drinks before lunch at the Royal Lodge after Sunday morning services was the usual time for the queen mother to buttonhole her eldest daughter. "Her mindset was pre-war," argued a former private secretary, suggesting that the monarchy would have modernized much sooner but for the interference of the queen mother.[14] Courtiers soon realized that the queen had to be firmly convinced of a course of action in case she was waylaid by her mother. Her views, however old-fashioned, had to be taken into account. Though at heart the queen was also a traditionalist who regularly followed the precedents set by her late father, the queen mother was always around to reinforce this mindset, particularly with regard to family matters. She was not always successful, notably the schooling of the queen's children.

Even if she failed to convince her daughter she invariably found a willing ally in the heir to the throne. He doted on her, seeing her as his surrogate mother while she thought of him as the son she never had and spoiled him accordingly. As historian Graham Turner observed: "Although she was deeply fond of her mother the queen often felt thoroughly irritated at the Queen Mother's indulgence of Charles's foibles and resented the fact that she too often gave him a soft ride when a gentle word of reproof might have helped him more."[15] During his twenties, the Prince of Wales imitated the grand comfort of his grannie with an indulgent lifestyle that included a valet among whose duties was to iron his money for the collection at Sunday church services and squeeze the royal toothpaste onto the royal toothbrush each night. He had a love for high living that neither his mother nor father could understand.

Though the queen mother lost out in her contention that the queen's children should be educated in the palace, where her voice was heard loudest was in relation to the Duke and Duchess of Windsor. It was the queen mother's fixed view that her husband's life was cut short because of the stresses and strains of his unwanted position as king. That he was a heavy smoker who died of lung cancer had little to do with it.

The queen mother's stern attitude ensured that since the abdication of 1936, the duke and duchess had enjoyed only very occasional contact with members of the royal family. The queen had briefly and reluctantly visited the duke and duchess at the London Clinic in 1965 in order to discuss their funeral arrangements. He informed the queen that he had bought a burial plot in Baltimore for them both if the royal family insisted on the current arrangement that he be buried alone at Frogmore on the grounds of Windsor Castle. The prospect of a king of England and his wife being buried outside the country was a proposal that the queen could not countenance—whatever her mother might say. After some back-and-forth, it was agreed that Wallis Simpson would lie next to her ducal husband at Frogmore. The only other occasion the Windsors mingled with the royal family was when the queen invited the ducal couple to the unveiling of a plaque in memory of Queen Mary at Marlborough House in 1967. Apart from that, silence.

From time to time a brave courtier would suggest inviting the Windsors to a social function such as Royal Ascot but the queen, knowing what her mother would say, quickly blocked any such proposal. Even Prince Charles lobbied his grandmother to invite them to Windsor for the weekend but he, too, dropped the idea when he realized how difficult she would find a prolonged encounter with a man whom she blamed for her husband's premature death.

In May 1972, with the ex-king's health rapidly deteriorating, the queen did agree to a deathbed meeting with the ailing duke during a state visit to France. There was more than a touch of the macabre about this fifteen-minute encounter. The purpose behind the state visit was to ensure Britain's smooth entry into the Common Market, the precursor to the European Economic Union. Nothing could overshadow this diplomatic triumph for Prime Minister Edward Heath—and that included the dying duke. The duke's physician Jean Thin was summoned to Paris and bluntly informed by the British ambassador

Sir Christopher Soames that he could die before or after the state visit but not during. That would be politically disastrous. As a result Soames would call the French doctor every evening at six o'clock for a medical update.

In the end he was well enough to see the queen and insisted on dressing and receiving her in his sitting room on the second floor. When she arrived he stood and bowed, leaving the doctors worried that his various drips—"this damned rigging" as he called it—would come apart. The queen was deeply moved not only by her uncle's gallantry but by his remarkable similarity in looks to her own father. It brought back a cascade of memories that, according to one observer, left her with "tears in her eyes."[16]

He died nine days later on May 28, 1972, his body returned to Britain where he lay in state for two days at St. George's Chapel, Windsor Castle. More than sixty thousand people filed past his coffin to pay their respects. The funeral service itself left the queen with a tricky question of protocol. It was due to take place two days after the annual ceremony of Trooping the Colour. The question was raised as to whether the popular time-honored parade should be canceled. If he had been a reigning monarch that would of course been the case, but as a private citizen living abroad, court mourning was no longer appropriate. The queen, though, insisted that his passing should be marked. Knowing that the duke loved the skirl of the bagpipes and was a keen practitioner himself, Trooping the Colour went ahead but with a lament played by pipe bands as a sign of respect.

The funeral service itself, which took place in St. George's Chapel on June 5, lasted just half an hour. Despite its brevity, Prince Charles described the ceremony as "simple, dignified to perfection, colorful and wonderfully British."[17] However, the achingly thin duchess was nervy and disoriented throughout. It got to the point where the queen, who was seated beside her, showed, according to the Countess of Avon, wife of the former prime minister, Sir Anthony Eden, "a motherly and nanny-like tenderness and kept putting her hand on the Duchess's arm or glove." It was a rare sign of affection in public.[18]

That said, later that same year the queen spoke with humor and feeling about her long marriage when the royal couple celebrated their silver wedding anniversary with a service at Westminster Abbey and lunch at the Guildhall in central London. In her speech she told her audience: "If I am asked what I think about family life after 25 years of marriage, I can answer with equal simplicity and conviction, I am for it.[19]

For all the platitudes, theirs remained a sparky marriage, with plenty of fireworks on the way. The queen had long since realized that Philip's flashes of temper came and went like a summer rainstorm. When he said to her "You're talking rubbish," which he did on numerous occasions, she either ignored him or smartly changed the subject. During one altercation on board the royal yacht *Britannia*, she told her private secretary Martin Charteris: "I'm simply not going to appear until Philip is in a better temper."[20] Whatever their disagreements, at the end of the day they still climbed into the same king-size double bed at Buckingham Palace.

The queen's ringing public endorsement of her marriage failed to stop the persistent rumors about Philip and his alleged extramarital affairs. Ever since the "party girl" rumpus in the mid-1950s, which prompted an official denial, there had been continued speculation that Philip had not been faithful.

Evidence, though, was circumstantial: His office was staffed by pretty girls, he always made a beeline for the most attractive girl in the room at private and even public functions, and he enjoyed flirting with good-looking women on the dance floor. Though biographer Sarah Bradford did break cover and suggested that he had affairs, she later backtracked. Sacha, Duchess of Abercorn, twenty-five years his junior, was in the frame for a time, as was Penny Romsey, who was his partner in carriage-driving. Sacha Abercorn conceded she had a passionate friendship for more than twenty years, but it wasn't a full relationship. She was his intellectual "playmate," bonded by an interest in Swiss psychiatrist Carl Jung. "When I see the tabloids, he once grumbled to Lady Mountbatten, "I think I might as well have done it."[21]

The queen always gave him the latitude to be himself and, in common with many men, he enjoyed the company of pretty, interesting women. As Michael Mann, the former dean of Windsor, observed: "He is attracted by very good-looking women but I don't think he's ever fallen in love with anyone else since they married."[22]

The queen had a number of close male friends she had known since the war years, most notably Patrick Plunket, the Deputy Master of the Household. During the war he was a regular visitor to Windsor Castle, a welcome guest who made every party go with a swing. He had brought this zest for life to organizing the queen's social life, be it weekend shooting parties or grand balls at Windsor Castle. During social gatherings he always kept an eye out for his boss to make sure she was being properly looked after. If Prince Philip was dancing with some attractive guest and the queen was looking a little lonely, he would whisk her onto the dance floor and keep her amused.

As Plunket's cousin Lady Annabel Goldsmith recalled: "He adored her from the outset. They enjoyed a very special connection. He was the one member of her staff who could talk to her on equal terms."[23]

They would go to the cinema together, dine at discreet Italian restaurants, and watch her favorite TV programs in her apartment at Buckingham Palace. When he died prematurely in 1975, a sign of her closeness to him was that, in a break with tradition, she attended both his funeral and memorial service. She even had a hand in writing his obituary in the *Times*. Later she had a pavilion built in his honor in Windsor Great Park. Months after his death she still keenly felt his loss.

The queen and her consort enjoyed a very royal marriage; Philip and Elizabeth were from a generation that expected loyalty, if not fidelity. She was prepared to forgive him almost anything because he had been such a supportive and steadfast consort.

Her sister, however, was not as fortunate in her choice of marital partner. The lengthy disintegration of her marriage to photographer Lord Snowdon involved not just the warring couple but the queen, who had to navigate the best course for the monarchy. As Snowdon himself pointed out, in the beginning all went swimmingly. They were glamorous, modern, and hardworking, the very symbols of the Swinging Sixties as they raced round London on his motorbike or Mini car. Together they wrote speeches, learned to water-ski, and traveled the world. They also had two much-loved children, David, born in November 1961, and Sarah in May 1964. Eventually though, things started to unravel. After a few years Snowdon, as his close friends had predicted, tired of the straitjacket of royal life. He abandoned his role as royal consort to pursue his photographic career. Possessive and lonely, Margaret would track him down, only for him to pull farther away. While Margaret could be imperious, having been raised to expect deference, Snowdon became cruel and mocking toward her, leaving malicious notes on her pillow or dressing table. They both took lovers and began leading separate lives. In public they were all smiles and maintained an impeccable display of togetherness.

Snowdon, though, refused Margaret's demand, made in the winter of 1974, that he move out of Kensington Palace and agree to a formal separation. Instead, the couple suffered several more years of dramatic and bitter scenes, many in front of embarrassed friends, servants, and members of the family.

The breakdown of Margaret's marriage was deeply upsetting and troubling for the queen and the queen mother. The queen loved her sister but was also very fond of Tony. She appreciated his creative abilities as well as his efforts on behalf of the monarchy, particularly his stewardship of Prince Charles's investiture in Wales. The queen mother, who had an eye for a good photograph and painting, admired his talent as a documentary maker and a photographer. In turn his behavior toward them was always cheerful, charming, and correct without being obsequious. They knew from lifelong experience that Margaret could be capricious, imperious, and downright rude, and so, as evenhanded as they tried to be, their sympathies tended toward Snowdon.

Or more accurately their sympathies lay with the children. Both the queen and her mother worried about the impact on David and Sarah, and the queen paid particular attention to her young niece. She took her to Balmoral on holiday and would take her horse riding, watching from the sidelines when she took part in gymkhanas.

As much as she indulged her sister, even the queen was taken aback when in the summer of 1973 she heard that Margaret had taken up with a rather aimless young man, Roddy Llewellyn. He was seventeen years her junior, which made him just a year older than her future son-in-law, Captain Mark Phillips, who was betrothed to her daughter Princess Anne. Roddy's arrival, the archetypal "Toy Boy" of popular imagination, complicated an already fraught situation and drove a wedge between the sisters. The queen believed that if news of her sister's behavior became public, it would have a devastating effect on the monarchy and open the institution up for ridicule. In a moment of despair she asked her private secretary Martin Charteris how they were going to get his sister "out of the gutter."[24]

Despite the brewing behind-the-scenes drama, Princess Margaret and Lord Snowdon were all smiles at the wedding of Princess Anne and Olympic equestrian Captain Mark Phillips at Westminster Abbey in November 1973, a televised spectacular with an estimated worldwide audience of a hundred million. Though the queen may have had reservations about Anne's choice of husband—Prince Charles called him Fog because he considered him to be wet and thick—she readily gave her permission to the marriage. Drily, she suggested that, given the couple's enthusiasm for all things equine, their children would be four-legged. Horses were very much on her mind around this time as she had, for once, hit a winning streak. Jockey Joe Mercer received a grateful note from the queen, the owner of the filly Highclere, after winning the 1000 Guineas at Newmarket in May 1974. She wrote: "For once I don't remember much about the race owing to the excitement but I do know that a homebred Guineas winner has given me more pleasure than anything for a long time."[25] But Highclere wasn't finished, in June 1974 going on to win the Prix de Diane, the French equivalent of the Oaks at Chantilly Racecourse, north of Paris. Winning jockey Joe Mercer and trainer Dick Hern flew back to London on a private plane. They were polishing off a bottle of champagne when the pilot was diverted to Heathrow airport in west London. The queen had invited the rather bedraggled duo to dinner at Windsor Castle. When they arrived the queen was standing outside in the rain waiting to greet them. "Come in my warriors," she said and led them into dinner with her, Princess Margaret, Prince Philip, and Lord Mountbatten.[26]

Pride of place on the center of the table was the gold Prix de Diane cup presented to the winning owner. As racing writer Sean Smith observed, "It was a privileged peep into the queen's private world of simply relaxing family enjoyment."[27] Appearances, though, were deceptive. The absence of Lord Snowdon from this family tableau was noticeable. At this time the queen was encouraging her sister and her husband to try to resolve their differences—at least for the sake of the children. She soon realized that matters were too far gone for a cosmetic makeover and was forced to deal with a sister whose life was rapidly unraveling. This emotional messiness was new territory for the queen. Such was Margaret's parlous medical state that she canceled all royal engagements in November 1974. On one occasion she phoned a friend, who happened to be hosting a dinner party, and threatened suicide: "If you don't come over, I'll throw myself out of the window." Her friend rang the queen who replied: "Carry on with your house party. Her bedroom is on the ground floor."[28]

Her sister's ill health, both mental and physical, was of continued concern for the queen. Though her ladies-in-waiting kept an eye on Margaret's behavior, they could only recommend a course of treatment. Her sister could command. In the end her lady-in-waiting contacted the queen and asked her to intervene. She delayed her engagements and drove to Kensington Palace to see her sister. "I feel exactly like the night nurse taking over from the day nurse," she said drily before taking Margaret for a quiet weekend at Windsor Castle.[29]

The situation was increasingly untenable. In late November 1975, Lord Snowdon wrote an anguished letter to the queen stating that he could no longer tolerate living at Kensington Palace. "The atmosphere is appalling for all concerned—the children, the staff, the few remaining loyal friends and she and I both."[30]

His letter genuinely shocked his sister-in-law, who had to admit that her sporadic efforts at counseling had come to naught. All that now remained was to oversee the practicalities of when the separation should be made public. It was decided that in the interests of the children the news be announced during Easter 1976 so that they were on holiday and could spend time with their parents. All concerned now faced the sad fact that Margaret was about to become the first member of the royal family to divorce since Henry VIII and Anne Boleyn in 1540.

Any hopes that the split could be managed by the palace were shattered when the *News of the World* published pictures of the princess, clad in a swimsuit, and her "tanned toy boy" Roddy Llewellyn on holiday together in Mustique. She was now seen as the adulterer in the failed marriage while her hardworking professional photographer husband was cast as the injured and innocent party. Though this was a grotesquely unfair narrative, it was one that stuck. Even the queen and queen mother felt that Margaret had not done enough to try to save her marriage. "They didn't realize the depths of Margaret's despair," observed her friend and biographer Christopher Warwick. "They remembered her as the trickster, the prankster, the little girl getting things her way. There was a feeling it was mainly her fault."[31]

There was, too, concern that the acrimonious breakup could overshadow the fast-approaching Silver Jubilee celebrations. The queen worried that no one would turn up to see them—or her. With the economy in free fall, inflation rampant, and rising unemployment, the first signs were not hopeful.

Local councils reported few applications to stage street parties, the demand for souvenirs, no matter how tacky, was weak, and events were canceled.

She need not have worried. The welcoming crowds during

an initial eleven-day tour of Scottish cities suggested that her jubilee was, after all, going to be well received. A million people filled the Mall to see the queen and Philip ride in the state coach from the palace to St. Paul's Cathedral for a service of celebration. This was followed by hundreds of local parades and thousands of neighborhood street parties. The proliferation of red, white, and blue bunting and Union Flags was reminiscent of Britain's war victory celebrations in 1945. She visited thirty-six counties in the three kingdoms, England, Wales, and Scotland, with millions of people taking to the streets to greet the passing royal parade. The queen was genuinely touched by the reception. "I am simply amazed, I had no idea," one courtier recalls her saying over and over again.[32]

Her fourth kingdom, Northern Ireland, proved much more dangerous. It was riven by sectarian conflict—the Protestant majority wanted to continue the centuries-old union with mainland Britain while the Catholic minority wanted to become part of Ireland. Before the queen and Prince Philip arrived there were death and bomb threats as well as violent street demonstrations. On the eve of her two-day visit in early August a demonstrator and a soldier were shot dead. When she arrived thirty-two thousand troops were on active duty with the Provisional Wing of the Irish Republican Army vowing that the British would pay dearly for the "Queen's champagne parties on a few acres of Irish soil."[33]

Such was the security surrounding the brief visit—she only spent a total of six hours on Irish soil at a cost of millions of dollars in security—that the queen stayed aboard the royal yacht *Britannia* before being whisked to a highly regulated public engagement at Hillsborough Castle by helicopter, the first time in her reign she had used this form of transport, which she considered dangerous. This was a sign, if any more were needed, of the concern for the queen's safety. She was, a British minister later confided, very anxious and "terribly, terribly tense." When she had completed her last engagement at the University of Ulster, he recalled that Prince Philip patted her hand and said: "There now, it's over. Unless they sink the *Britannia* we're safe."[34]

If that was the low point, the crowning personal glory of the Silver Jubilee celebrations was when the queen received a phone call on November 15, 1977, informing her of the birth of her first grandchild, Peter Phillips, the son of Princess Anne. It was a close-run thing regarding high points of the Silver Jubilee year also saw Dunfermline, her greatest-ever racehorse, win two classics, the Oaks and the St. Leger. The arrival of her first grandchild edged it, though. Indeed, such was her joy that she uncharacteristically delayed an investiture in the ballroom at Buckingham Palace for ten minutes so that she could call Prince Philip, who was in Germany. He had always been close to his straightforward daughter and admired her gung-ho spirit and robust independence. Four years later Zara was born and Anne signaled that she was going to raise her children very differently from her mother.

No governesses, palaces, or titles for these two. They were brought up in the country on a working farm, Gatcombe Park in Gloucestershire, purchased by the queen, and went to the local nursery. Anne was able to juggle motherhood with an exacting role as the hands-on president of the charity Save the Children, a position she had accepted in 1970. The queen and Prince Philip left Anne, fourth in line to the throne, very much to her own devices, proud of the way she managed to combine domestic and working life.

She was a successful product of the queen and Prince Philip's philosophy of "sink or swim." Their offspring were expected to set up their own administrative offices, choose charities that reflected their interests, and, perhaps most important, use their own judgment to find a partner. As a former private secretary observed: "They got the message that they were expected to overcome their difficulties for themselves and get on with it."[35] As the queen and Prince Philip were away so often, it was a policy born out both of necessity and belief. It enjoyed mixed results, particularly with their eldest son and heir.

While the queen and Prince Philip's dispassionate style of parenting worked for Princess Anne, she had neither the responsibilities nor expectations that came with being the heir to the throne. Charles had a much more public and tortuous journey, particularly when it came to his eventual choice of consort, where breeding and background were as important as romantic attachment.

As numerous courtiers have since observed, perhaps with the certainty of hindsight, if the queen had shown as much diligence about the choice of royal brides, particularly the future queen, as she did about the breeding of her horses, the House of Windsor may not have been in such a mess. Unlike Queen Victoria, who told her offspring who and when they were going to marry and that was that, the queen and her husband allowed her own children almost complete latitude.

Not that parental interference was a sure fire way of guaranteeing marital success. When the previous Prince of Wales, later Edward VIII, fell in love with Lady Rosemary Leverson-Gower, the daughter of a notorious aristocratic family he was told by his parents, King George V and Queen Mary, that she was not suitable as there was a strain of mental illness that ran in the family. If he had been allowed to marry her the course of the House of Windsor would have been very different.

The detached approach of the queen and Prince Philip gave others, notably the dynastically ambitious Lord Louis Mountbatten, the opportunity to interfere in the torrid love life of Prince Charles. In a letter to the prince, written shortly after Princess Anne's wedding, he advised him to "sow his wild oats" before marrying an unsullied virgin.[36] Of course the virgin he had in mind was a member of his own family, his granddaughter Amanda Knatchbull, nine years the prince's junior.

If the queen and Prince Philip shied away from matchmaking in their eldest son's love life, Mountbatten showed no such hesitation. He encouraged Charles to join Amanda and her family on holiday; he spent weekends with her at Broadlands, the Mountbatten family seat, as well as Balmoral and Sandringham. As they were second cousins, their budding romance passed mainly unnoticed. She was part of the aristocratic family furniture that surrounded the prince. In any case the media were much more interested in the many glamorous young women he produced at public and private events. Eventually his behavior as an erstwhile royal Lothario became so obvious that Prince Philip, rather than the queen, broke cover and wrote an admonishing note to his son for "parading" his paramours before the public.[37]

Whatever the public and private attempts the prince made toward finding a consort, his heart belonged to another woman, married mother of two Camilla Parker Bowles whose husband Andrew was a major in a household regiment, the Blues and Royals. Charles had dated her before she married, but she remained the one that got away.

His continued pursuit of a married woman offended many of his fellow officers. After discreet conversations between the palace and the regiment, senior royal officials formally informed the queen that the Blues and Royals were "unhappy" that her son was sleeping with the wife of one of their officers.[38] The queen made no comment—nor, crucially, did she speak to her son about his behavior. Such a confrontation would, according to courtiers, have been totally out of character.

Much rather an hour with her red boxes, which acted as the monarch's security blanket, than address such an intimate family issue. In the end she did act by putting out the word that Mrs. Parker Bowles was not to be invited to any royal events and that included Charles's thirtieth birthday party at Buckingham Palace. The queen mother followed suit.

In fairness, Mrs. Parker Bowles was, the queen hoped, but a temporary sideshow. As far as the queen and Prince Philip were concerned, the main romantic focus of the prince's life was his quiet pursuit of Amanda Knatchbull, a young woman they all knew and liked. Dickie Mountbatten, who was eager to cement his family's royal connections, gave the queen regular updates on the progress of the relationship. His zeal to make a match between Amanda and the future king extended to lobbying to have his granddaughter and himself added to a two-week tour of India that the prince was due to undertake in early 1980. Both the queen and Prince Philip expressed their doubts. Philip thought that Dickie would steal the limelight from his son, while the queen was concerned about Amanda. Her presence would merely excite wild press speculation about a possible engagement. If the relationship came to naught Amanda would be publicly humiliated. Her father John Brabourne agreed.

As it was the couple took matters into their own hands. Sometime later that fateful summer of 1979, Charles did propose to Amanda. She refused his suit and diplomatically explained that though they were great friends and would remain great friends, royal life was not for her.

There the matter rested at least for the time being. Everyone expected the indefatigable Dickie to try to revive the romance. Tragically it was not to be. In August while Dickie and his family were on holiday in Classiebawn Castle, his summer home on the west coast of Ireland, his family fishing boat was blown up by members of the Irish Republican Army. Of the seven people on board, only three survived. Mountbatten's daughter and son-in-law, Patricia and John Brabourne, and their fourteen-year-old son Timothy were seriously injured. Dickie, Timothy's twin brother, Nicholas, John's elderly mother, Doreen, and a local boy named Paul Maxwell all died.

The queen was at Balmoral when she heard the horrific family news. The Brabournes were among her closest friends. She had been a bridesmaid at the wedding of her childhood friend Patricia. Her husband John had been the guiding hand behind the tremendously successful *Royal Family* documentary. With Mountbatten's death the queen lost a living link to her father and his royal generation. She had known him all her life. He had been the family's éminence grise, adviser, and meddler in chief. A former courtier described their relationship in these terms: "The Queen's attitude was that he was her Uncle Dickie and she was very, very fond of him, but sometimes she wished he'd shut up. Once she said: 'I always say yes, yes, yes to Dickie, but I don't listen to him.'"[39] Prince Charles was devastated. "I have lost someone infinitely special in my life," he wrote later.[40] His uncle had been his friend, mentor, benefactor, and surrogate parent, and now he was gone.

As with Margaret's divorce, the queen's first thoughts were for the children. When she was told that her lifelong friend Patricia Brabourne was confined to her hospital bed as she recovered from her injuries she invited Timothy Knatchbull, then fourteen, and his sister Amanda to stay at Balmoral. Years later he could still remember the warm glow of the queen's greeting. He recalled the feeling of a "mother duck gathering up her lost young... [her] default setting of love and care... wrapping us up in a sort of motherliness."[41]

This then was the human side of the sovereign, the queen as family matriarch and consoler in chief.

9

Then Along Came Diana

The queen was hardworking, prudent, and abstemious. She weighed around 112 pounds, ate sparingly, and enjoyed good British fare: Welsh lamb, Scottish salmon, game from Sandringham, and freshly churned butter from the dairy at Windsor. Excess was never on the menu—either for herself or the monarchy.

She explained her rigorous dietary routine to President Jimmy Carter when he visited Buckingham Palace in May 1977. As he recalled: "She pointed out that her waist had to be watched very closely because she had [to wear] seven different tunics during the course of a year and that she couldn't afford to change the costumes and had to wear the same size for a number of years."[1]

The queen, who was one of the world's wealthiest women, meant of course that she couldn't afford the time and upheaval to have these elaborate costumes altered every year.

It was not only her formal regalia that caused her to watch her weight. As the most traveled monarch in history, she recognized that planning for her visits took place months, sometimes years, in advance. She might be being fitted for gowns and dresses that would not see light of day for many months. Hence the careful diet to avoid unnecessary alterations. If her wardrobe was a metaphor for her reign—steady, unchanging, and predictable—so was her daily routine. It had the cozy familiarity of a well-worn shoe, a shoe that a member of her staff would first break in.

At eight in the morning her personal maid would arrive with a calling tray with a pot of Earl Grey tea. Her bath was run to a depth of seven inches and a temperature of seventy-two degrees Fahrenheit—tested by thermometer. Her clothes were laid out, her hairdresser was waiting, and her personal piper would play beneath her windows at nine o'clock sharp.[2] So her day would continue: a modest breakfast of cereal, a ten o'clock meeting with her private secretary, matters of state discussed, correspondence considered, especially those memos and letters in the famous red boxes. Even late into her reign, when most people her age have retired, the queen is kept busy with the nation's business. This may have included a greeting or farewell to an ambassador, an investiture, or a lunch with charity and business heads.

If she is off duty, she eats a light lunch, finds time to walk her dogs, and settles down to afternoon tea at five o'clock during which members of her staff or her family may join her. It's here where she picks up the latest chatter about the doings of her family and the Upstairs, Downstairs staff. "A good gossip is a wonderful tonic," she once remarked.[3] When she was kept up to date with all the "scandal" by a loyal cohort led by her dresser Bobo MacDonald. In her day, Princess Diana was a regular visitor and often brought William and Harry along to see "Gan Gan."

At six o'clock a drinks tray appears, then at eight fifteen it's dinnertime. This regularity has always meant that everyone knows where they stand, from the footman to the chef. There are few, if any, surprises.

If she had decided to return, Queen Victoria would have found that little had really changed since her day. There was still the Order of the Garter ceremony, the state opening of Parliament, the reception for the diplomatic corps, Christmas at Sandringham, Easter at Windsor, and the much-relished family holiday at Balmoral, the queen's 50,000-acre estate which hugs the river Dee in the Scottish Highlands. This was perhaps the last royal kingdom, the one place where the queen was monarch of all she surveyed.

At this Scottish seat the rhythms and routines were unchanging—apart from the daily wardrobe. The queen has always liked the familiarity of the place, thankful that she is able to sleep in the same bed for six weeks continuously as she enjoyed what she called her "hibernation." It is a place where she is at her most secure and relaxed, surrounded by her beloved dogs and horses. Houseguests are usually friends of long standing or her and Philip's Hanoverian relations, those who were close enough to call her by the family name of Lilibet. They know the form and the codes and know how to treat her as queen, whether blood relation or lifelong friend. Even her staff are old Balmoral hands who know when to keep themselves scarce and when to provide attention. As the torrent of red boxes slows to a trickle the queen spends her days riding, roaming around the estate, checking on improvement works, walking, or, in the evening, stargazing. It is a place where the queen has always been able to commune with her God through nature.

Visitors are often surprised at how much she does herself, from feeding her dogs and horses to mucking them out. It was a trait noticed early on by her first riding master Horace Smith. He recalled: "Princess Elizabeth's progress was very far above the average. She was very conscientious and anxious to improve her horsemanship, and her standard of riding, considering the small number of lessons that she had, soon became very high."[4] For most of her life she has stuck to a familiar daily routine during her Balmoral visits. After dealing with state business with her private secretary, at ten thirty sharp she goes riding. Her chosen horse will already been taken out by a groom so that it was not too high-spirited. Afterward she may join the shooting party for a picnic lunch before taking a walk. After afternoon tea she changes for dinner, the fourth wardrobe variation in a day. Dinners are formal with ladies wearing long dresses and the men black tie or kilts, the queen's piper marching round the table at the end of the meal.

The pipes are not for show. She actually listens carefully and appreciates the art. During a dinner at her official residence, Holyroodhouse, she asked a regular guest, the former lord provost of Edinburgh, Eric Milligan, to listen to the pipes and tell her if he could hear anything off key. Milligan answered in the negative. The queen was quietly jubilant, going on to explain that her piper had lost a finger in a bomb explosion during a tour of duty in Iraq and had offered to stand down if he couldn't manage the correct phrasing.[5] The queen wouldn't hear of it and insisted he play on. Her faith in her piper was justified.

That decision would have been a relief for the queen's piper as the Balmoral retreat was seen as a busman's holiday for those members of staff who accompanied the royal family. Duties are light and time off plentiful; plus they enjoy frequent and informal day-to-day contact with the royal family without the presence of many of the household, essentially the managerial class, being present. They got up to all kinds of innocent pranks and games, sometimes involving younger members of the royal family. One evening was devoted to a mock trial, complete with judge, jury, and witnesses, who included Prince Andrew, which did not finish until the early hours. Another legendary story involved a drunken and comatose footman who was carefully carried into the royal dining room in his single bed and left there. When they came down for breakfast, the queen and Prince Philip, having been forewarned about the unwanted guest, put on a show of indifference that added to the general amusement.[6]

The Ghillies Ball is the much- anticipated climax to the royal family's Scottish holiday. It brought royalty and staff together in a blend of jovial informality, good manners, and earthy tradition. During Queen Victoria's day the balls were drunken affairs with servants collapsing in the ballroom and the diminutive sovereign whisked off her feet by kilted ghillies as the pipes whirled and skirled into the early hours.

Later it was the queen who chose her dancing partner, which made for a nervous evening for those who hadn't practiced their Highland dancing. Mischievously she would often choose someone known for having two left feet—her Scotland Yard bodyguards were favorite targets. If it was a novice she would indicate to the bandleader to slow the pace. She takes the Highland reels very seriously. On one occasion she was discussing a new dance and, to the surprise of the company, slipped off her shoes and manipulated her stocking feet in order to get into the correct position.

Picnics are another social ritual with traps for the unwary. Most evenings the queen and her family and guests enjoy a picnic in one of the shooting lodges on the estate. They are not rough-and-ready affairs, boiled eggs and blankets spread out on the heather, but rather grand occasions. Acknowledging the elaborate nature of the Windsor picnic, Princess Margaret once observed: "You can't possibly have a picnic without your butler."[7] The Windsor picnic arrived in a specially made mobile kitchen, designed by Prince Philip and towed by a Land Rover. Every table setting had its special place, and the queen carefully supervised the whole event.

Princess Margaret's former lady-in-waiting Lady Glenconner, a seasoned houseguest, liked to tell the story of the time she and her husband Colin started clearing up at the end of the meal. As they carried dirty plates back to the mobile kitchen, Princess Anne asked what on earth they were doing. She said fiercely that if they didn't put things back properly, "The queen will be bloody angry with you."[8]

Gulp. Even Lady Glenconner, onetime deb of the year, scion of Holkham Hall, and chat-show star, admitted she got sweaty-palmed at the very idea of HMQ being "bloody angry." It was a chilling family trait, one minute fooling around, the next glaring and grand. Of course Princess Margaret was the worst offender, but they all had that ability to turn it on and off in a heartbeat. A surefire way to glimpse the Windsor glare was, in conversation with Prince Charles, William, or any of the family, to refer to the queen as "your mother" or "your grandmother." Way too chummy and lacking in respect.

As Lady Glenconner was an old Balmoral hand and had attended numerous barbecues over the years, there may have been an element of exaggeration in her descriptions of both Princess Anne's and the queen's expected reactions in order to season the yarn. What is true is that the queen liked to take charge of the precise placement of dining utensils in the custom-made Land Rover.[9] This obsessive attention to detail is reminiscent of the childhood stories of the young princess carefully lining up her shoes several times each evening before she went to bed.

However, it was unusual for the queen to be "bloody angry." Her response to a faux pas or an internal palace cock-up was far more measured and modulated. She learned from an early age that a full-blown regal rebuke can make even the stoutest heart quail. When her father George VI was in the midst of one of his gnashes, his outbursts of uncontrolled anger, court-iers would be left ashen-faced and trembling.

A sharp look, a raised eyebrow, or a quizzical "Are you sure?" tended to be the regal lexicon of reproof. The queen was so controlled that when she did, very occasionally, lose her temper, those present remembered the moment for the rest of their lives.

❧

It was on one of her walks on her Scottish estate, in early August 1979, that she first encountered Lady Diana Spencer. She was somewhat perplexed as she half remembered her but assigned the third daughter of Earl Spencer, one of her equerries from the early years of her reign, as being part of the Sandringham quadrant of her life.

Diana had grown up in the grounds of the queen's twenty-thousand-acre Norfolk estate at Park House and as a little girl was invited over to play with Andrew and Edward and, during the Christmas holidays, to watch films. If she was mentioned at all it was as a playmate and later, a possible girlfriend for Prince Andrew, who was of a similar age.

During their conversation the winsome, rosy-cheeked eighteen-year-old explained that she was staying with her newly married sister Jane and her husband, the queen's assistant pri-vate secretary Robert Fellowes. She described Balmoral as "magical," a sentiment that found favor with the queen. The following summer the queen met Diana at Balmoral under quite different circumstances. This time she was a guest of Prince Charles. Everyone on the estate knew what that meant. She was undergoing what was colloquially known as the Balmoral test to see if she was suitable royal bride material. Could she divine the elusive Windsor country code or at least be a willing pupil? Those older and wiser than her had tried and failed. Some had not even bothered. Prince Charles's one-time girlfriend, Scottish heiress Anna "Whiplash" Wallace, so named because of her fiery temper, refused at the first fence, telling her royal boyfriend that the idea of going to the Windsor family seat was "too tedious for words."

For others the possible marital commitment implied by joining the royal family at Balmoral was an attachment too far. Lady Jane Wellesley, the daughter of the queen's friend the Duke of Wellington, bridled at the very idea of sacrificing her life on the altar of monarchy. "Do you honestly believe I want to be queen," she once said when cornered by inquisitive reporters.[10]

The bookies' favorite had been Amanda Knatchbull, Mountbatten's granddaughter who was even given a blank check by the ambitious patriarch to improve her wardrobe. Amanda, like a lengthening list of eligible young ladies, eventually decided a lifetime of sacrifice for the House of Windsor was not what she was put on this earth for.

Others, like Sabrina Guinness, accepted the invitation to Balmoral but then failed to crack the code. Even though her previous escorts included Jack Nicholson, Mick Jagger, and David Bowie, she found herself in an intimidating world. When she joined the royal family for drinks, she went to sit in a high-backed chair only to be told firmly by the queen: "Don't sit there—that's Queen Victoria's chair."[11] She never recovered her equilibrium after being admonished by the head of state. On a different occasion another member of the royal family delivered a similar reproof to a friend of the then Lady Diana Spencer and, according to others, the same happened to Tony Blair when he and Cherie arrived for the traditional prime minister's weekend.

This routine has the feeling of a long-running family in-joke, the Windsor equivalent of sitting on an embarrassingly placed whoopee cushion or skidding on a banana skin. Their sense of humor was somewhat Teutonic in the sense of laughing at another's misfortune or schadenfreude. The younger royals, in particular Prince Andrew, hailed from the bread-roll-throwing academy of schoolboy humor. It is a kind of bullying as the recipient, unless a very close friend, is uncertain how to react—throw one back or take it on the chin. During one raucous picnic on a beach during a cruise the royals and their guests, the queen excepted, threw small pellets of bird dung at one another, a jolly activity that culminated in everyone, once again the queen excepted, being thrown into the sea.

By contrast her humor was on the dry side, like her evening martini. She and her husband would smile conspiratorially at each other when things went wrong on a royal tour, the classic being her visit to California in 1983.

Unintentional irony always tickles the regal funny bone. There is a story, possibly apocryphal, that during a regal visit to a coastal town, the mayor, resplendent in his gold chains of office, proudly showed her around wooden cabinets displaying local treasures in the council chamber. In one was a splendid mayoral chain embellished with gold and gems. When the queen asked what it was, the mayor replied that it was a unique chain of office that was only brought out for very special occasions.[12] She needed all of Queen Mary's self-control not to burst into laughter.

Given her ingrained awareness of how those not in the immediate family can react to her presence, her admonishment of Charles's girlfriend for sitting on Queen Victoria's chair uncharacteristically jars. She has a well-deserved reputation of being a careful and thoughtful hostess, inspecting bedrooms before guests arrived and thinking of suitable books and flowers to place in their rooms. At pre-dinner drinks she is usually at her most relaxed, solicitous and humorous, such as the time Princess Margaret was chatting to thriller writer Denys Rhodes. She asked him how he was getting on with his latest book. "It's nearly finished," he replied, "but I desperately need a title." At which point a voice behind said gaily: "And I cannot think of a reason for giving you one." It was the queen, most amused with herself at this bon mot.[13] So why did she embarrass Charles's girlfriend Sabrina Guinness? The most benign explanation is that it was a social reflex, that she had said it so often over the years there was an assumption everyone knew what to expect. Or it was an unexpected lapse in someone who was constantly attuned to the sensitivities of others. Alternatively, she disapproved of Charles's cosmopolitan girlfriend with her rock-and-roll lovers and this was one way of making her feelings known.

Fortunately Diana did not get the Queen Victoria chair treatment. During the fateful visit in September 1980, the queen expressed her satisfaction with her eldest son's choice of houseguest. The Spencers were well known to the royal family, in fact Charles had dated Diana's older sister Sarah several years before. For her part, Lady Diana Spencer was jolly, jaunty, and joined in. Even when she fell into a bog on a long tramp she came up laughing. She had a dry sense of humor rather like, well, her own. Diana knew the form, fitted in, and, to Prince Philip's relief, wasn't a stranger. "She is one of us," the queen wrote to a friend. "I am very fond of all three of the Spencer girls."[14] That wasn't the whole story—Diana told me years later that before she arrived at Balmoral she was terrified-"shitting bricks" with nerves.

That, though, is not the impression she left with fellow guests, who admired her guile when she accompanied Prince Charles on a fishing expedition on the banks of the river Dee. Every summer photographers patrolled along the A93 road on the public side of the Dee hoping for a glimpse of Charles with his latest squeeze. Award-winning photographer Ken Lennox, who has been taking pictures of the royal family in Deeside for decades, spotted the prince and noticed that there was a girl lurking nearby. By the time he had gotten himself into position to take a picture, the young lady in question had spotted him and very calmly walked away up the bank out of sight. When Lennox next located her he could see that she was standing behind a tree using her compact mirror to watch him. In this curious cat-and-mouse game Diana proved herself to be no ordinary quarry.

Once he had discovered her name, though, the hunt was on, the *Sun* newspaper splashing with the headline: HE'S IN LOVE AGAIN. Within days there wasn't a man, woman, or child in Britain who didn't know that Lady Diana Spencer was a polite if rather bashful kindergarten teacher whose father was the Eighth Earl of Spencer and whose family home was Althorp Hall in Northamptonshire.

An earl's daughter at last. The queen mother was delighted, especially as Diana's grandmother Ruth, Lady Fermoy, was one of her ladies-in-waiting. The queen and Prince Philip also felt that Diana ticked all the boxes: white, Anglo-Saxon, Protestant, aristocratic, and without a known past. Her uncle Lord Fermoy trumpeted that she had never had a lover. In their eyes, too, it hopefully ended their eldest son's dangerous entanglement with Camilla Parker Bowles, the wife of fellow officer Andrew Parker Bowles.

All seemed to be going swimmingly in Charles's latest

courtship. While Diana was caught up in the excitement of it all, members of her family sounded notes of caution. Her grandmother Lady Ruth Fermoy articulated her concerns. "You must understand that their sense of humor and their lifestyle are very different and I don't think it will suit you."[15] It was a diplomatic way of saying that she had doubts about Diana and her suitability as Charles's wife and consort but also a warning that, even though she might be a member of the aristocracy, there was still a social and cultural divide between royalty and the upper classes.

There was also the looming presence of Mrs. Parker Bowles, which was a matter of concern for both Diana and the queen. In November 1980 Bob Edwards, editor of the *Sunday Mirror,* ran a story suggesting that Lady Diana had secretly joined Prince Charles aboard the Royal Train at Holt, Wiltshire. Acting on the personal instructions of the queen, the palace denounced the story and demanded a retraction. Edwards refused, quoting an "impeccable source."[16] Diana knew that she hadn't been on the Royal Train but had a jolly good idea who had been: Mrs. Parker Bowles. The scales were beginning to fall from her eyes. Unbeknownst to the queen and her court, another, ultimately calamitous narrative was developing.

During that fevered Christmas and New Year at Sandringham, the influx of national and international media was such that the queen herself felt under siege. She could not even ride out without being photographed. It was so frustrating that at one point she snapped, shouting at photographers to go away. It was a measure of her impotence and anger that her holiday was being interrupted in this unruly manner. The cause of the queen's unease was the innocent presence of Lady Diana Spencer in the house party—again at the invitation of Her Majesty. As she later told me: "The Queen was fed up." For his part the Prince of Wales was indecisive and confused about his romantic future. This was nothing new. His romantic prevarication toward Camilla Shand, now Parker Bowles, was now a matter of profound regret.

As he pondered his next move, his circle of friends weighed in on Diana's suitability. The endorsement was hardly enthusiastic. Princess Anne thought the third Spencer daughter a "silly girl"[17]—perhaps in retaliation for Charles's own dismissal of her choice of husband as "Fog"—while Mountbatten's grandson Norton Romsey and his wife Penny felt Diana was in love with the position rather than the man.

Years later when I was researching my biography *Diana: Her True Story*, which was written with the complete participation and enthusiastic support of the late princess, I asked Diana and her best friend Carolyn Bartholomew that very question: position or man? Both, speaking at different times, unhesitatingly said, "Man." While Diana was certain in her mind about her love for Prince Charles, he was unsure. It was such an awesome commitment.

The queen was more matter-of-fact. She thought that Diana's supportive, positive nature and girlish high spirits would make an ideal foil for her often disconsolate, melancholic son. The young kindergarten helper would, she thought, make a perfect companion and helpmate. At the same time, after her encounter with the scruffy ranks of the mass media in her own backyard, the queen sympathized with Diana's situation. Every time she left her shared apartment in Coleherne Court, Earls Court, she was tailed by a phalanx of photographers. The queen accepted, even if her son did not, that this state of affairs couldn't continue for much longer. It was damaging both to the reputation of the crown and to Lady Diana. In part the situation was one of Prince Charles's own making as he had suggested in a magazine interview that thirty was a good age to marry. From the moment he celebrated that significant birthday the marital starting gun was fired, every girl he so much as looked at considered a future queen. During the siege of Sandringham, the queen spoke to Prince Philip and he, as was his custom, dealt with the matter by writing a letter. This was not unusual; all the royal children received letters of some sort or other from "Pa." It was a traditional way the family had of broaching delicate or emotional matters. In what he considered to be a sympathetic and understanding missive, Charles's father outlined the issues facing both sides. The relationship had gone far enough. Either it should be ended for the sake of the reputation of an innocent girl or the prince should ask for her hand in marriage. In short, stop dithering. When the full disaster of his marriage unfolded Charles would later tell friends that his father had bullied him into marriage, that the letter was an ultimatum. Even his circle didn't interpret it that way. They felt that his father was simply asking him to make a decision one way or another. Charles, used to his father's bombastic nature, read between the lines and concluded that Prince Philip, speaking also on behalf of his mother, wanted him to get on with it.

Ultimately his letter did have the desired effect of provoking his eldest son into action. Charles returned from a skiing trip and asked Diana to Windsor Castle as he had something important to say to her. They met in the nursery, a bare, unremarkable room with worn green carpet and matching colored walls studded with ancient family photographs. Hardly the stuff of a fairy-tale romance. Not a rose or flickering candle in sight. Even the gruff Prince Philip managed a proposal at Balmoral "beside some well-loved loch, the white clouds overhead and curlew crying."[18]

Diana arrived at Windsor Castle about five o'clock on February 6, 1981, to be asked by Prince Charles if she would marry him. Diana took up the story: "I laughed. I remember thinking: 'This is a joke,' and I said: 'Yeah, OK,' and laughed. He was deadly serious. He said: 'You do realize that one day you will be Queen.' And a voice said to me inside: 'You won't be Queen but you'll have a tough role.' So I thought: 'OK,' so I said: 'Yes.' I said: 'I love you so much, I love you so much.' He said: 'Whatever love means.' He said it then."[19] Then he rang the queen.

Whatever love means: three words that came to haunt him, especially as he repeated almost the same equivocal phrase during the engagement interview before the world's media on February 24, 1981, on the lawn at Buckingham Palace. Then he said "Whatever 'in love' means." His ambivalence was unnerving for the princess to be.

From an upper-floor window, the queen watched the couple and attendant media unnoticed. It was a moment of quiet triumph. After so many years of prevarication by her son, at last he had chosen a girl who had the pedigree, personality, and popularity to support and nurture the future king. At last the kingdom seemed secure.

At this moment of triumph, shadowy forces plotted to assassinate the head of state. The success, as the Provisional IRA saw it, of Mountbatten's murder eighteen months previously had encouraged them to aim higher.

This time the queen was in the crosshairs of their murderous campaign. As the palace planners prepared for the wedding of the year, the IRA began their own deadly plotting. On May 9, just over eleven weeks before the wedding, the queen was due to open Sullom Voe oil refinery on the Shetland Islands, a place so far north it was as near to Norway as Britain. Employing more than six thousand workers and costing £1.2 billion

($6.5 billion in 2021), the facility, which took six years to build, was one of Europe's largest construction projects.[20]

Unknown to the site's operators, the oil company BP, at least one of the workers there was a member of the Provisional IRA. When the queen was due to open the facility, tensions across the water in Northern Ireland were at an all-time high. The death of IRA hunger striker Bobby Sands at the Maze prison on May 5 sparked fierce rioting in nationalist areas and an upsurge in IRA attacks.

While violence raged in Northern Ireland, on the Shetland Isles the IRA unit at Sullom Voe received a parcel posted from Ireland. It contained seven pounds of gelignite and a twelve-day timer device. A second bomb was also due to arrive but was delayed in the post. The IRA operative, fearing that the second bomb had been intercepted by security services, hid the first bomb in a power station, set the timer, and then escaped back to Ireland.

As the band struck up the national anthem and the queen prepared to deliver her speech, there was a sharp bang from the power station five hundred yards away, the noise mainly masked by the band. Fortunately the first bomb only partially detonated, and BP was able to claim that the small explosion was just an electrical fault. If the Irish postal service had been more efficient, Saturday, May 9, would have gone down in infamy—especially as the queen was also accompanied by Prince Philip and King Olav V of Norway.

Given the confusion surrounding the "non explosion," the incident received scant attention, much to the fury of the Provisional IRA, which felt obliged to release two statements claiming responsibility. The second stated: "Had we managed to place Saturday's bomb close enough to the British Queen she would now be dead."[21] Their claims were overshadowed by the attempted assassination of Pope John Paul II later that month and the happier news that the queen had become a grandmother for the second time following the birth, on May 15, of Zara Phillips, the infant daughter of Princess Anne and Captain Mark Phillips.

Just a month later the queen faced another assault, this time with the world watching. As she rode along the Mall on her nineteen-year-old Canadian horse Burmese during the annual Trooping the Colour ceremony, six shots rang out from the crowd. The gun was fired by Marcus Sarjeant, then seventeen, who was quickly wrestled to the ground by two guardsmen, a police officer, and a St. John Ambulance volunteer. Amid a flurry of activity, the queen, who had seen her assailant for a split second before he fired at her, was a study in calm. Years of riding experience meant she was able to soothe her startled mount, who was more alarmed by horsemen of the Household Cavalry riding toward her than the initial gunshots, which it later turned out were blanks fired from a starting pistol.

The queen, who was riding sidesaddle, continued the ceremony without demur, smiling at the crowd and occasionally patting Burmese with her left hand. Lady Diana Spencer, who was attending her first Trooping as Charles's fiancée, recalled that everyone around the queen marveled at her sang froid. She seemed utterly unruffled by the experience, the sovereign airily dismissing the danger she had just faced. Prince Charles later commented that his mother was "made of strong stuff."[22] It took a lot to unsettle her equilibrium.

There was, too, a sense of fatalism about her behavior. Unlike other heads of state, she always made it clear that she wanted security kept to a minimum. Her personal protection officer knew to keep a discreet, unobtrusive presence. It was many years into her reign, for example, that she accepted the need for police outriders to stop traffic, as she didn't want to inconvenience fellow road users. She was backed to the hilt by Prince Philip, who had little time for the cocoon of security. There is, too, a streak of obduracy in her makeup. She is the queen and she will, for example, decide whether or not she will wear a hard hat while out riding. Well into her nineties, she insisted on an Hermès scarf as her only protection.[23] Safety campaigners were concerned, but as far as the monarch was concerned she didn't want to have to mess her hair in case she had to be on public parade shortly after her morning ride.

After the engagement was announced, the queen went out of her way to make Diana feel welcome. She had deputed several courtiers, notably her lady-in-waiting Susan Hussey and Charles's assistant private secretary Oliver Everett, to show her the ropes. When Charles was away on overseas visits, the queen took the future princess under her wing. She installed her in the principal guest room at Windsor Castle, and the couple dined together frequently and walked her pack of dogs around the grounds. By now Diana was suffering from the eating disorder bulimia nervosa, a condition of bingeing and forced vomiting. Though her wedding dress makers David and Elizabeth Emanuel and her close friends, particularly Carolyn Bartholomew, noticed her rapid weight loss, the queen seemed not to have seen the warning signs. At the time eating disorders were surrounded by ignorance; it would have been remarkable if the queen had even been aware of this condition. Even if she had noticed Diana's weight loss she would have instinctively put it down to the nerves felt by many brides, particularly one whose wedding day was about to be broadcast worldwide. Although she was busy, the queen did set aside time to, as a former courtier recalled, "make a big fuss over Diana."[24] In the run-up to the wedding Diana was based at Buckingham Palace, where the queen frequently invited her future daughter-in-law to join her for lunch or dinner. Diana, however, made endless excuses to avoid her company. She did not wish to alert the queen to her condition. The queen found her behavior perplexing and put it down to nerves. For her part, Diana found the queen friendly but intimidating. "I kept myself to myself," she recalled. "I didn't knock on her door and ask her advice because I knew the answers myself."[25]

In the weeks before the wedding, Diana would often visit the kitchens to while away a few minutes in idle conversation. Barefoot, wearing jeans and a sweater, she helped with the washing up and on one occasion buttered the toast of a junior footman. Her excursions behind the green baize door irritated several chefs who felt she was spying. Eventually the queen tactfully asked her to stop these visits as it was upsetting the equilibrium between Upstairs and Downstairs. What she didn't realize was that Diana visited the kitchens so that she could gorge on packets of cereal and cream. Then she would make herself sick afterward.

At the time the queen was fully and enthusiastically invested in her son's marriage. Not only did she pay £28,000 ($135,000 in 2021) for Diana's oval sapphire-and-diamond engagement ring, she footed the bill for the opulent wedding ball at Buckingham Palace where the extensive guest list included First Lady Nancy Reagan together with all the crowned heads of Europe. The splendid, extravagant affair was a personal triumph for the queen. It was certainly a night to remember, though the grand affair was set against a backdrop of high, and mounting, unemployment, riots in deprived areas of London and Liverpool, and a government, led by Prime Minister Margaret Thatcher, that preached and practiced austerity and low taxes. She saw the queen for an audience every week for eleven years, but the two women, though cordial, were never close. Thatcher's official biographer Charles Moore described the prime minister as "too nervous" during these meetings for them to be productive.[26]

While the juxtaposition of the two Britains was striking—particularly to foreign television crews—on the wedding day itself, July 21, 1981, the focus was on Diana's meringue of a dress with its record-breaking twenty-five-foot train, the romantic contention of the Archbishop of Canterbury Dr. Robert Runcie that this was "the stuff of fairy tales," and the enthusiastic crowds that lined the route from St. Paul's Cathedral to Buckingham Palace to watch the horse-drawn parade.[27] It was only later that the head of the Church of England admitted to doubts, the prelate believing that the couple were ill suited and that the marriage would not last. Inside the cathedral, there were others who were equally concerned about the marriage's foundation, including the bride herself. One of her abiding memories was spotting Camilla Parker Bowles, who was wearing a gray outfit with a matching pillbox hat, and hoping that that relationship was now at an end. It was a sentiment that would have found an echo with the queen, who had edged toward tackling her son on the subject only to be told by the Prince of Wales, according to a rumor recorded in historian Hugo Vickers's diary, "My marriage and my sex life have nothing to do with each other."[28]

For all the doubts, everything seemed well when they returned to Balmoral from their Mediterranean honeymoon aboard the royal yacht *Britannia*. They were healthy, suntanned, and all smiles as they greeted family and staff who formed a guard of honor along the castle drive. "It was a glorious afternoon," recalled a member of staff. "We cheered and we clapped and everything seemed so cheerful and bright."[29]

It was an illusion, the truth about their honeymoon

emerging over time in hints and whispers. The princess, who suffered from a combination of exhaustion, bulimia, and jealousy, worried that her husband's heart still belonged to another. When photographs of Camilla fell out of his diary and he wore cufflinks with C intertwined with C—a gift from Mrs. Parker Bowles—it was the prelude to an out-and-out row.

They were all smiles for a media photo call by the banks of the river Dee, the princess, in a response to a question about married life, saying that she could "highly recommend" it.[30] During their extended stay at the castle the couple would go for long walks together, or he would take out his easel and paints and Diana would practice her embroidery. On other occasions Charles read to her from the works of his friend, the South African philosopher Laurens van der Post, or from Carl Jung. To add to this scene of romantic tranquility, the prince would give his bride love notes or billets-doux.

Diana, though, was anything but content. She found her revised status and the family dynamic difficult to come to terms with. It was only years later that she expressed her true feelings. She told me: "All the guests at Balmoral just stared at me the whole time and treated me like glass. As far as I was concerned I was Diana, the only difference was people called me 'Ma'am' now, 'Your Royal Highness' and they curtsied."[31]

For her part she felt an outsider, her husband always deferring to the queen or queen mother rather than taking her needs into account. An early sign that all was not well with the fairy tale was that Diana stayed in her room rather than joining the rest of the family for picnics or barbecues. Her resolute refusal to join in irritated the queen not only because of the discourtesy to her as host but also because it interrupted the smooth running of the castle as it meant changing staff rotas so that someone was available to attend Diana herself.

Princess Margaret came to her rescue, suggesting to the queen that Diana was having difficulties adjusting to her role and that she should cut her some slack. "Let her do what she likes," said Margaret. "Leave her alone and she will be all right."[32]

But the issues she faced involved much more than cutting Diana some slack. She had been overtaken by what she later called "the dark ages" of her life. Diana was consumed with jealousy, whether warranted or not, regarding Charles and Camilla, her bulimia was rampant, and she suffered wild mood swings. Nor did it help that it was one of the wettest and windiest Balmoral holidays on record. Diana agreed to seek professional counseling and advice. A doctor was summoned from London and, after a confidential consultation, concluded that she needed time and space to adjust to the drastic change in her circumstances. She had drawn a similar conclusion herself. Drugs were prescribed but she refused them. Instead she and Charles moved out of the big house to Craigowan, a small shooting lodge on the estate. She invited friends, including her former flat mate Carolyn Bartholomew, to stay. At the end of October she was able to announce that she was expecting her first child. The queen and the rest of the family were delighted, their happiness tempered by hope that motherhood would end Diana's "little local difficulties."

10

❦

Marriages Under the Microscope

Everyone from the queen downward was taken aback by the intense and continuing interest in the Princess of Wales. The queen and her advisers thought that, once the excitement of the wedding had dissipated, the princess would fade into the background and Prince Charles would renew his position in the royal limelight. It just didn't happen. Even newspaper and magazine editors were surprised by the public's reaction to the latest addition to the royal family. No matter how flimsy the story or grainy the image of the future queen, Diana sold and kept on selling, the princess seen as the golden goose who laid the circulation eggs. As she succinctly put it: "One minute I was nobody, the next minute I was Princess of Wales, mother, media toy, member of this family, you name it, and it was too much for one person at that time."[1]

The consequences were ominous. Diana, suffering badly from bulimia and morning sickness, found herself followed every time she left Balmoral, Kensington Palace, or Highgrove. A visit to the shops or the gym became an unpleasant obstacle course as she navigated her way past the numerous photographers who harassed her.

By instinct and convention the queen held back from interfering in the marriages of her children. However, seeing the daily trial by media endured by the pregnant princess, the queen felt that she could address that particular problem. She tended to agree with her daughter-in-law, who emphasized that she needed "time and space" to come to terms with her new royal role. The queen's press secretary Michael Shea was asked to organize a cocktail party for newspaper, TV, and wire services editors. Only Kelvin MacKenzie, editor of the *Sun*, the most aggressive of the tabloids, refused the invitation for the pre-Christmas gathering.

Shea told the assembled throng that Diana was "increasingly despondent" about the fact that she could not leave her front door without being followed by photographers.[2] He asked for restraint and the queen, in an unusual show of support and concern for her daughter-in-law, appeared and spoke to various groups of editors to reinforce that message.

It was hardly a mutual appreciation society. Barry Askew, then editor of the now defunct *News of the World*, told the queen that if the princess wanted privacy she should send a servant to buy sweets from the shops instead of going herself. The queen tartly responded: "That was the most pompous remark I have ever heard, Mr. Askew."[3]

The irony of the queen, who rarely visited shops, criticizing the Sunday editor's insensitive remarks was lost in the general and gleeful condemnation of the hapless Askew, who shortly afterward was sacked.

Within a matter of weeks, the queen's personal appeal to

the media was in tatters. In February 1982, two tabloids, the *Sun* and the *Daily Star,* published pictures of Diana, then five months' pregnant, running through the surf in a bikini on the island of Windermere in the Caribbean where she and her husband were enjoying a holiday in the sun. The prince and princess were livid while the queen described the intrusion as "one of the blackest days in the history of British journalism."[4] The honeymoon between the royal family and the media, such as it was, was very firmly over. Though both newspapers affected contrition, the plain facts were that photographs of the princess, especially the princess in a bikini, sold like hotcakes. The queen and her advisers were in direct conflict with the immutable laws of the market.

Thankfully the ever-eager media had not gotten wind of the real drama that was taking place beneath the queen's roof. With every passing day, it became clearer that the marriage of the Prince and Princess of Wales, the future king and queen, was not working. A tearful confrontation between the two at Sandringham in January 1982, several weeks before they headed off for their holiday in the sun, exposed the growing divide.

They had a blazing row about Charles and his indifferent behavior toward his young wife. What took place next shocked the queen and those present. Diana, according to her account, threw herself down the stairs at the North End staircase that leads to the queen mother's rooms. Even though she was in tears, Charles accused her of crying wolf and stalked out of the house to go riding. As she lay in a crumpled heap on the stairs, the queen was one of the first to arrive. Diana later told me: "The Queen comes out, absolutely horrified, shaking—she was so frightened."[5] Her concern was that Diana could possibly suffer a miscarriage.

Others who were present recall a less dramatic encounter.

They remember that Diana seemed to trip as she was walking down the stairs and ended up by the corgi food bowls at the bottom of the staircase, which the queen mother was replenishing at the time. The queen and other members of the family were alerted to the incident by the queen's page. When they arrived, Diana was dusting herself off, said that she was absolutely fine, and apologized for causing a fuss. As a precaution she was examined by a doctor to confirm that all was well with the princess and her unborn child.

Even if the queen had taken her at her word, and it was a trip rather than a deliberate self-inflicted fall, Charles's indifference and Diana's emotional behavior were cause for alarm. She was in a predicament. The queen couldn't force the couple to love or even like each other. She had played that card with the calamitous marriage of her sister Princess Margaret and her husband Tony Snowdon. That had ended in the first divorce in the royal family since Henry VIII. The difference was that the Snowdons' marriage went wrong after a few years, not a few months. Her watchwords for her son and daughter-in-law were to be patient and show understanding. This marriage could not conceivably end in the divorce courts.

❦

In March 1982 the arrival of a group of Argentinian scrap metal workers on the isolated and inhospitable British island of South Georgia in the South Atlantic put an end to these concerns—at least for the time being. Ostensibly the party landed to demolish an old whaling station, though diplomatic sources suspected that they were a provocative advance party sent at the behest of the ruling Argentinian military junta, which had long claimed dominion of this remote territory and the larger Falkland Islands some miles west. Matters quickly escalated and the islands, which were guarded by a small contingent of Royal Marines, were overrun by massed Argentine forces. Prime Minister Margaret Thatcher vowed to retake the British colony and mustered a task force to reassert Britain's dominion.

The hastily assembled naval armada included Sub-Lieutenant Prince Andrew, who was a Sea King helicopter pilot based aboard the aircraft carrier HMS *Invincible*. On Thursday, April 1, Thatcher traveled to Windsor Castle to warn the queen about the potential conflict in the South Atlantic and the government's intent to defend Britain's sovereign territory. When the issue of Prince Andrew and his role in the conflict was raised, the queen, speaking on behalf of her son and her husband, who saw active service during World War Two, insisted that Andrew be treated like any other naval officer.

According to one report the prince threatened to resign his commission if the *Invincible* sailed without him. Shortly after the mini summit, Buckingham Palace released a short statement from the queen: "Prince Andrew is a serving officer and there is no question in her mind that he should go." On April 5 the prince and his fellow officers sailed off to an uncertain and dangerous future in the South Atlantic.

What neither he, the queen, nor Mrs. Thatcher realized at the time was that the Argentinian junta considered the capture or death of Prince Andrew and the sinking of the *Invincible* as their primary war aim. At a meeting of the Argentinian chief of staffs in Buenos Aires, Admiral Jorge Anaya explained to his colleagues, "This is an easy war to win. All we have to do is sink one ship—the *Invincible* and Britain will crumble." His plan was to launch an audacious air raid and concentrate the entire Argentinian air force on the British aircraft carrier.[6]

Prince Andrew's role was already inherently dangerous. Not only was his unit, the 820 Naval Air Squadron, involved in search and rescue, submarine reconnaissance, and airborne supply, but his Sea King was assigned the role of an Exocet decoy. The Argentine air force was armed with French-made Exocet missiles, and the theory was that when one was launched at the *Invincible* from an enemy jet, the helicopter would attract the projectile away from the ship. Once it was spotted heading for the helicopter, the pilot would soar upward and the Exocet fly harmlessly underneath before falling into the water. At least that was the theory. In reality the Sea King was a sacrifice to save the aircraft carrier. It was such a terrifying assignment that years later when he gave an interview to the BBC regarding his friendship with convicted pedophile Jeffrey Epstein, Prince Andrew admitted that the adrenaline rush he suffered while under fire in the Falklands conflict left him unable to sweat.

The "frightening" incident that prompted this condition came during the much-vaunted attack on HMS *Invincible*. Instead of hitting the aircraft carrier, the assault, which took place on May 25, ended with the sinking of the 695-foot container ship *Atlantic Conveyor* and the deaths of twelve crew members.

In Buenos Aires the junta falsely claimed that they had sunk the *Invincible* and issued doctored photographs to the world media. Like any parents, the queen and her husband were concerned about their son, especially knowing the precarious position of the task force.

The next day, May 26, 1982, at the opening of the giant Kielder Water in Northumberland, the queen told the crowds. "Before I begin, I would like to say one thing. Our thoughts today are with those in the South Atlantic, and our prayers are for their success and safe return to their homes and loved ones."[7] Days later the queen was shaken once more by further claims from Argentina that her son was wounded and in enemy hands and that *Invincible* was a blazing hulk. Even Princess Anne made a rare visit to her local church in Gloucestershire to join a prayer service for the well-being of the fighting men in the South Atlantic.

The British task force ultimately prevailed, and following the Argentinian surrender on June 14, Andrew took the opportunity visit the islands' capital, Port Stanley, where he spoke to his "surprised" mother using one of the few satellite phones.[8]

He was another two months at sea and during that time he suffered a demotion to third in line to the throne after his sister-in-law gave birth to Prince William on June 21. One of the first visitors was the queen, who inspected the mite at St. Mary's Hospital in central London. "Thank goodness he hasn't [got] ears like his father," was the queen's droll observation.[9] Her eldest son's ears were so prominent that not only were they the subject of media ridicule but the prince had considered an operation to pin them back.

In a truly momentous summer, cartoonists struggled to depict an episode in the queen's life that was as comic as it was bizarre. In the early morning of July 9, Michael Fagan, an unemployed laborer with mental health issues, broke into Buckingham Palace and, after a series of flukes, managed to find his way into the queen's bedroom. The queen, who was startled awake, twice rang for the police for help and, in an effort to placate him, listened intently as he told her about his marital and financial issues. This was the queen behaving not as figurehead but as mother figure.

This was the second time Fagan had managed to break into the palace undetected, and if nothing else his incursion showed the wholly inadequate security system that was in place. On the second occasion he specifically wanted to see the queen, in his mind an idealized maternal symbol, to help sort out the mess he found himself in. He later told me: "I wanted her to be the woman I could communicate with, who would understand me and my everyday aspirations. I wanted her to know me. This woman is the pinnacle of our society, the summit of our dreams. We are tribal animals and the Queen is the head of the tribe. I wanted to speak to our chieftain."[10]

The queen recognized her mythical status and once remarked that she accepted that she was seen as a Jungian archetype, a concept developed by the psychologist Carl Jung whereby society projects its dreams of motherhood, justice, and leadership on the figure of the monarch.

During his self-imposed quest Fagan walked from his home in Islington, north London, to the perimeter of Buckingham Palace.

He easily scaled the wall, got through an open window, and before long found himself in the Throne Room. By good fortune he accidentally pressed a hidden handle in the dado rail that opened a secret door leading to the queen's private apartments.

His good luck continued. Normally a policeman would be sitting outside the queen's bedroom but he had gone off duty and the queen's footman, Paul Whybrew, had just taken the royal corgis for their early-morning walk. By a million-to-one chance the queen was alone and unguarded and, after quietly opening a door, Fagan found himself in her bedroom. He hid himself behind the curtains as he assessed the person in the bed, thinking at first the figure was so small it must be a child. He pulled the curtains aside to get a better look. The shaft of light woke the queen who saw, not her female maid, but a barefoot Fagan, in jeans and T-shirt, clutching a broken ashtray that had cut his thumb.

She pressed the alarm bell and then, according to the official report by Assistant Commissioner Dellow of Scotland Yard, made the first of two calls to the palace telephonist to send police to her bedroom. As the queen waited for the police, she reacted in textbook style, remaining calm and collected while she engaged the intruder in polite conversation. She listened to Fagan's tale of woe and in turn chatted about her own children, noting that Prince Charles was about Fagan's age.

Six minutes later the queen made a second call, coolly asking why there had been no response. Then she used the pretext of Fagan's craving for a cigarette to summon a maid, Elizabeth Andrew, to her bedroom. When she saw Fagan sitting on the edge of the sovereign's bed the startled housemaid uttered the immortal phrase: "Bloody hell, Ma'am. What's he doing here?"[11] Afterward her broad northern accent became part of the queen's own comic repartee.

Fagan's version, which has varied, is somewhat different. According to him, there was no conversation. Instead the queen grabbed the white telephone, asked for help, and then shouted, "Get out, get out," before she jumped out of bed herself ran across the room and out of the door. The confrontation was all over in seconds, Fagan left alone and crying by the empty bed. A few minutes later he was ushered into a pantry by Paul Whybrew who had just returned from walking the dogs.

He recalls the queen saying: "Can you give this man a drink?" The footman, astonished by the queen's calm demeanor, took an unprotesting Fagan into the Page's Vestibule and poured him a Famous Grouse whiskey.

As he did so he heard the queen screaming down the phone demanding to know why the police hadn't arrived. "I have never heard the Queen so angry," he later told colleagues.[12]

The subsequent inquiry revealed a whole catalog of

blunders, from exterior cameras and other detection devices not working on the palace perimeter to the duty police officer changing into a smarter uniform after being summoned by the monarch.

The queen was as annoyed that her domestic affairs had become a matter of consuming public interest as she was that security had allowed Fagan all the way into the royal bedroom. "Give her a cuddle, Philip," pleaded the *Daily Mirror* as the nation gleefully discussed the separate sleeping arrangements of the sovereign and her consort.[13] The reality was that the royal couple did share the same bed but, by ill luck, Prince Philip had slept in his own quarters before leaving very early to exercise his horses.

He was furious at the incompetence of the police and complimentary of his wife's bravery. She dismissed the plaudits and told friends that the entire event was too surreal to be taken seriously. There were further unhappy consequences. Michael Rauch, a male prostitute, read about the Fagan incident and visited the offices of the *Sun* newspaper to tell them about his own affair with the queen's bodyguard, Commander Michael Trestrail. The officer, nicknamed Aquarius as he carried the Queen's Malvern water, promptly resigned.[14]

It was a deeply distressing time. A few days later not only did her childhood friend and Prince Philip's private secretary Lord Rupert Nevill die but the IRA planted bombs in Hyde Park and at a bandstand in Regent's Park that killed and injured soldiers and horses of the Queen's Household Cavalry Blues and Royals and the Green Jackets. The initial blast killed four Blues and Royals soldiers and injured a further twenty-three. Seven horses were killed outright or had to be put down. One horse, Sefton, survived an eight-hour operation to removes nails and other pieces of shrapnel from his bloodied frame. A second bomb hidden in a bandstand where musicians from the Royal Green Jackets were playing killed seven and wounded more than fifty. That night the queen was heard repeating: "The poor horses, my poor soldiers," as the horror of that day sank in.[15]

Though she affected to make light of the Fagan incident, this was, according to friends, a distressing and disconcerting time that unsettled her famous equilibrium for several months. "She said she met so many dotty people that one more made no difference," recalled her friend Margaret Rhodes, who thought she was putting on a brave face to hide the shock.[16] Her instincts proved correct as the queen, feeling overwhelmed, decided for the first time in her life that she needed medical advice and counseling. She asked Betty Parsons, the no-nonsense childbirth guru who helped teach her breathing exercises before the birth of Prince Edward, to come to the palace to give her some further instruction to help restore her peace of mind.[17] Parsons's mantra was simple but effective: Drop the shoulders, breathe gently, pause, and then let the breath come in. Then repeat. The soothing repetition, which became a kind of meditation, helped restore a much-needed sense of calm in the heart of the monarch.

Her equilibrium was further improved when, on July 21, Prince Andrew returned to Portsmouth aboard HMS *Invincible*. The prince sauntered down the gangway, a red rose between his teeth, to be met by his parents who were clearly delighted, like many other families, that he had come home safe and sound. He was now celebrated as a bona-fide war hero and one of the world's most eligible bachelors.

During his leave the queen gladly gave the go-ahead for her second son and a party of friends, which included actor Kathleen "Koo" Stark whom he had been quietly dating for a while, to stay at Princess Margaret's clifftop retreat on the tiny island of Mustique. As luck would have it, a Fleet Street photographer and his girlfriend were on the same British Airways flight to Barbados as the royal party. He discovered that Andrew and Koo were traveling together under the names Mr. and Mrs. Cambridge. At the time no one could be sure that the prince had not secretly married the American actor. When it was later discovered that Koo had appeared in a tepidly erotic rite-of-passage movie called *Emily,* there was a global hue and cry orchestrated not just by newspapers but by British lawmakers who were horrified that the queen's son could have married a "soft porn star"—a description that was disgracefully wide of the mark.[18]

Such was the international media hysteria to take the first picture of the lovebirds together in paradise that one cameraman from an American supermarket tabloid considered hiring a submarine and photographing the couple through the periscope. Headlines suggesting that the queen was "furious" at Andrew's choice of partner were way wide of the mark. She had met Koo before when she was invited to Balmoral and, like Diana and other members of the family, had found her polite, bright, and conversationally adept. Her only comment when their romance became public was: "Oh, I do wish they would call you Kathleen and Andrew." In her own way the queen, who could see that Kathleen was good news for her son, tried to change the narrative about the couple. She showed her support of her son's choice when, according to Kathleen, she invited the couple for a picnic tea where they could be photographed by the paparazzi. She recalled: "Her Majesty made a point of snapping open the *News of the World* [front-page headline: QUEEN BANS KOO]. Her actions spoke volumes as she poured tea."[19] In 1983 the queen took the unusual step of going to court and accepted an out-of-court settlement over newspaper claims that Andrew's girlfriend had regularly stayed overnight at Buckingham Palace.

Perhaps inevitably the couple went their separate ways though they stayed friends.

But for an ill-judged choice early in her acting career it is likely that Kathleen Stark would have been the first American actress to marry a member of the royal family, rather than Meghan Markle.

Meanwhile the Queen's only daughter was working through tricky marital issues. The official release of photographs of Princess Anne and Captain Mark Phillips to celebrate his thirty-fourth birthday was seen by those in the know as another attempt to alter perceptions about the royal couple. They had been beset by rumors about the state of their marriage, especially after stories emerged in the tabloids that Anne's bodyguard Peter Cross had been removed from royal protection duties and transferred back to the uniformed branch after becoming "over familiar" with the queen's daughter. Even after he was pulled from royal duties, Cross and the queen's daughter kept in contact by phone or used safe houses. She used the code term Mrs. Wallis, presumably a reference to Wallis Simpson, when she called. How far the queen was privy to Anne's behavior is a matter of debate. As affairs are usually conducted in secret, it is doubtful that Anne would have confided in her mother. The queen may well, though, have been aware of the bigger, more concerning picture that her daughter's marriage was in trouble.

Equally troubling was the negative narrative about Diana that was snowballing in the popular prints. A fairy-tale princess no more, she was accused of being a "fiend" and a "monster" by influential gossip columnist Nigel Dempster, the princess deemed responsible for a wave of staff departures including Charles's bodyguard, valet, private secretary, and others. The princess, stung by this criticism, told journalists during a public engagement: "I don't just sack people."[20]

The queen showed her confidence in her daughter-in-law and agreed to her request, turned down by her private secretary Sir Philip Moore and Prince Charles, that she should represent the family and the monarchy at the funeral of Princess Grace of Monaco, who was killed in a car accident in September 1982.

Her demure and dignified manner during the emotional funeral convinced the queen that her policy of quiet understanding of and support for the Princess of Wales was paying dividends. The real turning point was the royal couple's highly successful six-week tour of New Zealand and Australia in April and May 1983. The grueling visit—the couple took over fifty flights during the tour—demonstrated to the queen that Diana had the stamina and sparkle to make these visits a success.

However, a green-eyed monster lurked beneath the surface. As the tour gathered momentum, Prince Charles became increasingly jealous of his wife's popularity. During walkabouts the crowd groaned if Charles went to their side of the street, cheering only if Diana came to shake hands. Though he made light of it in speeches, privately it rankled. It was but another indication of their growing estrangement. These scudding storm clouds gave way to a shaft of sunshine when Diana discovered that she was pregnant with her second child. A new life, a new beginning was always a source of pleasure for the queen, a sense of history in the making. Prince Harry was born on September 15, 1984, and with his arrival the queen hoped that the teething troubles of their marriage were now behind them.

She invited Andrew, a keen amateur photographer, to take her sixtieth-birthday photograph and the result was a relaxed, smiling mother, arms crossed and dressed in a twinset. She was more mumsy than monarch.

To celebrate this personal milestone, postage stamps were issued, laudatory documentaries edited, and a short musical commissioned by Prince Edward. The high point was a gala at the Royal Opera House where Frederick Ashton choreographed an eight-minute-long ballet, *Nursery Suite,* which reflected the happy childhood of the queen and her sister. Princess Margaret, knowing the character of her no-nonsense sister, warned him not to make the work too whimsical. The short ballet was a triumph; the queen, her mother, and sister all "ended up in floods of tears," Margaret wrote, after watching this affectionate portrait, sunny memories triggered by this dance to the music of time.[21]

Indeed, contrary to popular belief, the queen was not immune to tears. A week later on April 29, the Princess of Wales described her astonishment as the queen wept at the graveside of the Duchess of Windsor, a woman she had met infrequently and barely knew. She surmised that it was the passing of a somewhat tragic figure who lived her last years as a bed-bound recluse that sparked the emotion. Her tears perhaps of remembrance and regret. Her brief outburst was enough to shock Diana, who later told author Ingrid Seward: "We were at the graveside, Charles and me and the Queen and when she started crying I said to myself, 'I can't believe this is really happening.'"

She added that the queen had been "incredibly kind" to the duchess in her last years, particularly with regard to paying all her bills.[22] From that day Diana never saw her cry again in private or public.

She was, though, entitled to shed tears of joy a few weeks later when, on a sunny day in July 1986, she looked on as a beaming Prince Andrew watched Sarah Ferguson, now Her Royal Highness the Duchess of York, walk down the aisle of Westminster Abbey on their wedding day. Their marriage was a source of satisfaction for both the queen and Prince Philip. After his romance with Koo Stark ended, Prince Andrew had garnered a reputation as a playboy prince with a roving eye. One of his casual girlfriends had sold her story about late-night sexual exploits under a palm tree on a sandy beach in the Caribbean. Her disclosures coincided with Princess Anne's detective lover, Peter Cross, selling his story to a Sunday tabloid in September 1985. The queen and Prince Philip could do little about the detective's allegations other than ride out the storm, but with Andrew they were prompted into action. A few admonishing words from a stern Philip seemed to have done the trick. From then on the prince dated the "right sort" of girl. Sarah definitely came into that category. The daughter of Major Ronald Ferguson, who was Prince Charles's polo manager, Sarah was a familiar face in royal circles. Ginger-haired and freckle-faced, she was ebullient, energetic, and game for a laugh. During Ascot week she was invited to stay at Windsor Castle as a guest of her friend the Princess of Wales. It was over lunch that Sarah and Andrew first bonded, Andrew feeding her chocolate profiteroles, much as she protested that she was dieting. As he later recalled: "It had to start somewhere."[23]

Though she had had boyfriends and clearly had a "past," no one inside the royal family seemed especially worried. She was clearly one of them. The queen mother liked her at once. "She is so English," she commented. In a letter to the queen, dated April 10, she complimented the bride-to-be on how well she had fit in during the Easter break at Windsor. "She is such a cheerful person, and seems to be so thankful and pleased to be part of a united family & and is truly devoted to darling Andrew. It seems most hopeful which is a comfort."[24] Unspoken but understood was the implication that their union would not be hopeless, unlike certain other members of the family, namely the Prince and Princess of Wales. By 1986 they were living separate lives, Charles back together with Mrs. Parker Bowles, "us both having tried" as he would later declare on prime-time television.[25] Diana found comfort in the arms of her bodyguard Barry Mannakee, and later army captain James Hewitt. During the wedding ceremony Diana looked unusually distracted. It was because she had just learned that, following a complaint from a fellow protection officer, Mannakee had been moved from her detail.

It was the queen's hope that Fergie, jolly, jaunty, endlessly upbeat Fergie, would jolt Diana out of her sullen moods and help her to join in with the rest of the clan. The duchess went carriage driving with Prince Philip, who described her as a "great asset," rode horses with the queen, and regularly joined the queen for lunch at Buckingham Palace.[26] She was such a contrast from Diana.

The arrival of Fergie did indeed mark a change in Diana's behavior, though it was not a change the queen ultimately welcomed. It began at Andrew's stag night just before the wedding. Diana, Fergie, and several friends dressed as policewomen and tried to "arrest" the prince at the private house where his party was taking place. When that failed they ended up in Annabel's nightclub, where they drank mimosas. One customer asked Diana if she wanted another drink, to which she replied, "I don't drink on duty."[27] Clearly she did, as there was already a glass in front of her. Once the story got out the queen was deeply annoyed that the future Queen of England was roaming

around London dressed as a police officer, which was technically a criminal offense. When she spoke to the princess, Diana
defended her behavior as no more than lighthearted fun.

She explained that there was no intention of demeaning
either the queen or the monarchy. Not wanting a confrontation, the queen accepted her benign explanation. The general
silliness, though, continued; Fergie and Diana prodded their
friend Lulu Blacker's rear with their rolled umbrellas at Ascot,
they pushed and shoved each other at a photo call on the
ski slopes, earning a rebuke from Prince Charles, and they
danced the can-can during a dinner at Windsor Castle. Diana
was even criticized for wearing red leather trousers at a David
Bowie concert.

The watching world chorused its disapproval. "Far too much
frivolity," sniffed the *Daily Express* while other commentators
accused the women of behaving like actresses in a soap opera.[28]
With her poor fashion choices, her greedy enjoyment of royal
life—champagne-fueled parties in her quarters at Buckingham
Palace were regular events—and her blatant freeloading, the
duchess was singled out for especial criticism. It was not long
before she was dubbed "freebie Fergie" and described as "vulgar" by palace insiders. The tide was beginning to turn.

Ironically the event that ignited a critical firestorm and
marked a step change in public attitudes toward the queen and
her family was organized by the queen's youngest child, Prince
Edward. After completing his degree at Cambridge University,
he had joined the Royal Marines. After a few months he realized that he had made the wrong choice and, much to the
disappointment of the queen, Prince Philip, and the queen
mother, he resigned his commission. During his college days
he had enjoyed acting and decided to make his mark in the
theater world.

In early 1987, before embarking on this new career, he began organizing a TV game show called *It's a Royal Knockout*, with the aim of raising money for four charities. He roped in three other royals: the Duke and Duchess of York as well as Princess Anne, who would join him as captains of four teams comprising assorted celebrities including *Superman* actor Christopher Reeve, singer Meat Loaf, and film star John Travolta. The plan was for the four teams, decked out in mock-Tudor fancy dress, to compete in a series of slapstick games.[29] While the intent was benign, Prince Charles thought that this meshing of pantomime and monarchy was a disaster waiting to happen. He refused to take part and forbade his wife from getting involved. Initially Diana was resentful at missing out but would later have cause to thank her husband for stopping her from making a fool of herself.

Charles spoke to his mother and counseled against giving his younger brother permission to continue. When the queen was first approached, her instincts were in line with those of her eldest son. She was supported by her senior managerial staff who felt the show, filmed in June 1987, would open the royal family up to ridicule.

Edward secured a face-to-face meeting with his mother and, with a combination of youthful enthusiasm and emphasis on the charity contribution, convinced the queen to change her mind. The royal children and their partners knew that a personal meeting with the queen often derailed advice from courtiers. A case in point was when Diana went directly to the queen, over the head of her husband and the queen's private secretary, to secure permission to attend the funeral of Princess Grace of Monaco. (More recently when Meghan and Harry were planning to leave the royal world, other members of the royal family and the queen's courtiers worked hard to ensure that the prince would not secure a planned face-to-face meeting at Sandringham, with the queen knowing that she was "a soft touch" for family members.)

For once Prince Charles's instincts proved spot-on. Reaction to the show was wholly negative, the program seen as puerile slapstick that demeaned the royal family. The queen mother was so incensed that she summoned Andrew, Edward, and Anne and read them the riot act, accusing them of, in one evening, destroying the reputation of the monarchy that she and the later king had spent a lifetime building up. The queen's reaction was rather more benign. Even though the show had been made for altruistic reasons, she agreed that it was turning the royal family into a soap opera.

The internal postmortem was matched by a sea change in the attitude of the media and the public. It was felt that the younger royals were frivolous and irrelevant, doing little to justify taxpayers' largesse at a time of mass unemployment and growing social division. The decision by the queen to spend $5 million for the Duke and Duchess of York on the construction of Sunninghill Park, a sprawling ranch-style house dubbed "Southyork" after the *Dallas* TV show, seemed to suggest that she was out of touch with the mood of her people. Even though there were plenty of smaller and more appropriate "grace and favor" houses that could have served the royal couple, the queen once again gave in, her generosity outweighing her judgment. As one courtier observed: "The Queen is tight in her own financial affairs but she has been very extravagant with her children, she has indulged them terribly financially."[30]

The immature behavior of the younger royals allowed critics to take pot shots at the queen, the first salvo coinciding with the wedding of Andrew and Sarah. Just days before the big day, the *Sunday Times* informed its readers that the queen found

Mrs. Thatcher's style of government "uncaring, confrontational and divisive."[31] For the first time the story, quoting anonymous sources, addressed the constitutional elephant in the room—that the queen, who was by instinct and training conciliatory and compromising, was alarmed by the contentious style of the prime minister who had deliberately fostered strikes, particularly in the coal industry, in order to crush the trade unions. Under her tenure, the north had suffered while the south had prospered. In the political shorthand of the time, the queen was a "wet," Mrs. Thatcher a "dry." Whatever the queen might think of her government's policies, it was not her place to articulate a view, one way or the other. To do so was a constitutional no-no and for thirty-four years she had been, as her mother would say, "utterly oyster" in her political views. The hunt was on for the "anonymous source" who turned out to be the queen's press secretary Michael Shea. He vehemently denied making the statement ascribed to him, but the damage was done and a few months later he left royal employment. The episode jolted the hitherto seamlessly secret relationship between the queen and her prime minister. Such was the concern on both sides that the queen called the prime minister to apologize for the embarrassment the episode had caused her. For her part Mrs. Thatcher worried that the story might affect her grassroots support, while others, of the dry persuasion, felt that a politically biased monarch was also a dispensable one.

Her husband's behavior hardly helped matters. A few months later, in October 1986, the queen and Prince Philip flew to China on their first-ever state visit to the country. During the tour the prince firmly put his foot in his mouth when he told a group of students that they would go "slitty eyed" if they stayed in China much longer. Not only was the off-the-cuff remark blatantly racist, it was insulting to their hosts. They chose to ignore the remark. Not so the British media, who dubbed the queen's husband "the Great Wally of China."[32] Until his death in 2021, it remained top of the list of his many gaffes.

In the midst of this largely self-inflicted bombardment of negative headlines, one member of the family managed to evade the fallout. Princess Diana was forgiven any Fergie-inspired silliness after she shook hands, ungloved, with an AIDS patient at the Middlesex Hospital in London in April 1987. At a time when AIDS was dubbed "the gay plague" with no cure in sight, her behavior gained international headlines and approval.

When it eventually emerged that the queen and her advisers had counseled caution, Diana's courageous steadfastness was seen as a positive counterpoint to the self-indulgent silliness of the other royals, a view that became more pronounced after the airing of the *It's a Royal Knockout* show. The emerging consensus was that Diana was different and that she cared for the man and woman in the street.

This narrative of a family out of touch with modern realities was amplified during the latter part of the 1980s after a series of disasters, notably the Piper Alpha explosion, the Zeebrugge ferry sinking, and the Lockerbie air crash in December 1988. Though the queen sent Andrew as her representative to the air crash on the border of England and Scotland, his insensitive remarks suggesting that the American passengers suffered more than those killed on the ground led to renewed calls for the queen herself to visit these scenes. It seemed that not much had changed since Aberfan. She later admitted to her private secretary Robert Fellowes that she should have taken his earlier advice and gone herself.[33]

At the memorial service for the Lockerbie victims it did not escape notice that the queen was not represented by any member of the royal family. "Where are the royals," asked the *Sun*, helpfully showing pictures of the royal family out riding, skiing, and sunbathing.

This negative image was conflated with the debate about the introduction of the poll tax. Because the measure taxed individuals rather than property, it disproportionately affected poorer sections of society while providing the wealthier with substantial savings. The introduction of the poll tax provoked widespread rioting and effectively ended Prime Minister Thatcher's career. During this time of social uproar it was revealed that Prince Charles's butler paid as much poll tax as his master while the prince saved thousands of dollars on his privately owned properties. The same was also true for other members of the royal family. In addition it was reported that, during this time of national belt tightening, the queen paid no tax on her private income.

A leader in the *Sunday Times*, penned by editor Andrew Neil, argued that now was the time for the queen to pay tax and for unproductive junior members of the royal family to be taken off the payroll.[34]

Not only did Elizabeth find herself criticized for her tax privileges, she also found herself blundering in the world of horse racing where she had an impeccable reputation, enjoying unrivaled respect and admiration. The saga began in 1982 when the queen, acting on the advice of her racing manager Lord Carnarvon, bought the racing stables at West Ilsley with funds from the sale of her filly Height of Fashion to Sheikh Hamdan al Maktoum of the Dubai royal family.

One of the trainers using the facility was the highly respected Major Dick Hern, who had worked for the queen since 1966. He lived in a nearby rectory, which was also purchased by the queen. In 1984 following a hunting accident he was confined to a wheelchair but continued training and produced several notable winners. Four years later he had open heart surgery. He was still recovering in hospital when, in August 1988, Lord Carnarvon told him that he had two weeks to leave the stables and that he would also have to vacate his home. The racing world was horrified at the treatment of this popular figure. Such was the concern that fellow trainer Ian Balding tracked down the queen's private secretary Robert Fellowes on holiday in the Bahamas and warned him that unless the queen revised the arrangements for Hern she was in danger of having her horses booed in the winners' enclosure. What shocked racegoers the most was the queen's seemingly hardhearted behavior toward a loyal trainer. "The queen has done something I thought was impossible," observed Woodrow Wyatt, a right-wing politician and close friend of the queen mother. "She is turning the Jockey Club and the racing world into republicans."[35]

Though the matter was eventually resolved to everyone's satisfaction, it revealed an unexpected side of the queen, that she far too readily took the advice of those she trusted— in this case her racing manager, now the Seventh Earl of Carnarvon—without question. She eventually countermanded his advice and allowed Hern to stay in his home and to use the West Ilsley stables as well. More galling for the queen, as a competitive racehorse breeder, was the fact that a Hern-trained horse, Nashwan, galloped to a five-length victory in the June 1989 Derby, the one big race on the sporting calendar that the queen has never won.

These issues faded into the background when on August 2, 1990, Iraq invaded Kuwait and five months later the First Gulf War began. Before Allied troops went into battle the queen gave her first-ever televised address to the nation. It was a low-key, sober talk, the queen expressing her hope for a swift resolution of the conflict with minimum loss of life. As a counterpoint to the queen's address, newspapers continued to focus on the self-absorbed behavior of other members of the royal family.

"This country is at war," said the *Sunday Times* editorial, "though you would never believe it from the shenanigans of some members of Her Majesty's clan."[36]

The newspaper cited the Duchess of York skiing, the Prince of Wales pheasant hunting, the Duke of York golfing, and Lord Linley, the queen's nephew, at a nightclub on a Caribbean island, wearing red lipstick and standing alongside other men dressed in drag. Even though it was pointed out that the picture was taken long before the Gulf War conflict, the damage was done.

Royal expert Harold Brooks-Baker, the publishing director of Burke's Peerage, said the war in the gulf had only served to crystallize what he described as building public resentment over the behavior of some members of the royal family.[37]

The queen, stung by accusations that her family was not supportive of the British troops, authorized a statement in her name: "All members of the royal family are behind British forces every inch of the way." This was followed by a long inventory of the visits and events attended by members of the royal family that were intended to lend support to service personnel and their families.[38]

❧

It was time, somewhat belatedly, to take back the narrative, to demonstrate the importance in national life of the monarchy. The queen and her family might have been right behind the military forces but there was one future member of the House of Windsor who had other ideas. Six thousand miles away in a Los Angeles suburb, a nine-year-old girl led a school-yard march of her classmates agitating to stop the Gulf War. Their banners and placards were filmed by local news station KTLA. The freckle-faced girl leading the march was none other than Rachel Meghan Markle.

11

⚜

One's Annus Horribilis

O n the evening of February 6, 1992, the fortieth anniversary of the queen's accession to the throne, Britain's electric grid and water companies experienced a historic and alarming surge. Emergency reserves were tapped to keep up with demand. The reason behind the rush was the screening of a remarkable television documentary that had viewers making a cup of tea or using the bathroom when it ended. Around thirty million people—half the population—had tuned in to watch a year in the life of the most famous pensioner and grandmother on the planet, Her Majesty the Queen. As Eddie Mirzoeff, the director of *Elizabeth R*, observed: "At a time when the Queen was rather disregarded, there was a need to remind the nation what she was like."[1]

For years she had been overshadowed by her children, whose television antics had done little to burnish the crown. This documentary was different. Mirzoeff, who spent eighteen months filming the monarch at state banquets, with her grandchildren at Balmoral, meeting world leaders, and even having a flutter on the horses, ensured that the queen was star of the show. Her husband made a fleeting appearance but that was it. Her children were nowhere to be seen, unlike the first fly-on-the-wall documentary, *Royal Family*, which was broadcast in 1969.

Mirzoeff focused on her status as the head of state, a post she held for life. It was a unique and solitary position, one that several portrait artists, notably Pietro Annigoni, had previously tried to capture. Though she was small and unimposing in stature, she exuded a sense of majesty. Staff called encounters with the monarch entering "the presence." A presence, though, with a sense of humor, a characteristic Mirzoeff captured at the Derby. During the race the viewer glimpsed the almost girlish, wry, and knowing individual behind the mask of monarch.

She was seen watching the horse race on TV in her private box, then running to the balcony as the horses approached the finish line. She cried out excitedly: "That's my horse... I've won the sweep!" Her takings were around $20 and in spite of being one of the world's richest women, she was genuinely thrilled. As she pocketed her winnings, she flashed a confiding grin at the camera.

She later told Mirzoeff that the documentary was the "only good thing" that happened to her in that year. In her voice-over for the documentary the queen gave an unintentional hint about the coming crisis when she reflected on the difficulties faced by the younger members of the royal family in getting used to living within an institution governed by tradition and continuity.

This was something of an understatement. In the months leading up to the broadcast, she had a full-scale royal rebellion on her hands. The first signs came during the Balmoral holiday in August 1991, when both Diana and Fergie seemed frustrated and anxious. There was a wildness about their behavior that did not go unnoticed. One evening they took the queen mother's Daimler and a four wheel drive vehicle out for a spin and raced one another along country roads.

Another time they commandeered a quad bike and went racing over the golf course and in the process churned up the greens. It was a manifestation of the chaos and unhappiness in their lives.

At the time both girls discussed leaving their marriages and the royal family in tandem. At family gatherings they took the opportunity to speak separately to the queen about their marital problems. They acted almost like a wrestling tag team, taking it in turns to bend the queen's ear. "They were the kind of chats the queen had come to dread," noted a former servant. "Her big worry was for the grandchildren."[2]

As well as the queen they consulted with a small army of astrologers and soothsayers for guidance on making their next step. Diana told Princess Anne that Fergie was so disillusioned with married life that this would probably be the last time she came to Balmoral as a married member of the royal family. Her prediction proved to be accurate.

In any case Fergie was skating on very thin ice. She had embarked on an affair with Steve Wyatt, the adopted son of a Texan oil tycoon, while five months' pregnant with her second daughter, Princess Eugenie. During the time she arranged for Dr. Ramzi Salman, the head of marketing for Iraq's state oil, to pay a private visit to Buckingham Palace shortly before the First Gulf War. There he enjoyed dinner with the duchess and her lover Steve Wyatt, whose family had continuing business ties with the regime of Iraqi dictator Saddam Hussein.

Once the queen and her advisers learned of her imprudent behavior she was summoned to the office of the queen's private secretary Sir Robert Fellowes for a formal dressing-down.

"You have abused Her Majesty and her kindness," he told her, emphasizing that he and his two colleagues had the queen's full authority to speak to her in this manner. The following Sunday, Fergie spoke to the queen at Windsor Castle and asked why she had been given such a tongue-lashing.[3] Rather than confront her daughter-in-law about her behavior, the queen feigned ignorance, thus weakening the authority of her officials in future confrontations. Her inability to face down members of her extended family even when they were demonstrably in the wrong was a quality that quietly enraged her senior officials—and her husband. Philip always knew when his wife had avoided an unpleasant scene as he could see her taking her pack of dogs for a walk.

Even Philip was left breathless at the behavior of the Ferguson family. Fergie's lover Steve Wyatt two-timed the duchess when he embarked on an affair with polo-playing businesswoman Lesley Player, who was also the mistress of Fergie's father, Major Ronald Ferguson. He had earlier resigned as Prince Charles's polo manager after he was pictured leaving a massage parlour of dubious repute in Marylebone, central London. Shortly afterward Fergie began another affair, with Wyatt's friend and financial adviser John Bryan.

Though Fergie's marriage was firmly on the rocks, she consoled herself with the notion that her friend the Princess of Wales would leave the royal family at the same time. The princess, though, had other ideas.

Unknown to the duchess, Diana was secretly working on a no-holds-barred biography of her life. She openly discussed her eating disorders, her halfhearted suicide attempts—or desperate cries for help—as well as her husband's long-running relationship with Mrs. Parker Bowles. During this time her own affair with army captain James Hewitt, who served in the Gulf War, was petering out.

Even as she worked on her biography, titled *Diana: Her True Story*, she had not been idle in discussing her marriage with the queen. While she kept silent about the book, the princess had spoken to the queen face-to-face on numerous occasions about Charles and his behavior. Scarred by the bitter divorce between her own parents, which left her father Earl Spencer winning custody of the four children, Diana had a morbid fear of being blamed for the collapse of her own marriage. Ideally she wanted the queen to side with her and condemn her son for his infidelity. This of course would have ignored her own conduct.

Between the queen and Diana there was an uncomprehending respect. While the queen recognized Diana's popularity and her ability to physically embrace the public, a quality that was not part of her own DNA, she found her tears and tantrums hard to grasp. For her part Diana admired and respected the queen because of her unrelenting stoicism, a characteristic that was not part of her personal makeup. On one very hot day in July 1991 before a garden party at Buckingham Palace, for instance, a friend suggested that Diana take a fan to keep cool. Diana wouldn't hear of it. She knew that the queen would be there, heat wave or not, wearing tights and gloves and carrying a large handbag, a model of dutiful self-control. "She has dedicated her whole life to Britain," she told her friend Simone Simmons.[4]

Diana's takeaway from these often unproductive meetings was the queen's observation that Diana's bulimia was the *cause* rather that the *symptom* of her son's estrangement. At the same time, the queen confided that she found the direction of her eldest son's life unfocused and his behavior at times odd and erratic. It did not escape her notice that Charles was as unhappy and frustrated with his marriage as his wife.[5] There were no easy answers to this vexing issue, the queen reduced to offering bromides in the face of Diana's tears.

The queen's fortieth year as sovereign was not turning into a happy anniversary. Not by any means. In January 1992, Fergie and Andrew finally managed to make an appointment to discuss their failed five-year marriage with the queen. Even though Andrew was nominally the queen's favorite son, it had still taken him three weeks to arrange a summit. It was not a jolly gathering as the couple tried to explain how things had gone wrong and how they had let down the queen. Fergie confessed that her own behavior had not been befitting that of a duchess of the realm. For once it was not entirely the fault of the royal system. During their marriage Andrew, as a serving navy officer, spent only eighty days a year on shore leave. For the rest of the year, Fergie was left to her own devices and Andrew was not around to advise and guide her while she made blunder after blunder. For her part she felt that she had not been given the support she deserved from courtiers, though her own greed combined with her newly elevated position did, as her father observed, "go to her head. She didn't read the rule book properly."[6]

The queen somewhat reluctantly read the pair the riot act and convinced them to give their marriage another six months. They agreed to her wishes, in part, as Fergie reflected, because they had never seen her looking quite so sad.

Her Majesty's hope for a reconciliation was dashed within weeks when a cache of photographs from 1990 of the duchess on a Mediterranean holiday with her lover Steve Wyatt and her daughters were stolen from a central London apartment and made their way to the front pages of the tabloids. In March 1992 divorce lawyers were called in and Fergie was effectively banished from royal circles. As the BBC's court correspondent Paul Reynolds broadcast: "The knives are out for Fergie." A former private secretary described her as "vulgar, vulgar, vulgar" and Prince Philip made it clear that he never wanted to be in the same room as her again.[7] It would, according to Fergie's friend Ingrid Seward, be more than a quarter of a century before the two met again, in October 2008 at the wedding of Fergie's younger daughter, Princess Eugenie, to Jack Brookbank. It was the prelude for a better relationship between the duke and the duchess.

As Fergie and Andrew wrestled with their future, Diana and Charles flew to India in February on an official visit that laid bare their marital disconnect. It was symbolized when Diana sat on her own in front of the Taj Mahal, the temple to love, while her husband was at a business conference. After a polo match, when Charles was presented with the trophy by his wife, Diana deliberately moved her head when he went to kiss her cheek and his face ended up by her ear. The queen, who was still at Sandringham, was a concerned spectator of this unhappy tableau, which was broadcast on TV news around the world.

Soon enough Her Majesty became the reluctant referee between the warring parties. In March, Diana's father Earl Spencer died unexpectedly while she, Charles, and the boys were on a skiing holiday in Austria. When Diana was told about her father's death she refused to return to Britain with her husband, saying that she wanted the right to grieve for her father without going through a hypocritical masquerade. Such was the ice-cold atmosphere in the ski resort of Lech that Charles asked her bodyguard Inspector Ken Wharfe to convince her to allow him to accompany her back to England.

At first Diana refused point-blank. She only relented after a phone call to Windsor Castle where the queen insisted that the couple put on a united front.

As Diana predicted the journey home together was purely for the sake of appearances. Once they landed in London, Charles headed to Highgrove while Diana was left alone at Kensington Palace to mourn her departed father.

There was more bad news for the queen when, shortly after Earl Spencer's funeral, the palace announced the divorce of Princess Anne and her husband of nearly nineteen years, Captain Mark Phillips. Under normal circumstances the breakup would have captured the front pages, but these were not ordinary times as all eyes were on the Prince and Princess of Wales. The dam burst on June 14, 1992, with the publication of the biography *Diana: Her True Story*. What was shocking was the book's depiction of a royal world where the emotional temperature was chilly and the social landscape forbidding. When the book was first serialized in the *Sunday Times* under the front-page headline DIANA DRIVEN TO FIVE SUICIDE BIDS BY "UNCARING" CHARLES, the response was explosive.

Criticism of the book—which came from all sectors of society—was severe and unrelenting. The Archbishop of Canterbury, the chairman of the Press Complaints Commission, assorted Labour and Conservative members of Parliament, and rival newspaper editors joined in condemnation. Various bookshops and supermarkets banned the book. However, the Princess of Wales refused to put her name to a statement, to be issued by Buckingham Palace in both their names, denouncing the book as inaccurate and distorted.

Though Charles's friends were instructed to remain silent, the queen and Prince Philip could not. The day before the serialization in the *Sunday Times*, Prince Charles saw the queen at Windsor Castle to discuss the possibility of seeking a separation. He had already lined up the prominent lawyer Lord Goodman, who had a reputation as a conciliator, to explore the legal and constitutional ramifications of a royal divorce.

On the Sunday of the first serialization the queen was the guest of honor for a polo match at Windsor Great Park in which Prince Charles was playing. Her decision to invite Andrew and Camilla Parker Bowles into the Royal Enclosure as the nation was digesting the implications of the Waleses' miserable marriage was seen by Diana and her supporters as a public rebuke of the princess.

As a matter of prudence, Prime Minister John Major was briefed on the marital crisis as, too, were the lord chancellor Lord Mackay, and the Archbishop of Canterbury George Carey. All the mood music suggested that the prospects of a positive resolution were not good.

Though the queen had been painfully aware of the marital rift for some time, she was unprepared for such a detailed public exposition. While the palace was searching for a suitable strategy, outwardly it was business as usual. Diana stood beside the queen on the balcony at Buckingham Palace for the official birthday salute and joined the royal family at Windsor Castle for Ascot week.

Behind the scenes the queen and her aides tried to manage the unhappy situation. Her private secretary Robert Fellowes asked the princess point-blank if she had cooperated with the book. She looked him in the eye and told him a bald-faced lie: "No." When he subsequently learned that she had been involved, he offered his resignation, which the queen refused to accept.

Instead she and Prince Philip brokered a meeting with the prince and princess at Windsor Castle. During the conversation

Diana was alarmed when Prince Philip mentioned that there was a tape recording of the princess discussing the serialization, an assertion that puzzled her as she had nothing to do with negotiations with the *Sunday Times*. While the duke may have been incorrectly briefed by aides, in Diana's eyes, it confirmed her long-standing suspicions that her phone calls were regularly monitored by the shadowy security forces.

The central point during what was a difficult and tetchy meeting was that the queen and Prince Philip insisted that the Waleses give their marriage some more time and that they make a real effort to resolve their differences. According to Diana's account, their wishes conflicted with an earlier decision made between her and Prince Charles where they had agreed that an amicable separation was the only practical way forward. The princess was horrified when her husband remained silent and agreed with his mother's proposal. Such was the concern of the queen and Prince Philip that they suggested a date for a second meeting. To their lasting irritation, Diana did not show up.

Nonetheless Philip continued the conversation by post, sending the princess a series of letters, cajoling, pointed, conciliatory, where he asked her to look at her own behavior and to acknowledge that there had been faults on both sides. The duke signed them: "affectionately, Pa." While he modestly admitted that he was not a professional marriage guidance counselor, her father-in-law asked her to think very carefully about her marriage and the implications for herself, her children, her husband, and the monarchy.

In one blunt note he implied that the queen shared his view of Mrs. Parker Bowles. He wrote: "I cannot imagine anyone in their right minds leaving you for Camilla. Such a prospect never even entered our heads."[8] It remained the popular view for many years to come.

In a dismal summer where calamity followed upon calamity Fergie was next in the firing line. "The redhead is in trouble," Diana texted a friend on his pager messenger, at the time a rudimentary form of texting.[9] It was August 1992 and the "trouble" in question involved long-range paparazzi pictures of a topless Duchess of York having her toes sucked by her "financial adviser" John Bryan at the side of a swimming pool in the south of France while her children looked on. As luck would have it the duchess, now formally separated from Prince Andrew, had returned to Balmoral to discuss access arrangements for the children just when the story appeared on the front pages.

As she walked in to breakfast the rest of the royal family was studiously examining the tabloid story. It was a moment of excruciating embarrassment even by her own standards. As she recalled in her autobiography: "It would be accurate to report that the porridge was getting cold. Eyes wide and mouths ajar, the adults were flipping through the *Daily Mirror* and the rest of the tabloids...I had been exposed for what I truly was. Worthless. Unfit. A national disgrace."[10] There was little sense of irony in her final description.

The queen was furious and summoned her to her study. In her eyes even though the disgraced Duchess of York was now separated, she still had a royal title and the appellation Her Royal Highness. Her behavior had exposed herself to ridicule and the monarchy to contempt. The queen was cold, ice cold, as she listed her transgressions and the damage she had done to the institution to which the queen had devoted her life. She was also deeply upset on behalf of her son who had been made, according to one close figure, "to look such a cuckolded fool before the entire world."[11] Fergie later recalled: "Her anger wounded me to the core."[12]

The almost weekly accumulation of family scandal severely

jolted the queen's habitual equanimity. One guest at Balmoral during this unhappy period described the queen as looking "gray, ashen and completely flat. She looked so awful."[13] As a rather unusual pick-me-up she and Prince Philip went off ferreting, the couple and their gamekeeper using ferrets to catch rabbits and rats on the estate. She drove off all smiles, a brief break in the unrelenting pace of bad news.

In a kind of emotional ping-pong, three days later it was Diana's turn to face the music. In August 1992 a tape recording was published of her speaking on her mobile phone to longtime admirer James Gilbey. In the early days of these brick-size devices, radio hams were able to listen in to other people's conversations and, if they wished, make a recording. This was Diana's worst phone-tapping fear come true. Suspicions that she was and had been targeted by her enemies seemed to be borne out by the tape. The embarrassing twenty-three-minute conversation with Gilbey was recorded on New Year's Eve 1989 but was not published for another three years and then at a sensitive time in the marriage of the Prince and Princess of Wales. During the late-night chat Gilbey referred to Diana affectionately as Squidgy, which led to this latest scandal being dubbed Squidgygate. In the surreptitiously taped conversation Diana criticized Prince Charles as well as the Duchess of York and the queen mother. She told Gilbey that her husband made her life "real, real torture." She also complained that she was not properly appreciated by the royal family for her work on their behalf.

Though not as humiliating as the Fergie photos, the Squidgygate tape seriously compromised the future queen. Her comments about members of the royal family were injudicious but for many, including the princess, the prime takeaway was that the tape, which was apparently made by a radio ham, was introduced into the public conversation at a moment that weakened Diana's position with regard to her future dealings with the royal family now that separation and divorce were spoken of openly. Many thought the tape was a setup, so much so that Stella Rimington, the head of MI5, Britain's secret service, was eventually forced to formally deny involvement.

During this fevered summer the queen summoned Harry Herbert, the son of her racing manager the Earl of Carnarvon, to Balmoral. He was liked and trusted by both Diana and the queen, who wanted to get a friend's honest opinion on the state of her daughter-in-law's marriage. As they looked out over a "beautiful" scene of rolling hills and heather, he explained to Her Majesty that it was a bad time for Diana. "The light had gone out," he recalled. "The queen wanted to talk to me about it because she was so worried. It was a sad discussion, a sad moment, because that was when everything was at its worst."[14]

The queen had a further sense of how bad the situation had become when the princess declined to accompany her husband on the first-ever royal visit to South Korea. She was impervious to all entreaties even though she realized her absence would create a media firestorm. At Balmoral the queen implored her to change her mind. Initially Diana was deaf to reason and it was a sign of the queen's waning authority with her daughter-in-law that a royal command no longer inspired instant obedience. It was only after a concerted campaign by the queen and Prince Charles that she finally agreed to go.

She shouldn't have bothered. The tour was a disaster from the moment they landed, the royal couple barely able to raise a smile or a glimmer of enthusiasm. "We've lost this one," palace press officer Dickie Arbiter said out loud as he watched their distant body language as they walked down the aircraft steps.[15]

They were dubbed "The Glums" by the media, who

inevitably focused on their disintegrating marriage rather than the purpose of the tour, which was to improve trade and cultural links between the two countries.

During this tumultuous period the monarchy faced an existential crisis. Opinion polls revealed the general public's growing dissatisfaction with the institution. Numerous church figures castigated the royal family for failing to provide a healthy example of family life. Walter Bagehot's "interesting" notion of "a family on the throne" no longer seemed so appealing.

Around this time the queen's financial lawyer, Sir Matthew Farrer, was deep in negotiations with Downing Street over secret proposals for the queen to pay tax on her private income. It was considered the minimum needed to stay the slew of criticism.

In the midst of this correspondence, Prince Philip visited Argentina on official business. While he was away, the queen suffered the greatest physical catastrophe of her reign. On November 20, 1992, which by chance was their forty-fifth wedding anniversary, Windsor Castle caught fire. The inferno was started by a temporary lamp setting alight a curtain. It quickly engulfed St. George's Hall and the queen's private chapel. The blaze could be seen for miles and needed over 200 firefighters and thirty-nine fire engines to bring under control.

It was a devastating event. Ever the pragmatist, the queen would later remark that the three positive takeaways were that no one was injured, most of the most precious artifacts had already been removed in advance of rewiring work, and it was a still evening so the blaze did not spread as quickly as it might have.

As a further slice of luck Prince Andrew was on hand to take charge of the removal of paintings, antique furniture, and other works of art. Workers formed a human chain to carry them to safety.

When the queen, dressed in a green mackintosh and matching hat, came to visit the smoldering ruin she looked and was utterly devastated, shocked beyond words—and tears. The castle, an icon of Britain's history, had also been her home for most of her life. She retreated to the Royal Lodge and spent the weekend with her mother and sister, almost inconsolable. "The symbolism of the fire at Windsor Castle was not lost on anyone inside the family," Diana recalled.

Four days later, nursing a heavy cold but with her husband now by her side, she addressed the Guildhall in London to celebrate her forty-fifth wedding anniversary. In a voice hoarse with coughing, she spoke sadly about the events of the year. "Nineteen ninety-two is not a year on which I shall look back with undiluted pleasure. In the words of one of my more sympathetic correspondents, it has turned out to be an *annus horribilis*." Or as the *Sun* newspaper, one of the queen's chief tormentors, translated: "One's Bum Year."

She went on to acknowledge that any institution must expect criticism but hoped that it was done "with a touch of humor, gentleness, good humor and understanding." There was little on offer. The initial response that the taxpayer would pay for the restoration of the castle, which was a national monument, was angrily dismissed by the media and the public. A rancorous debate ensued about who was responsible for footing the bill. Several lawmakers and parts of the media insisted that the queen pay even though Windsor Castle was legally owned by the nation.

In response, the queen, who was shocked by the public's hostile attitude, eventually agreed to open up parts of Buckingham Palace to the public for the first time, with money raised from the entry charge going toward Windsor's restoration. This covered around 70 percent of the repair bill. In addition the queen donated £2 million ($2.7 million) of her personal wealth toward the costs of refurbishment.

Unfortunately for the queen, the debate over who paid for Windsor Castle became conflated with the announcement by the prime minister on November 26 that the monarch and Prince of Wales had agreed to pay tax on their private income and that the Civil List, the taxpayers' contribution to the upkeep of the monarchy and all its trappings, was to be reduced.

Given the sour public mood, many argued that the queen had been forced into this position as a result of the outcry over the Windsor Castle fire rather than, as was the case, as a result of months of earlier discussions. "The Queen pays tax and it's a victory for people power," boasted the *Sun*.[16]

In this republican atmosphere it was clear that, whatever she did, the queen couldn't catch a break. Her earlier invitation to a firm of accountants to look for savings in the workings of the monarchy—she accepted without demur two-hundred-plus recommendations—was seen as too little too late. Her own dry suggestion to members of her household that they no longer dot their *i*'s and cross their *t*'s in order to save ink was not received with as much mirth as in previous times.

The queen had little to smile about. An irate phone call from Prince Charles capped off a miserable year. He had arranged a shooting party with friends at Sandringham. William and Harry were scheduled to join the group. Not only did Diana refuse to go but she insisted on taking the boys to Windsor Castle. For the prince it was the final straw and he explained his exasperation to the queen. Once again, as was her policy, she counseled patience. Charles, though, had reached the end of his tether. In an uncharacteristic outburst he shouted down the line to the queen, "Don't you realize

she's mad, mad, mad," and slammed down the phone.[17] Everyone, including the queen, was now coming to accept that a
separation—the solution for which Diana had been arguing for
months—was the only workable way forward for the warring
prince and princess. On November 25, just five days after the
Windsor fire, the couple met at Kensington Palace to confirm
this agreed course of action and sort out access to the boys and
other matters before passing on their decision to their families
and lawyers.

Just two weeks later, on December 9, Prime Minister John
Major stood up in the House of Commons and announced the
separation "with regret" of the Prince and Princess of Wales.
He went on to say that the split was amicable and that it had no
constitutional implications. But the prime minister drew puzzled gasps from lawmakers when his carefully worded remarks
included the assertion that "there is no reason why the Princess
of Wales should not be crowned Queen in due course." This
made no sense. As MPs and commentators quickly concluded
the facts of life were that separation was a prelude to divorce.
Moreover a divorced princess could not possibly be the queen
of England. The idea of a divorced, or even separated, king
and queen sitting beside each other during their coronation
was grotesque.

In sixty years the royal family—and society—had come full
circle. Edward VIII, as head of the Church of England, abdicated in 1936 in order to marry the twice-divorced American
Wallis Simpson. Now it seemed there was no let or hindrance
to allow a divorced Prince of Wales to claim the throne.

The queen was, according to a friend, at her "wit's end,"
wondering aloud when her family and the institution that was
her lifeblood would be given some respite. A clergyman who
has known the sovereign for years observed her mood at this

difficult time. "She felt that things were slipping away from her, that so many horrible things were happening, and when would it end? In a sense, she was feeling that she was losing control. It was the cumulative weight of all the personal disasters."[18] Staff noticed, too, that her modest consumption of alcohol— she enjoyed a dry martini in the evening—had increased.

The run-up to Christmas, a traditional time of good cheer, brought little reprieve. Days after the separation announcement Diana made an appointment to see the queen at Buckingham Palace. When she entered the queen's suite, she burst into floods of tears, Diana claiming that everyone was against her.

"The Queen didn't know what to do," recalled a lady-in-waiting afterward. "She has always hated this kind of emotional confrontation and, frankly, has never had to deal with it before or since."[19]

During their hour-long conversation, which was punctu-ated by tears, the queen was able to reassure Diana that, come what may, she would never be challenged regarding custody arrangements for her two boys. This was a profound relief for the princess, who had fretted about this issue long before the actual separation.

Early the following year they were at their boarding school when yet another scandal about their parents burst into the open. This time it was Prince Charles's feet that were held to the flames. "Just when we thought things couldn't get any worse," remarked the queen wearily.[20] Once again it was a late-night mobile telephone conversation, illicitly recorded by radio hams who listened in as a form of titillation, that was the cause for royal embarrassment. In the so-called Camillagate tapes, which were released in January 1993, the prince and his lover Mrs. Parker Bowles were recorded in a lovey-dovey chat. During their conversation, which took place in 1989, Prince Charles made distasteful references to his desire to be a tampon inside his lover, a sentiment Diana described as "just sick."[21]

It was clear to listeners that Charles and Camilla had enjoyed a passionate and long-standing relationship that fully justified Diana's suspicions. If they didn't think so before, the majority of the public believed that Diana was indeed the wronged wife. As his popularity ratings plummeted, some churchmen and politicians publicly declared that Charles was not fit to be king. The cry arose that the crown should skip a generation and go directly to Prince William. While the queen was resolutely opposed to any change in the rules of succession, it is not a clamor that has abated overmuch in the ensuing decades.

For the next few years the "War of the Waleses" consumed the media and agitated the queen and the rest of the royal family. Everyone tiptoed around Diana, concerned that the unpredictable princess, referred to as a loose cannon, would further damage the already listing institution. Much against the better judgment of her mother and sister, the queen tried to keep Diana within the fold, quietly hopeful that at some point Charles and his wife could effect a reconciliation. At this delicate period the olive branch was ever present.

The queen's somewhat forlorn wish for a positive resolution echoed her behavior during the marital convulsions of her sister Princess Margaret and Lord Snowdon. Long, long after the couple had accepted that their marriage was dead and buried, the queen refused to inter the corpse, hoping against hope that something would turn up.

Her policy fed into her personality. The queen's unwillingness to grasp the nettle would unnecessarily drag out difficult issues, especially those involving the family. Sometimes playing for time did work. She had done so when Margaret fell in love with divorced Group Captain Peter Townsend at a time when divorce was not acceptable to either the state or the Church of England. She had played the long game, a strategy that ultimately helped resolve this vexatious issue.

The Waleses situation was quite another matter as the drip, drip, drip of bitterness and anger seeping into the media slowly corroded respect for the monarchy. The queen was, though, clinging to the words of Prime Minister Major, who asserted in the House of Commons that the couple had no plans to divorce. As long as that policy held good there could still be light at the end of the dark tunnel.

Long after other members of the royal family had given up, the queen always lent a listening ear to the princess, the monarch concerned about her well-being. She would recieve messages via her private secretary Sir Robert Fellowes, whose wife Jane was Diana's older sister, or call her up at Kensington Palace to ask if she was all right.

In April 1983 the queen invited the Princess of Wales to a state banquet held at Buckingham Palace in honor of Mario Soares, the president of Portugal. She did so without telling any other members of the royal family—including Charles—about the invitation. They were furious but the queen clung to the hope that somehow a truce could be called in the increasingly bitter War of the Waleses. After all, the separated princess continued to perform royal duties and even made overseas visits on behalf of the monarchy.

She invited the princess to Sandringham for Christmas in 1993 when the Waleses had been officially parted for a year. Diana stayed overnight and went with her sons and the other royals to church, but she left before Christmas lunch. Servants recalled that the atmosphere lightened after her departure.

Again the queen insisted on inviting Diana, whom the rest of the royal family called "evil in their midst," to the D-Day celebrations in June 1994.[22] Before the event the princess was anxious and nervous, wondering aloud to her private secretary Patrick Jephson how the royal family would greet her. Ironically it was not the hostility of the royal family that made her decide to temporarily step back from formal duties but the behavior of the tabloid media.

The previous November 1993 a Sunday newspaper published covertly taken pictures of the princess as she worked out in a private gym. The gym owner Bryce Taylor had rigged his workout equipment with cameras to snap the princess during her early-morning routine. Diana was shocked, the queen horrified. "Oh my God, no," was her response as she reviewed the Sunday papers over breakfast at Windsor Castle.[23] As a result of this intrusion Diana decided to retire for a time from public life, the princess giving what was known as the "Time and Space" speech on December 3, 1993, at the Headway trust for brain injuries.

She announced that this unwarranted invasion into her private life had forced her to step back and reconsider her public role. While she publicly thanked the queen and Duke of Edinburgh for their kindness and support, her husband's name was conspicuously omitted. For the next months Diana kept a low profile.

As much as she worried about the prince and princess, the queen's focus was also on William and Harry. She always cleared her diary if there was a possibility of Diana bringing them to Buckingham Palace or Windsor Castle for afternoon tea.

Her private secretary Patrick Jephson observed: "The Princess also used these opportunities to express loyalty and give assurances about her wish to do no harm either to the institution or to her husband who would inherit it."[24] Her protestations of loyalty were met with skepticism by both the queen and her private secretary though they cautiously continued the collaboration.

For her part Diana, somewhat naively, continued to see the queen as a family referee with regard to her separation from Princes Charles. She was frustrated that she had not intervened to end Prince Charles's relationship with Camilla Parker Bowles. The queen and the queen mother had shown their disapproval of this long-running affair by refusing to invite Mrs. Parker Bowles to any court functions. It was, as far as Diana was concerned, not enough. "My mother-in-law has been totally supportive but it's so difficult to get a decision out of her," she observed diplomatically.[25] Essentially she was playing a waiting game, prepared to sit on the sidelines until her husband took the initiative and asked for a divorce. She felt that as he had asked her to marry him, he should be the one to initiate proceedings. It was a view she made clear to the queen in the hope that she would push her son in the direction of divorce.

After giving her "Time and Space" speech Diana was nervously anticipating her husband's authorized book and television documentary about his life and work, which had been two years in the making. So, too, was the queen. While relations between the sovereign and heir are historically regarded as difficult—Queen Victoria and the Prince of Wales, later Edward VII, for example—at this time they were racing toward a head-on collision. The queen and her advisers felt that Charles's decision, encouraged by his private secretary Richard Aylard, to work with broadcaster Jonathan Dimbleby on a "warts and all" biography was a gross mistake. His strategy to air his dirty linen in public by confessing his adultery with Mrs. Parker Bowles was viewed with horror by the palace.

Charles and his camp argued that only by addressing the issue directly could a line be drawn to enable him to move forward. It was by no means a unanimous view even among his supporters. Camilla Parker Bowles thought it a great mistake and told him so. It was an issue in which both estranged wife and mistress were in agreement. Diana, too, thought the documentary would diminish Charles's reputation. Both women were proved correct.

The result, *Charles: The Private Man, the Public Role*, appeared on television on June 29, 1994, the same night that Diana had been invited to the summer party at the Serpentine Gallery. The princess arrived in a flirty black Christina Stambolian number that was forever known as "the revenge dress" as it overshadowed Charles's prime-time confessional. Though the documentary focused on his good works, it was defined in the public's mind by his strangled admission of adultery. When Dimbleby asked the question, "Did you try to be faithful and honorable to your wife when you took on the vow of marriage?," the prince answered, "Yes.Until the marriage had irretrievably broken down, us both having tried."[26]

Neither the television profile nor the confession went down well, either inside or outside Buckingham Palace. The queen's former press secretary Dickie Arbiter observed: "The program was a complete whinge, a terrible own goal that not only affected relations between the prince and princess but St. James's Palace and Buckingham Palace."[27] That is to say, between the queen and her eldest son.

If the television documentary was divisive, the authorized biography was, in many ways, so much worse. Not only had his friends and staff been given license to speak freely, but the prince had allowed Dimbleby access to official papers.

Once the queen heard of this ploy, the papers were retrieved and those sections of the book based on confidential state papers excised.

The queen was fighting a rearguard action to save her son from himself—and from damaging the monarchy. She could though do little about the serialization date, which coincided precisely with her historic visit to Russia, the first by a British sovereign.

Charles was doing to the queen exactly what he complained his wife often did, overshadowing his work by her own behavior.

This tactless diary clash paled into insignificance when the contents of the biography were made public. Dimbleby, with the approval of Prince Charles, described his subject as suffering from a lack of appreciation and affection from either of his parents. His mother was remote, his father was a bully. Thus the reason for the breakdown of his marriage was forged in the crucible of his childhood, where he wanted for nothing except love and parental warmth. In other words his marital collapse was not his fault. It was laid at the door of the queen and Prince Philip. That neatly sidestepped his long-term relationship with Mrs. Parker Bowles.

For her part the queen was disappointed at the way Charles had drifted back to Camilla amid the turmoil of his own marriage. He was taking the easy way out, she thought. What is more he made himself a hostage to fortune when he stated that Camilla's presence in his life was "non negotiable."[28]

Two absent words run like a river through the recent history of the royal family: *Well done.* During her brief stay in the royal family Meghan Markle complained she was never praised by anyone in the system. So, too, did Diana. For Charles, he would have done anything to hear those words from his mother. But he never did. As one of his circle noted: "He can't understand the total absence of motherly genes in her."[29]

Other friends repeated this refrain: "Charles is absolutely desperate for his mother's approval and knows he'll never really get it. He's the wrong sort of person for her—too needy, too vulnerable, too emotional, too complicated, too self-centered."[30]

The tragedy of Charles's upbringing is that he repeated his memory of his father's behavior toward him with his own sons. Prince Harry explained in a television interview: "My father used to say to me when I was younger, 'Well, it was like that for me, so it's going to be like that for you.'" Harry took issue with this parental philosophy, saying, "That doesn't make sense. Just because you suffered, that doesn't mean that your kids have to suffer, in fact quite the opposite."[31]

If Prince Charles was looking for sympathy from his siblings after the publication of his biography, he was profoundly disappointed. His brothers and sister were furious at this unfair and one-sided portrayal and told him so. They had very different memories of their upbringing, cherishing the times their father read to them or made up a story at bedtime, took them swimming in the palace pool, and taught them country pursuits. In their eyes Charles was articulating *his* truth about his childhood, not necessarily the truth, or the truth as his siblings remembered it.

Inevitably the queen, because of her unique role as mother, head of state, head of the Commonwealth, and head of the household, had to ration her time, especially during Charles's early years. It could, though, be argued that she delegated too much parental control to her husband, his bluff, brusque behavior at odds with his son's sensitive spirit.

The queen and her husband had no right of reply. By instinct and training, the public confessional was anathema to them. "We did our best," was all Prince Philip would say about the couple's parenting skills when asked by biographer Gyles Brandreth.[32] They had to take their son's public criticism on the chin.

Not so when the Princess of Wales decided to go public as

well. At last the queen was stirred into action over an issue—the separation of the Prince and Princess of Wales—that had paralyzed the entire royal system for years.

In November 1995 Diana appeared on BBC's *Panorama* show, where she spoke candidly about her loves and her life. Wearing striking black eye makeup that gave her a haunted look, she discussed her eating disorders, her failed marriage, her depression, and her husband's adultery. She talked about her lover James Hewitt, her belief that Charles was not up to the "top job" of king, and her desire to be the "queen" of people's hearts. She reserved her most devastating zinger for her love rival Camilla Parker Bowles. When interviewer Martin Bashir asked about Camilla's role in the marriage, she said sweetly: "Well, there were three of us in this marriage so it was a bit crowded."

She shot the devastating interview on a quiet Sunday at Kensington Palace. Her only stipulation she wanted was that she tell the queen before the BBC announced its coup.

When she spoke to the queen's private secretary Robert Fellowes he asked innocently if it was an interview for the popular charity Children in Need. When she told him that it was for the hard-hitting current affairs show *Panorama* he visibly blanched. His response, "Oh," said it all. Despite entreaties from her private secretary, lawyer, and others in her dwindling circle, Diana steadfastly refused to divulge the contents.

When it was broadcast her television confessional was both shocking and, as far as the royal family was concerned, unforgivable.

From the perspective of the queen and other royals, notably Princess Margaret, Diana crossed a line when she spoke of her wish to be the "queen of people's hearts" and articulated her doubts about Prince Charles's fitness to be king. She told Martin Bashir: "Because I know the character I would think that the top job, as I call it, would bring enormous limitations to him, and I don't know whether he could adapt to that."

At the time the interview was seen as a devastating riposte to Prince Charles's Dimbleby interview, a fatal ratcheting of the couple's escalating feud that finally prompted decisive action from the queen. Diana, in the eyes of many, had gone too far. Her behavior was seen as inexcusable, both questioning Charles's right to be king and challenging the sovereign herself. There was only one queen, and she had served the nation dutifully for more than forty years.

When the queen finally watched a recording of the show, she was despairing, her husband apoplectic. Something had to be done, for the sake of not just the monarchy but also their grandchildren.

The queen, having held out the olive branch for so long, was now determined to cut the marital Gordian knot. She spoke to the prime minister, the Archbishop of Canterbury, and historian Lord Blake, who advised the palace on constitutional issues. "The present situation in which they seem to be giving a sort of tit-for-tat, running each other down, really has become almost intolerable," warned the historian peer.[33]

Once the queen had made up her mind, matters moved quickly. On December 18 Diana received a handwritten note from the sovereign delivered by a uniformed courier to Kensington Palace from Windsor Castle. It was, Diana noted ruefully, the first letter she had ever received from her mother-in-law. In part the letter said: "I have consulted with the Archbishop of Canterbury and with the prime minister and, of course, with Charles, and we have decided that the best course for you is divorce."[34]

Shortly afterward she had a letter from Prince Charles personally requesting a divorce. In the letter, which began "Dearest Diana," the prince described the failure of their relationship as a "national and personal tragedy."[35] She duly forwarded both missives to her lawyer Anthony Julius and sent holding responses saying she would need time to reflect and consider her options.

The timing of the queen's historic letter reflected a genuine sense of crisis and exasperation felt by senior royals and their courtiers. It also exposed the failure of the queen's previous policy of prevarication and conciliation. It had merely served to drag out this marital conflict and done long-term damage to the crown. As royal historian Sarah Bradford observed: "The Wales' divorce was undoubtedly the most damaging event since the abdication. It brought into question the reality of the monarchy and the queen's personal attributes as a mother and as a monarch."[36] Even in this personal crisis, the queen invited Diana to stay with the family at Sandringham for Christmas. Diana declined, telling friends that she would "[go] up in my BMW car and come out in a coffin."[37] Instead she spent Christmas on her own at Kensington Palace before flying off for a holiday in the Caribbean.

The princess's decision to decline the sovereign's invitation, normally viewed as a command, marked the nadir of her relationship with the queen. It was an affront too many.

From now on, the queen was not always available to take her phone calls or ready to invite her to afternoon tea. Their dealings were necessarily more business-like than before as the queen was one of the interested parties in divorce negotiations.

Discussions with Prince Charles focused on the financial settlement while the queen dealt with Diana's future title, her continued residence at Kensington Palace, and custody arrangements for her boys. At a meeting at Buckingham Palace in February 1996 the queen, once again, assured her about the custody and care of William and Harry and indicated that it was "highly unlikely" that Charles would ever marry Camilla Parker Bowles.

Diana's future title did, though, become a matter of dispute. It was reported that she had decided to be known as Diana, Princess of Wales, and had told friends that she had agreed to drop the appellation Her Royal Highness.

The queen intervened, making clear that Diana's "decisions" were still requests and that she had not been pressured to give up the HRH. "It is wrong that the Queen or the Prince asked her," said an official palace spokesman.[38] She may have given up her title, which meant curtsying to junior royals, but she had become a very rich woman in her own right, with a settlement of around £17 million ($20.5 million). As for her title, Prince William told her: "Don't worry mummy, I will give it back to you one day when I am king."[39]

In the months that followed her divorce the absence of a royal appellation seemed to help rather than hinder her popularity. She was now seen as a strong, independent, and glamorous humanitarian in her own right, a feature of her life that had developed since her earlier separation. Diana was routinely courted by the likes of American statesman Henry Kissinger, former secretary of state Colin Powell, and media queen Barbara Walters. Diana was now a global superstar, her causes and concerns eclipsing those espoused by the House of Windsor. The queen always appreciated that the monarchy survived by the consent of the people. She fully recognized that, after a bruising few years, now was the time to regroup.

12

⚜

Flowers, Flags, and Fortitude

William and Harry had just come down from the hills and were playing with their cousin Zara Phillips in the grounds of Balmoral Castle during their annual summer holiday in August 1997 when the phone rang. It was their mother, who had just landed in Paris. She was due back in London the following day and wanted to touch base. Harry was too involved in his game to want to spend much time chatting. The conversation was short and staccato, the princess suffering the frustration every mother knows when their children would rather be doing something else. "I can't really, necessarily, remember what I said," said Harry years later. "But all I do remember is probably, you know, regretting for the rest of my life how short the phone call was."[1]

William was a little easier to communicate with, as he wanted to speak to his mother about an issue that was on his mind. The prince was worried about a proposed photo call that had been arranged to mark his third year at Eton, his exclusive fee-paying school. Harry had been held back a year at Ludgrove preparatory school and he felt that the staged event would overshadow his brother. Diana promised to discuss it with his father when she returned the following day.

She had spent the last few days on an idyllic sunshine cruise with her boyfriend, Dodi Fayed, sailing round the Mediterranean aboard *Jonikal,* the yacht owned by his controversial businessman father, Mohamed Al-Fayed. Now she was looking forward to seeing her boys. The couple flew from Sardinia to Paris on a private jet. After they landed they briefly stopped at Villa Windsor, the former home of the Duke and Duchess of Windsor, in the Bois de Boulogne, then inspected Dodi's apartment before they drove to the Ritz hotel where they planned to stay for the night. During the journey they were surrounded by motorbike-riding cameramen, who were desperately trying to get shots of the couple. Late into the evening they were still waiting by the front entrance of the Ritz when, in a change of plan, Dodi, Diana, and their bodyguards left by the hotel's rear entrance to drive to Dodi's apartment. Five minutes later the hired Mercedes hurtled into the thirteenth pillar of the Place de l'Alma underpass by the river Seine, killing Dodi and driver Henri Paul instantly. Diana and their bodyguard Trevor Rees-Jones were grievously injured.

❧

At one o'clock in the morning of August 31, the queen's assistant private secretary Robin Janvrin, who was staying on the Balmoral estate, was woken up by a telephone call from the British ambassador in Paris, Sir Michael Jay, informing him about the accident. Janvrin was confounded. He hadn't even known that Diana was in Paris. He immediately threw on some clothes and alerted the staff in the "big house" to wake the queen and other senior royals. By the time he got there the whole castle was stirring, the mood one of bewilderment and confusion. As the queen asked: "What is she up to now?"

In a rare show of affection, the queen and her son physically consoled each other, perhaps sensing that this event was going to be emotionally off the grid. The queen ordered a pot of tea but never touched a drop, she, Prince Philip, and Prince Charles pacing the tartan-carpeted corridor asking what should be done. First reports suggested Diana had only suffered a broken arm and had walked away from the accident. The queen's initial response to the news was extraordinary: "Someone must have greased the brakes."[2]

Her gnomic reaction shocked and puzzled her staff, who rarely heard her use such colloquial language. They interpreted her words, which were out of character, as an indication of just how shaken she was.

An alternative view was that she was referring not to Diana, but to the possibility that one of Mohamed Al-Fayed's many avowed enemies had taken lethal action against his son and that Diana was innocent collateral damage. Sinister schemes, murderous intrigues, and coldhearted conspiracies: Anything was possible in the uneasy hours before dawn.

As the minutes ticked by the news became ever bleaker. They were told that paramedics were fighting to keep the princess alive. At that time she was already on artificial respiration, her blood pressure was very low, and she had suffered major cardiac arrest. Even as Prince Charles arranged to fly to France to be by Diana's side, Ambassador Jay relayed the terrible news that Diana was dead.

The news triggered all the swirling emotions that the Prince of Wales had kept under control. He wept, saying over and over: "What have we done to deserve this?" His first instincts were about how the public would blame him for the tragedy, an assumption that was largely accurate.

It was an issue he discussed at length with Camilla, who was at her Wiltshire home, and with his London-based aide Mark Bolland. He feared that the world would go mad, and it could destroy the monarchy.[3] It was a measure of his character and position, torn between duty and self-interest, that his fears for the future of the monarchy became conflated with his concern and sorrow for his boys who had just lost their mother.

As the respective staffs of the queen and the Prince of Wales tried to decide the official response to Diana's death, the queen wisely ordered the removal of the radio and television from the boys' nursery. She did not want the princes to hear about the news from anyone but their father. William and Harry were her immediate and continuing priority.

The queen was also at Balmoral when Mountbatten was assassinated. After the initial shock and disbelief, the royal family and their advisers knew that there was a road map for the funeral arrangements. Uncle Dickie had meticulously planned his own funeral, right down to the last medal and insignia.

For a disaffected Princess of Wales who had voluntarily relinquished her formal appellation Her Royal Highness during the divorce negotiations, everyone, including the queen, was entering unknown territory.

Although Diana was the mother of the future king and his brother, since the divorce she was technically no longer a member of the royal family. Not only did she spend much of her time in America, but she had not attended family gatherings for several years. The last time the queen had seen her was at William's confirmation in March, some five months before.

In the early going it was the express wish of the Spencer

family that the funeral service be a private affair, followed by a memorial service.

"When I rang up," said one ex-courtier who was out of the country, "there was genuine uncertainty about whether it [the funeral] was going to be public or private. If it had been private, guidance wouldn't have been needed."[4]

In the meantime, the circumstances surrounding the interment of Diana's boyfriend Dodi Fayed were swift and straightforward, the businessman laid to rest in a private ceremony at a Muslim cemetery in Woking, south London, within hours of returning home from Paris.

Unlike Dodi, Diana was an internationally-known personality as the queen's senior advisers, including the new prime minister Tony Blair, were quick to recognize.

The prime minister, who was at his Sedgefield constituency in the north of England, immediately appreciated the global implications. He told his press secretary Alastair Campbell: "This is going to unleash grief like no one has ever seen anywhere in the world."[5] After further discussion among the Spencers, the palace, and Downing Street, the family accepted that a private funeral was inappropriate for a much-loved public figure.

The queen's private secretary Sir Robert Fellowes was pivotal. Because he was married to Diana's sister Jane, he was able to steer the Spencer family toward accepting a more regal and public send-off for the princess.

Back at Balmoral, Charles readied himself to break the tragic news to his sons. At seven fifteen, Charles woke fifteen-year-old William and relayed the devastating story. "I knew something was wrong," William later recalled, "I kept waking up all night."[6] His father explained that he had to fly to Paris and that the boys would stay with their grandparents at

Balmoral. "Thank goodness we're all together," was the queen mother's immediate response. "We can look after them."[7] Her mood, according to a courtier, was "steely." Like the rest of the family she was trying to cope with the tragedy by sticking to routine. Fortunately Princess Anne's son Peter Phillips and the boys' official companion, Tiggy Legge-Bourke, were guests at the castle so they could help keep the young princes occupied.

Before the queen left for church she spoke to the prime minister. By now the family had released a brief statement saying: "The Queen and Prince of Wales are deeply shocked and distressed by this terrible news."[8] When she spoke to Blair she made it clear that no further statement would be made, but she had no objection to him making a public tribute that morning.

He later recalled: "She was most worried about the impact on the boys, obviously sad about Diana, and concerned about the monarchy itself because the Queen has a very strong instinct about public opinion and how it plays out, and, in that first conversation, we agreed to keep closely in touch with it."[9] He had only been prime minister for four months, and he now had to navigate treacherous social terrain that was essentially unknown to the Labour politician, namely the tensions between the Spencers and the Windsors and between the Prince of Wales and the queen. In an emotional tribute on the Sunday morning, Blair captured the national mood of shock and bewilderment at losing such a radiant individual so young. In a telling sentence he said: "She was the people's princess and that's how she will stay, how she will remain in our hearts and in our memories forever."

Though his words were well intentioned, the phrase *people's princess* would not be received favorably in certain quarters.

As Archbishop Carey watched his tribute he felt that Diana's alternative iconography would be set against the royal family. So it proved. As he recalled: "These fears were soon realized. There seemed to be mounting hysteria, fuelled by the media's focus on this beautiful but essentially ordinary person."[10] Political observers believed that the prime minister's phrase, *people's princess,* was not entirely welcomed by the queen. It led initially to a degree of strain that was, as the week progressed, largely dissipated.

At the time Prince Harry, then twelve, was bewildered. He and his elder brother had attended the Sunday-morning church service at Crathie at the queen's suggestion but there was no mention of his mother's passing, in either prayers or the sermon. Instead visiting minister Reverend Adrian Varwell stuck to his prepared sermon about moving house and joked about Scottish comedian Billy Connolly. Little wonder that Harry asked: "Is it true that Mummy's dead?"[11] While the kirk's minister Reverend Robert Sloan explained later that he did not mention the late princess for fear of further upsetting the boys, it played into an emerging narrative that the royal family was cool to indifferent about their mother's death.

Certainly not every member of the family felt Diana's death as keenly as others. Princess Margaret had fallen out badly with her after she appeared on the TV show *Panorama* questioning Charles's fitness to be king and talking of her ambition to be a "queen of people's hearts." Not only did Margaret consider these sentiments a betrayal of the Prince of Wales but, as far as she was concerned, there was only one queen—and it was her sister. From then on Margaret would have nothing to do with Diana and expected her children David and Sarah to ignore her, too. As a result she was deeply irritated that she had to stay at Balmoral in court mourning instead of flying off to

Tuscany where she was looking forward to her annual cultural holiday in the sun.

While she complained about the "fuss" Diana had caused, Margaret was, like her sister, concerned about the impact on William and Harry. "Terrible to lose your mother at that age, and with little Harry's birthday only a few days away," she said.[12]

Like Harry and William, millions of people worldwide were disbelieving of Diana's death. It was only at the sight of the British Aerospace 146 of the queen's flight, with the princess's coffin aboard, making its final approach from Paris to RAF Northolt in west London that the enormity of her loss began to sink in. Her coffin, draped with her own Royal Standard, was borne in silence across the tarmac by six RAF pallbearers, watched by the prime minister and other government and military dignitaries. If the Spencer family needed any further convincing that a private ceremony was wholly inappropriate, then the drive into central London along the A40 dual carriageway was further proof. Thousands of people, some openly weeping, lined the roadside or watched from bridges and other vantage points as the cortege drove past, her body taken first to a private mortuary in west London and then to the Chapel Royal at St. James Palace where she lay in state.

The outpouring of grief took everyone, not just the royal family in their Scottish home, by surprise. Early on that fateful Sunday morning, Princess Margaret's chauffeur Dave Griffin was at Kensington Palace discussing the tragic events with the duty police inspector. The officer predicted a handful of bouquets from a few well-wishers, not appreciating for a moment that the woman he waved through the gates every day had touched a nerve in the global psyche. By the late afternoon

Kensington Palace was a floating moat of cellophane-wrapped floral tributes, poems, pictures, and lighted candles.

As Carey predicted, the contrasting iconography of Diana and the royal family came into play, the perceived warmth, accessibility and normality of the princess conflicting with the cold, indifferent and aloof House of Windsor whose members used duty and tradition as a shield.

Over the next few days Britain succumbed to flower power, the scent and sight of countless bouquets bearing witness to the love and respect that people felt for a woman who, they believed, had been scorned during her lifetime by the Establishment. Thousands of people, most of whom had never met the princess, made their way to Kensington Palace to pay homage.

In a spontaneous outpouring of feeling, they expressed their grief, their sorrow, their guilt and regret. Total strangers hugged and comforted one another. Others prayed. Some mourned Diana with a greater intensity and feeling than they had done for their own lost family members.

While the church service at Crathie, where Diana's name was not mentioned, jarred with the public, resentment was beginning to build up as the palace seemed more interested in maintaining protocol than reaching out to the grieving population. At first the police would not allow the public to place bouquests outside the royal palaces while those wishing to pay written tribute were waiting many hours to sign one of the handful of books of condolence. The fact that the flagpole at Buckingham Palace was naked—traditionally only the Royal Standard is flown and then only when the sovereign is in residence—soon became a focal point, the absence of a raised flag or one flying at half-mast seen as a sign of the royal family's invisibility.

The *Sun* newspaper was typically blunt: "Where is the Queen when the country needs her? She is 550 miles from London, the focal point of the nation's grief."

∽

There was a bitter irony in this criticism of the queen. In the past she had been accused of putting duty above motherhood, particularly during the childhoods of Prince Charles and Princess Anne. Now she was being attacked for placing her compassion and concern for her grandchildren above her obligation to the nation. At Balmoral the queen's priority was to keep the boys occupied just as she had in 1979 when she had shown Timothy Knatchbull "unstoppable mothering"[13] as he recovered from the Mountbatten assassination. Prince Philip was a constant presence, reassuring and consoling. He set the boys to work preparing food for barbecue picnics, Princess Anne took Harry out exploring the Balmoral wildlife, while Peter and Zara Phillips and the boys went quad biking, horse riding, fishing, and shooting.

In between endless meetings, their father brought out the old family albums to take them on a trip down memory lane. Harry also took solace in the arms of Tiggy Legge-Bourke, the woman he called his "second mother."[14]

During that fateful week William and Harry valiantly tried to absorb their family's fortitude and stoicism: "I kept saying to myself that, you know, my mother would not want me to be upset," William recalled years later. "She'd not want me to be down. She'd not want me to be like this. I kept myself busy as well—which is good and bad sometimes—but allows you to kind of get through that initial shock phase."[15]

If they had returned to Kensington Palace they would have been kicking their heels and listening to the wailing and keening outside the gates. "Thankfully, we had the privacy to mourn and to try to collect our thoughts and have that space away from everybody," William later recalled. "We had no idea the reaction to her death would be quite so huge."[16]

At the business end of planning Diana's funeral, the queen's management team together with officials from the prime minister's office in Downing Street and representatives from the Spencer family had worked into the early hours to come up with a proposal tailored to remember and celebrate a unique human being. Early on Monday morning her senior officials, Fellowes, Janvrin, and the lord chamberlain, the Earl of Airlie, outlined what they considered to be an appropriate commemoration of Diana's life. Working, as Airlie put it, de novo as there were no precedents, the idea was to create a funeral that neatly meshed the ancient and modern with the traditional and innovative.

Diana's coffin would be pulled on a horse-drawn gun carriage, flanked by twelve pallbearers from the Welsh Guards. The standard military procession would be replaced by five hundred workers from Diana's charities.[17] Airlie argued: "It was important to bring a cross-section of the public not normally invited to the Abbey—the people Diana associated with." Everyone nervously awaited the sovereign's verdict. Thankfully the queen agreed to the proposals and made it clear that the royal family was not detached from this major event. "She was very happy with the charity workers," courtier Malcom Ross recalled.[18] Blair's press secretary Alastair Campbell was impressed by the queen's flexibility, creativity, and even risk taking—hardly words normally associated with the head of state.

There were some elements she refused to move on, in particular her family's wish to grieve in private in Scotland. She also objected to Earl Spencer's demand that Diana be buried at Althorp rather than Frogmore.

This spikiness between the House of Spencer and the House of Windsor continued throughout the week, as the Archbishop of Canterbury recalled: "I had sent a first draft of the prayers I proposed to read at the service to the Dean of Westminster for comments from those directly involved. I was taken aback when the reaction revealed intense bitterness. It was reported to me that the Spencer family did not want any mention of the Royal Family in the prayers, and in retaliation Buckingham Palace had insisted that they must have a separate prayer for the Royal Family, and that the words 'people's Princess' be removed. While I was saddened by this, I considered it essential to get the prayers right, for everyone's sake. It was a time of exceptional bewilderment, and the strain was affecting everybody."[19] The archbishop was also concerned that Earl Spencer had been invited to give the address when traditionally only members of the clergy preach at funeral services. Though he contacted Diana's brother and urged him to bring out the Christian message of hope and life evermore in God, he got the impression that the earl had other ideas about what he wanted to say.

There was another conflict brewing that had the potential to be far more damaging than Windsor versus Spencer, namely the disagreements between St. James Palace and Buckingham Palace. Or the advisers of the queen and of Prince Charles. In the early going the prince's spin doctors attempted to portray Charles as decisive and democratic while all the queen's men dithered, delayed, and hid behind precedent and tradition.

In their misleading narrative Elizabeth was depicted as initially opposed to the use of an aircraft of the queen's flight to bring her body home. Such was the anger generated by this intransigence that her deputy private secretary Robin Janvrin is said to have told the queen: "What would you rather ma'am that she came back in a Harrods van?" (The department store Harrods was owned by Mr. Al-Fayed.) Again the original idea was for Diana to remain in a public mortuary in Fulham, west London, but Charles, on his own initiative, countermanded the order.

In reality both the queen and her private secretary Sir Robert Fellowes agreed from the beginning that a plane should be sent to Paris, that she lie in state at the Chapel Royal, and there should be a full ceremonial funeral.

As an official who was present during that week recalled: "One of the most dangerous things that took place during those fraught days was that the two palaces were totally at odds with each other."[20] In short Charles's camp was prepared to throw anyone under the bus in order to protect their man—and that included the queen and other members of the royal family. This conflict continued long after Diana's burial.

As well as the flag flying—or lack of it—at Buckingham Palace, the issue of the boys walking behind the funeral cortege was the most contentious. Earl Spencer said he should be the only one to walk while representatives of the royal family pointed out that traditionally all the close male relatives accompany the coffin. This tussle was not resolved until the evening before the funeral. The boys became something of a shuttlecock among the different parties.

As one Downing Street aide recalled: "There was an amazing moment when we were on speaker with who we thought was Janvrin alone and Prince Philip came booming over the squawk box. The Spencer side had been saying what the role of the children had to be and Philip suddenly blasted, 'stop telling us what to do with those boys! You're talking about them as if they are commodities, have you any idea what they are going through!' It was rather wonderful. His voice was full of emotion, a real voice of the grandfather speaking." Later in the week, the duke again made an impromptu contribution. "Our worry at the moment is William. He's run away up the hill and we can't find him. That's the only thing we are concerned about at the moment."[21]

Twenty years later William tried to explain his confused feelings during that terrible week. "There's nothing like it in the world. There really isn't. It's like an earthquake has just run through the house and through your life and everything. Your mind is completely split. And it took me a while for it to actually sink in."[22] During this time he found consolation from his grandmother who, as he described later, "understood some of the more complex issues when you lose a loved one."[23]

As the boys sought solace with their family and the senior royals and their officials tried to work out a unique funeral for a unique individual, on the streets of London the mood had turned genuinely nasty. The initial target was the tabloid media for hiring the paparazzi who apparently chased Diana to her death, and then the royal family, not only for their slow and muted response to the tragedy but for their indifference to her during her lifetime.

With the crowds swelling around the palaces at a rate of six thousand an hour, Downing Street officials feared that rioting could break out. It was taking ten hours standing in line to sign books of condolence. Still no flag. *Where is the queen?* asked mourners in the Mall. WHERE IS OUR QUEEN? chanted the tabloids. SHOW US YOU CARE, they hysterically demanded in ninety-six-point type. Still the queen refused to budge and return to the capital.

Courtiers tried in vain to convince the queen and Prince Philip to recognize the increasingly precarious situation and fly back to the nation's capital. Tony Blair, sensing matters were genuinely getting out of hand, called Prince Charles to make clear that tide of public opinion could not "be turned back, revisited or ignored."[24] In the end an alliance of the Prince of Wales, the prime minister, and every royal adviser came together and, over a conference call, managed to persuade the queen of the magnitude of the situation. Once she was convinced that inaction was harmful to the monarchy, everything changed. She agreed to return to London a day early, go for a walkabout outside the palace, broadcast to the nation, and, for the first time in history, allow the Union Flag to fly at half-mast at Buckingham Palace.

On that final evening at Balmoral, Prince Philip suggested the family attend the service at Crathie Kirk. This time Diana was mentioned in a prayer for the family. On their way back to the castle, the boys were photographed looking at the mounds of flowers and reading the notes outside the gates.[25]

In this highly charged atmosphere the queen's return from Scotland and her decision to broadcast her own tribute to Diana from Buckingham Palace immediately helped to heal the evident dislocation between monarch and the people. The prime minister advised her to show that she was vulnerable. He told her: "I really do feel for you. There can be nothing more miserable than feeling as you do and having your motives questioned."[26]

On Friday afternoon, after flying down from Scotland, the queen and Prince Philip finally made their much-anticipated appearance among the grieving crowds. A momentary expression of anxiety flashed across her face, betraying her uncertainty as to how her people would react. "We were not confident," an ex-courtier stated, "that when the Queen got out of the car, she would not be hissed and jeered at."[27] As soon as the queen walked among her people the ugly atmosphere evaporated and the crowds erupted into spontaneous if polite applause. When an eleven-year-old girl held out a bouquet of red roses the queen asked: "Would you like me to place them for you?" The girl replied: "No, Your Majesty, they're for you."[28]

Back in the palace, the queen and her husband spent a long time talking about the public mood. The royal couple could barely process what was going on. It was like entering another world. As a senior aide explained: "At Balmoral, she hadn't taken it in. You never know what it is like until you are actually there. All the remarks and people hugging each other, sobbing—the whole nation seemed to have gone bananas. The Queen and Prince Philip felt utterly bewildered."[29]

They would have understood the national mood more keenly had they been in London, at Buckingham Palace or Windsor Castle, when the tragedy happened. It was their fortune or misfortune, depending on perspective, that they were staying at Balmoral, which is remote and beautiful but is truly like entering a time warp. Nor did they fully appreciate, along with many others, the impact of Diana's death on the national psyche. "The world has lost the plot," wrote commentator Gyles Brandreth at the time.[30] Yet for the public, who had keenly watched the upward trajectory of Diana's life, it was the suddenness of her death that was so difficult to bear. It was an unequal end to everything that had gone before in her life. The queen and her family did not see what the public saw. They mourned someone whom they all knew, the family lamenting the flawed individual rather than the saintly icon. Years later Harry discussed his own confusion. He heard people sobbing when he couldn't bring himself to cry for his late mother. His father felt a similar sense of bafflement, the Prince of Wales recalling: "I felt an alien in my own country."[31]

At the time the queen was preparing for only the second special televised address of her reign—the first was in February 1991 before the First Gulf War. "She knew it was something she should do," noted one senior adviser.[32] Her speech was initially drafted by her private secretary, then discussed with the queen, Prince Philip, and other courtiers before being sent to Downing Street for final approval. As Blair and Campbell read the draft, one of the duo suggested that the sovereign should speak not only as the queen but as a grandmother. It was a touch of genius.

The queen agreed to be filmed live in the Chinese Dining Room in front of a large window overlooking the Mall, which was teeming with flowers and mourners.[33]

Her three-minute-and-nine-second speech was one of the most effective of her reign. Her uncomplicated authenticity, clear reading, and respect toward the late princess meant that there was an immediate "dissipation of hostility to the Windsors."[34]

She spoke of the disbelief, incomprehension, and sense of loss. "We have all felt those emotions in these last few days. So what I say to you now as your queen and as a grandmother, I say from my heart. First, I want to pay tribute to Diana myself. She was an exceptional and gifted human being. In good times and bad, she never lost her capacity to smile and laugh, nor to inspire others with her warmth and kindness. I admired and respected her—for her energy and commitment to others and especially for her devotion to her boys."

With a nod to the criticism of herself and her family she continued: "I for one believe that there are lessons to be drawn from her life and from the extraordinary and moving reaction to her death."[35]

She had been slow to change direction when it became clear she was out of step with the nation, and though the boys were the focus of the family and her own concerns there had been nothing to stop a camera crew filming a similar message at Balmoral several days earlier. This would have stopped criticism of the royal family and the monarchy in its tracks.

Her speech, though several days late, had done the trick. George Carey remarked that "it showed her compassion and understanding, it went a very long way toward silencing her critics and removing the misunderstanding that had developed."[36] Support for republicanism dropped after the speech.

At dinner that evening, one final question needed to be answered—would William and Harry walk behind their mother's coffin and follow royal tradition? While the final decision was left to the princes themselves, in the end it was the intervention of their grandfather Prince Philip that proved decisive. "If I walk, will you walk?" he asked.[37] When William agreed, Harry followed his lead. "The boys are very close with their grandparents, adore them," observed press secretary Dickie Arbiter. "Significantly, they walked for their grandfather, not their father or uncle."[38] There was also the fear that if only Prince Charles and Charles Spencer walked, the future king, who had received numerous threatening letters during the week, could be jeered at or physically attacked by a member or members of the crowd who blamed the prince for Diana's death.

On the day of the funeral the queen and her family assembled outside the gates of Buckingham Palace. As the funeral cortege passed the royal party, the queen bowed her head in a moment of obeisance, acknowledging Diana herself but also perhaps what she represented about the changing values of modern Britain.

As the queen and other members of the family bowed their heads in respect, Princess Margaret remained upright and upstanding, looking like she would rather be somewhere else. Somewhat bizarrely, as the queen and Margaret waited for the arrival of the cortege, she had been nagging the queen about improving the lavatories at Kensington Palace.[39] It was a moment that symbolized the estrangement between two former royal neighbors.[40]

Paradoxically it was the fact that the boys displayed the traditional royal virtues of stoicism and fortitude amid a sea of tears that lent the funeral such an emotional resonance. They adhered impeccably to the maxim of Princess Alice, Countess of Athlone: "You don't wear private grief on a public sleeve." Prince Philip comforted his grandsons on that lengthy walk by quietly pointing out historic landmarks and explaining their background.[41]

A worldwide audience of two and a half billion watched as Tony Blair read from the Bible and Diana's sisters Jane and Sarah read poems inside Westminster Abbey while Elton John gave an emotional rendition of his hit song "Candle in the Wind," which he dedicated to the late princess.

It was Charles Spencer who publicly threw down the gauntlet to the royal family and the mass media, implicitly rebuking the royal family for stripping the princess of her appellation Her Royal Highness, and for the cool way they raised their children. "Diana," he said, "needed no royal title to continue to generate her particular brand of magic." He pledged to William and Harry that the Spencers, their "blood family," would continue the imaginative way in which Diana was steering her sons "so that their souls are not simply immersed by duty and tradition, but can sing openly as you planned." He highlighted too the way the media was on a quest to "bring her down." As he finished his peroration, praising his sister as the "unique, the complex, the extraordinary and irreplaceable Diana, whose beauty, both internal and external, will never be extinguished from our minds," applause rippled from the crowd outside the open doors of the abbey. Inside the abbey, after a moment of recognition, the congregation, including William and Harry, also applauded his address. It was, however, unclear whether the applause was in acknowledgment of the earl's assessment of his sister, the mass media, or the royal family.

The queen stared ahead, stony-faced, as did her husband. Prince Charles was so incensed that he had to be restrained from issuing a public statement. As Dickie Arbiter recalled: "The mood inside the royal family was very angry about what he said and the courtiers were apoplectic, shell-shocked."[42] The queen felt that Diana's brother should have made more of Diana's evident Christian qualities, a point the Archbishop of Canterbury made before the service. It was an opportunity missed, she felt.

After the funeral and Diana's burial at Althorp, the royal family returned to Balmoral. The next day, exactly a week after the accident, Tony and Cherie Blair flew to the queen's Highland home for an abbreviated prime minister's weekend. During his private audience with the queen, Blair spoke about the possible lessons to be learned from Diana's death. He recollected that the queen was "reflecting, considering and adjusting."[43] Before she headed off on her delayed Italian holiday, Princess Margaret sent her older sister a note of thanks for "how kindly you arranged everybody's lives after the accident and made life tolerable for the two poor boys. There, always in command, was you, listening to everyone and deciding on all the issues. I just felt you were wonderful."[44]

After such a bruising week, the queen appreciated the

loyalty and support of a sister who knew her so intimately. Brought up not to show emotion in public, Margaret, like the queen, found the wailing and keening hard to understand.

In another private letter, this time a reply to a close confidant, Lady Henriette Abel Smith, the queen spoke of the negatives and positives that had emerged from the funeral week. In a typed portion she wrote: "It was indeed dreadfully sad, and she is a huge loss to the country. But the public reaction to her death, and the service in the Abbey seem to have united people around the world in a rather inspiring way. William and Harry have been so brave and I am very proud of them."

In her own handwriting she continued: "I think your letter was one of the first I opened—emotions still so mixed up but we have all been through a very bad experience!"[45]

Even though the queen had been on the throne for more than forty-five years, following Diana's death it felt as if the queen, or rather the monarchy, was on probation. She had gone head-to-head with her people and by and large the people had won.

While the mantra from Buckingham Palace was that lessons had been learned, a skeptical nation watched warily—and reserved judgment. It was recognized that the disconnect between sovereign and society during the tumultuous funeral week would take some healing, although the polls clearly showed that the people didn't want a republic. They wanted to see a modernized monarchy more in touch with multicultural Britain. For a woman schooled in precedent and tradition with the unspoken question *What would my father have done?* always hanging in the air, any reform would be sensible and incremental. She was also stubborn when under threat. When Lord Altrincham argued for the abolition of the presentation of debutantes at Buckingham Palace, the queen delayed the decision for a year so as not to give the radical lord the satisfaction of saying: *I told you so.*

And Britain was changing. While new Labour prime minister Tony Blair praised the queen as "the best of British" at a lunch to celebrate her fiftieth wedding anniversary in November 1997, he was on the cusp of overseeing a remodeling of the political landscape, with closer European integration, devolution of powers to Scotland, Wales, and Northern Island, an elected mayor of London and London Assembly, as well as integration into European laws. With a growing movement for Scottish devolution and the queen's beloved Commonwealth of Nations something of a political afterthought, the nation was fundamentally evolving—and not in a way that necessarily enhanced the monarchy.

Amid calls for a "People's Monarchy" to mirror the work of the "people's princess," the queen gradually adjusted her public persona, often with the advice of pollsters, well-connected diplomats, and media mavens. Prince Philip was especially interested in the new monarchy website, www.royal.uk, while the inception of the Way Ahead Group, which comprised senior members of the family and their advisers, was designed to give early warning of problems ahead and chart a safe course for the monarchy in the future.

◠

Though the queen said, "I don't do stunts," meaning that she wouldn't play up to the camera or the prevailing view, the media pack was now swollen with correspondents looking for signs of the "Diana effect." Had the queen truly learned lessons from Diana's life and altered her tone and style accordingly? The omens seemed positive.

When the queen visited a school she now sat with the

children rather than standing with the head teacher. At a drive through McDonald's in Ellesmere Port in 1998 she allowed herself to be photographed with excited staff, and on a 1999 visit to the Craigdale estate in Glasgow she joined pensioner Susan McCarron for tea and chocolate biscuits in her neat-as-a-pin bungalow.

During a tour of Malaysia in September 1998 she signed a Manchester United football for fans and even allowed glimpses of humor to shine through her normally impassive facade. She let it be known that when England had a goal disallowed during a World Cup match with Argentina she had thrown her arms up in the air in disgust at the decision and declared "one is not amused." As a further nod to egalitarianism, she took the train to and from King's Lynn in Norfolk for her annual festive holiday in Sandringham. Several commuters expressed their shocked delight at walking past her first-class carriage and seeing the queen quietly looking out at the passing parade.

As the *Sunday Telegraph* observed, "We are not seeing a new Queen. What we are gradually noticing is the same Queen reflecting the changing society around her."[46]

In a further nod to Diana, the Union Flag was now routinely raised over unoccupied royal residences. The bare flagpole that caused so much concern during the funeral week was no more. "The princess was very good at picking issues," a palace official reflected, "and we have to learn from that. She was very good at keeping abreast of topics of public concern. That was one of her strengths and a lesson that could be learned."[47]

In December 1997 the royal yacht *Britannia*, the floating country home and safe haven on overseas visits, was decommissioned in Portsmouth after half a lifetime's service. The queen was reluctant to say goodbye as the yacht held so many memories of happy times as a family, particularly the annual

Western Islands cruise. Before the formal service, the queen and her family took one last lingering look around the yacht. It was an emotional private farewell, the queen seen dabbing away tears before retiring for lunch in the state dining room. Later at the public ceremony on the quayside the queen and the princess royal, who was also distressed, watched tearfully as the Royal Marines Band played the highly evocative "Highland Cathedral" during their final farewell. It was quickly pointed out by several media pundits that they never shed a tear for the princess though they cried over a floating piece of metal.

The yacht was stripped of all its royal memorabilia, including a narwhal tusk and oil paintings by Prince Philip, before she was sailed to Leith Harbor in Scotland where she is now a popular tourist attraction. Most of the artifacts have been reinstated.

At Kensington Palace a similar operation had been undertaken by the Spencer family. Everything in Diana's apartment was removed lest trophy hunters sell Diana memorabilia. Her butler Paul Burrell complained that Diana's mother, Frances Shand Kydd, had even shredded the blotting paper on her daughter's desk.

Within a matter of months all traces of her had been removed from her former royal home.

13

⚜

Two Weddings and Two Funerals

While Diana was gone but not forgotten, Camilla Parker Bowles, now divorced, was very much around and Prince Charles made it abundantly clear that she was not going anywhere.

His obdurate attitude placed the palaces of St. James and Buckingham on a collision course. The prince had already laid the groundwork for her continuing presence in his life; publicly in his 1994 documentary where he said that Camilla was a good friend then and would be in the future, and privately in her role as the mistress, albeit low-profile, of Highgrove.

This did not please the queen who had wanted Camilla gone, both before and after Diana's death. Her senior officials, notably her principal private secretary Sir Robert Fellowes, were in firm agreement. They felt that the prince's desire for self-fulfillment was in danger of jeopardizing the monarchy.

As Camilla's biographer Penny Junor noted, "It was nothing

personal. She had been very fond of Camilla in all the years she had been married to Andrew but it was Camilla who had been responsible, wittingly or not, for all the disasters that had befallen the prince since his marriage."[1]

The queen could be forgiven for thinking that Charles had not spent enough time working on his marriage before going back to Camilla's soothing ministrations. However difficult Diana had been—and the queen knew all about her wayward behavior—she had deserved more than the four or five years he had devoted to married life before going his own way. The now unanswerable question was whether Charles and Diana would have remained married had Camilla not been on the scene.

Few at the official fiftieth birthday party for Charles held at Buckingham Palace would have sensed the familial tension in the air. An estimated 850 guests including Prime Minister Tony Blair and former premier Margaret Thatcher, toasted his achievements and life in the presence of the queen and Prince Philip. The queen praised her son for his "diligence, compassion and leadership."[2] It all seemed so friendly and easygoing. Prince Charles referred to the queen as Mummy, a description that always got an amused reaction—so much so that he used it often.

Behind the public smiles, relations between "Mummy" and "darling" could not have been worse. The first issue was the thudding absence of Charles's companion Camilla Parker Bowles, who had deliberately been left off the palace invitation list by the queen. Second was an ITV television documentary, broadcast to coincide with the prince's birthday, that had the fingerprints of his charming but ruthless deputy private secretary Mark Bolland all over it. A "senior official" had briefed the TV producers that Charles wanted a slimmed-down monarchy and would be "privately delighted if the queen abdicated."[3]

When confronted by the queen, Charles apologized and said the story was untrue. However, this was by no means the end of the matter. A rival BBC documentary, also well briefed by an anonymous official, emphasized that Charles was irritated with the queen for not stepping back from more of her official duties and letting him take over. To make matters even more awkward, one of the queen's aides anonymously briefed the BBC show on the queen's attitude toward Camilla. "The Queen has not and will not formally meet with Camilla. She will not even appear at the same social function."[4] In fact she had not been on the guest list of either the queen or the queen mother for the last fifteen years or so.

It was a similar reason behind the queen's refusal to meet Princess Margaret's boyfriend, Roddy Llewellyn, who came into her life while she was still married, albeit very unhappily. In the court of public opinion Roddy, rightly or wrongly, was seen as the catalyst who exploded the royal marriage and led to the first royal divorce since Henry VIII. In a comparable situation, at least as far as the queen and her private secretary were concerned, Charles's continuing association with Mrs. Parker Bowles was damaging the monarchy: The public, again rightly or wrongly, believed that Camilla, as the third wheel in the Waleses' marriage, had precipitated their divorce.

Though Camilla was omitted from the Buckingham Palace guest list, she did appear at Highgrove on Charles's actual birthday, November 14, 1998, where she and the prince hosted a party for 250 guests including actors, politicians, and comedians. The queen and Prince Philip turned down the invitation as did his three siblings. However, Princess Margaret did attend along with various crowned heads of Europe. As Charles and Camilla greeted the array of guests it was clear to fellow partygoers that they were in it for the long haul.

So, too, was Charles's public relations guru and now deputy private secretary Mark Bolland, whose brief was to grasp the nettle and make Camilla acceptable to the queen and the British public. If it meant treading on toes to make the Prince of Wales look good—so be it, even if those toes were wearing size-four Anello & Davides, makers of the queen's shoes.

He and other supporters of Prince Charles were aware that the "love her but leave her" attitude of the queen and Sir Robert Fellowes was not universally accepted by all senior advisers, who felt that an olive branch should be proffered to the couple. The world had moved on since the abdication and Princess Margaret's renunciation of her lover, Group Captain Peter Townsend, because of divorce.

The Archbishop of Canterbury George Carey and his wife Eileen had privately met with Camilla on several occasions and he came to appreciate the deep and affectionate relationship that existed between Prince Charles and herself. "Subsequent meetings gave us no reason to change our opinion that her future was irrevocably bound up in his," he recalled.[5]

While Prince Charles was in no rush to remarry, it was not a situation that could continue indefinitely. Even though the queen was in robust health there was no point in tempting fate. A king living with his divorced mistress would not find approval among clerics, churchgoers, and those who still carried a torch for the late princess. The strategy therefore was to navigate a pathway that would allow Charles to marry Camilla without their union being seen to harm the monarchy. As for the prospect of "Queen Camilla," that was some way down the road.

Bolland realized that Camilla's rehabilitation would be accelerated if she was recognized in a positive light by Diana's sons. They were her living representatives, her flagbearers. If they could accept Camilla, why not the British public who, according to opinion polls, opposed Camilla becoming queen by a slim majority.

On a sunny day in June 1998 Camilla was about to find out. William arrived unexpectedly at York House, next to St. James's Palace, while Camilla was present. She offered to leave but Charles insisted she say hello to his eldest son. They were formally introduced and then spoke privately for about thirty minutes. The meeting went well, though afterward Camilla announced that she needed a gin and tonic to calm her nerves.

The queen's men were not so easily swayed. Shortly after Prince William had been introduced to Camilla, the queen's deputy private secretary Sir Robin Janvrin also happened to be in the building. Charles, who felt he was on a regal roll, asked his private secretary Stephen Lamport to organize another meeting, this time between Camilla and Sir Robin. Janvrin refused, saying that he would have to ask the queen first. Some time later, after Sir Robert Fellowes had retired, the queen did give Janvrin, now her private secretary, leave to privately meet Mrs. Parker Bowles and take the constitutional temperature.[6]

The temperature outside the Ritz hotel in central London was freezing on January 28, 1999, when Charles continued his campaign to make the public feel warmer toward his companion. That night Charles and Camilla were guests at her sister Annabel Elliot's fiftieth birthday party at the hotel. They arrived separately but left together, their path to a waiting limousine illuminated by scores of camera flashbulbs. The unofficial photo call was organized by Mark Bolland, whom William and Harry now dubbed Lord Blackadder, after the devious character in a TV comedy.

This was the first of a series of highly orchestrated public moves to introduce Camilla to the nation. Over the next few months the couple appeared in the audience at West End plays, the Royal Shakespeare Theatre at Stratford-upon-Avon, and a classical piano concert, as well as on the hunting fields of East Yorkshire. There was a sign of a thaw from Buckingham Palace. In January 1999 the engagement of Prince Edward to public relations executive Sophie Rhys-Jones was announced. During their six month engagement the couple, with the queen's consent occupied adjoining rooms at Buckingham Palace. The times were indeed a-changin'.

In May 2000, Camilla's appearance at the General Assembly of the Church of Scotland in Edinburgh where the Prince of Wales gave the keynote address was a further indication of her wider acceptance. At dinner that evening Camilla told Janis Milligan, the wife of the lord provost of Edinburgh, Eric, that this was a big moment for her. It did not escape anyone's notice that the Church of Scotland, which is considered to be more liberal than the Church of England, was willing to marry the divorced Princess Anne and her second husband, Commander Tim Laurence.

Finally on June 3, 2000, Camilla came face-to-face with the queen for the first time since 1992. When the queen accepted her son's invitation to attend a barbecue lunch at Highgrove to celebrate the sixtieth birthday of King Constantine of Greece, she was fully aware of the consequences. She was acknowledging, if not yet accepting, Charles's companion at court. The queen smiled, Camilla curtsied, and they made brief small talk before retiring to their separate tables.

Though Camilla was now referred to as the prince's "companion," there was still no place for her at formal royal functions. At a grand black-tie ball at Windsor Castle, the first since the devastating fire, in June 2000, the queen hosted a combined birthday party for her mother's one hundredth, her sister's seventieth, her daughter's fiftieth, Prince Andrew's fortieth, and Prince William's coming of age. Camilla was not invited. With public opinion becoming more favorable to Camilla, though, the queen was in danger of looking out of step with her subjects. Even members of her own family, especially the younger generation, felt that Camilla should be formally recognized.

Nonetheless Camilla was notably absent from the queen mother's hundredth birthday celebrations where her beloved grandson Prince Charles accompanied her in a horse-drawn carriage on Horse Guards Parade in July before a cheering crowd. Acceptance came in increments. In February 2001 both Prince Charles and Prince William attended the tenth anniversary of the Press Complaints Commission at Somerset House. As Camilla arrived with the prince, the ladies and gentlemen of the mass media were invited to conclude that if Camilla was publicly accepted by William, Diana's torchbearer on earth, then everyone else should follow suit. Not so the queen mother, who did not invite her to celebrate her 101st birthday. Inadvertantly the Countess of Wessex indicated the prevailing mood at Court some months previously when she was trapped in a tabloid sting by the notorious Fake Sheik, a tabloid reporter impersonating a wealthy Arab. During the secretly taped conversation the countess described Charles and Camilla as "number one on the unpopular list" who would only marry after the death of "the old lady," meaning the queen mother.[7]

Terrible events in New York, Washington, and Pennsylvania overshadowed all thoughts of "Queen Camilla" when al Qaeda terrorists carried out the 9/11 atrocities. The queen, who was in Balmoral, acted with alacrity. Her robust decisions were in sharp contrast with the paralysis that affected the royal family following Diana's death. She agreed to the Union Jack

flying over Buckingham Palace at half-mast and prepared to
fly to London for a special service at St. Paul's Cathedral to
honor the dead who included sixty-seven Britons. The queen
also approved a suggestion that at the next Changing of the
Guard, the Coldstream Band play the "Star Spangled Ban-
ner." It was a deeply emotional few minutes that left many of
the crowd outside the gates of Buckingham Palace in tears. In
her message of condolence, which was read out by the British
ambassador at a memorial service in New York, the ringing
phrase "Grief is the price we pay for love," which was penned
by her private secretary Sir Robin Janvrin, struck just the right
tone.[8]

The queen felt the tragedy more keenly as her great friend
and racing manager Henry "Porchie" Carnarvon died of a heart
attack on the same day. He was watching television coverage of
the attacks on the World Trade Center when he suffered what
proved to be a fatal episode. It was all the more devastating as
it was so sudden and unexpected. Porchie and the queen had
been friends since the war and at one point he was considered
as a possible romantic partner. Besides her immediate family, he
was one of only a handful of people who would be put through
by the Buckingham Palace operator to speak to her on the
telephone. He would bring her up to speed with news from her
stables and gossip from the equine world. His death was a real
blow not just for the queen but for the world of racing. As well
as grieving the loss of her great friend, the queen had a great
deal to worry about with regard to her two dearest relatives.

The health of both the queen mother and Princess Margaret
was deteriorating, so much so that they were brought together
by helicopter to spend the 2001 festive season at Sandringham.
Both were confined to wheelchairs; the queen mother had
previously broken her hip in a fall while Margaret had suffered

several strokes, which had left her visually impaired. Though the queen encouraged her sister to try walking rather than rely on her wheelchair, her jaunty blandishments got her nowhere.

For the most part Margaret retired to her room and listened to the radio, a sad shell of the vibrant, glamorous woman who graced nightclubs and glossy magazine covers. The queen tried her best to encourage her sister to join the family throng but she "looked so awful" that she declined. It was seen as a minor triumph when her lady-in-waiting Lady Glenconner enticed her to eat a jam tart. At one point Margaret complained to her maid: "If only I were a dog, I could be put down."[9]

On February 8, 2002, she suffered yet another stroke and died early the next morning in King Edward VII's Hospital with her children by her bedside. "We four" were now "we two," the queen losing another member of the family quartet whom she was able to trust and rely on completely. Her mischievous little sister had proved a loyal and dutiful adviser who enjoyed an instinctive bond of blood and shared experience. Now she was gone.

The funeral service was held at St. George's Chapel, Windsor, with the queen mother flown to the service by helicopter and taken to the funeral in a wheelchair. After the service, as the coffin was borne out of the chapel, the queen mother, with great difficulty, struggled to her feet in a final sad acknowledgment of her daughter. The queen, too, seemed overwhelmed by the loss of the sister she spoke to on the telephone nearly every day. As the coffin was placed into a hearse, one hand gripped that of her niece Sarah Chatto, and the other brushed away a tear.

Her coffin was taken to Slough Crematorium and her ashes interred in the King George VI Memorial Chapel in St. George's next to her father—as she always wanted.

There was little respite for the queen. As it was her Golden Jubilee year, she was touring extensively. After she bade a sad farewell to Margaret, she and Prince Philip flew on an official visit to New Zealand, Australia, and Jamaica. During the two-week tour the queen telephoned her mother every day, and as soon as she arrived back at Heathrow airport she drove immediately to Royal Lodge to check on her well-being. She discovered that her mother was still seeing people, eating little, drinking champagne, and telephoning old friends and associates in a long, last goodbye.

A few days later the queen was out riding in Windsor Great Park when her groom had word from the castle on his radio that the queen mother was sinking fast. Immediately she headed to Royal Lodge where she found her mother, her eyes closed, seated in a chair, her dresser and a local nurse by her side.

In between the comings and goings of medical personnel, Canon John Ovenden, the parish priest of the royal chapel, arrived. He held her hand and recited a Highland lament. Later the queen mother was put to bed.

By her bedside were the queen, Princess Margaret's children David Linley and Sarah Chatto, as well as Lady Margaret Rhodes, who was always considered the queen mother's third daughter. Canon Ovenden returned later and uttered a poignant word of prayer: "Now lettest thou thy servant depart in peace."

She died at three fifteen in the afternoon of March 30, 2002. "We all had tears in our eyes and to this day I cannot hear that being said without wanting to cry," recalled Margaret Rhodes.[10]

Her death was the signal for Operation Tay Bridge, the code name for the queen mother's funeral arrangements, to be put into effect. On Friday, April 5 an estimated quarter of a million people lined the streets as the queen mother's oak coffin was taken from St. James's Palace to lie in state at Westminster Hall. Next to her crown and Royal Standard on the coffin was a wreath saying IN LOVING MEMORY, LILIBET. As the queen was driven back to Buckingham Palace, the crowd burst into spontaneous applause, a gesture that stirred her profoundly. The queen mother's official biographer William Shawcross recalled: "She was visibly moved and she said to one of those with her that this moment was one of the most touching things that had ever happened to her."[11]

In only her third special address to the nation, the queen reflected on that particular experience and singled out the mourners whose "kindness and respect" had given her great comfort. "This is what my mother would have understood, because it was the warmth and affection of people everywhere which inspired her resolve, dedication and enthusiasm for life."[12] She later told friends that if she had had to speak about the loss of her sister as well she would not have been able to maintain her composure. The next day, April 9, 2002, the queen mother's coffin was placed on a gun carriage and taken to Westminster Abbey for the funeral. Following the service her body was driven to St George's chapel to lie beside her husband, George VI. We four was now reduced to one.

With the queen mother laid to rest with due pomp and dignity, the auguries seemed propitious for the queen's Golden Jubilee. Any remaining doubts that this was going to be an impressive national celebration were stilled during a fourteen-week crisscrossing of the country.

The enthusiasm was infectious. Women were seen running out of hairdressers, their hair in curlers, in order to catch a glimpse of the queen as she passed by. At one point she tapped on the glass ceiling of her limousine and apparently told her chauffeur to slow down as she wanted to savor the atmosphere for a little longer.[13]

In early June 2002, after a weekend of street parties and pageantry, the highlight of the celebrations was the rock concert held at Buckingham Palace. Guitarist Brian May opened the proceedings from the roof of the palace with an iconic rendition of "God Save the Queen." Pop aristocracy, including Paul McCartney, Elton John, Annie Lennox, and Ray Davies, played to the largest audience—estimated to be over one million—since Live Aid in 1985. When he was introduced to the queen, Ozzie Osborne was so nervous he called her "your worship, your holiness."

Prince Charles got the biggest cheer when he began his speech of appreciation by saying: "Your Majesty.... Mummy." He went on to praise her for embodying continuity in the lives of the nation. "You have been a beacon of tradition and stability in the midst of profound and sometimes perilous change," he said.[14]

At the first major royal event since the death of the queen mother, Camilla was at last included with the royal party, seated in the row behind Princes William and Harry. She sang along to the Phil Collins song "You Can't Hurry Love," lyrics that, as columnist Caitlin Moran observed, must have been of great comfort to her over the years.[15] At the end of the show, she joined the queen and the rest of the family in a celebratory dinner at the Ritz hotel.

Of wider import was the decision in July by the Church of England to allow divorced couples to marry in church even if a former spouse was still alive in exceptional circumstances. Modern domestic realities combined with greater tolerance were changing the landscape regarding divorce and remarriage.

The beneficiaries seemed to be the Prince of Wales and his companion.

There was, too, a major change in the queen's manner. Those who had known her for some time remarked on how she seemed more relaxed, more approachable and at ease now that she was no longer having to second-guess what her mother might say or think. She was the undisputed matriarch of the family, free to carve out her own path. As historian Hugo Vickers observed: "After the Queen Mother's death suddenly the queen did blossom there is no doubt about it."[16]

Peace was also breaking out between the various royal palaces following the departure of contentious courtiers who had polarized opinions inside the royal court. With the death of the queen mother, the Prince of Wales had taken over her London home, Clarence House, and Birkhall in Scotland.

As part of the renovations of his new London home he had hired interior designer Robert Kime, who had restored Highgrove, to decorate a suite of rooms for Camilla and guest quarters for her father Bruce Shand. It was clear he intended to live with his companion.

Work was still ongoing in Charles's new home when the ghost of Diana came to haunt the royal family once more. This time the queen was center stage, the monarch involved in a high-profile court case at London's storied Old Bailey that revolved around Paul Burrell, Diana's former butler, who was accused of stealing property belonging to the late princess, her sons, and Prince Charles. The allegedly stolen items included signed pictures and letters, designer clothes, and other personal memorabilia. When he was arrested two years before he insisted that he had only taken the property, valued at £6 million ($7.8 million), for safekeeping. He was eventually charged with theft in August 2001.

After several days of evidence at the famous Number One Court there was an extraordinary twist that defied even the script contortions of a Hollywood movie. Just before Burrell was due to take the stand, the trial was halted. Enter the queen.

On October 25, 2002, while traveling to the memorial service at St. Paul's Cathedral for victims of the Bali bombing, the queen, Prince Philip, and Prince Charles were discussing the case when the queen recalled a lengthy audience with Paul Burrell five years earlier in which he had referred to safekeeping some of Diana's documents. She had not considered this relevant as they formed only a small proportion of the large amount of allegedly stolen property he had taken.

This revelation fatally undermined the prosecution's case that Burrell had never told anyone that he was taking Diana's property for safekeeping. Now it seemed he had.

When the queen was further questioned by Prince Charles's new private secretary, Sir Michael Peat, she confirmed that Burrell was going to look after Diana's papers as he was concerned that Diana's mother, Frances Shand Kydd, was shredding important documents relating to her life and legacy.

While the queen's intervention added to the surreal nature of the trial, equally bizarre was the fact that in the two years since his arrest Paul Burrell had not once mentioned to his lawyers this conversation with the queen even though the thrust of the prosecution case against him was that he told no one that he had taken Diana's property.

On November 1 the trial was halted and all charges dropped. As he left the court in relieved triumph he told the milling throng: "The Queen came through for me."[17] Commentators immediately seized on the fact that the trial was halted just before Burrell was due to take the stand in order to ensure his silence. During his testimony he was widely expected to reveal potentially embarrassing details about the late princess, Prince Charles, and the dark side of the monarchy. As the royal family had had numerous opportunities to resolve this matter before trial, these allegations seemed exaggerated.

What was intriguing, though, was Burrell's assertion that he had enjoyed a ninety-minute conversation with the queen in her private apartments where they had discussed everything from Diana's personality to her relationship with Dodi Fayed and his concerns about the behavior of the Spencer family in destroying Diana's artifacts.

During their lengthy conversation the queen issued a somewhat melodramatic warning: "Be careful, Paul. No one has been as close to a member of the Royal Family as you have. There are powers at work in this country about which we have no knowledge. Do you understand?"[18] Then she ended the conversation by saying: "I must take the dogs for a walk."

Burrell later told the *Daily Mirror*: "She made sure I knew she was being deadly serious. I had no idea who she was talking about. There were many things she could have been referring to. But she was clearly warning me to be vigilant."[19]

While Burrell did not explain or know what "powers" may have posed a threat to him, it was all of a piece with Diana's suspicions about her personal safety when she was alive. She had her apartments swept on several occasions. While the queen did not jump at shadows, in the early 1990s she, too, had been unnerved by the rash of illicit tape recordings of private conversations made about members of her family.

A year later, in October 2003, Burrell had his moment in the sun when he released his biography A *Royal Duty*, which revisited the turbulent life of Diana, Princess of Wales, and her relationship with the royal family. One of the more contentious issues was the publication of a letter from Prince Philip to Diana, Princess of Wales, concerning Prince Charles's affair with Mrs. Parker Bowles. He wrote: "Charles was silly to risk everything with Camilla for a man in his position. We never dreamed he might feel like leaving you for her. I cannot imagine anyone in their right mind would leave you for Camilla. Such a prospect never even entered our heads."[20]

Written in the previous decade, it neatly encapsulated the queen's objections to her son's choice of partner and also demonstrated Camilla's uphill struggle to be accepted inside and outside the royal family.

Her inside-outside status continued to cause embarrassment and offense as members of society took their cues from the queen. The wedding of Lady Tamara Grosvenor and Edward van Cutsem, the son of Charles's longtime friend and prominent Catholic Hugh van Cutsem, in 2004 proved to be a turning point. It was the society wedding of the year, with a guest list that included the queen and Prince Philip as well as Prince Charles, who was godfather to Edward van Cutsem, and Camilla Parker Bowles. As the big day approached the groom's mother Emilie van Cutsem informed Camilla, who was a friend, that to avoid giving offense to the queen she had been seated separately from her partner who was in the front pews with other members of the royal family. In addition she would be obliged to travel separately from Prince Charles.[21] The prince was furious at what he interpreted as a snub and withdrew their acceptance of the wedding invitation. Instead Charles visited his regiment, the Black Watch, while Camilla spent the day at home, doubtless pondering how long this social uncertainty would last. It would not be long.

Aside from the niceties of etiquette at social events such as weddings, there were serious constitutional matters to consider. It was a question of becoming not just man and wife, but also king and queen. What would Camilla's status be if Charles succeeded and they were still unmarried?

Though Prince Charles wanted a church wedding, the new Archbishop of Canterbury, Dr. Rowan Williams, argued against. He felt that a church wedding would offend many Anglican priests and parishioners. Instead a compromise was reached: They could marry in a civil ceremony followed by a service of prayers and a blessing in church.

Once the ecumenical matters were resolved, it was a matter of formally asking the queen under the Royal Marriages Act of 1772 for permission to marry. He received the queen's blessing and those of his sons at Sandringham that Christmas. Finally, over New Year at Birkhall, a rather more grown-up setting than the nursery at Windsor where he had asked Lady Diana Spencer to marry him, the Prince of Wales got down on one knee and asked Camilla to be his bride. He presented her with an art-deco-style diamond ring that he had inherited from the queen mother.

It was almost the end of a long, uncertain march with the prospect of a happy future together now beckoning.

After publicly announcing their engagement in February, the couple married on Saturday, April 9, 2005, in a civil ceremony at the Guildhall in Windsor. When the big day arrived, Camilla was so nervous that it took four friends to coax her out of bed and help her into her Anna Valentine dress.

Once suitably dressed, she was driven to the Guildhall in Windsor where the civil ceremony was due to take place. When she emerged from the queen's maroon Rolls-Royce, she looked pensive, the newest member of the royal family worried that she might be heckled by someone in the crowd.

They were on her side, onlookers applauding as she and Prince Charles walked into the Guildhall where, in the company of close friends and relatives, they exchanged their vows as well as rings of Welsh gold. Prince William and Camilla's son Tom Parker Bowles were witnesses.

The queen did not attend though her grandsons and other family members did. As the head of the Church of England it was not her practice to ever attend civil ceremonies. While some interpreted her decision as a snub, it was predicated on her decision to put her duty before any family feelings. She did not want to set a precedent that could compromise her position as the supreme governor of the Church of England. She did attend the service of dedication inside St. George's Chapel, which was conducted by the Archbishop of Canterbury Dr. Rowan Williams. As a further gesture of goodwill she hosted and paid for the wedding reception.

It was a very relaxed party that, after the service of dedication, walked to the historic Waterloo Chamber where the queen had organized celebrations for the seven hundred guests. In a deft and witty speech the queen, who had a horse running at the Grand National at Aintree that day, told the rowdy throng that she had two announcements. The first was that Hedgehunter had won the National and that she was delighted to be welcoming her son and his bride into "the winners' enclosure."

"They have overcome Becher's Brook and The Chair [two famous jumps at the National] and all kinds of other terrible obstacles. They have come through and I'm very proud and wish them well. My son is home and dry with the woman he loves."[22] Though she could have taken the title Princess of Wales, out of deference to Diana's memory, Camilla was granted the title Duchess of Cornwall with the appellation Her Royal Highness.

It was late afternoon when Charles's Bentley, festooned with JUST MARRIED signs, headed to Birkhall for their honeymoon.

This marked the end of a historic day that had finally seen the resolution of an issue that had blighted the queen's reign for more than a decade.

$\sim$

It was a moment of unadulterated joy and celebration. Red, white, and blue ticker tape showered the cheering crowd in Trafalgar Square while the Red Arrows aerial display team screamed past overhead leaving a red, white, and blue vapor trail of triumph. Even Prime Minister Tony Blair admitted to dancing a jig of excitement. After years of planning, presentations, and private arm twisting, for the first time since 1948 London was chosen to stage the summer Olympic Games. The next day jubilation turned to horror when, on July 7, 2005, four suicide bombers exploded themselves, three on the subway, one on a London bus, leaving fifty-two dead and hundreds injured.

The queen was quick to respond. Next day she visited the Royal London Hospital in Whitechapel and met with the emergency responders and nursing staff as well as some of the injured. Then she made an "unusually forthright" speech in the informal setting of the hospital canteen where she praised Londoners for calmly resuming their normal everyday lives.[23]

"Atrocities such as these simply reinforce our sense of community, our humanity and our trust in the rule of law. That is the clear message from us all." She referred to the outrage again during the commemoration services for the sixtieth anniversary of the end of the Second World War. As with the earlier 9/11 atrocity, she ordered the flag at Buckingham Palace to fly at half-mast. At times of national crisis the queen was now much more proactive than earlier in her reign. With her mother no longer around to remind the queen of precedent and tradition, Elizabeth relied much more on her own judgment. In the past it had been her habit to sit on the sidelines, most notably after the Aberfan disaster. Now she was much more willing to adopt the role of grandmother to the nation, the consoler in chief during times of national calamity. She clearly felt at ease in her position as royal matriarch.

As she approached her eightieth birthday she looked younger, more relaxed, and much more stylish. "She's reached a stage in her life where she has complete confidence in who she is," her designer Stewart Parvin said. "The Queen looks squarely in the mirror and she likes what she sees. She has a confidence that transcends beauty—that's the most fascinating thing with her."[24] The daughter of a Liverpool dockworker, haute couture designer Angela Kelly was largely responsible for that transformation by encouraging the cautious sovereign to take chances.

It paid off. The queen went from a place on the Worst Dressed List to being voted one of *Vogue* magazine's Most Glamorous Women, included in the same company as supermodel Naomi Campbell, Twiggy, and actor Helen Mirren who played her in the movie *The Queen*.

Understated elegance and attention to detail were her recipe for late-blooming fashion success. When the queen agreed, after some hesitation, to wear a monochrome black-and-white outfit for her arrival at the White House in 2007 to meet President Bush, the striking ensemble, which was designed by Angela Kelly and Alison Pordum, earned wide praise.

While Kelly, who joined the queen's staff as assistant dresser in 1994, could never take the place in the queen's life of Bobo MacDonald, who was her childhood maid and eventually dresser, over the years they forged a close bond. "You know we could be sisters," the queen once said to her.[25] It was a remarkably relaxed and intimate comment, even to a long-serving senior official.

Those who saw this double act in action pointed out that Angela was never servile, made the queen laugh, and, perhaps most important, filled in a lot of the lonely time, the waiting hours, in the queen's life. She came to the queen with solutions, not problems. When, for example, the queen forgot to buy a birthday present for her eldest son, it was Angela who offered to fix it. Such was her influence that before the queen's long-haul flight to Australia to open the Commonwealth Games in March 2006, she accepted her advice to rest for thirty-six hours beforehand. Unusually she granted Angela permission to write two books about her life as the queen's dresser and even posed for exclusive photographs to illustrate the tomes. As a general rule those who worked for the royal family were legally obliged to a vow of silence about their royal relationships. This was a sign of the queen's confidence in the woman she chose to guard her jewelry—and her burgeoning fashion reputation.

The confluence of the queen's eightieth and Prince Philip's eighty-fifth birthdays in 2006 led to speculation that the royal double act would choose this moment to abdicate or retire. Her lifelong friend Margaret Rhodes quickly stifled this talk. "When she took her Coronation vow all those years ago, she promised to serve her country whether her life be long or short. As we have seen, her life is proving to be very long, healthy and productive. It is not a responsibility she will ever—if at all—give up lightly. I am sure that she will never abdicate."[26] The queen, in her own subtle way, endorsed her friend's ringing statement when she allowed herself to be photographed out riding with her groom Terry Pendry in Windsor Great Park. These days she rode smaller fell ponies and, despite advancing years, she resolutely refused to wear a hard hat. As they joked at the palace, the only thing coming between Prince Charles and his destiny was an Hermès scarf.

The queen was a picture of health when compared with the other two octogenarian monarchs, King George III and Queen Victoria, who were both physically frail during their eighties. She made lighthearted reference to her age at a celebration lunch, stealing a line from Groucho Marx: "Anyone can get old—all you have to do is to live long enough."[27] In the same vein she turned down the invitation to be the Oldie of the Year, *Oldie* being a magazine for folk of a certain age, with the logic: "You are only as old as you feel."[28]

In a televised appreciation Prince Charles remembered how she would tuck him up in bed at night while practicing wearing her coronation crown in order to get used to the weight.

He praised her steadfast nature, saying that she was "an example to so many of service, duty and devotion in a world of sometimes bewildering change and disorientation."[29]

As the diamond wedding anniversary approached, those who had known Prince Philip for a number of years noticed that old age had mellowed him. Never an easy man, friends noted that he had aged "benignly." His mind remained sharp, his bearing erect, and he seemed closer to and more supportive of the queen than in the past. He was always fiercely protective of her, a one-man icebreaker always on hand to ensure that she was conversationally comfortable. At the endless receptions they attended, they were an effective double act, the duke confident that he could get a reaction, normally laughter, within a few seconds of meeting a member of the public. He remained provocative and challenging, what some considered rudeness often his way of putting someone on their mettle to see if they could rise to the challenge.

She still told him to "shut up" if he overstepped the mark,

while he mocked her use of her dogs to avoid serious discussion. For all his rattiness, she relied heavily on his judgment particularly with regard to family matters. As Lady Penn, widow of Sir Eric, former queen's comptroller, observed: "They've always leaned on each other. How else do you think she managed to cope so incredibly well through such tough times? They are very good friends and that is their secret. The Queen has had a lot to contend with and the fact she has coped so wonderfully is largely thanks to him."[30]

Even after a long marriage, there was still a spark between them, still a glint in the eye. As a former lady-in-waiting observed: "I was watching them teasing each other and giggling just the other day and I thought how lucky they are to have each other. They've always been different—he's sharp, decisive, bold and she's cautious and slow to make up her mind—and they don't always like the same things but they fit like hand in gloves."[31] British television presenter Carol Vorderman, who dined privately with the couple, felt a similar chemistry, remembering how they were "flirting with each other madly and laughing."[32]

Along with her faith and her family, her relationship with the Duke of Edinburgh was at the core of her life. In short Prince Philip was the only man in the world to treat her like a normal human being, a quality that she truly valued. Appropriately they spent their sixtieth wedding anniversary on Malta, the island they called home when they were a young married couple.

Now grandparents and great-grandparents, they enjoyed a close relationship with their young brood. They would join them for afternoon tea or sit on the sofa and watch Mickey Mouse and other Disney cartoons. The palace switchboard knew to patch the youngsters through to the queen wherever she might be in the world.

Though the queen paid special attention to Harry after he lost his mother at such a young age, she carefully monitored the development and well-being of her eventual heir, Prince William. Their relationship blossomed when he was a boarder at Eton, just a short walk from Windsor Castle. Every Sunday he joined the queen and Prince Philip for lunch or afternoon tea. Once they had finished the meal, the duke would make a discreet exit so they could talk further. In between chitchat about his schoolwork, their meetings were an early chance to impress upon the thoughtful teenager the need to protect and sustain his birthright, the monarchy.

As the queen's friend Lady Elizabeth Anson once observed: "The Queen spent a huge amount of time with William. They are exceptionally close and the Queen has been a wonderful mentor for William over the years."[33] Her thoughtful conduct was reminiscent of the way her own father, George VI, gradually inducted his eldest daughter into the family "Firm."

She and the Duke of Edinburgh always ensured that their diaries were free in order to watch William mark the major milestones in his life. They were present at the University of St. Andrews on the northeast coast of Scotland on June 23, 2005, when, at the formal graduation ceremony, he was presented with an upper-second-class degree in geography. His girlfriend Catherine Middleton earned the same grade for her subject, the history of art. Though she and her parents were introduced to the queen and Prince Philip, few palace insiders expected the romance to last long after college.

Catherine confounded the critics and stuck around to the point that the queen invited William and his girlfriend for a quiet dinner at Windsor Castle. This time around she was not going to leave anything to chance. The queen took a particularly close interest in the woman who might one day become queen consort. And the mood music was almost entirely favorable. A lady-in-waiting gave her the thumbs-up. She reported: "The Queen has taken genuine delight in Kate Middleton. She sees in Kate a young woman who has no interest in being royal but loves William for himself. The Queen is very positive about the match. She sees in them two young people who are capable of capturing the affection of the people."[34]

Such was the hysteria surrounding the possibility of an engagement announcement on Catherine's twenty-fifth birthday in January 2007 that she was mobbed by paparazzi as she walked down the street to her car before driving to her job in a retail fashion company. A seething Prince William, astonished that the paparazzi had learned nothing from his mother's untimely death, issued a statement condemning the harassment. The incident was a turning point. William was so concerned that Catherine did not truly realize what she was getting herself involved in that, in April 2007, he ended the relationship.

He later explained: "I wanted to give her a chance to see in and back out if she needed to before it all got too much. I'm trying to learn from the past. I just wanted to give her the best chance to settle in and to see what happens on the other side."[35]

After the well-publicized breakup Catherine simply kept smiling and carried on having a good time. It was not long before William realized his mistake and renewed the romance. This time he was back for good. The queen kept a watchful but benign eye on the burgeoning romance, for example inviting Kate to watch William when he was inaugurated as a royal knight companion in the Order of the Garter during a ceremony at St. George's chapel. She also suggested that Catherine affiliate herself with a charity. She took the point, involving herself in raising funds for Starlight Children's Foundation, a charity for seriously and terminally ill children.

When William trained as a search-and-rescue pilot based at Valley station in Anglesey, an island off the northwest coast of Wales, the queen gave her approval for Catherine to live with him in a rented cottage. This courtship was so very different from that of his father. Charles only spent a few weeks romancing Lady Diana Spencer before asking her to marry him. His eldest son was much more circumspect. William followed his mother's advice, which was to "marry your best friend." He had spent years with Catherine before he finally asked her to marry him during a fishing expedition on a holiday in Kenya. Shortly after the engagement announcement on November 16, 2010, he was calling the queen for advice.

At the first meeting with palace officials he was presented with a list of 777 candidates to be invited to the wedding. He had never heard of most of them let alone met them. The prince and his bride wanted to organize the wedding their way. Noticeably he went to the queen rather than his father for advice. She suggested he scrap the first list and begin by writing down the names of those he and Catherine actually wanted to share their big day. Then work from there.

The wedding day itself, on April 29, 2011, was a splendid confluence of pomp, pageantry, and family intimacy. Catherine looked stunning in her Sarah Burton satin-and-lace gown while William seemed nervous as he watched the bride make her way down the aisle in Westminster Abbey. Their departure in a vintage Aston Martin for Clarence House following their balcony appearance at Buckingham Palace was a brilliant coup de théâtre.

The queen was positively playful on the wedding day, "practically skipping" said one observer, absolutely thrilled at the way the public responded to the royal newlyweds.[36] It seemed that, in her eyes, the future of the royal family, her family, was now secure. The monarchy was once again held in admiration and affection by the public. Prince Edward reflected on her response some time later. "The Queen was surprised at how the public took William and Catherine to heart. I don't think my mother ever expected the public response or thought people would come out in such support of her family as they did during William and Catherine's wedding. It was wonderful. My mother really cares about the British people and their welfare. It was wonderful to see the warm and heartfelt support."[37]

Clear skies however rarely lasted long over the House of Windsor. The buildup to the wedding had overshadowed an embarrassing family matter. Prince Andrew came under intense scrutiny over his position as special representative for trade and investment. Concerns were raised about the costs of his extensive travel and the people he was linked with, who included the son of the Libyan dictator General Gaddafi and another associate who was described as a gun smuggler. Most damning was his continued relationship with New York millionaire sex offender Jeffrey Epstein. Even though Epstein was convicted in 2008 for procuring a child for prostitution, in 2010, after his release, Andrew was photographed together with him in Central Park in New York.

Much as the queen indulged her second son, both financially and emotionally, the media and political criticism was unrelenting. It went up a gear when it was learned that Fergie, the Duchess of York, had accepted a loan from the sex offender. Shortly after a difficult hour-long conversation with the queen Andrew resigned from his position as trade envoy. His surrender was, noted BBC royal correspondent Peter Hunt, "inevitable." This was a classic example of a witless royal falling prey to the generosity of wealthy friends of dubious provenance.

William and Catherine knew little of the brooding scandal as they enjoyed their honeymoon on an island in the Seychelles in the Indian Ocean. Prince William spent time on his computer trying to find out about a visit that had the queen, a veteran of dozens of royal tours, very excited. For the first time since 1911 when George V visited Dublin during its days as part of the British empire, a reigning monarch was about to step foot on Irish soil.

The long history of animosity, resistance, and revolution between these two neighboring islands had previously made an official royal tour unthinkable—until now. After months of back-and-forth, the two countries agreed an agenda that placed the emphasis on peace and reconciliation, a key element of the Good Friday Agreement.

As Prince William told writer Robert Hardman: "She was so excited about it and really looking forward to it. It was quite sweet."[38] From the moment she stepped off the aircraft wearing an emerald coat, dress, and hat, Irish eyes were smiling, cooing at the compliment paid to the Irish nation in her choice of color scheme.

During the four-day state visit, the queen and Prince Philip visited the Trinity College Library in Dublin where they saw the Book of Kells, one of the world's most ancient volumes, laid a wreath at the Garden of Remembrance dedicated to those who died in the struggle for liberation from Britain, visited a trio of stud farms—and watched a pint of Guinness being carefully poured. At the state banquet the queen began her speech in Gaelic, which earned warm applause from President McAleese and other dignitaries.

In a careful and well-judged speech, the queen acknowledged the "sad and regrettable" mistakes of Britain's troubled relationship with Ireland, referring to the "heartache, turbulence and loss" of the past. "We can all see things which we would wish had been done differently or not at all."[39] Prime Minister David Cameron described the queen's visit as a "game changer"[40] that heralded a new era of Anglo-Irish relations. This official tour helped embed the peace process between the peoples of Ireland and Northern Ireland. The queen continued to play her part. Three years later, in June 2014, she visited Belfast where she shook the hand of Martin McGuinness, deputy first minister of Northern Ireland and former hard man of the Provisional IRA terrorist group. It was one of the most symbolic actions of her reign. Her handshake was seen as a gesture of forgiveness and reconciliation with a man whose terrorist organization had killed Lord Mountbatten and others. The simple act demonstrated how far the peace process had come.

There was constitutional housekeeping taking place much nearer to home. As the Diamond Jubilee of the queen's reign approached, she agreed to sweeping but long-overdue reforms to the royal succession. At the heads of Commonwealth meeting in Perth, Western Australia, in October 2011 British prime minister David Cameron put forward proposals, unanimously agreed by the other fifteen leaders, to change the law so that firstborn girls could become queen. It meant that should William and Catherine's first child be a girl, she would be the sovereign. In fact their firstborn was a boy, Prince George.

The leaders unanimously agreed to reform the 1701 Act of Settlement, which discriminated against women, and also repeal the Royal Marriages Act of 1772. The scrapping of the latter act lifted the ban on a monarch marrying a Roman Catholic and also removed the requirement for all those in line to the throne, apart from the first six, to obtain permission to marry from the sovereign. They were made law in the 2013 Succession to the Crown Act.

Not only did these constitutional changes bring the House of Windsor into the twenty-first century, they also deliberately coincided with a radical change in the funding of the monarchy. The age-old Civil List was replaced by the Sovereign Grant, the monarchy now subsidized by a percentage from the profits of the Crown Estate, the independent corporation that is owned by the monarch but is not the private property of the sovereign. These much-needed reforms effectively wiped the constitutional slate clean for the queen's immediate heir, Prince Charles.

For some years he had been a firm advocate of a supple, slimmed-down monarchy. During the Diamond Jubilee celebrations in June 2012, the future direction of travel for the monarchy was on full display. When the queen and Prince Philip stood on the deck of the lavishly decorated royal barge, *Spirit of Chartwell*, to review the stunning thousand-boat flotilla on the river Thames in central London, they were joined only by the Duke and Duchess of Cambridge, the Duke and Duchess of Cornwall, and Prince Harry. The remaining senior royals, Princes Andrew and Edward and Princess Anne, were assigned to other boats for the pageant.

It was noticeable, too, that the Duchess of Cornwall, for so long a royal outsider, was now on easy and convivial terms with the queen and every other member of the royal family. As the specially built royal row barge *Gloriana* passed the National Theatre the queen nudged her daughter-in-law to point out Joey, the puppet realization of Michael Morpurgo's *War Horse*, which had reared up in greeting. The queen was a fan of the production, having seen the original play in London and hosting a special screening at Windsor Castle for members of the Household, the performance also attended by director Steven Spielberg.

The one casualty of the four-hour festival, which took place in chilling June rain and wind, was Prince Philip, who was subsequently hospitalized with a bladder infection. He never really fully recovered. He missed the spectacular three-hour firework concert outside Buckingham Palace with performances from, among others, Elton John, Paul McCartney, and Kylie Minogue. In a symbolic moment, the band Madness played their hit "Our House" from the roof of Buckingham Palace, a clever light show turning the frontage into a block of downmarket apartments.

In a touching speech to his mother, Prince Charles paid tribute to the queen's selfless duty, service, and "making us proud to be British." The grand finale of the celebration was the reappearance on the Buckingham Palace balcony of the Magnificent Seven (minus Prince Philip). The signal was clear—the succession was assured.

"An incredible day, absolutely wonderful,"[41] the queen said to her eldest son as they watched a flypast by the Red Arrows display team as well as World War Two fighter planes. The experience had been, she said in a short broadcast of thanks, "a humbling experience."[42] The jubilee festivities marked not only the queen's magnificent sixty years on the throne, but also the beginning of a new era for the royal family.

14

❧

Good Evening,
Mr. Bond

On a balmy summer's night the eighty-six-year-old queen gave herself a license to thrill and surprise a worldwide audience eager to watch the opening ceremony of the 2012 Olympic games.

"Her Majesty," wearing a peach dress and pearls, leapt from a hovering helicopter, her Union Jack parachute illuminated in the night sky as she fell safely to earth, somewhere offstage. The next shot was of her in that same colored dress and fascinator walking to the podium at the specially built Olympic stadium in east London to formally open the games.

There were many among the watching millions who genuinely thought that the real queen had made the most daring and dangerous entrance of her reign. Former health secretary Jeremy Hunt later told Elizabeth that a Japanese tourist remarked that it was wonderful for the queen to be involved in the Olympics in such a daring manner as back home they would never get their emperor to jump out of a plane.[1]

In the beginning there were some inside Buckingham Palace who never thought that the queen would agree to becoming the highest-profile "Bond girl" ever and, for good measure, agree to utter the immortal lines: "Good evening, Mr. Bond."

Yet the longer the queen reigned, the more willing she seemed to kick back and take a chance. Irish film director Danny Boyle, who had the daunting task of arranging the choreography for the opening Olympic ceremony, wondered if she would take a chance on him.

Some months before he had the idea of using the queen in a short promotional film just before the official opening ceremony. She was to be rescued from some unseen threat by 007 himself. James Bond, in black tie, would meet her at Buckingham Palace and escort her to a helicopter where "the queen" would fly over and under various London landmarks, such as Tower Bridge and the Houses of Parliament, before dramatically jumping out of the helicopter into the night sky.

Would the idea fly with Her Majesty? Initially Boyle put the scheme to Lord Coe, the London 2012 chief, who in turn spoke to Princess Anne. In her matter-of-fact manner she said simply: "Why don't you ask her?"[2]

Within days Boyle was inside Buckingham Palace sketching out the scenario to the queen's deputy private secretary Edward Young and her dresser Angela Kelly. She loved the idea and went upstairs to speak to the queen in person.

It found immediate royal approval but with one proviso: She had to speak the iconic—and much parodied—line "Good evening, Mr. Bond," as actor Daniel Craig, who played the evergreen hero, stood at attention waiting for her to finish some paperwork at her desk. Then the queen, her corgis, and her page, followed by Commander Bond, would walk to a waiting helicopter, ending with that iconic parachute jump in an evening gown.

Not only was the sketch one of the highlights of a memorable Olympic games but it revealed a daring, almost mischievous, side to the queen's personality that came to the surface from time to time. During that Olympic year she told her dresser Angela Kelly that ever since she was young she had harbored a secret wish. As a child her elders, especially Queen Mary, had insisted that she keep her hands out of her pockets. Just to make sure, the pockets in all her clothes were sewn up.

For years she wanted to make a childhood dream come true and to be photographed more informally, with her hands in her pockets. However, the queen mother as well as her advisers had always suggested it was not an appropriate look for the sovereign. Then, as with so many things, she had given in to their arguments.

Not this time. Kelly brought in photographer Barry Jeffery who shot her as she mimicked the poses of a professional model—with and without her hands in the pockets of her white dress.

For several years the pictures remained private. Officials from the Royal Collection argued, according to Kelly, that these more candid informal photographs of the queen could bring down the monarchy and therefore were not suitable for the public.[3] Some years later the whole set of photographs was released—and the sky did not fall in on the institution.

Though the dead hand of protocol and proper form was ever present in the queen's life, occasionally she was able to show flashes of a very different queen, such as the time she entertained President Barack Obama and First Lady Michelle Obama at a Buckingham Palace reception in 2009.

It seemed like a routine meet and greet until the queen reached over and slipped her arm around the waist of Michelle Obama who at five foot eleven towered over the diminutive monarch. In turn she placed her arm around her shoulder telling the queen: "I really enjoyed our meeting."[4] Later Michelle Obama explained that they bonded over their sore feet.

As the traditional image of Elizabeth was of someone who discouraged intimacy, the sovereign holding her oversize handbag in front of her like a shield, this show of amiable familiarity was startling. In the past acres of newsprint had been spilled in baying disapproval when a host had so much as touched the queen's back to help guide her through the throng.

Her willingness to take a risk was rewarded when in April 2013 the British Academy of Film and Television Arts conferred an honorary BAFTA on the queen for her "sensational" appearance at the opening ceremony of the Olympics as well as her support for the world of arts and entertainment. Actor Kenneth Branagh, who made the presentation, joked that several colleagues were so impressed by her performance at the Olympics that they had further scripts ready for her perusal.

During the event, which was held at Windsor Castle, actor Helen Mirren, who played the queen in Peter Morgan's eponymous movie, was reprising her regal role once more in Morgan's new play *The Audience* in London's West End and so missed the royal engagement. Her depiction of the queen as imperious, no-nonsense, and drily witty was so realistic that when Prince William subsequently presented her with a BAFTA Fellowship award, he described her as "an extremely talented British actress who I should probably call 'Granny.'"

In turn Mirren admitted that, though she had performed as the monarch both on stage and film, she experienced a "lesson in embarrassment" when she joined the queen and Prince Philip for afternoon tea at Buckingham Palace. She found herself reduced to speaking "gobbledeegook."[5]

"You're thinking 'it's the Queen, it's the Queen.'" In a cute inversion of roles, Mirren admitted that she was now even more starstruck when meeting the woman she had played so successfully. "I am genuinely always astounded by her aura, her twinkle, her presence. It never fails to surprise me."[6]

The fact that so many, even Oscar-winning actors, were reduced to talking gobbledeegook in "the presence" helped explain her lifelong love of horses and racing. As the novelist Jilly Cooper observed: "A horse wouldn't know she was the queen; a horse would just treat her like any other human. She would have had to earn a horse's love and respect, not expect it as a given. That must have been such a release for her."[7]

More than a hobby, breeding and racing horses was her refuge from the endless problems that passed across her desk. It was a positive relaxation to spend a few minutes with the comforting columns of the *Racing Post* or to talk about horses, discussing the personalities, auctions, and pedigrees with knowledgeable experts. It was a world where she felt utterly at home. Horses were her hinterland, an engrossing world that provided an enriching alternative to the day-to-day royal world. So while she was pleased with her honorary BAFTA, there was no mistaking the sheer unadulterated excitement on the queen's face two months later, in June 2013, when she and her racing manager John Warren roared home Estimate to win the Gold Cup at Ascot. In so doing she became the first reigning monarch in its 207-year history to take the prize. Her lifelong passion had yielded her biggest win since 1977. A few years later in 2021 it came as no surprise to the racing community that she became the first "special contributor" inductee into the QIPCO British Champions Series Hall of Fame.[8]

The queen celebrated another unique milestone when on September 9, 2015, she toppled Queen Victoria's record of sixty-three years, 216 days on the British throne. She became the longest-reigning female monarch in world history, although she treated the historic moment as just another day in the office when she opened the new Borders Railway at Tweedbank in the Scottish Borders. Her lengthy service was, as her daughter, the princess royal, observed, a double-edged sword. "People tend to forget when she passed the longest reigning monarch mark that was only because her father died so young. For her that's a very mixed blessing and it's a record that she would much rather not have been able to pass."[9]

Though Prince Philip had talked about retiring when he reached the ripe old age of ninety, he was by her side when the queen reached her own date with destiny. A three-day visit to Malta in November 2015, where she and Prince Philip spent much of their early married life, brought back happy memories. The queen was visiting as head of the Commonwealth Heads of Government Meeting (CHOGM), and though the queen and Prince Philip no longer undertook long-haul flights, the three-hour trip from London was deemed acceptable.

For the queen, Prince Philip, and those who knew the couple in the 1940s this was truly a trip down memory lane. During a tour of the island the couple made time to visit the polo field where Philip and Dickie Mountbatten played. As they looked around the queen spotted Elizabeth Pulé, the daughter of her former housekeeper Jessie Grech, in the crowd. Another familiar face was Freddie Mizzi, a clarinet player with the Jimmy Dowling Band who used to play their favorite tunes from the musical *Oklahoma* at the Phoenicia hotel.

When she told her audience that she spent some of the happiest years of her life there, she was not exaggerating. She genuinely remembered those who worked for her and kept up with current affairs on the Mediterranean island with a regular delivery of the *Times of Malta*.

The queen was always interested in and appreciative of those who worked for or with her. From the palace, to Parliament, Balmoral, Sandringham, and the Commonwealth beyond, she liked to keep her finger on the pulse. As former Edinburgh lord provost Eric Milligan observed: "She knows what is going on and cares for the people who have cared for her."[10]

Her extensive knowledge of the social scene also impressed Prince Andrew. "Her intelligence network—of who's done what, what's happened, who's ill, who's died, who's had a birth—is extraordinary. How she finds out is a mystery."[11]

Of course her own brood mattered most, as she demonstrated on her ninetieth birthday when American photographer Annie Leibovitz was invited to take a family portrait of the queen, Prince Philip, her two youngest grandchildren and all of her great-grandchildren at Windsor Castle. Leibovitz also had time to fit in a shot of the queen on her own with her corgis and dorgis. This time her left hand was resolutely in her cardigan pockets.

Like her horses, her great-grandchildren were not fazed in her presence—though at a certain age they came to realize whom they were dealing with. Elton John watched the queen in action at one party where she asked Princess Margaret's son David Linley to look in on his sister Sarah, who had been taken ill and had retired to her room. When he tried to wriggle out of doing his duty the queen playfully slapped him across the face, saying, "Don't"—SLAP—"argue"—SLAP—"with"—SLAP—"me"—SLAP—"I"—SLAP—"am"—SLAP—"THE QUEEN!" When the queen noticed Elton John staring at this family scenario she gave him a wink and walked off.[12]

During their childhoods and teenage years William, Harry, and her other grandchildren viewed the queen as a wise woman, at times slightly forbidding but always there for help and advice. In their eyes she was a briskly no-nonsense figure who commanded respect and never treated them with kid gloves. William remembered the day at Balmoral when he received the "most mighty bollocking" from the queen after he and Peter Phillips chased his cousin Zara, who was driving a go-kart, into a post during high jinks on the Balmoral estate.[13] The queen, dressed in her kilt, was the first person out of the house to help the shocked youngster and then to deliver a tongue-lashing to the boys.

Horse riding, rather than go karting, of course is a bond that spans the generations. The queen herself was given her first Shetland pony aged just four while Princess Anne and her daughter Zara have both ridden at the Olympics. Following in the footsteps of her grandfather, Prince Edward's daughter Lady Louise Windsor has followed in the footsteps of her grandfather and taken up competitive carriage driving. On gentler occasions, Princesses Beatrice and Eugenie recall picking raspberries with Grannie and then finding their haul turned into jam for afternoon tea.

As the Duke of York recalled: "She's been a fantastic grandmother to Beatrice and Eugenie and probably revels in that more than being a mother to some extent; always interested and concerned for what the girls are up to."[14]

The birth of the Duke and Duchess of Cambridge's first born Prince George in July 2013 and then, in May 2015, the arrival of Princess Charlotte ensured the stability of the dynasty, an often unstated but crucial feature of the monarch's role. "The Queen can see continuity with William, Catherine, George and Charlotte," said her friend Lady Elizabeth Anson. "That has changed her life."[15]

As the nation celebrated her ninetieth birthday, a jaunty Prince Harry managed to inveigle his way into her sitting room at Windsor Castle and get her to take part in a stunt to publicize the Invictus Games of which he was patron.

The queen had a genuine soft spot for Harry, the grandchild who had the knack of being able to jump the line to see the queen—much to the frustration of royal officials. This time, in a video that went viral, Harry convinced the birthday girl to watch a message on a camera phone from President Barack Obama and First Lady Michelle Obama ahead of the games, which were due to be held in Florida in May 2016.

A stern-faced First Lady Michelle Obama pinged into view and challenged Harry with regard to the inter-service rivalry between America and Britain as injured military personnel from several countries aimed to take part in the games.

"Careful what you wish for," interjected the president, waving his finger as a team of servicemen joked around in the background before one said, "Boom." The queen remarked: "Oh, really, please." A red-faced Harry then looked at the camera and said rather sheepishly: "Boom."[16]

Beneath the grandmotherly levity and the confetti of souvenir newspaper editions celebrating the queen's milestone year, there was a growing sense of transition. It was a change that Harry wanted to be part of.

The following summer in 2017 Prince Harry told writer Angela Levin that he was eager to "get on with" an overhaul of the monarchy. "We are involved in modernizing the British monarchy. We are not doing this for ourselves but for the greater good of the people."[17]

A reminder of just why the monarchy still mattered came in the days following the terrible Grenfell Tower block fire in west London on June 14, 2017, which left seventy-two dead and hundreds homeless. The queen and Prince William were quick to visit the survivors and first responders, the monarch there as a listening ear and a comforting presence during a national calamity.

"The Queen looked at me. There was compassion, it was caring and sincere," concluded one survivor after outlining her own ordeal in a face-to-face meeting with the queen.[18] Here was the nation's grandmother in action, bringing comfort and acknowledgment of loss.

She had always made it crystal clear, despite years of speculation, that she would reign as long as she had health and strength. As she told the Archbishop of Canterbury George Carey upon his retirement: "That's something I can't do. I'm going to carry on to the end."[19]

That did not prevent thinking and action with regard to the inevitable change of reign. Her private secretary Sir Christopher Geidt earned a second knighthood as early as January 2014 for masterminding this work. His citation read: "for a new approach to constitutional matters…[and] preparation for the transition to a change of reign."[20]

There were other straws in the wind. In 2016 the queen elevated Camilla to the Privy Council, the sovereign's most senior advisory body. It meant that she was entitled to be present at the Accession Council to hear the proclamation of the new sovereign.

As for the Prince of Wales, he now routinely received despatch boxes on a read-only basis so that he was fully up to speed with government policy. Though there were those who believed the queen was still as sprightly and energetic as in her middle years, the truth was that she was slowing down and spending much more time at Windsor Castle and rather less at Buckingham Palace.

While the queen had no intention of abdicating, she recognized that it was time for her husband, five years her senior, to step down. His eyesight, hearing, and memory were failing to the point where it was only his legendary stubbornness that kept him going. In May 2017 he told the family of his intentions and in August he made his final appearance on the forecourt of Buckingham Palace in his role at captain general of the Royal Marines.

Prince Philip deserved his rest. During his royal career he had shaken hundreds of thousands of hands; had given thousands of speeches roaming over his interests in science, the environment, and religion; and had, since 1952, attended some 22,219 engagements in his own right.

At an Order of Merit reception at St. James's Palace shortly after the announcement, mathematician Michael Atiyah, then eighty-eight, said to the prince: "I'm sorry to hear you're standing down." In typically irreverent fashion the duke joked, "Well, I can't stand up much longer."[21]

He retired to Wood Farm, the spacious but modestly furnished cottage on the Sandringham estate, where the ninety-six-year-old patriarch spent his days reading, painting watercolors, writing letters, and having friends and family to stay and sample his cooking—he liked to make recipes he spotted on TV cooking shows. An old friend observed: "He is enjoying reading things he's always wanted to read and gets up to what he wants without an equerry telling him he has to be elsewhere or a camera following him around."[22]

The move came entirely with the queen's blessing even though she recognized that they would see much less of each other. They spoke on the phone daily and she visited Sandringham more frequently. She was initially alarmed when he was involved in a car crash in January 2019 but was grateful that the incident forced him to give up his driving license. In her eyes he had always driven too fast—his driving habits a source of decades-long conflict and sharp words.

With the family's enforcer out to pasture, it fell to the queen's private secretary, Sir Christopher Geidt, to propose changes in the monarchy.

He promoted the policy of centralizing the structure of the monarchy so that Buckingham Palace would take the lead, supported by Clarence House, the London home of Prince Charles, and Kensington Palace, the home of Prince William and Prince Harry. His command and control proposals did not find favor from the princes, who wanted the autonomy to do their own thing rather than constantly defer to Buckingham Palace. Each company, or rather household, wanted to operate from their own silo, thus weakening the authority at the center. Charles, William, Andrew, and Harry favored a collegiate system, the princes decisively rejecting the Geidt plan for centralization. Though he had planned to step down, Lord Geidt, who had served the queen for ten years, decided to leave early rather than fight it out with the queen's children. "This summertime bloodless palace coup means Prince Charles can now exercise more control over the monarchy's direction of travel," noted BBC royal correspondent Peter Hunt.[23]

Part of the argument marshaled by the royal princes was that Prince Charles, rather than the queen, should be responsible for shaping the monarchy. There were unconfirmed proposals that he wanted Buckingham Palace to be open year-round for visitors while the new king would live in an apartment in the palace, similar to the prime minister's flat above Downing Street. His main home would be Highgrove in the West Country while William and Catherine would move from Kensington Palace to Windsor Castle. Balmoral Castle would be turned into a museum though Prince Charles would still keep nearby Birkhall Lodge.

While the consequences of the behind-the-scenes power

struggle were not immediately apparent, it was clear that the queen's authority had been diluted and that the princes had a freer hand to shape their own vision of the monarchy going forward. While her institutional authority was diminished, she was still held in considerable respect not to say awe by her family and staff.

Though there were tensions between the households there was cooperation, too, no more so than with the queen's beloved Commonwealth, an organization she had nurtured and supported throughout her reign.

At a London gathering of the Commonwealth Heads of Government in 2018, she spoke of her "sincere wish" that one day the Prince of Wales should carry on the important work started by her father in 1949.[24] Before the conference ended the leaders gathered and unanimously agreed to accept her recommendation for Charles to be the next head of the Commonwealth. It was a welcome success for the House of Windsor.

The diversity of race, creed, and color that was the cornerstone of the Commonwealth came closer to home with the warm acceptance into the royal family of Prince Harry's girlfriend, Meghan Markle, a divorced, biracial American actor. During the run-up to the May 2018 wedding she thoughtfully recognized how much the Commonwealth mattered to the queen when she incorporated the national flowers of the fifty-three nations of the organization into her bridal veil. It was a gesture the queen much appreciated, as she did Meghan's decision to be baptized into the national faith, the Church of England, before her wedding day. As she watched Meghan, from a different country, color, and culture, walk down the aisle of St. George's Chapel, Windsor, she was witnessing history in the making. At a stroke their marriage made the monarchy seem more relevant and inclusive in an ever-changing world.

However, their brief journey at the heart of the institution would test the patience of the queen, expose her familial indulgence, and stretch and strain the bonds of blood and sinew.

At first all seemed well. A few weeks after the wedding the queen invited Meghan on the Royal Train for a day's engagements in Cheshire in the northwest of England. On the journey there she presented her with a beautiful pearl necklace with matching earrings. "I just really loved being in her company," Meghan said later, comparing her warm and welcoming persona to that of her own grandmother Jeanette.[25] To ensure that Meghan was properly briefed for future events, the queen assigned to her office her own experienced assistant private secretary Samantha Cohen to explain the workings of the monarchy and the Commonwealth. She appointed Harry as a Commonwealth youth ambassador while months later Meghan became patron of the Association of Commonwealth Universities. These appointments would give the couple an international role and leave the domestic scene largely to the future king and queen, Prince William and Duchess Kate. It seemed a shrewd strategy especially as Harry seemed determined to carve out a role very different from that of his brother, a mindset that set the brothers on a conflicting path.

A story in the venerable *Times* of London in November 2018, shortly after Meghan and Harry had returned from a successful first tour Down Under, gave an intimate flavor of the relationship between the prince and his sovereign. It revolved around the tiara, held under lock and key in the vaults of Buckingham Palace, that the queen had loaned Meghan before the wedding. The story stated that before the wedding Harry was angry when it was not immediately available for a hair fitting with Meghan's hairdresser Serge Normant who had flown in specially from New York. The queen's dresser, the redoubtable Angela Kelly who is also guardian of her private jewelry collection, explained that certain security protocols had to be adhered to in order to access the priceless piece. Harry would have none of it and angrily told staff: "What Meghan wants Meghan gets."[26] In the end he went to see the queen, who agreed to make the tiara available for the hair fitting.

Though the media focus was on Meghan's alleged prima donna behavior, the most telling takeaway from the "tiara tantrum" story was the way Harry was able to go over the head of a trusted royal aide directly to the queen and to convince her to do his bidding.

In an organization where it can take weeks to gain an appointment with the queen, this access was remarkable. Family came first. It was both a strength and a flaw. As an aide observed: "It has to be remembered that this is a family and a court not a corporation."[27]

A family where ultimately position, not popularity, mattered most. Meghan joined the institution at a period when it was undergoing the gradual but nonetheless seismic change that inevitably comes with the passing of the crown from one generation to the next. As popular as they were, Meghan and Harry would in time slide down the royal totem pole, like Prince Andrew who, from once being second in line to the throne, was now a member of the supporting cast.

The royal couple wanted to shape an alternative future for themselves, one that eventually placed them in direct conflict with the existing order.

As the rifts inside the family, particularly between Harry and William, became ever more pronounced, the queen's theme for 2019 mutual respect and conciliation, seemed as appropriate for her warring family as for a Britain still licking its wounds following the fractious vote to leave the European Union.

Conciliation was a theme the queen returned to often: in a speech to the Women's Institute, the visit to Britain by America's President Trump, and the twentieth anniversary of the opening of the Scottish Parliament. She saw it as her role to try to cool political passions and soothe the brow of a nation turning in on itself.

Her wisdom and judgment were needed much closer to home. Ever since "her strength and stay," Prince Philip, had retired, her second son Prince Andrew had done his best to fill in the gap. He accompanied her to church on Sundays and ensured that his daughters, Beatrice and Eugenie, kept in contact.

In her eyes her second son had, at times of crisis, shown qualities of courage and leadership, notably during the Falklands conflict and the Windsor fire. Though he had a reputation for arrogance, his loyalty to the queen was unswerving. She appreciated his dogged support, even if his judgment was somewhat simplistic. During the week of Diana's funeral, for instance, when passions were running hot inside Balmoral about how to deal with the crisis, Andrew declared to a roomful of warring palace advisers: "The Queen is the Queen. You can't speak to her like that,"[28] meaning that her view should be accepted without question.

Though he had become a reassuring and welcome presence, distracting the queen from her two grandsons at war, his own issues soon dominated the royal agenda. Try as he might, he could not lay to rest his association with the banker and convicted pedophile Jeffrey Epstein. Matters became much worse when, in August 2019, Epstein, after being accused by numerous women of further sex crimes, committed suicide in a Manhattan prison cell.

One of his most prominent and persistent accusers was

Virginia Roberts Giuffre, who claimed that when she was seventeen years old Epstein forced her to have sex with his friends, including Prince Andrew. She said that she had sex with the prince on three separate occasions. As proof of their relationship she released a picture that showed a smiling Prince Andrew with his arm around her at Ghislaine Maxwell's central London home.

While the duke denied any sexual contact with Giuffre, the negative headlines continued. In November 2019, Andrew, after discussions with his lawyers and private secretary Amanda Thirsk, decided to consider giving an extended interview to BBC *Newsnight*'s presenter Emily Maitlis. When the *Newsnight* team came to the palace to make their final pitch for the interview, Andrew stated that he must "seek approval from higher up," meaning the queen herself.[29] The final decision, therefore, would be up to the queen and Prince Charles, who were both nervous about the possible fallout. His mother knew from past experience with her family, notably Prince Charles's prime-time confession of adultery and Diana's *Panorama* interview, that royalty did not fare well on TV. However, following internal conversations, the queen and Prince Charles were sufficiently reassured to give the interview the go-ahead.

After the hour-long grilling by Emily Maitlis, Andrew thought the conversation, which took place in a palace ballroom, had gone well and called the queen to tell her: "Mission accomplished." He thought it such a success that after the interview he took the *Newsnight* team on a tour of Buckingham Palace.

A cacophony of criticism soon stilled that wrongheaded belief. Andrew's interview was a disaster; "car crash TV" was one of the kinder descriptions.[30] The prince didn't appear to regret his relationship with Epstein; nor did he express any sympathy for the disgraced banker's victims even though he was given ample opportunity to do so. The queen was said to be horrified, for she, too, was in the firing line for allowing Andrew to go ahead with an interview that not only wrecked his reputation but also damaged the standing of the monarchy. PRINCE ANDREW'S TV CALAMITY SUGGESTS QUEEN IS LOSING HER GRIP ON "THE FIRM" was the headline in the *Times*, the Establishment's paper of record.[31]

Her advanced age, the absence of Prince Philip, the family "enforcer," from the fray, and the queen's fondness for Andrew were suggested as factors contributing to the debacle. However the fact that the prince had not been able to provide a convincing reason for his continued friendship with the millionaire pedophile or explain away the picture with his arm around Giuffre's waist after he stated he could not remember meeting her, proved damning. Moreover his breezy responses and unreflective manner suggested a man totally out of touch with the MeToo generation.

As his charities, colleges, businesses, and other organizations washed their hands of him, within days of the November broadcast the prince became the first member of the royal family in history to be forced to retire from royal duties. He made the decision following crisis talks with the queen and Prince Charles, who was consulted during a tour of New Zealand.

As far as the queen was concerned, those last few days forced her to choose between the demands of her family and the institution they served. Andrew's historic statement announcing his departure was released just a few minutes before the queen arrived at Chatham House to present her friend, the naturalist Sir David Attenborough with an international award regarding his work to highlight ocean plastic pollution.

Nothing in the queen's demeanor suggested anything other

than delight at honoring her old friend. She smiled broadly and as she signed the visitors book she asked for the date. It was November 20, her seventy-second wedding anniversary. "Oh I knew that," she deadpanned.[32] No one present would have had an inkling that just a few minutes before she had been party to ousting Andrew from the front ranks of the family.

She demonstrated that she remained ruthless when necessary in order to protect the institution to which she had sacrificed her whole life. Andrew was a problem, and she and her eldest son had moved swiftly to exorcise him from the public realm. Andrew now had the rest of his life to reflect on his folly. Though he publicly regretted his "ill-judged association" with Epstein and expressed his "deep sympathy" for the victims, it was all too little too late. (Matters only got worse for the disgraced duke. After a month-long trial in December 2021 his friend Ghislaine Maxwell was found guilty of sex trafficking while in January 2022 he lost his bid to have Virginia Giuffre's case against him thrown out. Days later he was, with the queen's "approval and agreement," stripped of his Royal patronages and military titles. He eventually reached an out-of-court settlement with his accuser, which left many unanswered questions.)[33]

Within days of managing her second son's folly the queen was plunged into a crisis at the opposite end of the scale. Whereas Prince Andrew was desperate to hang on to the trapping of royalty and was devastated by his abrupt relegation, Prince Harry made it abundantly clear he would like to resign from the family "Firm." Harry had always been a reluctant royal. Ever since the death of Diana, he found public appearances a trial, breaking into a nervous sweat when faced with camera flashes. He would have much preferred to continue his career in the army rather than glad-handing well-wishers at royal engagements. The problem was that he was a natural, the public seeing in him shades of his much-loved, much-missed mother. As the BBC's royal correspondent Jonny Dymond noted: "To watch Prince Harry is to observe a man who comes alive with crowds, with love, with those who need him. But it is also to see a man entirely unhappy with his lot. A man who desperately wants to get away from cameras, observers, outsiders, looking and filming and exploiting him."[34] He had, at his brother's suggestion, gone for psychological counseling to help him cope. The queen had kept a weather eye on him, as far as time allowed, and he was always welcome to see her.

Though the arrival of Meghan Markle in his life was looked upon rather doubtfully by some, including Prince William, there were others who hoped she would bring Harry to safe harbor. History was not on their side, as evidenced by the abdication of Edward VIII so that he could marry the twice-divorced American Wallis Simpson.

Though it started brightly, royal life for both of them soon began to unravel and they began crafting a road map for their future that ran parallel to that of the royal family. The family and their officials had been aware since around May 2019 of their plans to live in both America and Britain, to be financially independent, and to focus on their own humanitarian mission. It had been apparent for some months that Harry and Meghan were unhappy with the unrelenting media criticism and what they considered to be a lack of support from inside the institution. Prince Harry had spoken to the queen and his father about stepping back as senior royals and raising funds privately so that they would not need the Sovereign Grant or moneys from the Duchy of Cornwall, Prince Charles's estate, to subsidize their lifestyle. As private citizens they would not be beholden to the media but be able to serve the monarchy, albeit in a limited capacity.

The queen's initial reaction to this idea was that it was impossible to be half in and half out of the royal family; it was like being slightly pregnant.

The couple, who spent Christmas at a borrowed Canadian mansion, watched the smoke signals emerging from Buckingham Palace and realized that the message did not include them. First came the release of the official photograph, taken at Buckingham Palace, of the reigning monarch and the three princes, Charles, William, and George, who were directly in the line of succession. It was only the second time the existing and future sovereigns had been pictured together.

Then, when the queen gave her Christmas message, there was no photograph of Harry, Meghan, and Archie Harrison Mountbatten-Windsor, her most recent great-grandchild, on her desk with the other members of her family. Prince Harry, notoriously thin-skinned at the best of times, interpreted this in the most conspiratorial way possible: that they were no longer part of the royal family.

It all fed into their decision making as they carefully gamed out their future. On January 8, 2020, the couple announced, with minimal notice to the queen, Prince Charles, and Prince William, that they were indeed "stepping back" from royal duties and dividing their time between Britain and North America.

Their official statement, which was issued against the queen's express wishes, read in part: "After many months of reflection and internal discussions, we have chosen to make a transition this year in starting to carve out a progressive new role within this institution. We intend to step back as 'senior' members of the royal family and work to become financially independent, while continuing to fully support Her Majesty the Queen." They aimed to "collaborate" with the queen and the rest of their family to make this happen. This choice of wording clearly demonstrated how weakened the queen's position had become. The idea of a junior member of the royal family "collaborating" with the head of state on an equal footing left historians, royal officials, and commentators aghast. If it was anything, the royal family was a hierarchy, not a republic of equals.

The couple's declaration of independence, some 244 years after the original, was met with disbelief by the rest of the royal family and their officials. A new front in the War of the Windsors was about to break out. Though increasingly incapacitated, Prince Philip's indignant and mystified response summed up the feelings of many inside and outside the family: "What the hell are they playing at?"[35] The idea of a royal not wanting to be a royal anymore nor willing to accept the queen's authority without question was simply incomprehensible, particularly to a man who had sacrificed his whole life in supporting the queen and upholding the monarchy.

The sovereign agreed to a meeting at Sandringham a few days later with herself, Charles, William, Harry, and their senior staff. Officials were told to work "at pace."[36] For once she was not prepared to let this matter drag on as she had with the separation of her sister Princess Margaret and the damaging War of the Waleses that had erupted when Charles and Diana separated in December 1992. Nor was there any "ostriching"— that is to say, the queen's habit of avoiding unpleasant realities.

From the off it was clear that the queen wanted to carve a workable solution to accommodate the Sussexes while maintaining the integrity of the monarchy particularly with regard to finances. The idea that Meghan and Harry could monetize their royal brand, Sussex Royal, for example, was a nonstarter. Subsequently, however, they were able to craft deals for themselves as individuals, the couple surprising the family and the wider world by quickly snagging multimillion-dollar agreements with the likes of Netflix, Spotify, and other media outlets.

In a warm and friendly statement following the talks the queen said: "My family and I are entirely supportive of Harry and Meghan's desire to create a new life as a young family. Although we would have preferred them to remain full-time working members of the Royal Family, we respect and understand their wish to live a more independent life as a family while remaining a valued part of my family."

It was clear from the start of negotiations that if they wanted freedom, they had to give up their royal privileges. After much back-and-forth, the couple agreed to pay for the renovations of Frogmore Cottage, the home they had moved into after their marriage, underwrite their own security, abandon the Sussex Royal brand, and relinquish Harry's honorary military patronages, notably his position as captain general of the Royal Marines, a post he had held since 2017.

On January 18, just ten days after Meghan and Harry's stepping-back announcement, the way forward was mapped out, drawn up, and agreed. While Charles and William had doubtless pushed matters along, in the end it was still the queen who issued the statement about the departing royal couple.

While in her final statement the queen hoped that the young couple would have a happy life, not everyone was so fulsome. The awkwardness and tension among the quartet once dubbed the Fab Four after the Beatles pop group was on public display at the televised Commonwealth Day service at Westminster Abbey on March 9, 2020. The brothers barely exchanged a word. Shortly afterward Meghan and Harry headed west, keeping out of sight at a waterside mansion on Vancouver Island.

They had a secret weapon already primed once they had made their great escape. Just six months after their wedding, in December 2018, Harry had held secret discussions in a London hotel with talk-show queen Oprah Winfrey, a guest at their wedding, about the possibility of an interview. When they flew to Canada for the winter, the media deal was already in the bag.

Then the term Covid-19 was on everyone's lips. And nothing was ever the same again. Just two days after the Commonwealth Day service, the World Health Organization formally announced a pandemic, the government responding by shutting down schools, retail stores, and public gatherings as well as discouraging any but vital travel. Within weeks the nation was on lockdown and the royal drama was suddenly forgotten in the midst of a life-or-death struggle the British nation had not seen since the Second World War.

In the days before there was an effective vaccine the staggering numbers of those dying from Covid-19 in the nation's capital were higher than the worst week of the Blitz in 1940 when Nazi bombers rained down death and destruction on London, killing more than four thousand in a week. Frontline National Health Service doctors, nurses, and others, some of whom gave their lives, were compared to the heroic Spitfire pilots who thwarted the Nazi invasion. Thursday nights at eight o'clock became a regular time for the nation to show their appreciation by standing in their doorways to applaud NHS staff and other carers.

For the queen, who had lived through the Blitz, it was a moment to remind the nation of what they were made of. With her son and heir at Birkhall in Scotland suffering from the illness and Prime Minister Boris Johnson admitted to St.

Thomas' Hospital in central London, where he ended up fighting for his life in intensive care, the queen spoke to a deeply anxious and nervous nation. At the same time it was a country united in the face of a common enemy.

While the queen may have been in the autumn of her reign, she was perfectly positioned to speak to the nation with knowledge and empathy. Her Sunday-night address on April 5, 2020, lasted only four minutes, but the impact was long-lived, the queen evoking Britain's wartime stoicism, quiet courage, and ability to meet deadly calamity with a smile. Many of the 23.3 million who tuned in to what was only her fifth non-festive special address in her sixty-eight-year reign admitted that they had a lump in their throat and tears in their eyes as she echoed the famous words of wartime favorite Dame Vera Lynn: "We will meet again."

The queen, who wrote the evocative speech together with her private secretary Sir Edward Young, began by saying: "I am speaking to you at what I know is an increasingly challenging time.

"A time of disruption in the life of our country: a disruption that has brought grief to some, financial difficulties to many, and enormous changes to the daily lives of us all."

After thanking those on the front line, she continued: "I hope in the years to come everyone will be able to take pride in how they responded to this challenge. And those who come after us will say the Britons of this generation were as strong as any. That the attributes of self-discipline, of quiet good-humored resolve and of fellow-feeling still characterize this country. The pride in who we are is not a part of our past, it defines our present and our future."

She finished on a note of encouraging positivity: "We should take comfort that while we may have more still to endure, better days will return: we will be with our friends again; we will be with our families again; we will meet again."

It was a speech of hope, consolation, inspiration—and steely resolve. Her long experience with crises and dramas gave her words a resonance and authority that a younger voice would not have had. She was the right person with the right speech at the right time. In that moment the queen was truly the grandmother to the nation.

From now on she and Prince Philip, who returned from Sandringham, spent their days in a protective bubble at Windsor Castle. Though they had a staff of twenty-two, the couple found themselves spending more time together than at any time since their early married days.

The pandemic tested the ingenuity of everyone—including the queen and her family. For all her life the queen had been in the waving and hand-shaking business. As she liked to say: "I have to be seen to be believed."[37] Not anymore. The queen and the rest of the family had to adapt to a world of video calls and talking to a computer or television screen. This was the new normal. The queen was able to keep in touch with her subjects via the very medium she had once opposed: television. Besides the "We'll Meet Again" speech, she used television to deliver her Easter message and to commemorate the seventy-fifth anniversary of Victory in Europe or VE Day.

At Easter she called for hope and light in a darkened world. "We know that Coronavirus will not overcome us. As dark as death can be—particularly for those suffering with grief—light and life are greater. May the living flame of the Easter hope be a steady guide as we face the future."

She looked back fondly on VE Day as the nation, under lockdown, remembered those who laid down their lives in the cause of freedom: "Today it may seem hard that we cannot mark this special anniversary as we would wish. Instead we remember from our homes and our doorsteps. But our streets are not empty; they are filled with the love and the care that we have for each other. And when I look at our country today, and see what we are willing to do to protect and support one another, I say with pride that we are still a nation those brave soldiers, sailors and airmen would recognize and admire."

Her grandson Prince Harry, himself hardened by warfare in Afghanistan, had another battle to fight. It concerned what he considered to be the unfair treatment meted out to Meghan and himself by his family and their officials. After several fraught conversations with members of the family and their officials, he had concluded that he could never resolve his complaints privately. Waiting in the wings was Oprah Winfrey, eager to discuss their royal lives. Their hour-long conversation, which was broadcast in March 2021, for once lived up to the billing. It was a bombshell, the couple accusing the royal family of racism as well as indifferent and callous treatment in the face of Meghan's mental illness, isolation, and "imprisonment." Many of their claims, such as suggesting they were formally married three days before the televised wedding ceremony, were subsequently shown to be false or exaggerations. It was hurtful for the queen who had shown continuing good faith in her support of Harry both before and after his marriage. She was, as a friend of Diana's observed, "disappointed" by his behavior. Her formal response was classic HMQ—modulated, loving, but firm—while her phrase "some recollections may vary" spoke volumes about the accuracy of the recollections of Meghan and Harry. The queen's decision to investigate the allegations of racism in private indicated her preferred direction of travel.

Once again television had proved that it was a fair-weather friend, marvelous for royal spectacle, highly damaging for the monarchy once a member of the royal family clipped on a voice microphone.

Covid, though, constrained everything. Like Mountbatten, Prince Philip had painstakingly planned his funeral right down to the color of the Land Rover designed to carry his coffin. When he died on the morning of April 9, 2021, just weeks short of his one hundredth birthday, his elaborate plans had to be severely cut back.

His passing was described as "gentle and peaceful," though it left the queen with, according to Prince Andrew, "a huge void" in her life.[38] It was as if, said the Countess of Wessex, "somebody took him by the hand and off he went."[39] His funeral at St. George's Chapel in Windsor Castle was, due to Covid-19 regulations, a limited celebration of his life. Only thirty members of the family could take part in the service, which saw the queen, a diminutive lonely figure in black, sitting apart as she made her final goodbyes. "To see Her Majesty on her own," said the Countess of Wessex, "it was very poignant."[40] The service was brisk and to-the-point, like the man himself. *Just get on with it,* he would have said. The queen followed his wishes, the sovereign returning to royal duties two weeks after his death. After the funeral she was phlegmatic and reflective but never left alone. Senior members of the royal family, particularly Sophie Wessex, the wife of Prince Edward, were regular visitors to Windsor Castle. The arrival of Lilibet "Lili" Diana Mountbatten-Windsor, the daughter of Meghan and Harry, on June 4 was a welcome addition to the clan, demonstrating once again that in death there is also life, especially a life who bore the queen's childhood nickname, Lilibet. In the early going the queen had to make do with Zoom shots of the baby rather than the real thing.

By contrast her trusted and loyal ladies-in-waiting were a

constant physical presence. On the journey to bid farewell to Prince Philip, it was Lady Susan Hussey, who had known the queen since 1960, who accompanied her to St. George's Chapel in the state Bentley. Her ladies-in-waiting were not just unpaid helpers but genuine friends who had suffered family loss themselves. The queen proved herself remarkably stoical and, as the Countess of Wessex noted, "always thinking of others before herself."[41]

It was a comment made about her many years before in a tone of some wonderment by the king's gruff private secretary Tommy Lascelles during the famous tour of South Africa in 1947.[42] He was used to members of the royal family thinking of themselves before others. Not Elizabeth Alexandra Mary Windsor.

She became a young adult in wartime, witnessing at first hand the many guises of bravery. During those dark days of hardship and sacrifice, her steadfast Christian faith lit the way. Her quiet conviction sustained her through the many challenges she faced, often at a young age.

Her own memories of VE Day, dancing with strangers in the crowd, stayed with her throughout her life, as did her days living as a navy wife in Malta with the hope and expectation of a normal life stretching out before her.

Normal was a word she embraced. Her life was uniquely privileged but uniquely constrained, always on the inside looking out. She never allowed her heart to rule her head and yet, ironically, it was matters of the heart that defined her reign. Protocol and tradition were her safety net—and at times proved her undoing, most notably after the death of Diana, the Princess of Wales.

Her initial instinct was to clam up and retreat, though in later life she was far more her own person, more relaxed and willing to let her hair down, her wit as dry as her evening martinis. The older she became, the greater grew her capacity to surprise.

She put up with excessive amounts of praise and equally excessive criticism, though she was an instinctive conciliator, a follower of the middle way, an apostle of tolerance. She was wise, shrewd, and, in her own way, beneath the brittle facade, rather softhearted.

Though she, too, suffered health issues she made it clear that she had an appetite for business as usual. The prospect in 2022 of becoming the first monarch ever to celebrate her platinum anniversary, seventy years on the throne, was an undeniably enticing prospect. During the weekend of the seventieth anniversary of the accession, February 6, 2022, the queen issued an official statement expressing her "sincere wish" that Camilla be crowned queen consort when Prince Charles became king. It was the most public indication of Her Majesty's wish to ensure a smooth, orderly and uncontroversial transition of reign.

Queen Victoria earned herself the title grandmother of Europe, while Queen Elizabeth II has become grandmother to the United Kingdom and the Commonwealth. The longest-serving monarch in history has devoted herself to her family, her people, and the wider family of nations. Through the many shocks and surprises that have studded her record-breaking reign, she has stood for service and dedication, patiently watching the passing parade, often with a twinkle in her eye. In the good times and the bad she has been a steady presence, ready to celebrate or commiserate, her own life reflecting our island's journey in war and in peace. Much loved and immensely popular, she will go down in history as perhaps our greatest ever queen.

Epilogue

Though she had been the star of the show for as long as anyone could remember, over the passing months the queen gradually relinquished her role as top of the bill and took on a more frequent role as a much beloved background character. This gave other members of the Windsor cast list, notably her son and heir, Prince Charles, and her grandson Prince William the chance to shine on center stage.

Her decision to step back from important royal occasions, often at the last minute, was mainly due, as the palace stated, to "episodic mobility issues" that made standing for long periods difficult. In February 2022 she also contracted a mild dose of Covid-19, which caused her to cancel numerous public and private engagements. Her frequent bouts of ill health gave the watching world the chance to gain a sense of what the shape and composition of the monarchy would be in the not-too-distant future.

Though it was announced in advance that the queen would miss the annual Buckingham Palace garden parties, there was a genuine sense of concern when, for the first time in her long reign, she decided, on health grounds, to miss the traditional state opening of Parliament. In her stead she deputed another member of the royal family, namely Prince Charles, to attend this ancient ceremony, which is a key duty in the sovereign's role as head of state.

The decision was much more than asking her son to step into the breech at short notice. Important constitutional and legal procedures, known as Letters Patent, were enacted in order for Prince Charles to read the queen's official address, which laid out the government's plans and policies for the coming parliamentary term. These included its strategy for growing the economy, making Britain's streets safer, and clearing patient backlogs then in the health service due to Covid-19.

During the state opening, held in May 2022, Prince Charles, who delivered the speech from the consort's throne, was flanked by his eldest son, a very somber-looking Prince William, and his wife and future queen consort, the Duchess of Cornwall. Though the imperial state crown was present during the ceremony, the queen's slightly larger throne remained empty, a physical sign of the slow but steady transition of power from the sovereign to her successor.

In recognition of the queen's age and physical health, her formal role was rewritten by Buckingham Palace to reflect that change. The annual duties of the monarch such as the state opening of Parliament were no longer defined as "must fulfill." Instead, according to the report by the Sovereign Grant, which monitors royal spending, greater responsibility was placed on the support of the wider royal family. It was a sensible but necessary change to ensure the smooth transition of the reign as the queen increasingly stepped back from royal duties.

Stepping back but not stepping away. The queen used the

seventieth anniversary of her accession in February 2022 to renew her lifelong pledge to the nation. "My life will always be devoted to service," she confirmed. Her service continues, but it is beginning to look different with Charles and now William taking on a more prominent role than ever before.

Like the state opening of Parliament, the official four-day celebration of her platinum jubilee in June 2022 was a party where the guest of honor was largely absent. The queen was present for two brief balcony appearances at Buckingham Palace and a private lunch at Garter Day, and she also sent a message of thanks to racegoers at the traditional Royal Ascot meeting in June. For the most part it was the Prince of Wales aided by Prince William who led the traditional public elements, notably reviewing the various regiments at Trooping of the Color. He also stood in for his mother at the Royal Maundy Service. Following the Jubilee celebrations, the queen issued a message of thanks in which she said: "While I may not have attended every event in person, my heart has been with you all, and I remain committed to serving you to the best of my ability, supported by my family."

As with everything involving the House of Windsor, there was always a "but," a ticklish issue that invariably involved her family. Her health issues. which placed greater responsibility on Prince Charles and Prince William as counselors of state, also exposed a family vulnerability. Currently there are four counselors of state, whom the queen calls "my substitutes." The other two are the princes Andrew and Harry.

As one was in disgrace due to his relationship with millionaire pedophile Jeffrey Epstein and the other no longer an active member of the family, this arrangement had the potential to cause difficulties should either Charles or William be abroad on official duties when their presence nearer home was required due to the queen's incapacity. In those circumstances, technically Andrew and Harry would be left minding the store. Not a prospect welcomed by anyone.

This awkward state of affairs touched on the unsettled family dynamic at the heart of the House of Windsor. Just as at the beginning of her long reign when the queen had to confront the issue of Princess Margaret's love for divorced equerry Group Captain Peter Townsend, so in her reign's twilight years, family conflicts generated the most intractable and heartfelt problems.

The presence of Prince Andrew, always said to be her favorite, was now a constant thorn in the side of the institution. Days after the jubilee celebrations in June, which he missed due to a bout of Covid-19, his scheduled involvement with the ancient Order of the Garter ceremony, held at Windsor Castle, laid bare a family struggling to cope with his toxic persona due to the legal fall-out from the Epstein sex scandal. Although the queen had given her permission for her second son to take part in the public procession, Prince William warned his grandmother that he would feel uncomfortable joining his tainted uncle in this time-honored procession of chivalry. He feared that the optics of Andrew—who paid an estimated $15 million in an out-of-court settlement to his principal accuser, whom he claimed he never met—taking part in such an occasion would excite criticism and ridicule. William was later joined in this opinion by his father. The duo convinced the queen to rescind her invitation, even though the program for the order of service and the procession arrangements had already been printed. Though the queen informed Andrew that he was allowed to join his family for the private aspects of the ceremony—where no photographers were present—it was another manifestation of a scandal that continued to morph and gnaw at the fabric of the monarchy, the familial equivalent of the ever-changing virus Covid-19. So, for example, when Andrew's friend Ghislaine Maxwell was later sentenced to twenty years in jail for her part in the procurement and sexual exploitation of underage girls inevitably the spotlight returned to him. Months after he stepped down from royal duties, the fallout continued. In July 2022 the BBC announced that it was making a film about the genesis of Andrew's famous "car crash" interview with journalist Emily Maitlis, in which he showed little sympathy for the victims and little regret over his friendship with Epstein.

The episode further demonstrated Prince William's increased authority inside the family, as the prince, now forty, flexed his constitutional muscles. That he could tackle the monarch directly regarding her decision to invite her favored son to the Garter ceremony spoke volumes about the shift in the balance of power inside the royal family. It also underlined the queen's trust in his judgment regarding difficult issues. He was proving himself to be decisive and forthright, a future successor with an instinctive feel for protecting the monarchy in the modern age.

The arrival from California of Meghan, Harry, and their children, Archie and Lilibet, for the jubilee celebrations also had the potential to become a family calamity and a media circus. There were fears, inside and outside the palace, that the couple, who have contractual deals with Netflix and other media outlets, would say or do something that would take the spotlight away from the queen. Royal observers cited a previous trip to London in April 2022 when Prince Harry was on his way to the Netherlands to preside over the Invictus games.

At that time he told NBC that he had visited the queen to make sure that she was protected and "has got the right people around her."

His words were seen as a swipe at the courtiers close to Her Majesty, notably her private secretary, Sir Edward Young, and her influential dresser, Angela Kelly. It was Kelly who clashed with the prince over access to a tiara that the queen loaned to Meghan for her wedding day.

During their brief visit the couple deliberately maintained a low profile and watched the traditional Trooping of the Color ceremony from inside a government building, where the couple were photographed marshaling some of the noisier royal youngsters during the occasion. There was, however, no place on the Buckingham Palace balcony for Harry, Meghan, their children, nor the sprawling cast of junior royals. Those invited to watch the spectacular flypast were limited to "working royals" only, the queen standing with her immediate successors—Princes Charles, William, and George—in a public demonstration of continuity.

Privately the California-based couple introduced Lilibet to both the queen and Prince Charles. After an "emotional meeting" Charles described himself as "absolutely thrilled" to see his granddaughter for the first time and to be reacquainted with his grandson, Archie. Though the couple brought along a photographer to capture the scene of one Lilibet meeting another, the queen indicated that she was too tired and, as her eyes were bloodshot, she was not up to a photo session. More cynical media observers suggested that this was a diplomatic way of preventing the Sussexes from exploiting the historic family meeting.

Within hours of that brief family reunion, the Sussexes boarded a private jet to take them to back to California with little if any sign of a rapprochement between the feuding brothers. Instead there was the inevitable realization that though Harry and Meghan had previously pledged their undying allegiance to Her Majesty while criticizing the institution she presided over, one day in the not-too-distant future their most affectionate, forgiving, and influential supporter would no longer be around to defend them. It is doubtful that Harry's brother and father will lend the couple the same welcome as the queen. Indeed it would be an indulgent king who gave his querulous and critical son the same easy access as the previous incumbent. It is almost history repeating itself: George VI's relationship with his elder brother, Edward VIII, who later became the Duke of Windsor, was never the same after Edward abdicated the throne to marry the twice-divorced American Wallis Simpson.

Just as Prince Andrew's folly will cause problems for the monarchy for some time to come, so the Sussexes' rival royal court in California may provide a more overtly political and radical counterpoint to the House of Windsor. Meghan and Harry have already dipped more than a toe in the American political scene; the couple joined in the widespread condemnation of the Supreme Court's dismantling of the *Roe v. Wade* decision regarding abortion rights. A speech by Harry to the United Nations celebrating the life of the late South African president Nelson Mandela in July 2022 demonstrated the prince's continued reach and relevance—with or without an HRH title. Similarly George VI and Queen Elizabeth were always wary that his charismatic elder brother and wife who, like Meghan and Harry, lived abroad, would steal the spotlight away from them.

Ironically it was not the behavior of her family but her fourteenth prime minister, Boris Johnson, that threatened to cast a pall over the jubilee celebrations and drag the monarchy into a national crisis. Even as the crowds sang the queen's praises, other voices in his own ruling party urged Johnson to go. This was in response to numerous scandals that had assailed his premiership. In the heady days of the crisis it was thought that Johnson would refuse to resign. Like a scene out of an action movie, the cry went up: "Activate the queen," suggesting that if Johnson stayed put in spite of losing the confidence of his cabinet and party the queen would be dragged into the political arena. She would be obliged to sack him. It was a murky constitutional area that was never tested. In early July Johnson tendered his resignation, which was duly, perhaps gratefully, accepted by the queen. It was proof, if any were needed, that the queen had to be on her constitutional toes, no matter how long she had reigned.

During her reign the monarchy has moved away from platitudes and bromides to commitment to and concern about some of the most challenging issues of our times, notably the environment. Planting trees, not just the odd ceremonial sapling but entire forests, was the overarching theme of the jubilee. The queen was acutely aware of the symbolism of a growing tree; like the institution to which she has devoted her life, it represented change amid continuity.

She was an enthusiastic exponent of the green monarchy, a sentiment symbolized by the "tree of trees" which was planted outside Buckingham Palace. During the jubilee celebrations she referred to the pioneering environmental work of her late husband and indicated that she couldn't be more proud of his legacy and the work of princes Charles and William. As William told the boisterous crowd gathered outside Buckingham Palace for the jubilee pop concert, "The pressing need to protect and restore our planet has never been more urgent." He shared his grandmother's optimism that the planet could be saved for future generations. The focus on the environment, arguably the greatest issue of our time, was a further sign of how far the monarchy had changed during the queen's reign,

⁓

While the constitutional importance of the monarchy has waned, the queen has presided over the transformation of the institution into a national cheerleader with members of the family becoming enthusiastic activists and promoters for causes they hold dear. The days of the white-gloved, big-handbag, do-not-touch monarchy are long gone.

Just before his fortieth birthday in June 2022, Prince William gained global headlines when he went on the streets of London to sell the *Big Issue*, a magazine sold by the homeless to help them get a hand up out of poverty. He admitted that he was inspired by the work and example of his late mother, Diana, Princess of Wales, who took him and his brother on excursions to meet rough sleepers. At the time, her work with the underprivileged and marginalized was seen as unconventional.

Now it is mainstream. The queen presided over this important change in royal work, and the behavior of the coming generation helps to ensure the continued relevance of the monarchy long into the future. As William observed in an interview with the *Big Issue*: "I have always believed in using my platform...to bring attention and action to those who are struggling. I plan to do that now that I'm turning forty, even more than I have in the past."

It is deeply satisfying for the queen to know that her successor not only shares her commitment to service but enjoys a solid, committed family life that is reminiscent of her own happy childhood. As she observed in a BBC documentary,

Elizabeth: The Unseen Queen, which she narrated herself: "In my experience a happy family is one of the positive features of human existence that has not changed." She revealed, too, the bedrock values that have sustained her during the triumphs and disasters of her long reign: "Faith, family, and friendship have not only been a constant for me but a source of personal comfort and reassurance," she said.

A single sentence in her televised reflections gave a telling insight into her character and helped explain why the queen excites such universal respect from world leaders to the men and women in the street: "It is not enough to do our job, service demands sacrifice."

This sentiment has served as a lodestar throughout her long reign, comprised of sterling values she has endeavored to pass on to the generation who will come after her. For most of her reign she has seemed impregnable and immovable, the "golden thread" who has linked disparate and often competing nations, organizations, and constitutions to one another. The monarchy has always been based on contradictions, ambiguities, and paradoxes, conflicts that have been largely left untouched.

With thoughts turning to the prospect of King Charles and Queen Camilla, fundamental questions about the future of the monarchy will be raised in a very different political climate to that which existed in 1952, when Elizabeth first became queen. With the waning of deference and the questioning of ancient and modern institutions from the church to Parliament, the monarchy and its purpose and relevance will come under close scrutiny at the beginning of the new reign. Why, for instance, should a white, Anglo Saxon Christian family automatically represent a diverse multiethnic nation and Commonwealth ? With Scottish independence still a live political issue, could King Charles realistically reign over this independent northern realm? How, too, will Queen Camilla be accepted by the general public, given her part in Charles's divorce? And will the Commonwealth, so carefully tended by Elizabeth, still have a purpose in the long-term? Will a pared-down, streamlined monarchy, which is Charles's aim, be able to cope with a demanding international constituency?

Though the queen will have left a formidable legacy of service, selflessness, and respect, it remains to be seen how the new players will respond to these challenges when Queen Elizabeth II finally leaves the stage. One thing is certain, though; she will be a hard act to follow.

Acknowledgments

For more than forty years I have been, along with other topics, reporting on and writing about the British monarchy. During that time I have met with members of the royal family, with varying degrees of brevity, as well as their managerial staff, popularly known as courtiers, and their Downstairs employees: the valets, chauffeurs, bodyguards, chefs, gardeners, maids, and others who keep the wheels of this ancient institution turning. On the way some have become friends, while others have remained acquaintances. They have one thing in common—a story to tell, often about the woman the late Diana, Princess of Wales, referred to as "the chief lady," Her Majesty the Queen, the longest-reigning monarch in British history. In reviewing her life and times, some have preferred to remain in the background but others are happy to be acknowledged for their contribution to this biography of a remarkable woman.

I would like to thank Dickie Arbiter, Sarah Bradford, Phil Dampier, Grania Forbes, Dave Griffin, Patrick Jephson, Richard Kay, Ken Lennox, Eric Milligan, former lord provost of Edinburgh, Katie Nicholl, Professor Jonathan Petropolous,

Dr. Frank Prochaska, Paul Reynolds, Ingrid Seward, Professor Andrew Stewart, Noreen Taylor, Ken Wharfe, and Christopher Wilson.

In Malta my thanks to Charles Azzopardi, general manager, Phoenicia hotel, Michael Bonello, Carmen Glenville, Tony Grech, the late Dr. Joseph Micallef Stafrace, and Robert and Dee Hornyold-Strickland, as well as Marisa Xuereb for her splendid organization.

I would like to thank my agent Steve Troha as well as researchers Claudia Taylor, Camille J. Thomas, and Andrina Tran for their sterling efforts during the pandemic. Thanks, too, to Gretchen Young, my editor at Grand Central in New York, for bringing a fresh and perceptive focus to the project. My appreciation, too, to assistant editor Haley Weaver and copy editor Laura Jorstad at Grand Central and my editor Louise Dixon, copy editor Helen Cumberbatch, and picture researcher Judith Palmer at Michael O'Mara Books in London.

In this marathon pandemic, I have much appreciated the patience and forbearance of my wife, Carolyn.

—London
January 2022

Notes

Introduction: Surfing with Her Majesty

1. *Prince Philip: The Royal Family Remembers*, directed by Faye Hamilton and Michael Hill (UK: Oxford Films, September 22, 2021), BBC One.
2. Kiron K. Skinner, Annelise Anderson, and Martin Anderson, eds., *Reagan: A Life in Letters* (New York: Free Press, 2003), 48.
3. Joan Goulding, "Queen Elizabeth II Left Her Luxury Yacht Today," UPI Archives, March 5, 1983.
4. Henry Samuel, "Teetotal Sarkozy Uses Dutch Courage to Grill Queen," *Independent*, October 7, 2010.
5. "Obituary: Sir Kenneth Scott," *Times*, March 2, 2018.

1: Shirley Temple 2.0

1. Marion Crawford, "The Day the Queen Threw a Tantrum and Tipped a Pot of Ink Over Her Own Head," *Daily Mail*, May 18, 2012.
2. Edwards, *Royal Sisters*, 11.
3. Duchess of Windsor, *The Heart Has Its Reasons*, 225.
4. Dennison, *The Queen*, 100.
5. Dismore, *Princess*, 104.
6. "A Young Princess Elizabeth: The Early Years," *Australian Women's Weekly*, September 5, 2015.

7. Margaret Rhodes, "The Day the Queen Did a Conga into the Palace," *Daily Mail*, June 18, 2011.
8. Eliana Dockterman, "Elizabeth Didn't Expect to Be Queen. Here's How It Happened," *Time*, June 1, 2018.
9. William Safire, ed., *Lend Me Your Ears: Great Speeches in History—Updated and Expanded* (New York: W. W. Norton, 2004), 422.
10. Morrow, *The Queen*, 15.
11. Crawford, *Little Princesses*, 63.
12. Lydia Starbuck, "The Queen's Birth: What the Papers Said," *Royal Central*, April 21, 2021.
13. Shawcross, *The Queen Mother*, 257.
14. Pimlott, *The Queen*, 3.
15. Shawcross, *The Queen Mother*, 307.
16. Shawcross, *The Queen Mother*, 302.
17. "Featured Document: Letter from Princess Elizabeth to WSC," International Churchill Society, June 5, 2018.
18. Countess of Airlie, *Thatched with Gold*, 180.
19. Richard Kay and Geoffrey Levy, "The Queen of Mischief," *Daily Mail*, March 16, 2016.
20. Ian Lloyd, "Revealed: The Little Girl the Queen Chose to Be Her Best Friend," *Daily Mail*, July 25, 2014.
21. Dismore, *Princess*, 91.
22. Shawcross, *The Queen Mother*, 316.
23. Shawcross, *The Queen Mother*, 320.
24. Edward Owens, "'This Is the Day of the People': The 1937 Coronation," in *The Family Firm: Monarchy, Mass Media and the British Public, 1932–53* (London: University of London Press, 2019), 133–98, http://www.jstor.org/stable/j.ctvkjb3sr.9.
25. Crawford, *Little Princesses*, 22.
26. Rhodes, "The Day the Queen Did a Conga."
27. Box 6, File 30, Bruce and Beatrice Blackmar Gould correspondence, Rare Books and Special Collections, Firestone Library, Princeton University, Princeton, New Jersey.
28. Box 6, File 30, Bruce and Beatrice Blackmar Gould correspondence.
29. Pimlott, *The Queen*, 28.
30. Crawford, *Little Princesses*, 26.

31. Maria Coole, "The Queen's Ruined Childhood and Why She Won't Let Prince George Suffer the Same Heartbreak," *Marie Claire*, December 25, 2019.

32. Crawford, *Little Princesses*, 19.

33. Untitled, Box 6, Folder 32, Bruce and Beatrice Blackmar Gould correspondence, Rare Books and Special Collections, Firestone Library, Princeton University, Princeton, New Jersey.

34. Crawford, *Little Princesses*, 28.

35. Crawford, *Little Princesses*, 21.

36. Crawford, *Little Princesses*, 72.

37. Royal Collection Trust, RCIN 1080431.

38. Dismore, *Princess*, 110.

39. Crawford, *Little Princesses*, 84.

40. Crawford, *Little Princesses*, 79.

41. Crawford, *Little Princesses*, 102.

42. Brandreth, *Philip and Elizabeth*, 68.

43. Crawford, *Little Princesses*, 103.

2: Bombs at Bedtime

1. Henry Holloway, "Nazi Plot to Kill Winston Churchill with Spy Parachuted into Britain to Win WW2," *Daily Star*, July 3, 2017.

2. Richard M. Langworth, "How Many Assassination Attempts on Winston Churchill? Ask Walter Thompson," Churchill Project: Hillsdale College, September 18, 2019.

3. Comer Clarke, "Kidnap the Royal Family," *Sunday Pictorial*, March 22, 1959.

4. Stewart, *King's Private Army*, 124.

5. Hannah Furness, "Queen Mother Learned to Shoot Buckingham Palace Rats in Case Nazis Tried to Kidnap Royal Family," *Telegraph*, April 30, 2015.

6. Shawcross, *Counting One's Blessings*, 277.

7. Stewart, *King's Private Army*, 127.

8. Longford, *Queen Mother*, 80.

9. Stewart, *King's Private Army*, 127.

10. John W. Wheeler-Bennett, *King George VI: His Life and Reign* (London: Macmillan, 1958), 464.

11. Wheeler-Bennett, *King George VI*, 468.

12. Caroline Davies, "How the Luftwaffe Bombed the Palace, in the Queen Mother's Own Words," *Guardian*, September 12, 2009.
13. Shawcross, *Counting One's Blessings*, 298.
14. Julia Labianca, "17 Wild Secrets You Never Knew About Windsor Castle," *Reader's Digest Canada*, May 31, 2021.
15. Howard, *Windsor Diaries*, 35.
16. Shawcross, *The Queen Mother*, 586.
17. "Wartime Broadcast, 1940," royal.uk, published October 13, 1940.
18. Glenconner, *Lady in Waiting*, 18.
19. Duff Hart-Davis, ed., *King's Counsellor: Abdication and War: The Diaries of Sir Alan Lascelles* (London: Orion Publishing, 2006), 208.
20. "Sir Geoffrey de Bellaigue," *Telegraph*, January 8, 2013.
21. Gill Swain, "My Picnics with the Queen," *Daily Mirror*, September 19, 1998.
22. Stewart, *King's Private Army*, 94.
23. Shawcross, *Counting One's Blessings*, 361.
24. Shawcross, *Counting One's Blessings*, 354.
25. Henry Wallop, "Her REAL Highness," *Daily Mail*, February 4, 2018.
26. Crawford, *The Little Princesses*, 134.
27. Ibid., 126.
28. Howard, *Windsor Diaries*, 100.
29. "ER's Press Conference in Canterbury, England, 18 November 1942," reprinted in Maurine Beasley, ed., *White House Press Conferences of Eleanor Roosevelt* (New York: Garland, 1983).
30. F. J. Corbitt, *My Twenty Years in Buckingham Palace*, 188.
31. Shawcross, *Counting One's Blessings*, 366.
32. Maclean, *Crowned Heads*, 32.
33. "Queen Mum Falters on Memory Lane: Writer Accused of Ill Table Manners in Reporting Anecdote," *Los Angeles Times*, July 11, 1990.
34. Duff Hart-Davis, ed., *King's Counsellor*, 85.
35. Tim Heald, "A Very Contrary Princess—Why Did the Charming Margaret Turn into the Most Unpopular Royal?" *Daily Mail*, June 29, 2007.
36. Brandreth, *Philip*, 171.
37. Howard, *Windsor Diaries*, 131.
38. Rhodes, *Final Curtsey*, 87.
39. Dismore, *Princess*, 193.

40. Dismore, *Princess*, 145.
41. Dismore, *Princess*, 194.
42. Philip Eade, "The Romances of Young Prince Philip," *Telegraph*, May 5, 2017.
43. Seward, *Prince Philip Revealed*, 66.
44. Annie Bullen, *His Royal Highness the Prince Philip, Duke of Edinburgh (1921–2021): A Commemoration* (London: Pitkin Publishing, 2021), 23.
45. Seward, *Prince Philip Revealed*, 69.
46. Crawford, *Little Princesses*, 150.
47. Howard, *Windsor Diaries*, 217.
48. Howard, *Windsor Diaries*, 282.
49. Valentine Low, "VE Day: Queen Recalls Joining the Party with Margaret," *Times*, May 9, 2020.
50. Chris Pleasance, "Don't Look Now Your Majesty!" *Daily Mail*, March 17, 2014.
51. Low, "VE Day."
52. "The Way We Were," BBC Radio 4, December 24, 1985.

3: A Walk in the Heather

1. Sarah Bradford, *George VI* (New York: Viking, 2011), 346.
2. Thorpe, ed., *Who Loses, Who Wins*, 177.
3. *Prince Philip: The Plot to Make a King*, directed by Richard Sanders (UK: Blakeway Productions, July 30, 2015), Channel 4.
4. Seward, *Prince Philip Revealed*, 75.
5. Andrew Hornery, "Happy 99th Birthday to Philip," *Sydney Morning Herald*, June 14, 2020.
6. Michael Thornton, "Was Philip Really a Philanderer?" *Daily Mail*, March 18, 2017.
7. Dismore, *Princess*, 195.
8. Maclean, *Crowned Heads*, 34.
9. Thorpe, ed., *Who Loses, Who Wins*, 319.
10. Seward, *Prince Philip Revealed*, 73.
11. Dismore, *Princess*, 244.
12. Corbitt, *My Twenty Years in Buckingham Palace*, 204.
13. Seward, *My Husband and I*, 70.
14. Tom Utley, "Grandad's Words Made Churchill and the Queen Cry," *Daily Mail*, June 7, 2012.

15. Viney, *Last Hurrah*, 274.

16. Viney, *Last Hurrah*, 270.

17. "A Speech by the Queen on Her 21st Birthday, 1947," royal.uk, published April 21, 1947.

18. Viney, *Last Hurrah*, 275.

19. Viney, *Last Hurrah*, 273.

20. Viney, *Last Hurrah*, 273.

21. "95 Years, 95 Jewels: Part 2 (March–April 1947)," *Court Jeweller*, March 29, 2021.

22. Viney, *Last Hurrah*, 153.

23. *Prince Philip: The Plot to Make a King.*

24. Peter Townsend, *Time and Chance: An Autobiography* (London: Collins, 1978), 147.

25. Glenconner, *Lady in Waiting*, 275.

26. Dermot Morrah, *The Royal Family in Africa* (London: Hutchinson, 1947). See also Edwards, *Royal Sisters*, 160.

27. *Prince Philip: The Plot to Make a King.*

28. Reiss Smith, "The Crown: Why Did King George Call Queen Elizabeth His Pride and Margaret His Joy?" *Daily Express*, December 7, 2016.

29. Bradford, *Elizabeth*, 116.

30. Shawcross, *The Queen Mother*, 626.

31. Steph Cockcroft, "How Prince Philip Curtsied to King George VI," *Daily Mail*, July 31, 2015.

32. *Prince Philip: The Plot to Make a King.*

33. Seward, *Prince Philip Revealed*, 82.

34. Ingrid Seward, "So What Is the Truth About Philip and Those 'Affairs'?" *Daily Mail*, November 15, 2017.

35. Jonathan Mayo, "Minute by Mesmerizing Minute, Relive the Queen's Most Joyous Day," *Daily Mail*, November 10, 2017.

36. Mayo, "Minute by Mesmerizing Minute."

37. Pamela Hicks, "Philip's Risque Party Trick and My Mischievous Friend Lilibet," *Daily Mail*, December 14, 2012.

38. Elizabeth Grice, "Royal Wedding: A Marriage Made in History," *Telegraph*, March 25, 2011. See also "'Alles sal reg kom': Churchill on the Royal Wedding," Richard M. Langworth website, April 29, 2011.

39. Erin Hill, "'I Lost Something Very Precious': Read King George VI's Touching Letter to Daughter Elizabeth on Her Wedding Day," *People*, November 20, 2015.

40. Kate Nicholson, "The Heartwarming Speeches Prince Philip and the Queen Gave on Their Wedding Day Revealed," *Daily Mirror*, November 20, 2019.

41. Shawcross, *The Queen Mother*, 631.

42. Rhodes, *Final Curtsey*, 44.

4: The Barefoot Princess

1. *The Private Lives of the Windsors*, directed by Ben Reid (UK: Renegade Pictures, October 7, 2019), Smithsonian Channel.

2. Seward, *Prince Philip Revealed*, 95.

3. Vanessa Thorpe, "Queen Mother Was 'Ruthless' to Royal Nanny," *Guardian*, June 24, 2020.

4. Bradford, *Elizabeth*, 151.

5. Vicky Spavin, "Was Crawfie Victim of Royal Conspiracy?" *Scottish Daily Record*, June 24, 2000.

6. Pimlott, *The Queen*, 159.

7. Chloe Foussianes, "New Letters by Princess Margaret Reveal Love for Her 'Heavenly Nephew,' Prince Charles," *Town and Country*, March 13, 2019.

8. Queen mother to Mabel Strickland, February 7, 1972, private papers, estate of Robert Hornyold-Strickland, Malta, GC.

9. Joan Alexander, *The Life of Mabel Strickland* (Malta: Progress Press, 1996), 194.

10. Janet Morgan, *Edwina Mountbatten: A Life of Her Own* (London: HarperCollins, 1991), 444.

11. Richard Kay and Geoffrey Levy, "The Surprising Truth About the Queen's Very Amorous Marriage," *Scottish Daily Mail*, March 8, 2016.

12. Philip Ziegler, *Mountbatten: The Official Biography* (London: William Collins Sons, 1985), 492.

13. Morgan, *Edwina Mountbatten*, 444.

14. Jebb, ed., *Diaries of Cynthia Gladwyn*, 92.

15. Dismore, *Princess*, 256.

16. Camilla Tominey and Phil Dampier, "'Forget Protocol, Darling!'" *Daily Express*, November 18, 2012.

17. Princess Elizabeth memo to Jessie Grech, September 15, 1950, author collection.

18. Father Geoffrey Attard, "Queen Elizabeth II's connection to Gozo," *Times of Malta*, November 23, 2015.

19. Queen Elizabeth II to Mabel Strickland, January 5, 1975, private papers, estate of Robert Hornyold-Strickland, Malta, GC.

20. Seward, *My Husband and I*, 82.

21. Turner, *Elizabeth*, 5.

22. Seward, *My Husband and I*, 85.

23. Seward, *My Husband and I*, 84.

24. Hartley, *Accession*, 128–29.

25. Hartley, *Accession*, 128.

26. Hartley, *Accession*, 113.

27. Hartley, *Accession*, 130.

28. Hartley, *Accession*, 131.

29. Hartley, *Accession*, 131–32.

30. Pimlott, *The Queen*, 179.

31. Hartley, *Accession*, 131–32.

32. Hartley, *Accession*, 136.

33. *Queen and Country*, directed by John Bridcut, written by William Shawcross (UK: Crux Productions, May 1, 2002), BBC.

34. Holly Evans, "Queen Responded with Brutal Swipe After Royal Family Tragedy," *Daily Express*, May 19, 2021.

5: Crowning Glory

1. Wheeler-Bennett, *Friends, Enemies and Sovereigns*, 133.

2. Smith, *Elizabeth the Queen*, 66.

3. Smith, *Elizabeth the Queen*, 66–67.

4. Pimlott, *The Queen*, 176.

5. Andrew Roberts, *Churchill: Walking with Destiny* (New York: Penguin, 2018), 929.

6. Williams, *Young Elizabeth*, 47.

7. Shawcross, *The Queen Mother*, 658.

8. Shawcross, *The Queen Mother*, 658.

9. Pimlott, *The Queen*, 199.

10. Box 314, Sir Fitzroy Maclean Papers, MSS 11487, Albert and Shirley Small Special Collections Library, University of Virginia, Charlottesville, Virginia.

11. Ingrid Seward, "So What Is the Truth About Philip and Those 'Affairs'?" *Daily Mail*, November 15, 2017.

12. Author interview with anonymous source, June 2019.

13. Michael Bloch, *The Secret File of the Duke of Windsor* (New York: HarperCollins, 1988), 264.

14. Lacey, *Monarch*, 175.

15. Dimbleby, *Prince of Wales*, 18.

16. "His People's Day," *Courier-Mail*, February 11, 1952.

17. Charles Drazin, ed., *The Journals / John Fowles*, volume 1, *1949–1965* (Evanston, IL: Northwestern University Press, 2003), 172.

18. Laura Connor, "How Last Victoria Cross Holder 'Big Bill' Hurled Rocks and Beer Cans to Keep the North Korean Army at Bay," *Daily Mirror*, June 22, 2018.

19. Smith, *Elizabeth the Queen*, 73–74.

20. Lacey, *Crown: Official Companion*, volume 1, 76.

21. Longford, *Elizabeth R*, 238.

22. Bradford, *Elizabeth*, 220.

23. Smith, *Elizabeth the Queen*, 93.

24. Edwards, *Royal Sisters*, 246.

25. Edwards, *Royal Sisters*, 247.

26. Pimlott, *The Queen*, 185.

27. Bradford, *Elizabeth*, 170–71.

28. Strober and Strober, *The Monarchy*, 80.

29. Williams, *Young Elizabeth*, 275.

30. Seward, *My Husband and I*, 89.

31. Brandreth, *Philip and Elizabeth*, 254.

32. Longford, *Elizabeth R*, 192.

33. *Prince Philip: The Plot to Make a King*.

34. *Daily Express*, October 20, 1952.

35. *Elizabeth: Our Queen*, directed by Mick Gold, Suzy Boyles, Karen McGann, and Nicola Seare (UK: ITN Productions, February 6, 2018), Channel Five.

36. Peter Townsend, *Time and Chance: An Autobiography* (London: Collins, 1978), 198.

37. Smith, *Elizabeth the Queen*, 81–82.

38. Edwards, *Royal Sisters*, 257.

39. Dominic Midgley, "The Coronation of Queen Elizabeth II: How the Daily Express Reported It 61 Years Ago," *Daily Express*, September 18, 2014.

40. Smith, *Elizabeth the Queen*, 67.

41. Pimlott, *The Queen*, 209.

42. Katy Winter, "The Queen Asked, 'Ready Girls?'" *Daily Mail*, April 16, 2013.

43. Smith, *Elizabeth the Queen*, 85.

44. Smith, *Elizabeth the Queen*, 85.

45. Lacey, *Crown: Official Companion*, volume 1, 125.

46. Glenconner, *Lady in Waiting*, 74.

47. Maclean, *Crowned Heads*, 40.

48. Ellen Castelow, "The Coronation 1953," Historic UK website, undated.

49. Brandreth, *Philip*, 282.

50. Glenconner, *Lady in Waiting*, 77.

6: Hearts and Coronets

1. Peter Townsend, *Time and Chance: An Autobiography* (London: Collins, 1978), 188.

2. Shawcross, *The Queen Mother*, 684.

3. Christopher Warwick, *Princess Margaret: A Life of Contrasts* (London: Andrew Deutsch, 2000), 190. See also Williams, *Young Elizabeth*, 293.

4. Williams, *Young Elizabeth*, 262.

5. Pimlott, *The Queen*, 219.

6. Christopher Warwick, "Princess Margaret Letter Changes How We View Her Life," *Telegraph*, November 7, 2009.

7. Karen Kissane, "It Happens Even in Royal Marriages," *Sydney Morning Herald*, September 28, 2011.

8. Hardman, *Our Queen*, 195.

9. Warwick, *Princess Margaret*, 197.

10. Roya Nikkhah, "Princess Margaret Recently Unearthed Letter Sheds New Light on Decision Not to Marry," *Telegraph*, November 7, 2009.

11. Katie Sewell, "Princess Margaret: Unearthed Letter Reveals Peter Townsend Split Not All as It Seemed," *Daily Express,* January 4, 2021.

12. Sarah Pulliam Bailey, "Fact Checking 'The Crown': Queen Elizabeth's Faith and Her Close Relationship with Preacher Billy Graham," *Washington Post,* January 9, 2018.

13. Marshall Frady, *Billy Graham: A Parable of American Righteousness* (Boston: Little, Brown, 1979), 372.

14. Paul Reynolds, "Did the Queen Stop Princess Margaret Marrying Peter Townsend?" *BBC News,* November 19, 2016.

15. Townsend, *Time and Chance,* 234.

16. Seward, *Prince Philip Revealed,* 135.

17. Townsend, *Time and Chance,* 236.

18. Maclean, *Crowned Heads,* 42.

19. Seward, *My Husband and I,* 139.

20. Bradford, *Elizabeth,* 264.

21. Seward, *Prince Philip Revealed,* 256.

22. Bradford, *Elizabeth,* 268.

23. Seward, *My Husband and I,* 137.

24. Andrew Pierce and Richard Kay, "Princess Margaret's Very Private Correspondence," *Daily Mail,* February 20, 2015.

25. Jebb, ed., *The Diaries of Cynthia Gladwyn,* 207.

26. Bradford, *Elizabeth,* 240.

27. Bradford, *Elizabeth,* 240.

28. Smith, *Elizabeth the Queen,* 128.

29. Untitled, Box 6, Folder 32, Bruce and Beatrice Blackmar Gould correspondence, Rare Books and Special Collections, Firestone Library, Princeton University, Princeton, New Jersey.

30. "Christmas Broadcast 1947," royal.uk, published December 25, 1947.

7: Secrets, Scandals, and Spies

1. Seward, *Prince Philip Revealed,* 150.

2. Seward, *Prince Philip Revealed,* 145.

3. Dennison, *The Queen,* 240.

4. *Prince Philip: The Royal Family Remembers,* directed by Faye Hamilton and Michael Hill (UK: Oxford Films, September 22, 2021), BBC One.

5. Bradford, *Elizabeth,* 282.

6. Christopher Wilson, "Punched as He Slept, Friends Tortured with Pliers," *Daily Mail*, February 1, 2013.

7. Bradford, *Elizabeth*, 276.

8. Hugo Vickers, *The Quest for Queen Mary* (London: Hodder & Stoughton, 2018), 222.

9. Smith, *Elizabeth the Queen*, 188.

10. Abbie Llewelyn, "Prince Philip's Staggering Confession About Prince Andrew Exposed," *Daily Express*, August 4, 2020.

11. Smith, *Elizabeth the Queen*, 146.

12. Seward, *My Husband and I*, 144.

13. Tim Heald, *Princess Margaret: A Life Unravelled* (London: Weidenfeld & Nicolson, 2007), 121.

14. Thorpe, ed., *Who's In, Who's Out*, 160.

15. Dennison, *The Queen*, 311.

16. Dennison, *The Queen*, 311.

17. "Watch: Queen Elizabeth II's 1961 Visit to Ghana," British Heritage Travel, December 3, 2021. See also Dennison, *The Queen*, 307–08.

18. Dennison, *The Queen*, 307.

19. Valentine Low, Hugo Vickers, and Alice Foster, "Queen Dancing in Ghana: The Story Behind Her Iconic Visit to Save the Commonwealth," *Times*, March 26, 2018.

20. Tom Parfitt, "Yuri Gagarin's Brush with Royalty Revealed in New Biography," *Guardian*, April 12, 2011.

21. Craig Brown, *Ninety-Nine Glimpses of Princess Margaret* (New York: Farrar, Straus and Giroux, 2017), 7.

22. Andrew Glass, "Jackie Kennedy Adopts Sardar, March 23, 1962," *Politico*, March 23, 2011.

23. Jack Whatley, "Remembering the Beatles' 1963 Royal Variety Performance," *Far Out*, November 4, 2019.

24. Queen Elizabeth II to Mabel Strickland, March 1964, private papers, estate of Robert Hornyold-Strickland, Malta, GC.

25. Bradford, *Elizabeth*, 308.

26. Miranda Carter, *Anthony Blunt: His Lives* (New York: Farrar, Straus and Giroux, 2001), 376.

27. Turner, *Elizabeth*, 57.

28. "How Many Prime Ministers Has the Queen Had in Her Reign?" inews.co.uk, December 13, 2019. See also Marr, *Real Elizabeth*, 158.

29. Hardman, *Our Queen*, 205.
30. Marcia Falkender, *Inside Number 10* (Worthing, UK: Littlehampton Book Services, 1972), 17.
31. Matthew Francis, "Harold Wilson's 'White Heat of Technology' Speech 50 Years On," *Guardian*, September 19, 2013.
32. Nicole Stinson, "Revealed: Queen Broke Protocol for Winston Churchill by Bestowing Rare Honour on Prime Minister," *Daily Express*, February 22, 2018.
33. Reiss Smith, "The Crown: Who Is John Lithgow, the American Actor Playing Winston Churchill on Netflix?" *Daily Express*, December 7, 2016.

8: A Family Affair

1. Author interview with Victoria Charlton, December 2018.
2. Pimlott, *The Queen*, 371.
3. Pimlott, *The Queen*, 371.
4. Author interview with Grania Forbes, February 2015.
5. Abbie Llewelyn, "Princess Anne Loathed Royal Family Documentary: 'It Was a Rotten Idea,'" *Daily Express*, January 29, 2021.
6. Dennison, *The Queen*, 332.
7. Bradford, *Elizabeth*, 353.
8. Smith, *Prince Charles*, 43.
9. Anne de Courcy, *Snowdon: The Biography* (London: Phoenix, 2008), 192.
10. Bradford, *Elizabeth*, 397.
11. Lacey, *Monarch*, 238.
12. Turner, *Elizabeth*, 91.
13. Turner, *Elizabeth*, 91.
14. Turner, *Elizabeth*, 97.
15. Ibid.
16. Bradford, *Elizabeth*, 112.
17. Smith, *Prince Charles*, 63.
18. Bradford, *Elizabeth*, 415.
19. Katie Frost, "The Queen and Prince Philip's Best Quotes on Married Life,: *Harper's Bazaar*, April 9, 2021.
20. Hardman, *Our Queen*, 270.
21. Turner, *Elizabeth*, 110.

22. Turner, *Elizabeth*, 111.

23. Sheila Langan, "The Irish Lord Who Captured Queen Elizabeth's Heart," *British Heritage Travel*, July 6, 2021.

24. Lisa Waller Rogers, "Princess Margaret and Her Guttersnipe Life," *Lisa's History Room*(blog), April 30, 2020.

25. Sean Smith, "Will She Finally Be Elizabeth the First?" *Daily Mail*, May 16, 2011.

26. Smith, "Will She Finally Be Elizabeth the First?"

27. Author interview with Sean Smith, October 2021.

28. Theo Aronson, *Princess Margaret: A Biography* (London: Thistle Publishing, 2013), 276.

29. de Courcy, *Snowdon*, 230.

30. de Courcy, *Snowdon*, 234.

31. *Elizabeth and Margaret: Love and Loyalty*, directed by Lucy Swingler and Stephanie Wessell (UK: Outpost Facilities, September 26, 2020), Channel Five.

32. Shawcross, *The Queen Mother*, 850.

33. R. W. Apple Jr., "Northern Ireland, Awaiting Jubilee Visit by the Queen, Erupts in Violence Fatal to Two," *New York Times*, August 10, 1977.

34. David McKittrick, "Northern Ireland: Memories of 1977 and a 'Terribly Tense' Royal Visitor," *Independent*, June 28, 2012.

35. Turner, *Elizabeth*, 117.

36. Dimbleby, *Prince of Wales*, 205.

37. Dimbleby, *Prince of Wales*, 260.

38. Sally Bedell Smith, "'A Sympathetic Ear and a Goofy Sense of humour,'" *Daily Mail*, April 2, 2017.

39. Ben Pimlott, *Elizabeth II and the Monarchy* (London: Harper Press, 2012; paperback version), 470.

40. Dimbleby, *Prince of Wales*, 267.

41. Dennison, *The Queen*, 384.

9: Then Along Came Diana

1. Jimmy Carter, *White House Diary* (New York: Farrar, Straus and Giroux, 2010), 49.

2. Dennison, *The Queen*, 415–16.

3. Catherine Armecin, "Queen Elizabeth Reportedly Loves 'Good Gossip' About 'Immoral Balmoral,' Biographer Says," *International Business Times*, February 24, 2019.

4. Smith, *A Horseman Through Six Reigns*, 144. See also Erickson, *Lilibet*, 58.

5. Author interview with Eric Milligan, February 2019.

6. Gordon Rayner, "Barbeques, Quips and Pranks at Balmoral: MPs Share Fondest Memories of Prince Philip," *Telegraph*, April 12, 2021.

7. Anne Glenconner, "Princess Margaret, Her Lover and Me," *Daily Mail*, September 27, 2019.

8. Glenconner, "Princess Margaret, Her Lover and Me."

9. Glenconner, "Princess Margaret, Her Lover and Me."

10. Seward, *The Queen and Di*, 41.

11. Seward, *The Queen and Di*, 47.

12. Author interview.

13. Rhodes, *Final Curtsey*, 114.

14. Seward, *My Husband and I*, 165.

15. Andrew Morton, *Diana: Her True Story—In Her Own Words* (New York: Simon & Schuster, 2017; orig. 1992), 25th anniversary edition, 56.

16. "Another Round in Prince Charles' Matrimonial Sweepstakes," UPI Archives, November 22, 1980.

17. Joel Day, "Princess Anne's Brutal Assessment of Diana Amid Relationship Tensions," *Daily Express*, July 14, 2021.

18. Seward, *The Queen and Di*, 46.

19. Seward, *The Queen and Di*, 63.

20. Paul Riddell, "MI5 Blamed BP for Security Lapse Before IRA Bomb Attack on Queen at Sullom Voe," *Shetland Times*, June 24, 2019.

21. Graham Strachan, "The IRA Plot to Bomb the Queen in Shetland Following the Death of Bobby Sands," *Press and Journal Evening Express*, May 7, 2021.

22. *Elizabeth at 90: A Family Tribute*, directed by John Bridcut (UK: Crux Productions, April 21, 2016), BBC.

23. Stephanie Linning, "The Queen Steps Out in Her Third Headscarf in as Many Days," *Daily Mail*, May 12, 2017.

24. Seward, *The Queen and Di*, 52.

25. Morton, *Diana: Her True Story*, 82.
26. Charles Moore, *Margaret Thatcher: From Grantham to the Falk-lands* (New York: Vintage Books, 2015).
27. Smith, *Elizabeth the Queen*, 303.
28. Vickers, *Elizabeth, the Queen Mother*, 424.
29. Seward, *The Queen and Di*, 59.
30. Morton, *Diana: Her True Story*, 184.
31. Morton, *Diana: Her True Story*, 67.
32. Seward, *The Queen and Di*, 65.

10: Marriages Under the Microscope

1. Andrew Morton, *Diana: Her True Story—In Her Own Words* (New York: Simon & Schuster, 2017; orig. 1992), 25th anniversary edition, 72.
2. Smith, *Elizabeth the Queen*, 306.
3. Smith, *Elizabeth the Queen*, 306.
4. "The Princess and the Press: Interview Ken Lennox," *PBS Front-line*, undated.
5. Morton, *Diana: Her True Story*, 71.
6. Andrew Morton and Mick Seamark, *Andrew: The Playboy Prince* (London: Corgi, 1983), 88.
7. "Queen Praying for Troops in Falklands," UPI Archives, May 26, 1982.
8. Erickson, *Lilibet*, 266.
9. Talia Shadwell, "Royal Baby: Queen Cracked This 'Mean Joke' When She Met Another New Arrival," *Daily Mirror*, May 9, 2019.
10. Andrew Morton, *Inside Buckingham Palace* (New York: Summit Books, 1991), 28.
11. "A Talk with the Queen," *Washington Post*, undated.
12. Morton, *Inside Buckingham Palace*, 84.
13. Brandreth, *Philip*, 226–27.
14. Michael Dennigan, "Queen's Former Bodyguard Cleared of Charges," UPI Archives, November 24, 1982.
15. Victoria Murphy, "60 Amazing Facts You Never Knew About the Queen," *Daily Mirror*, February 1, 2012.
16. Seward, *The Queen and Di*, 103.
17. Seward, *The Queen and Di*, 103–04.

18. "Andrew and Koo Reported Back on Track," UPI Archives, May 2, 1983.

19. Monica Greep and Chloe Morgan, "Prince Andrew's Ex-Girlfriend Koo Stark," *Daily Mail*, May 28, 2021.

20. Morton, *Diana: Her True Story*, 219.

21. Dennison, *The Queen*, 410.

22. Seward, *The Queen and Di*, 7.

23. Morton, *Diana: Her True Story*, 229.

24. Shawcross, *Counting One's Blessings*, 589.

25. Morton, *Diana: Her True Story*, 367.

26. Camille Heimbrod, "Prince Philip Saw Sarah Ferguson as 'Great Asset' to Prince Andrew," *International Business Times*, August 11, 2019.

27. Seward, *The Queen and Di*, 166.

28. Morton, *Diana: Her True Story*, 221.

29. Brandreth, *Philip*, 375.

30. Turner, *Elizabeth*, 91.

31. "Thatcher Declines to Answer Questions on Queen," UPI / *LA Times* Archives, July 23, 1989.

32. Brandreth, *Philip*, 15.

33. Anna Kretschmer, "Queen Heartbreak: Greatest Regrets of Her Majesty's Reign Revealed," *Daily Express*, December 14, 2019.

34. Andrew Neil, *Full Disclosure* (London: Pan Macmillan, 1996), 276.

35. Smith, *Elizabeth the Queen*, 350.

36. William E. Schmidt, "Far from Gulf, British Royalty Is Under Fire," *New York Times*, February 12, 1991.

37. William Tuohy, "A Royal Dilemma for Britain," *Los Angeles Times*, September 8, 1992.

38. Schmidt, "Far from the Gulf, British Royalty Is Under Fire."

11: One's Annus Horribilis

1. Alex Zatman, "Filmmaker Edward's Right Royal Legacy," *Jewish Telegraph*, 2012.

2. Richard Kay and Geoffrey Levy, "How Diana Broke the Queen's Heart," *Daily Mail*, March 6, 2016.

3. Seward, *The Queen and Di*, 193.

4. Author interview with Simone Simmons, August 2021.

5. Andrew Morton, *Diana: Her True Story—In Her Own Words* (New York: Simon & Schuster, 2017; orig. 1992), 25th anniversary edition, 298.

6. Seward, *The Queen and Di*, 168.

7. Rachel Borrill, "No Shock as 'Vulgarian' Fergie Leaves the Royal Fold," *Irish Times*, April 18, 1996.

8. Britta Zeltmann, "Pen Papa," *US Sun*, April 15, 2021.

9. Richard Kay, "The Night Diana Told Me 'The Redhead's in Trouble,'" *Daily Mail*, October 31, 2014.

10. Daniela Elser, "The Toe-Sucking Photo That Ruined the Duchess of York," news.com.au, July 28, 2019.

11. Kay and Levy, "How Diana Broke the Queen's Heart."

12. Anna Kretschmer, "Royal Rage: How Sarah Ferguson Faced Queen's Fury at Balmoral," *Daily Express*, November 1, 2019.

13. Turner, *Elizabeth*, 9.

14. *Diana, Our Mother: Her Life and Legacy*, directed by Ashley Gething (UK: Oxford Film and Television, July 24, 2017), ITV.

15. Dickie Arbiter, "Diana and Charles's Ex-Press Chief Reveals Advice He Gave," *Daily Mail*, September 21, 2014.

16. Pimlott, *The Queen*, 558.

17. Seward, *The Queen and Di*, 203.

18. Kay and Levy, "How Diana Broke the Queen's Heart."

19. Kay and Levy, "How Diana Broke the Queen's Heart."

20. Dennison, *The Queen*, 437.

21. Ken Wharfe with Robert Jobson, *Guarding Diana: Protecting the Princess Around the World* (London: King's Road Publishing, 2017).

22. Andrew Morton, *Diana: In Pursuit of Love* (London: Michael O'Mara Books, 2004), 111.

23. Morton, *Diana: In Pursuit of Love*, 87.

24. Morton, *Diana: In Pursuit of Love*, 107.

25. Morton, *Diana: In Pursuit of Love*, 109.

26. John Darnton, "Prince Charles, in TV Documentary, Admits to Infidelity," *New York Times*, June 30, 1994.

27. Morton, *Diana: In Pursuit of Love*, 137.

28. Robert Jobson, "Charles: Camilla Is Central to My Life," *Evening Standard*, April 12, 2012.

29. Graham Turner, "The Real Elizabeth II," *Telegraph*, January 8, 2002.

30. Turner, *Elizabeth*, 169–70.

31. Andrew Morton, *Meghan: A Hollywood Princess* (New York: Grand Central Publishing, 2018), 319.

32. Brandreth, *Philip and Elizabeth*, 225.

33. Morton, *Diana: In Pursuit of Love*, 209.

34. Jennifer Newton, "Queen's Letter to 'Furious' Princess Diana That Finally Ended Marriage to Charles," *Daily Mirror*, June 28, 2021.

35. Morton, *Diana: In Pursuit of Love*, 211.

36. Morton, *Diana: In Pursuit of Love*, 210.

37. Morton, *Diana: In Pursuit of Love*, 213.

38. Smith, *Elizabeth the Queen*, 387.

39. Matthew Kirkham, "Prince William's Promise to Princess Diana Revealed," *Daily Express*, February 15, 2019.

12: Flowers, Flags, and Fortitude

1. Naomi Gordon, "Prince William and Prince Harry Speak of Their Regret at 'Rushed' Last Call with Princess Diana," *Harper's Bazaar*, July 23, 2017.

2. Seward, *The Queen and Di*, 14.

3. Penny Junor, *The Duchess: Camilla Parker Bowles and the Love Affair That Rocked the Crown* (New York: HarperCollins, 2017), 150.

4. Pimlott, *The Queen*, 2012 paperback, 609.

5. Deirdre Fernand, "Diana, the Queen and a Final Royal Family Reckoning," *Times*, September 17, 2006.

6. Beth Whitehouse, "The Lives of 'the Heir and the Spare,' With and Without Diana," *Los Angeles Times*, August 22, 2001.

7. Pimlott, *The Queen*, 2012 paperback, 615.

8. Robert Seeley, "Britain Shocked by Princess Diana's Death," AP News, August 31, 1997.

9. *Diana: 7 Days* (UK: Sandpaper Films, August 27, 2012), BBC One.

10. George Carey, *Know the Truth: A Memoir* (New York: Harper-Collins, 2004), 407.

11. Siofra Brennan, "'Is It True That Mummy's Dead?'" *Daily Mail*, May 30, 2017.

12. Christopher Warwick, *Princess Margaret: A Life of Contrasts* (London: Andrew Deutsch, 2000), 285.
13. Frances Hardy, "My Twin Brother Was Dead," *Daily Mail*, August 6, 2010.
14. Katie Nicholl, *William and Harry: Behind the Palace Walls* (New York: Weinstein Books, 2010).
15. *Diana, Our Mother: Her Life and Legacy.*
16. *Diana 7 Days*, BBC One.
17. Smith, *Elizabeth the Queen*, 397.
18. Smith, *Elizabeth the Queen*, 397.
19. Carey, *Know the Truth*, 409.
20. Turner, *Elizabeth*, 159.
21. Brown, *Diana Chronicles*, 472.
22. *Diana, Our Mother: Her Life and Legacy.*
23. "The Queen Starts Celebrations for Her 90th," *Sky News*, April 20, 2016.
24. "Princess Diana's Death Was 'Global Event' Says Blair," *BBC News*, September 1, 2010.
25. Smith, *Elizabeth the Queen*, 402.
26. Smith, *Elizabeth the Queen*, 401.
27. Pimlott, *The Queen*, 2012 paperback, 623.
28. Smith, *Elizabeth the Queen*, 403.
29. Pimlott, *The Queen*, 2012 paperback, 623.
30. Dennison, *The Queen*, 453.
31. Ann Leslie, "'So Tell Me, Ma'am, Why Do You Always Look So Grumpy,'" *Daily Mail*, September 17, 2008.
32. Smith, *Elizabeth the Queen*, 403.
33. Smith, *Elizabeth the Queen*, 404.
34. Pimlott, *The Queen*, 2012 paperback, 624.
35. Smith, *Elizabeth the Queen*, 404–05.
36. Smith, *Elizabeth the Queen*, 405.
37. Smith, *Elizabeth the Queen*, 406.
38. Author interview with Dickie Arbiter, January 2019.
39. Petronella Wyatt, "Taking Sides in the Battle Royal," *Daily Mail*, June 29, 2019.
40. Andrew Morton, "Destroyed: The Letters That Fuelled a Royal Feud," *Telegraph*, September 20, 2009.

41. Brown, *Diana Chronicles*, 471.

42. Andrew Morton, *Diana: In Pursuit of Love* (London: Michael O'Mara Books, 2004), 272.

43. Smith, *Elizabeth the Queen*, 408.

44. Camille Heimbrod, "Princess Margaret Wrote 'Secret' Letter to Queen Elizabeth After Princess Diana's Death," *International Business Times*, October 24, 2018.

45. Carolyn Durand, "Letter from Queen Elizabeth About Princess Diana's Death Comes to Light," *ABC News*, August 13, 2017.

46. Editorial, *Sunday Telegraph*, September 24, 1998.

47. Pimlott, *The Queen*, 663.

13: Two Weddings and Two Funerals

1. Penny Junor, *The Duchess: Camilla Parker Bowles and the Love Affair That Rocked the Crown* (New York: HarperCollins, 2017), 157.

2. Smith, *Prince Charles*, 345.

3. John Davison and Kathy Marks, "Prince's Charm Offensive Backfires," *Independent*, November 10, 1998.

4. *Prince Charles at 50: Heir to Sadness*, directed by Alan Scales, written by Margaret Holder (UK: Imagicians, October 12, 1998).

5. George Carey, *Know the Truth: A Memoir* (New York: HarperCollins, 2004), 412.

6. Anna Kretschmer, "Royal Bombshell: What the Queen 'Hates Above All Things' Revealed," *Daily Express*, April 21, 2019.

7. Smith, *Elizabeth the Queen*, 432.

8. Penny Junor, *The Firm: The Troubled Life of the House of Windsor* (London: HarperCollins, 2005), 363.

9. Thorpe, ed., *Who Loses, Who Wins*, 363.

10. Rhodes, *Final Curtsey*, 5.

11. Shawcross, *The Queen Mother*, 935.

12. "Queen Thanks Nation 'For Their Love,'" *Guardian*, April 8, 2002.

13. "The Queen Tells Driver to Slow Down," YouTube, July 31, 2012.

14. Smith, *Elizabeth the Queen*, 446–47.

15. Caitlin Moran, "The Best Bit Was Seeing Reactions in the Royal Box; Golden Jubilee," *Times*, June 4, 2002.

16. Gerrard Kaonga, "Queen 'Blossomed' as She 'Heralded New Era' of the Monarchy After Royal Family Death," *Daily Express*, January 14, 2021.

17. Caroline Davies, "The Queen Came Through for Me," *Telegraph*, November 2, 2002.

18. "What the Butler Paul Burrell Said About the Queen, Prince Philip, Charles…and Himself," *Daily Mail*, January 15, 2008.

19. Steve Bird and Sam Lister, "The Queen 'Warned Butler to Beware of Dark Forces at Work,'" *Times*, November 6, 2002.

20. Bronwen Weatherby, "Diana's Letters from Prince Philip Reveal He and the Queen 'Never Dreamed' Charles Would Leave Her for Camilla," *Daily Mirror*, September 8, 2018.

21. "War of the Wedding," *Daily Mail*, November 4, 2004.

22. Smith, *Prince Charles*, 400.

23. "Queen Condemns Bombing 'Outrage,'" *BBC News*, July 8, 2005.

24. Liz Jones, "Queen Elizabeth Looks in the Mirror and Likes What She Sees," *Daily Mail*, May 26, 2012.

25. Richard Kay, "Angela, We Could Be Sisters," *Daily Mail*, October 29, 2019.

26. Rebecca English, "The Queen will never consider abdicating," *Daily Mail*, April 20, 2006.

27. "A Speech Made By the Queen at Mansion House for Her Majesty's 80th Birthday," royal.uk, published June 15, 2006.

28. Valentine Low, "Royal Family: Queen Turns Down Oldie of the Year Award Because 'You Are Only as Old as You Feel,'" *Times*, October 19, 2021.

29. Poppy Danby, "A Birthday Like No Other," *Daily Mirror*, April 21, 2021.

30. Valentine Low, "What Now for the Queen Without Prince Philip at Her Side?" *Times*, April 9, 2021.

31. Geoffrey Levy and Richard Kay, "His Royal Grumpiness," *Daily Mail*, November 10, 2007.

32. Holly Fleet, "Carol Vorderman Describes Spark Between Queen and Philip," *Daily Express*, April 9, 2021.

33. Katie Nicholl, *William and Harry: Behind the Palace Walls* (New York: Weinstein Books, 2010), 61.

34. "Focus: The Girl Who Would Be Queen," *Sunday Times*, December 31, 2006.

35. Kate Nicholson, "Kate Middleton Heartbreak: Real Reason William Waited So Long to Propose Revealed," *Daily Express*, October 10, 2019.

36. Kate Nicholson, "How Queen Was 'Practically Skipping' on William and Kate's Wedding Day," *Daily Express*, April 29, 2020.

37. Sunday People, "Queen Will Protect Kate Middleton Says Prince Edward," *Daily Mirror*, March 25, 2012.

38. Hardman, *Our Queen*, 53.

39. Alan Cowell, "In Ireland, Queen Elizabeth Offers 'Deep Sympathy' for Past," *New York Times*, May 19, 2011.

40. "PM Says Queen's Visit to Ireland Was a 'Game-Changer,'" *BBC News*, December 27, 2011.

41. David Collins, "'An Incredible Day...Absolutely Wonderful': What Queen Told Prince Charles on Balcony as a Million Well-wishers Cheer," *Daily Mirror*, June 6, 2012.

42. Collins, "'An Incredible Day...Absolutely Wonderful.'"

14: Good Evening, Mr. Bond

1. Tom Sykes, "Jeremy Hunt Jokes with Queen, Queen Not Amused," *Daily Beast*, October 17, 2012.

2. Anne Pukas, "Transformed into Our Merry Monarch: How the Queen Never Seemed So Informal and Relaxed," *Daily Express*, July 19, 2013.

3. Kelly, *Other Side of the Coin*, 186.

4. Murray Wardrop, "Michelle Obama Hugs the Queen," *Telegraph*, April 2, 2009.

5. Rebecca English, "And I told Wills," *Daily Mail* 17 February, 2014.

6. "The Queen Welcomes A-List Actors at Palace Celebration," *BBC News*, February 18, 2014.

7. Jilly Cooper, "That's the End of the Ride, Ma'am," *Telegraph*, March 8, 2011.

8. Jack Haynes, "'She Loves the Sport So Much'—The Queen Inducted into Racing's Hall of Fame," *Racing Post*, October 12, 2021.

9. *Elizabeth at 90: A Family Tribute*, directed by John Bridcut (UK: Crux Productions, April 21, 2016), BBC.

10. Author interview with Eric Milligan, July 2019.

11. *Our Queen at 90*, directed by Ashley Gething, written by Robert Hardman (UK: Oxford Film and Television, March 27, 2016), ITV 1.

12. Carly Ledbetter, "Elton John Reveals He Once Saw Queen Elizabeth Jokingly Slap Her Nephew," *Huffpost*, July 10, 2019.

13. Nina Massey, "Prince William Recalls Moment the Queen Gave Him an 'Absolute B*****king,'" *Independent*, April 20, 2016.

14. *Elizabeth: Queen, Wife, Mother*, directed by Peter Higgins (UK: ITN Productions, June 1, 2012), ITV.

15. Smith, *Prince Charles*, 492.

16. Dan Roberts, "Obamas, Prince Harry and the Queen Trade Mic Drops in Comedy Sketch," *Guardian*, April 26, 2016.

17. Angela Levin, "Exclusive: Prince Harry on Chaos After Diana's Death and Why the World Needs 'the Magic' of the Royal Family," *Newsweek*, June 21, 2017.

18. Oliver Harvey and Emma Lake, "Queen of Hurts," *The Sun*, June 16, 2017.

19. Dennison, *The Queen*, 481.

20. Elizabeth Sanderson and Katie Nicholl, "Buckingham Palace Reshuffles Key Personnel in 'First Step to Bringing Prince Charles to the Throne,'" *Daily Mail*, January 18, 2014.

21. Martin Robinson and Amie Gordon, "Prince Philip Seals His 'Standing Down' Announcement," *Daily Mail*, May 4, 2017.

22. Richard Kay and Geoffrey Levy, "Prince Philip Downsizes for Retirement," *Daily Mail*, November 3, 2017.

23. "Buckingham Palace Plays Down 'Power Struggle' Claims," *BBC News*, September 16, 2017.

24. Laura Smith-Spark, "Britain's Queen Hopes Prince Charles Will 'One Day' Lead Commonwealth," CNN, April 19, 2018.

25. Rachel Brodsky, "Meghan Markle Says Queen Elizabeth Was 'Always Wonderful,'" *Independent*, March 8, 2021.

26. Luke May, "Queen DID Slap Down Meghan Markle Over Her Choice of Wedding Day Tiara," *Daily Mail*, July 29, 2020.

27. Sean O'Neill, "Prince Andrew's TV Calamity Suggests Queen Is Losing Her Grip on 'the Firm,'" *Times*, November 18, 2019.

28. Seward, *My Husband and I*, 210.

29. Mark Landler, "In Prince Andrew Scandal, Prince Charles Emerges as Monarch-in-Waiting," *New York Times*, December 1, 2019.

30. Rebecca English, "Prince Andrew's Regret Over 'Car Crash' TV Interview," *Daily Mail*, November 17, 2019.

31. O'Neill, "Prince Andrew's TV Calamity."

32. Valentine Low, "Prince Andrew Interview: Queen Does Her Duty Despite Disgrace of 'Favourite Son,'" *Times*, November 21, 2019.

33. "A Statement by His Royal Highness the Duke of York," royal.uk website, published November 20, 2019.

34. Jonny Dymond, "Harry and Meghan: The Royal Couple Are Looking for the Exit," *BBC News*, January 13, 2020.

35. Jemma Carr, "Fuming Prince Philip Was Left in 'Disbelief' at the Lack of Respect Shown to the Queen by His Grandson Prince Harry and Meghan Markle," *Daily Mail*, January 11, 2020.

36. Caroline Davies, "The Royal Showdown: Everything You Need to Know," *Guardian*, January 13, 2020.

37. Smith, *Elizabeth the Queen*, 494.

38. Daniel Uria, "Prince Andrew: Queen Elizabeth II Feels 'Void' After Prince Philip's Death," UPI Archives, April 11, 2021.

39. Victoria Ward and Jessica Carpani, "'It Was Like Somebody Took Him by the Hand and Off He Went,' Says Countess of Wessex of Prince Philip's Last Moments," *Telegraph*, April 11, 2021.

40. Naledi Ushe, "Prince Edward's Wife Sophie Shares Emotional Moment 'When Everything Stopped' During Prince Philip's Funeral," *People*, June 4, 2021.

41. Naomi Adedokun, "Sophie Wessex 'Proven to Be Queen's Most Reliable' Aide as Monarch Copes with Philip's Death," *Daily Express*, April 13, 2021.

42. Pimlott, *The Queen*, 119.

Select Bibliography

Airlie, Mabell, Countess of. *Thatched with Gold.* Edited by Jennifer Ellis. London: Hutchinson, 1962.

Barry, Stephen. *Royal Secrets: The View from Downstairs.* London: Random House, 1985.

Bradford, Sarah. *Elizabeth: A Biography of Her Majesty the Queen.* London: Penguin, 1996.

Brandreth, Gyles. *Philip and Elizabeth: Portrait of a Royal Marriage.* London: W. W. Norton, 2004.

——. *Philip: The Final Portrait.* London: Coronet, 2021.

Brown, Tina. *The Diana Chronicles.* New York: Penguin, 2007.

Corbitt, F. J. *My Twenty Years in Buckingham Palace.* New York: David McKay, 1956.

Crawford, Marion. *The Little Princesses.* New York: St. Martin's Griffin, 2020; orig. 1950.

Dennison, Matthew. *The Queen.* London: Head of Zeus, 2021.

Dimbleby, Jonathan. *The Prince of Wales: A Biography.* New York: William Morrow, 1994.

Dismore, Jane. *Princess: The Early Life of Queen Elizabeth II.* Guilford, Connecticut: Lyons Press, 2018.

Duncan, Andrew. *The Reality of Monarchy*. London: Pan Books, 1973.

Edwards, Anne. *Royal Sisters: Queen Elizabeth II and Princess Margaret*. Guilford, Connecticut: Lyons Press, 1990.

Erickson, Carolly. *Lilibet: An Intimate Portrait of Elizabeth II*. New York: St. Martin's Press, 2004.

Flamini, Roland. *Sovereign: Elizabeth II and the Windsor Dynasty*. London: Bantam Press, 1991.

Glenconner, Anne. *Lady in Waiting: My Extraordinary Life in the Shadow of the Crown*. London: Hodder & Stoughton, 2019.

Hardman, Robert. *Our Queen*. London: Hutchinson, 2011.

Harris, Kenneth. *The Queen*. New York: St. Martin's Press, 1995.

Hartley, John. *Accession: The Making of a Queen*. London: Quartet Books, 1992.

Hoey, Brian. *At Home with the Queen*. London: Harper-Collins, 2002.

Howard, Alathea Fitzalan. *The Windsor Diaries: 1940–1945*. Edited by Celestria Noel. London: Hodder & Stoughton, 2020.

Jay, Antony. *Elizabeth R*. London: BBC Books, 1992.

Jebb, Miles, ed. *The Diaries of Cynthia Gladwyn*. London: Constable, 1995.

Keay, Douglas. *Elizabeth II: Portrait of a Monarch*. London: Ebury Press, 1991.

Kelly, Angela. *The Other Side of the Coin: The Queen, the Dresser, and the Wardrobe*. New York: HarperCollins, 2019.

Lacey, Robert. *The Crown: The Official Companion*. Volume 1, *Elizabeth II, Winston Churchill, and the Making of a Young Queen (1947–1955)*. New York: Crown Archetype, 2017.

——. *Monarch: The Life and Reign of Elizabeth II.* New York: Free Press, 2003.

Longford, Elizabeth. *Elizabeth R: A Biography.* London: Weidenfeld and Nicholson, 1983.

——. *The Queen Mother.* New York: William Morrow, 1981.

Maclean, Veronica. *Crowned Heads: Kings, Emperors, and Sultans—A Royal Quest.* London: Hodder & Stoughton, 1993.

Marr, Andrew. *The Real Elizabeth: An Intimate Portrait of Queen Elizabeth II.* New York: Henry Holt, 2012.

Morrow, Anne. *The Queen.* New York: William Morrow, 1983.

Pimlott, Ben. *The Queen: Elizabeth II and the Monarchy.* London: HarperCollins, 1996.

Rhodes, Margaret. *The Final Curtsey: A Royal Memoir by the Queen's Cousin.* London: Umbria Press, 2012.

Seward, Ingrid. *My Husband and I.* New York: Simon & Schuster, 2017.

——. *Prince Philip Revealed: A Man of His Century.* London: Simon & Schuster, 2020.

——. *The Queen and Di: The Untold Story.* London: HarperCollins, 2000.

Shawcross, William, ed. *Counting One's Blessings: The Selected Letters of Queen Elizabeth the Queen Mother.* New York: Farrar, Straus and Giroux, 2012.

Shawcross, William. *The Queen Mother: The Official Biography.* New York: Knopf, 2009.

Smith, Horace. *A Horseman Through Six Reigns: Reminiscences of a Royal Riding Master.* London: Odhams, 1955.

Smith, Sally Bedell. *Elizabeth the Queen: The Life of a Modern Monarch.* New York: Random House, 2012.

——. *Prince Charles: The Passions and Paradoxes of an Improbable Life.* New York: Random House, 2017.

Stewart, Andrew. *The King's Private Army: Protecting the Royal Family During the Second World War*. Warwick, UK: Helion, 2015.

Strober, Deborah Hart, and Gerald S. Strober. *The Monarchy: An Oral Biography of Elizabeth II*. New York: Broadway Books, 2002.

Thorpe, D. R., ed. *Who's In, Who's Out: The Journals of Kenneth Rose*, Volume One: *1944-1979*. London: Weidenfeld & Nicolson, 2019.

———. *Who Loses, Who Wins: The Journals of Kenneth Rose*. Volume 2, *1979–2014*. London: Weidenfeld & Nicolson, 2019.

Turner, Graham. *Elizabeth: The Woman and the Queen*. London: Macmillan, 2002.

Vickers, Hugo. *Elizabeth, the Queen Mother*. London: Hutchinson, 2005.

Viney, Graham. *The Last Hurrah: South Africa and the Royal Tour of 1947*. Johannesburg, South Africa: Jonathan Ball, 2018.

Wheeler-Bennett, Sir John. *Friends, Enemies and Sovereigns*. London: Macmillan, 1976.

Williams, Kate. *Young Elizabeth: The Making of the Queen*. Berkeley, California: Pegasus Books, 2015.

Windsor, Duchess of. *The Heart Has Its Reasons*. London: Michael Joseph, 1956.

Photo Credits

Page 1: George Elam/*Daily Mail*/Shutterstock.

Page 2: Shutterstock (top); Design Pics Inc./Shutterstock (center and bottom).

Page 3: *Daily Mail*/Shutterstock (top); Richard Gardener/Shutterstock (bottom).

Page 4: Design Pics Inc./Shutterstock (top); Shutterstock (center); AP/Shutterstock (bottom).

Page 5: Eddie Worth/AP/Shutterstock (top); AP/Shutterstock (center); Everett/Shutterstock (bottom).

Page 6: AP/Shutterstock (all).

Page 7: Everett/Shutterstock (top); AP/Shutterstock (center); Shutterstock (bottom).

Page 8: *Daily Mail*/Shutterstock.

Page 9: Photo courtesy of Ken Lennox.

Page 10: Photo courtesy of Ken Lennox (top); AP/Shutterstock (bottom left); *Evening Standard*/Hulton Archive/Getty Images (bottom right).

Page 11: Reginald Davis/Shutterstock (top left); Central Press/Hulton Archive/Getty Images (top right); AP/Shutterstock (bottom).

Page 12: Mike Lawn/Shutterstock (top); Shutterstock (center); Mike Forster/ANL/Shutterstock (bottom).

Page 13: Gillian Allen/AP/Shutterstock (top left); AP/Shutterstock (top right); Shutterstock (bottom left); Santiago Lyon/AP/Shutterstock (bottom right).

Page 14: Tim Rooke/Shutterstock (top and center); David Fisher/Shutterstock (bottom).

Page 15: Paul Grover/Shutterstock (top); David Hartley/Shutterstock (center); Shutterstock (bottom).

Page 16: Jonathan Brady/AP/Shutterstock (top); Buckingham Palace/Shutterstock (center); Tim Rooke/Shutterstock (bottom).

Index

About the Author

Andrew Morton studied history at the University of Sussex, England, with a focus on aristocracy and the 1930s. Morton has written extensively on celebrity including biographies of Tom Cruise, Angelina Jolie, and Madonna, as well as the British royal family. He has written bestselling biographies of the Duke and Duchess of Windsor, Prince Andrew, and Meghan Markle. His #1 *New York Times* bestselling biography *Diana: Her True Story* won international acclaim, described by critics as a "modern classic" and "the closest we will ever come to her autobiography."